FLEXIBLE
SOFTWARE
DESIGN

Other Auerbach Publications in Software Development, Software Engineering, and Project Management

The Complete Project Management Office Handbook
Gerard M. Hill
0-8493-2173-5

Complex IT Project Management: 16 Steps to Success
Peter Schulte
0-8493-1932-3

Creating Components: Object Oriented, Concurrent, and Distributed Computing in Java
Charles W. Kann
0-8493-1499-2

The Hands-On Project Office: Guaranteeing ROI and On-Time Delivery
Richard M. Kesner
0-8493-1991-9

Interpreting the CMMI®: A Process Improvement Approach
Margaret Kulpa and Kent Johnson
0-8493-1654-5

ISO 9001:2000 for Software and Systems Providers: An Engineering Approach
Robert Bamford and William John Deibler II
0-8493-2063-1

The Laws of Software Process: A New Model for the Production and Management of Software
Phillip G. Armour
0-8493-1489-5

Real Process Improvement Using the CMMI®
Michael West
0-8493-2109-3

Six Sigma Software Development
Christine Tayntor
0-8493-1193-4

Software Architecture Design Patterns in Java
Partha Kuchana
0-8493-2142-5

Software Configuration Management
Jessica Keyes
0-8493-1976-5

Software Engineering for Image Processing
Phillip A. Laplante
0-8493-1376-7

Software Engineering Handbook
Jessica Keyes
0-8493-1479-8

Software Engineering Measurement
John C. Munson
0-8493-1503-4

Software Metrics: A Guide to Planning, Analysis, and Application
C.R. Pandian
0-8493-1661-8

Software Testing: A Craftsman's Approach, Second Edition
Paul C. Jorgensen
0-8493-0809-7

Software Testing and Continuous Quality Improvement, Second Edition
William E. Lewis
0-8493-2524-2

IS Management Handbook, 8th Edition
Carol V. Brown and Heikki Topi, Editors
0-8493-1595-9

Lightweight Enterprise Architectures
Fenix Theuerkorn
0-8493-2114-X

Outsourcing Software Development Offshore: Making It Work
Tandy Gold
0-8493-1943-9

Maximizing ROI on Software Development
Vijay Sikka
0-8493-2312-6

Implementing the IT Balanced Scorecard
Jessica Keyes
0-8493-2621-4

AUERBACH PUBLICATIONS

www.auerbach-publications.com
To Order Call: 1-800-272-7737 • Fax: 1-800-374-3401
E-mail: orders@crcpress.com

FLEXIBLE SOFTWARE DESIGN

SYSTEMS DEVELOPMENT FOR CHANGING REQUIREMENTS

Bruce Johnson, Ph.D.
Walter W. Woolfolk
Robert Miller
Cindy Johnson, PMP

PARK LEARNING CENTRE
UNIVERSITY OF GLOUCESTERSHIRE
P.O. Box 220, The Park
Cheltenham GL50 2RH
Tel: 01242 532721

Auerbach Publications
Taylor & Francis Group
Boca Raton   London   New York   Singapore

Published in 2005 by
Auerbach Publications
Taylor & Francis Group
6000 Broken Sound Parkway NW, Suite 300
Boca Raton, FL 33487-2742

© 2005 by Taylor & Francis Group, LLC
Auerbach is an imprint of Taylor & Francis Group

No claim to original U.S. Government works
Printed in the United States of America on acid-free paper
10 9 8 7 6 5 4 3 2 1

International Standard Book Number-10: 0-8493-2650-8 (Hardcover)
International Standard Book Number-13: 978-0-8493-2650-9 (Hardcover)
Library of Congress Card Number 2005043626

This book contains information obtained from authentic and highly regarded sources. Reprinted material is quoted with permission, and sources are indicated. A wide variety of references are listed. Reasonable efforts have been made to publish reliable data and information, but the author and the publisher cannot assume responsibility for the validity of all materials or for the consequences of their use.

No part of this book may be reprinted, reproduced, transmitted, or utilized in any form by any electronic, mechanical, or other means, now known or hereafter invented, including photocopying, microfilming, and recording, or in any information storage or retrieval system, without written permission from the publishers.

For permission to photocopy or use material electronically from this work, please access www.copyright.com (http://www.copyright.com/) or contact the Copyright Clearance Center, Inc. (CCC) 222 Rosewood Drive, Danvers, MA 01923, 978-750-8400. CCC is a not-for-profit organization that provides licenses and registration for a variety of users. For organizations that have been granted a photocopy license by the CCC, a separate system of payment has been arranged.

Trademark Notice: Product or corporate names may be trademarks or registered trademarks, and are used only for identification and explanation without intent to infringe.

Library of Congress Cataloging-in-Publication Data

Flexible software design : systems development for changing requirements / Bruce Johnson
    ... [et al.].
        p. cm.
    Includes bibliographical references and index.
    ISBN 0-8493-2650-8 (alk. paper)
    1. Computer software--Development. I. Johnson, Bruce (Bruce M.)

QA76.76.D47F596 2005
005.1--dc22   2005043626

Taylor & Francis Group
is the Academic Division of T&F Informa plc.

Visit the Taylor & Francis Web site at
http://www.taylorandfrancis.com

and the Auerbach Publications Web site at
http://www.auerbach-publications.com

Dedication

This book is dedicated to those information technology (IT) professionals who want the systems they develop to continue to serve the changing needs of their enterprises long after they have left the project. It is also dedicated to the business experts who wish to make critical system updates without being hamstrung by an IT backlog.

Contents

Acknowledgments

First and foremost, the authors would like to thank Auerbach for the opportunity to fulfill our aspiration to make this flexibility handbook available. Thanks are also given to Peter Ligezinski, Mark Murphy, Jack Scheuer, and an unnamed representative from Auerbach for taking time to read the manuscript and make valuable suggestions. Also, we want to thank Andrea Shultz for the computer graphics support.

Special thanks go to our families for their continued support and encouragement. We truly appreciate your understanding, patience, and forbearance as this project took much time away from family activities and responsibilities.

We have made extensive use of material that we have published earlier. Appreciation is expressed to the publishers of these earlier works for their gracious permission to use this material.

There are others along the way with whom we have shared ideas and who have influenced our thinking, including Dale Atkins, Chris Dent, Hahn Tram, Kevin Clanahan, Jeff Gruber, and Shaun Achmad. And there are others, although not acknowledged specifically by name, whose contributions are also appreciated.

We couldn't have completed this work without all of you.

Introduction

One of our colleagues reported the following (the airline name and locations have been removed).

I was sitting in the Airport VIP Lounge waiting for my flight and reviewing the manuscript for this book. I looked at the departures screen and saw that my flight was not listed; yet an earlier flight, which had already departed, was still showing. I went to the desk to get my flight information. When I asked why the discrepancy was shown on the display screen, I was told, "We've requested many times for that problem be fixed, but they keep telling us that it's too expensive to modify the program."

I suggested that perhaps a copy of the book should be made available to the Information Technology (IT) staff of the airline. With flexible software, this program modification would be easy and inexpensive to make [Scheuer 2004]!

Many IT experts talk about flexible software. They say that it is a good thing and that ease of modification of a software system is one of its most important attributes, but they do not say how to do it. We do. We understand techniques and principles of building flexible software as well as the theory behind these techniques. The authors are seasoned IT professionals with over 50 years of combined experience, much of it developing flexible systems and flexibility techniques.

The lack of flexibility has been recognized for a long time; we are bringing forward into present practice many of the critiques and design advances that have been offered over the years. Our references date from when we started our study of software flexibility almost 20 years ago up to the present, and their tone has not changed.

One expert reminds us that each dollar of development generates 20 cents for operation and 40 cents for maintenance. The need to maintain old systems is a primary driver of the IT growth curve, with old systems dominating budgets and schedules. Even with the advent of new technologies such as client/server, Web-enabled applications and the consequent replacement of legacy systems, the result is not new development; there is no net increase in automation coverage. Such technology-driven conversions reduce productivity while in progress, and it is always problematical whether they will succeed in positioning the enterprise for significant future productivity or competitive gains. In the meantime, maintenance goes on.

The premise of this book is that knowledge of a system's requirements is necessarily imperfect because a significant part of those requirements lies in the future and is unknowable at the time the system is designed — or built, for that matter. We must therefore rely on techniques for improving flexibility — the system's ability to change gracefully — rather than for improving our knowledge of requirements. The maintenance burden will be eased only when systems themselves can be modified easily to meet unanticipated requirements.

The purpose of this book is to identify, present, and demonstrate a set of design principles and techniques that empower IT professionals to design software that enables business staff to effectively manage operational changes to those systems with little or no further intervention by those same IT professionals. To do this, we concentrate almost entirely on design aspects of system development, the area where the flexibility leverage is to be found.

Our book is aimed at four audiences:

1. *Practitioners/IT professionals* who want satisfied customers, who want to get out of the maintenance and fire-fighting business, and who want to put fun, creativity, and joy (back?) into their careers.
2. *Business staff* who are tired of being told, "We can't do that. The computer system will not let us," who want not only to hear, "Yes, we can do that!" but wish to hear "Yes, you can do that yourself — you do not have to wait for IT to get to it!"
3. *Managers* who wish to end the war between what business staff expect and what IT professionals can deliver, and who want systems that will, over the long term, remain responsive to their organization's needs and opportunities.
4. *College professors* who want to teach their students to do it right the first time.

The book is organized into four parts:

■ Part I, Introduction to Flexibility, establishes the case for flexible software, locating the serious issue of software inflexibility within the context of a series of common misunderstandings, or myths, that cut across the entire field of IT business systems development, and introduces some fundamental background concepts and terms. It explains the reality of imperfect knowledge. It also points out how the various participants in the software development process will have to the change their thinking if they are to implement flexible software. We introduce the reader to UniverSIS, business software developed for the University of Cincinnati, using principles of flexibility. Overcoming imperfect knowledge, its designers implemented a flexible design that has responded gracefully to changing business requirements.

■ Part II, What Is Required to Achieve Flexibility, covers design guidelines for flexible software, the necessity of having stable identifiers, and the importance of what we call "regulation" — the management of artificial limits with minimal or no IT intervention. The last two chapters of Part II deal with the very important topic of stable information structures — an absolute necessity for flexible systems — and the Generic Entity Cloud, which automatically provides stable but flexible information structures.

■ Part III, How to Design Flexible Software Systems, starts at the very beginning of application software development — strategic planning — and presents a nontraditional view of what is required for flexible software. Next is shown how the elicitation of require-ments for a system differs when one is designing for the long term rather than just to satisfy current business requirements. Having discussed the necessity of stable identifiers in Part II, we show how to design stable identifiers under several scenarios. Part III includes thoughts on how testing flexible software differs from testing tradi-tional software. We focus particular attention on how maintenance and testing are done once the software is in operation and business staff are performing these functions. Part III ends with a discussion of project management, quality, and procurement for flexible systems.

■ Part IV, Flexibility: Delving Deeper, is for the really avid reader who likes details. The UniverSIS system and its Evaluator facility are described in detail. Several chapters explain applications and exten-sions of the Generic Entity Cloud originally introduced in Part II.

Concepts are presented clearly and concisely with liberal use of exam-ples. Because repetition is one of the laws of learning, the same concept is sometimes presented from different perspectives. We have been selective with nonstandard terms and sparing and consistent with acronyms. A bibliography of relevant works is provided. Please read this book carefully and apply its techniques and principles so that you, your organization, and your software will be the happy beneficiaries of the combination of smart design and smart work that this approach supports.

The Authors

Bruce Johnson resides in Estes Park, Colorado, and is a retired associate professor at Xavier University in Cincinnati, Ohio, where he taught information and decision sciences for 17 years. Prior to that, he operated his own software consulting company, held various positions with software firms as an independent consultant, and was manager of systems and programming for Billboard Publications. He started his career as an analyst and data center manager with Procter & Gamble. His technical interests include the management of technology and the effects of technical knowledge on decision making.

He is currently researching design and implementation principles of flexible computer systems and is developing (in Java) an information-structure generator for flexible systems. He has an M.B.A. and Ph.D. in operations management, information systems, and organizational behavior from the University of Cincinnati and B.S. and M.S. degrees in civil engineering from Washington State University. Bruce has been writing and researching the subject of flexible computer systems for more than a dozen years and has coauthored a number of papers dealing with the subject of computer software flexibility.

Walter W. Woolfolk is information systems director for Taylor Distributing in Cincinnati, Ohio. Prior to that, he was a systems architect with Unisys Europe-Africa, data administration manager for Federated Department Stores Corporate, held various other IT management and technical positions, and taught graduate and undergraduate database systems courses at the University of Cincinnati. His technical interests include the characteristics of flexible information systems, structure/process differentiation in systems, and dictionary-based systems. He has a B.A. in mathematics from Graceland College in Iowa and has done graduate work in philosophy and general systems theory at Indiana University and the University of Louisville.

Walt has been working in and researching the subject of flexible computer systems for more than a dozen years. At Federated Department Stores, for example, he designed the information structure for the company's financial reporting system, which enabled end-user maintenance of the changing organization and product structures of 20 disparate and decentralized retail divisions, including multiple concurrent future business planning scenarios. He has coauthored a number of articles on the subject of flexible software systems.

Robert Miller is director of information technology systems services at the University of Cincinnati. He has worked primarily in higher education. He has over 20 years of experience in information systems development. Previously, he was a senior systems analyst at Boston University and manager of application development at Xavier University in Cincinnati, Ohio.

He has implemented flexible systems that support a wide range of university administrative functions. These systems have provided key business staff with direct control over system behavior, including execution of complex business-decision logic, with a minimum of intervention by the technical staff. He has a B.S. in economics from the University of Pennsylvania, Wharton School, and an M.S. in occupational therapy from Boston University. He is the developer of the UniverSIS flexible software system at the University of Cincinnati and coauthored the paper describing its development and operation.

Cindy Johnson is the marketing manager for Enspiria Solutions, Inc., a company that provides IT systems integration services for electric and gas utilities. She was formerly a program manager with the Utilities Practices at SchlumbergerSema and Convergent Group. Prior to that, she was a principal in a management-consulting firm. She has a B.A. (Phi Beta Kappa) in energy management and policy from the University of Colorado, Boulder, Colorado.

Cindy is a certified project management professional (PMP) from the Project Management Institute (PMI). She has managed hundreds of IT system implementations and business consulting projects for a variety of clients such as Sempra, ESKOM, Southern Company, U.S. Department of Energy, PacifiCorp, Public Service Electric and Gas (NJ), and the Electric Power Research Institute. She also prepares project and industry publications and provides training courses to utility personnel. Cindy shares our common interest in improving the success of IT delivery. She contributes her experiences and perspective that the work be accessible to the non-IT manager.

INTRODUCTION TO FLEXIBILITY

I

This book offers an approach to system development that reduces the need for maintenance by the information technology (IT) department. For most organizations, the demand for increased automation of business processes exceeds the capacity of the IT function to deliver satisfactory results, and the gap is increasing. People and organizations are aware that there is a problem, but the identification of what is wrong is often incorrect. Incorrect diagnosis will not lead to effective treatment or cure. Part I provides the reader with an awareness of where the real problem lies — with inflexible software systems — and introduces the advantages of flexible software design.

- Chapter 1 examines from a fresh perspective the lack of success of many, if not most, of today's IT projects and systems. It exposes the lack of flexibility that results in maintenance backlogs, compounding costs, deferred development, customer dissatisfaction, and declining competitive position.
- Chapter 2 introduces flexibility as an improved approach for software design and system development. It discusses the characteristics of flexible systems and recognizes historical progress in the direction of flexibility. It also explores a series of pervasive and persistent misconceptions about IT, myths that impede the application of IT to a changing world.
- Chapter 3 addresses the shift in thinking that is required. We need to shift our objective from functional accuracy with regard to current business requirements to adaptability to future changes in business requirements. The specific outcome we are looking for is ease of maintenance. Systems that are easy to maintain permit

organizations to respond to changing business conditions quickly and easily.

■ Chapter 4 discusses the realignment of roles for flexible software. When compared with traditional systems, flexible systems represent a paradigm shift in the roles of those who are involved in its development, operation, and maintenance. End users, customers of IT, must be more involved in the development and maintenance of their software systems as well as in their operation. Developers must design and build so as to eliminate the developer's role in maintenance. Managers at all levels are responsible for seeing that this happens.

■ Chapter 5 takes a look at the University of Cincinnati (UC)'s University Student Information System (UniverSIS) — an information system that was developed with flexibility as the guiding principle. UniverSIS helps UC's business staff do their jobs better, with less effort, and easily accommodates current and future business requirements with little impact on the IT department.

Chapter 1

The Serious Problems with IT Today

Information technology (IT) publications chronicle the troubles with today's computer systems. These difficulties are also a topic of interest in the popular press. Most relevant statistics of these "troubles" deal with development or operational problems.

Whitmarsh [1995] and others quote disturbing statistics provided by the Standish Group International. Defining a successful computer application development project as "one that is delivered on time, on budget and with most of the features as originally specified," they reported the success rate in Fortune 500 companies as a shocking 9 percent. Among those companies with annual revenues exceeding $100 million, a 31 percent cancellation rate and a runaway project rate of 53 percent were reported.

The situation has not improved much, if at all, since these statistics were published in 1995. The Standish Group International more recently reported the following: 63 percent of information technology projects had time overruns, 45 percent faced cost overruns, and 23 percent were cancelled before completion or never implemented [Elkins, 2001].

In his study of system economics, Keen [1991, pp. 18, 44] reports that no large system fell into the "easy to deliver category, the average large system development lead-time being seven years." Little needs to be said about the perils of undertaking a large or even a medium systems development initiative. It is necessary only to read the newspaper or talk to industry colleagues.

We can build systems quickly or big or right — but not all three. If we build them quickly, they're bound to be small or wrong. If we build them big, they'll either be late or wrong. And for *really* big systems, they're guaranteed to be late *and* wrong [Hayes, 2001a].

Since 72% of large projects are late, over budget or don't deliver anticipated results, if you're a sponsor of a project you have a 28% chance of success [Mark Jeffrey in Brandel, 2004].

In attempting to combat these troubles, organizations rely increasingly on methods of accelerating systems development, when the real problem is systems maintenance. Maintenance applies not only to legacy systems, but also to new systems, whether written last year, last month, or even still under development.

The IT world has a problem: it is drowning in its systems maintenance backlog. The enterprise that employs IT has a problem: it cannot fully exploit its automated systems when necessary software modifications persistently remain undone. This is far more serious than how to do systems development faster. For example, Chabrow [2004] reports the following:

With executives who see IT as a growth enabler, 42% of IT spending goes to new systems and capabilities *versus* [emphasis added] maintaining existing platforms. But spending on new systems and capabilities drops to 30% in companies where managers judge IT as an inhibitor.

1.1 The Industrywide Maintenance Problem

For each dollar spent on development, typically 40 cents goes to nondiscretionary maintenance annually for the life of the system.

Systems maintenance is not a happy topic. Most executives say that their businesses are changing faster than their IT organizations can keep critical systems current. Yet IT cannot afford to make any major modifications because so much of the technology budget is devoted to incremental maintenance [Lytton, 2001].

The industrywide maintenance problem has people frustrated. The frustration is most acute at Fortune 1000 companies. A recent Crossroads-OSA poll of 200 executives showed that only about 3 percent of their companies' programmers are assigned to new systems development. Almost 52 percent are devoted to software maintenance. Just over 45 percent are dedicated to interface development and maintenance [Lytton, 2001]. One manifestation of this frustration is "unexpressed demand" — when system users just stop asking for new systems or features in existing systems or develop their own systems.

The erosion of development capacity by maintenance is accelerated as development is accelerated. Everywhere the backlog of maintenance is increasing, often reported as requiring 80 percent of IT resources. In fact, if unexpressed demand is taken into account, we would find in many installations a maintenance need exceeding 100 percent, where all resources could be devoted to maintenance and the backlog would still be increasing [Johnson et al., 1999].

Keen [1995, p. 258] reminds us that for each dollar spent on development, typically 20 cents goes to operational costs and 40 cents to non-discretionary maintenance annually for the life of the system. The need to maintain old systems is the primary driver of the IT growth curve, with old systems dominating budgets and schedules. Even when legacy systems are replaced, the result is not necessarily new development; there is no net increase in automation coverage. Such technology-driven conversions reduce productivity while in progress, and it is always problematical whether they will succeed in positioning the enterprise for significant future gains in effectiveness. In the meantime, maintenance goes on reducing the resources available for new development. Keen [1991] demonstrated the effect of this erosion of development resources over a five-year time horizon, using four different IT budgeting strategies. Exhibit 1.1 is derived from Keen's work [1995] and extends the erosion of development resources to a ten-year horizon for emphasis. Keen [2004] recently said "These figures are still accurate — I have not had a CIO challenge them."

Exhibit 1.1 shows four strategies for managing an IT budget. Strategy 1 keeps a level IT budget, and Strategy 2 keeps a level IT development budget. In Strategy 3, development is grown at 10 percent per year, and for Strategy 4, development is grown at 20 percent per year. Within each strategy, the current year's data for years one through five and ten is shown for each of the following: development, operations and maintenance, total budget, the percentage of the total budget that is development, and the development and maintenance that is due to this year's development.

Is this maintenance burden necessary? Is the current high level of maintenance an inevitable consequence of having automated systems? Hayes [1995, 1996] broadly defines maintenance as any modification, regardless of type or size, made to existing production-level code. This is a conservative perspective on maintenance. If you count as maintenance any rework to accommodate new requirements, then it usually starts before development is done. The world does not wait for us to finish development

Strategy 1: Maintain a Level IT Budget of $40 Million

Year	1	2	3	4	5	10
Development	10.00	4.00	1.60	0.64	0.26	0.00
Operations and Maintenance	30.00	36.00	38.40	39.36	39.74	40.00
Total Budget	40.00	40.00	40.00	40.00	40.00	40.00
Development %	25%	10%	4%	2%	1%	0%
Next year's Operation and Maintenance due to this year's Development	6.00	2.40	0.96	0.38	0.15	

Year 5: IT budget amount remains constant. Development cut by over 90%.
Year 10: Development effectively zero. Entire budget dedicated to maintenance.

Strategy 2: Keep Development Budget Level at $10 Million

Year	1	2	3	4	5	10
Development	10.00	10.00	10.00	10.00	10.00	10.00
Operations and Maintenance	30.00	36.00	42.00	48.00	54.00	84.00
Total Budget	40.00	46.00	52.00	58.00	64.00	94.00
Development	25%	22%	19%	17%	16%	11%
Next year's Operation and Maintenance due to this year's Development	6.00	6.00	6.00	6.00	6.00	

Year 5: IT budget amount increased by 60%. Development drops to 16% of budget
Year 10: IT budget amount increased by 135%. Development drops to 11% of budget

Strategy 3: Grow Development by 10% per Year

Year	1	2	3	4	5	10
Development	10.00	11.00	12.10	13.31	14.64	23.58
Operations and Maintenance	30.00	36.00	42.60	49.86	57.85	111.48
Total Budget	40.00	47.00	54.70	63.17	72.49	135.06
Development	25%	23%	22%	21%	20%	17%
Next year's Operation and Maintenance due to this year's Development	6.00	6.60	7.26	7.99	8.78	

Year 5: IT budget amount increased by 81%. Development drops to 20% of budget.
Year 10: IT budget amount increased by 238%. Development drops to 17% of budget.

Strategy 4: Grow Development by 20% per Year

Year	1	2	3	4	5	10
Development	10.00	12.00	14.40	17.28	20.74	51.60
Operations and Maintenance	30.00	36.00	43.20	51.84	62.21	154.79
Total Budget	40.00	48.00	57.60	69.12	82.94	206.39
Development	25%	25%	25%	25%	25%	25%
Next year's Operation and Maintenance due to this year's Development	6.00	7.20	8.64	10.37	12.44	

Year 5: IT budget amount increased by 107% to allow development to remain constant at 25% of budget.
Year 10: IT budget amount increased by 420% to allow development to remain constant at 25% of budget.

Exhibit 1.1. The Cost Dynamics of Information Technology (Source: Keen, P.G.W., *Every Manager's Guide to Information Technology: a Glossary of Key Terms and Concepts for Today's Business Leader,* 2nd ed., Harvard Business School Press, Cambridge, MA, 1995. With permission.)

before it introduces a new requirement. Hayes goes on to describe three types of maintenance: corrective (fixing bugs), perfective (upgrading technology), and adaptive (changing functionality). We are concerned here

At a large aluminum processing plant in the Midwest the new plant manager decided to "flatten" the organization and proceeded to eliminate a middle tier, to combine certain departments and to subdivide others. This was not a simple change, but neither was it an uncommon type of change in the life of an enterprise. Within six to eight weeks, most of those affected had adjusted to the new organization, changed their procedures, and altered their communications. The administrative costs of the reorganization were not insignificant, but neither were they considered large enough to budget for. However, a year later, the corresponding modifications to the plant's computer systems were "90% complete" at a cost exceeding a quarter million dollars. An expensive chain reaction of program modifications, testing, debugging, file reformatting and repopulating, history restating, and report redesigning had been triggered by the reorganization.

Exhibit 1.2.   90 Percent Complete at the Aluminum Processing Plant (© 2004 IEEE)

with the mostly nondiscretionary adaptive maintenance that arises from requirements changes. Organizations need to change, and change frequently. But in many organizations, change is inhibited by computer systems that are resistant to modification. Inflexible systems plus changing requirements equals costly maintenance. It is virtually every enterprise's experience with maintenance that it takes too long and costs too much.

1.2 What Is Wrong with Nonflexible Systems? Two Cautionary Tales

*This book is not about how to do maintenance. It is about how to **not** do maintenance.*

To illustrate the problem of inflexibility, we present two tales of problems caused by inflexible systems (Exhibit 1.2 and Exhibit 1.3). The first is true; the second is representative of many of the authors' frustrations in dealing with inflexible systems that we have inherited.

The problem at the aluminum plant was not a missed requirement in the traditional sense; the original systems accurately reflected the plant's organization. Rather, it was a failure to see the variability of the organization as a requirement on the system. Consequently, what was variable in the real world of the plant was designed as a static property of its computer systems (for example, by embedding the organization scheme in the identifiers of production, inventory, and financial files).

An analyst developing an order processing system is obtaining requirements related to sales force commissions:
- The first user interviewed explains that, "...we generally apply only one commission rate of 0.80% to all our business."
- The second user says that principally this is right, "...but some of our sales force get a higher rate for selling big-ticket products to corporate customers."
- A third user says, "...and when I had the difficult Conos account in '02, I negotiated a special rate for myself for the winter quarter, usually our slow time in sales."
- A fourth user reports, "...don't forget that in the past the sales people for a new territory have gotten a higher rate initially, except in soft goods, of course."
- The nth user says, "...yes, but ..."

Exhibit 1.3. Order Processing System (© 2004 IEEE)

The computer system that accurately implements the specific commission "requirements" has a problem. The problem is that the analyst never gets to the nth user, who is symbolic here of the "missed" requirement and the costly post-implementation modification. But does it make any difference if the nth requirement comes before or after requirements determination has been officially completed and the system has been designed, built, and placed into operation? Suppose that after the system is operational the company forms a total quality management (TQM) team, studies customer expectations, and revises its commission policies. The system now expresses all the symptoms of incomplete requirements.

1.3 The Typical IT Environment: No Time to Do It Right — Time to Do It Over!

As the maintenance backlog increases, costs compound, development is deferred, customer dissatisfaction grows, and competitive position declines.

The high maintenance costs, extensive project backlogs, and frequent service interruptions caused by inflexible software systems are painfully familiar. The experts agree.

For the most, part we're still using the same traditional design methodologies that were originally designed to address far more static business information needs. These static applications aren't flexible enough to meet our current needs and are forcing an upheaval on the application front.... You need a new approach that fully embodies the organic nature of what you're trying to build in each of the main development phases [Rubin, 1999].

Software systems are failing at increasing rates. In short, we cannot continue to use current system development paradigms. We must be able to build systems that can adapt to changing requirements and changing implementation environments on time scales from microseconds to years. This will let us more effectively manage resources, upgrade components, and tolerate failures [Kavi et al., 1999].

In this book we use the term "customer" to refer to anyone who uses a software system to do business-related work. Customer dissatisfaction is rampant in today's typical IT environment. Many types of dissatisfaction combine in ways that produce seriously unhappy customers. Of course, customers do not always perceive their distress in precise categories. They often place blame in a global way on either the IT organization or the vendor of the system. For purposes of simple expression, we will refer to this entire dissatisfaction complex as the typical IT environment, implying that the net effect is a less than desirable level of IT services and products so far as the IT customer is concerned.

IT customer dissatisfaction is multidimensional. We have identified ten key types of customer dissatisfaction (Exhibit 1.4), which fall into three major categories:

1. Dissatisfaction with the IT organization
2. Dissatisfaction with the systems
3. Dissatisfaction with senior management

All of the ten customer dissatisfiers listed in Exhibit 1.4 are directly or indirectly impacted by the persistence of high maintenance levels. We ask our readers to carefully think back to the last three troubles that you, your organization, or your enterprise has had with your IT systems or department and try to classify them into one or more of the ten customer dissatisfiers listed here.

1.4 Summary

- Many sources report disturbing statistics regarding the lack of success of many, if not most, of today's IT projects and systems.
- This lack of success appears to have been with the IT industry for a long time, and the reasons, in many cases, have not been properly diagnosed.

IT Dissatisfier	Description	System Maintenance Role
Target of Dissatisfaction: IT Organization		
Delivery	• Systems often take too long to develop and are too costly to maintain once developed. • And it is not all uncommon for systems to be scrapped almost immediately after development has been completed.	• Systems development costs are discretionary; operation and maintenance are not. • High maintenance levels erode the resources available for new development.
Changes	• Modifications to system functionality appear to take too long, and the cost seems excessive. Many system modifications are not made because the cost or potential business disruption are perceived as being too great.	• Systems maintenance that is perceived as too time consuming and too costly is an immediate source of customer distress.
Backlog	• This is the other side of the "Changes" coin. Modifications are often not made because the necessary resources have been completely absorbed by competing maintenance activities. • Time spent on a high-priority modification delays implementation of lower-priority modification accordingly. When high-priority items are introduced, they jump ahead of existing lower-priority modifications. As this scenario is repeated, the queue gets longer, resulting in what one organization called the eight-year backlog, the implication being that the lower-priority modification is never completed.	• Lower-priority modifications may be continually bypassed. • "Essential" system maintenance required for ongoing operation may supersede "Discretionary" enhancements that will bring improved operation or competitive advantage.
Budget	• Growing operational and capital budgets are out of proportion to the benefits. • The cost of keeping outdated legacy and nonflexible systems limping along can exceed the perceived benefit of these systems and drain resources needed to provide system support for current business needs.	• In order to sustain an acceptable level of development, resource levels must be raised to compensate, thus driving up overall IT costs.
Bureaucracy	• Administrative rules appear to impede rather than facilitate progress. • Procedures for the allocation of precious and limited IT resources absorb much time and effort that could be directed to achieving competitive advantage.	• As high levels of maintenance drive resources into short supply, they become subject to stricter controls—project approval becomes more highly regimented and its mechanisms grind more finely
Operating Errors	• Too many errors are encountered in the operation and technical management of production systems. • System modifications often lead to side effects such as lost data, inaccurate reporting, and even lost revenue and business.	• When an enterprise is running an applications inventory of mostly interface-coupled systems, modifications to the systems' parochial data structures often trigger costly maintenance chain reactions. This complex operating environment is difficult to manage and thus routinely requires frequent operator and user intervention, and is prone to errors that propagate disastrously.

Exhibit 1.4. The Role of System Maintenance in Customer Dissatisfaction

IT Dissatisfier	Description	System Maintenance Role
Target of Dissatisfaction: Systems		
Operational Profile	• Current user expectations for presentation, ease of use, reliability, and performance make the existing system appear inadequate and outdated. • Response time is perceived as unacceptable and resource consumption is perceived as excessive.	• High maintenance costs limit resource availability for system enhancements or new development.
Information Anomalies	• Related systems produce inconsistent information.	• A high level of IT maintenance activity increases the risk of operating error and of delivery of inconsistent information. • The cure becomes part of the disease. Remember the axiom "when the same data exists in more than one place—sooner or later, often sooner, it will differ from one place to another!" • Nonflexible, nonintegrated (interfaced) systems—often developed by non-IT business units to get around the backlog problem often lead to differing results between systems.
Processing Errors	• System processing produces incorrect results, either because of logic errors in programs or logic "holes" that stem from inadequate communication of business requirements.	• Maintenance activity introduces errors into systems.
Target of Dissatisfaction: Senior Management		
Resource Allocation/ Priority Setting	• Allocation of resources for system support and maintenance is perceived as inadequate. • Priorities for IT investment are perceived as unwise and unresponsive to what should be the business priorities of the organization.	• Hidden maintenance costs and the unexpressed demand that develops from a persistently high maintenance burden are information gaps that negatively impact IT investment decisions.

Exhibit 1.4. (continued)

- Much of this undiagnosed lack of success can be attributed to the industrywide maintenance problem.
- The cost dynamics of IT, given today's approach to IT, result in allocation of more and more resources to system maintenance and fewer and fewer to software development, even as the IT budget expands.
- It has been shown that the search for that "last requirement" is a never-ending and fruitless endeavor.
- The typical IT environment — with no time to do it right or time do it over — yields a host of dissatisfactions with IT and its environment, systems, and operation.

As the maintenance backlog increases, costs compound, development is deferred, customer dissatisfaction grows, and competitive position declines. The long-term result of inflexible systems is a growing crisis in the ability of information technology to support the enterprise. Most systems today, regardless of the technologies, methods, languages, or tools used for their development, are designed without sufficiently radical attention to the problem of change. They lack flexibility. The challenge is to reduce the cost of adaptive maintenance by designing flexibility into systems. This book is not about how to do maintenance. It is about how to *not* do maintenance.

Chapter 2

The Reality of Imperfect Knowledge

Flexible systems are needed because we cannot predict the future. Because organizations change over time, complete knowledge of a system's requirements, in the traditional sense, is necessarily imperfect. Some requirements lie in the future, and they are unknowable at the time the software system is designed or being built. The traditional objective of system design is functional accuracy, but when designers do not look beyond the current requirements, the result is often inflexible software. Acceptance of the reality of imperfect knowledge of requirements adds a new and fundamental objective — adaptability to functional change. That adaptability is essential to good system design.

Parnas [1979] perhaps overstates the case when he says, "Any design can be bent until it works. It is only in the ease of change that they differ," but the overriding importance of business change on system design is clear. The automated system is necessarily subject to continual modification to maintain synchronization with unfolding requirements. We want to design the software to cope with change affordably, so as to maximize the possibility of maintaining this synchronization without gross disruption or modification costs that are out of proportion to the magnitude of the corresponding real-world changes.

An improved approach — what we call flexible systems and others call organic or adaptable systems — is required. We have had favorable and ongoing experience with techniques that, when applied with care, allow automated systems to flex with their real-world counterparts.

2.1 Flexibility: An Improved Way of Thinking

> We have had favorable and ongoing experience with techniques that, when applied with care, allow automated systems to flex with their real-world counterparts.

Two basic approaches have been taken to flexibility in computer systems. Boogaard [1994] characterizes these as active flexibility and passive flexibility. Active flexibility is basically fast modification. Many techniques have been devised for speeding up the process of modifying computer systems to meet new functional or operational requirements, including automatic program modification as seen in application generators. Active flexibility focuses on the modification process. In recent years, this has been the approach taken almost exclusively. However, the continuing crisis level of the maintenance backlog demonstrates the futility of relying on the active-flexibility approach alone. In contrast, Boogaard's passive flexibility is built in. The computer system is designed to require inherently less modification, fast or otherwise; flexibility focuses on the system itself. We are concerned throughout this book with this latter approach of built-in or planned flexibility.

2.1.1 Real World/Automated World

> *We are concerned throughout this book with ... built-in or planned flexibility.*

A computerized information system can be viewed as a representation of a real-world (RW) system that is actually, relative to the real-world system, an automated-world (AW) system. Systems development is therefore a series of transformations [Wand and Weber, 1990, p. 123], as shown in Exhibit 2.1:

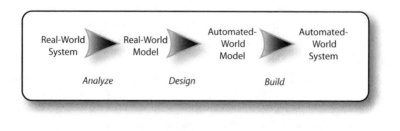

Exhibit 2.1. Real-World/Automated-World Transformation

1. From the real-world system to a model of the real-world system via analysis
2. From the real-world model to a model of the automated-world system via design
3. From the automated-world model to the automated-world system via construction

2.1.2 Synchronization and Resynchronization

The real world *changes*; the automated world is *modified*.

These transformations, taken together, synchronize the functionality of the automated-world system with that of the real-world system. When the real world subsequently undergoes some change in functionality, then the automated-world system needs to be resynchronized with it or else fail to continue to be useful [Weinberg, 1975, p. 254]. We will say that the real world *changes* and the automated world is *modified*. For example, the change in a payroll procedure that requires a new type of deduction in the real-world payroll system requires a corresponding modification to the automated payroll system. Synchronization and resynchronization are, of course, software development and software maintenance, respectively. Maintenance repeats the transformation steps of development, but starts with a changed real-world system, analyzes the change in the context of the existing automated-world system, and designs and builds a modification to the automated-world software.

The transformation-series concept is deceptively simple but fundamental, and it will be employed extensively throughout this book. Primarily, it reminds us that the real world and the automated world are different, with significantly different characteristics. The main intention of this book is to explore how, despite the differences, the inherent flexibility of the real world can be carried into the automated world.

IT people expect users to always know what they want, and they can get exasperated when they don't. Business people have a right to change their minds, because the business changes [Ellen Gottesdiener in Horowitz, 2004].

2.1.3 Flexibility and Local Modifiability

This book proposes that a flexible system, in basic operational terms, is one that can be resynchronized with changes in the real-world system almost entirely through user-controlled data-value modifications with minimal or no program code modification or information restructuring. Somewhat more formally, flexibility in a system is the characteristic of being able to sustain the minimum degree of modification in its components needed to accommodate a change in the behavioral requirements made upon it by its environment. Because the modification of some kinds of system components has more costly effects than others, the focus is on achieving a system design that enables subsequent modifications to be limited as much as possible to the least-cost-effect components.

Experience supports the contention that the least costly modification is a data-value modification; the next most costly is a procedural code modification; and the most costly is an information structure modification (Exhibit 2.2). That is, when the declaration of a primary access key in the database is modified, then all programs using that key are affected and will have to be modified to assemble the key value differently. (This is equally true for the object-oriented approach, because the custodial object type cannot hide the primary key.) This is the exponentially more costly nonlocal modification that occurred at the aluminum plant (Exhibit 1.2). In those cases where coding changes are necessary, we want them to be restricted to local modifications that do not result in a chain reaction of additional compensating modifications. Flexible systems reduce the need for Hayes's [2001a] adaptive code modification. Flexible systems directly attack Keen's [1995] estimate of 40 percent of development costs allocated to nondiscretionary maintenance annually for the life of a system.

(The authors have chosen to use COBOL (common business-oriented language) for some of the exhibits throughout the book (including Exhibit 2.2 in this chapter), as well as other languages, including Java. The last time we looked, there were more lines of COBOL in production than all other languages combined, and until at least recently, more COBOL was still being written every day than all other languages combined. It is not glamorous like Java, but it is in the back rooms where the vast majority of the processing occurs and where the databases are.)

2.1.4 Natural and Artificial Limits

We already know that most AW systems are not flexible enough. In contrast, we observe that RW systems are flexible enough.

> The organization as a whole is able to adapt more fluidly than the software upon which it has grown dependent. In fact, software systems are usually the least responsive element in many organizations today [Cox, 1986].

Let us agree that if AW systems could be modified as readily as the corresponding RW systems are changed, that would be flexible enough.

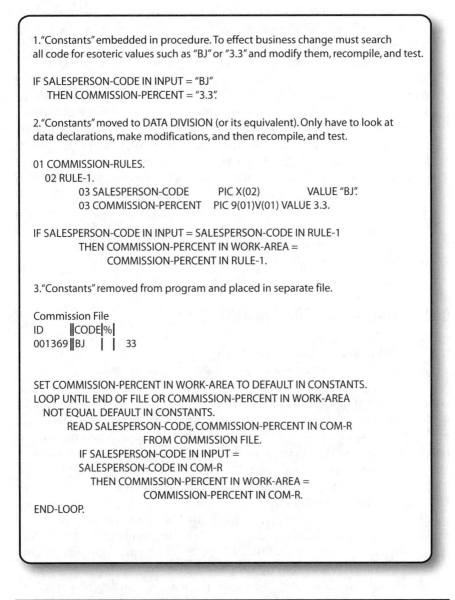

```
1."Constants" embedded in procedure. To effect business change must search
all code for esoteric values such as "BJ" or "3.3" and modify them, recompile, and test.

IF SALESPERSON-CODE IN INPUT = "BJ"
   THEN COMMISSION-PERCENT = "3.3".

2."Constants" moved to DATA DIVISION (or its equivalent). Only have to look at
data declarations, make modifications, and then recompile, and test.

01 COMMISSION-RULES.
   02 RULE-1.
         03 SALESPERSON-CODE        PIC X(02)             VALUE "BJ".
         03 COMMISSION-PERCENT    PIC 9(01)V(01) VALUE 3.3.

IF SALESPERSON-CODE IN INPUT = SALESPERSON-CODE IN RULE-1
      THEN COMMISSION-PERCENT IN WORK-AREA =
            COMMISSION-PERCENT IN RULE-1.

3."Constants" removed from program and placed in separate file.

Commission File
ID      ‖CODE|%|
001369 ‖BJ    |  |   33


SET COMMISSION-PERCENT IN WORK-AREA TO DEFAULT IN CONSTANTS.
LOOP UNTIL END OF FILE OR COMMISSION-PERCENT IN WORK-AREA
   NOT EQUAL DEFAULT IN CONSTANTS.
         READ SALESPERSON-CODE, COMMISSION-PERCENT IN COM-R
                     FROM COMMISSION FILE.
            IF SALESPERSON-CODE IN INPUT =
            SALESPERSON-CODE IN COM-R
               THEN COMMISSION-PERCENT IN WORK-AREA =
                     COMMISSION-PERCENT IN COM-R.
END-LOOP.
```

Exhibit 2.2. More Flexible Handling of "Constants"

An essential refinement on the transformation world concept is to distinguish between the RW system and the enterprise-world (EW) system. For example, let the RW payroll system include all physically and logically possible ways of arranging and performing the payroll function. Then the EW payroll system incorporates the current enterprise-specific rules for doing payroll. The RW system is what the enterprise can do; the EW system is what it is doing now. We will use the RW term by itself, with the EW subset implied.

A more rigorous mapping between the types of components of the RW system and those of the AW system is key to keeping the flexibility characteristic invariant through the analysis/design/construction transformations to the AW system. The source of most AW system modifications is a changed *processing* requirement. For example, management says, "We're going to institute a job-sharing program as part of our employee empowerment initiative." This is a change in how things are to be done. The problem is that, due to misdesign, the corresponding modification in the AW system is not isomorphic with the change in the RW system; it is not restricted to modifying a process but also often requires a modification of the information structure. Once that occurs, then programmed processes unrelated to job sharing must also be modified. We propose that AW systems be made more like RW systems.

2.2 What Is Flexible Software?

> *Designed well, flexible software can serve an organization over many decades and multiple technological generations.*

Let us begin with another question. What is the difference between "good" software and "bad" software? Good software serves an organization well, and bad software does not. Let us assume that any software that is successfully implemented is good initially. Does good software go bad? Yes. Good software goes bad when the cost of keeping it good is perceived as being greater than the cost of replacing it. By keeping it good, of course, we mean modifying it to accommodate changes in business requirements. Flexible software is good software that can be kept good at low cost by accommodating change with a minimum of IT intervention. Designed well, flexible software can serve an organization over many decades and multiple technological generations.

Throughout the book we use the term "generic" to describe software components that can be used in a variety of different ways, depending on the needs of the individual organization, with a minimum of intervention from the IT staff. The term "generic" may carry with it a connotation of vanilla, or basic, or unsophisticated. As we will demonstrate, this need not be the case. Careful analysis of business requirements, and equally careful design, can result in highly sophisticated software that is easily maintained by business staff.

The two most basic design characteristics of flexible software are:

1. Stable information structure
2. Processes that exploit that stability

2.2.1 Structural Stability

Flexible computer software requires stable information structures. This is not an oxymoron. In the design of a flexible information system, something static can and does serve as the foundation for something flexible. The more static a structure becomes (i.e., the more variability is excluded), the more generic it becomes, both in the things it represents and the relationships among them. Thus, in static structures, changes are viewed as new interpretations of software components rather than as modifications to those components. For example, a generic "person" entity in an information system can be interpreted variously as an employee, manager, or contractor without needing to alter the declaration of the entity itself. This is exactly what happens in real-world systems. Individuals wear different hats. Sometimes a single individual wears more than one hat. Sometimes new hats come into existence. Sometimes the hats need to be reassigned. Accommodating new hats or assigning hats differently should not require major software modification and the high cost that goes with it. Throughout this book, we will provide examples of how to achieve structural stability.

By way of preview, here are some key points of stable information structures. The characteristics of stable information structures are outlined in the following subsections.

2.2.1.1 Invariant, Unique, and Meaningless Identifiers

One of the deadly sins of software design is poor design of record identifiers, or keys. The use of unstable keys is a major source of maintenance as well as the cause of a host of other problems. There is more than simple uniqueness to better key design. We will discuss that better design.

2.2.1.2 Generic Entity Types

A major emphasis in designing a flexible software system is identifying entities, those real-world things about which we want to store information. The objective is to define only entities that are actually needed, distinguishing between things that truly differ from each other and things that are simply variations on a theme. For example, "employee" and "student" could be considered categories of a single entity — "person." "Building" and "automobile" appear to be truly different things, although in some systems, they could be treated as "assets."

Another emphasis is storing business rules as data rather than embedding them in program code. In addressing these topics, we show how some very basic business rules can be accommodated easily in the data structures in a way that allows them to be maintained without modification of programs

2.2.1.3 Generic Entity Relationships

Well-established techniques exist for maintaining information about relationships between entities. We will discuss techniques that go beyond much of current practice.

2.2.1.4 Recursive Entity Relationships

Relatively little attention has been paid to storing information about relationships between instances of the same entity. An organizational chart, for example, is essentially a listing of relationships among organizational units such as departments, divisions, etc. The same applies to parts such as car, chassis, frame, wheels, etc. We will cover techniques that allow information about such relationships to be maintained easily and flexibly.

2.2.1.5 Variable Cardinality

A common source of "I wish we had thought of…" is the need to modify the software because additional occurrences of an attribute are needed. You allowed for one address, and now you need two. You allowed for five children, and now you need six. We will discuss design techniques that prepare the software for changes of this nature.

2.2.1.6 Variable Typing

Typing corresponds to the "hats" mentioned earlier. Recognition of the need to allow for entity typing is critical to flexible design. We will discuss techniques for providing typing capability and for increasing the number of types available as business needs change.

2.2.1.7 Consistent Typing

If a type A organization can have only a type B organization as its parent, then organization 006, which is a type A, can have as a parent only an organization, whatever its identifier, that is a type B.

Each of these items will be presented in greater depth in subsequent chapters. And the chapter on what we refer to as generic-entity clouds (Chapter 10) addresses these items in a comprehensive way.

2.2.2 *Processes That Exploit Stable Structures*

When information structures remain constant, software developers can construct stable and reliable processes in which software behavior can easily be modified to handle most processing eventualities. Although the development costs of these processes may be higher than with traditional development, it is, by and large, a one-time investment. Some of the basic characteristics of this software are listed below. These points assume, of course, that stable, flexible data structures serve as the software foundation. Each is developed fully in subsequent chapters.

- *Assume the most general case with respect to cardinality*: If an attribute can potentially have multiple occurrences, write the program to handle multiple occurrences, even if today's records have only one occurrence.
- *Interact with an external cardinality regulation facility*: Store the rule for the number of allowable occurrences in the software and write the program to use that stored number to control processing. This is really powerful: imagine altering cardinality relationships without modifying structural declarations.
- *Provide generic explosion/implosion capability for bill-of-material-like structures, including recursive nested structures*: This will be explained later in the context of entity typing. It is possible to develop a general design that provides for nested recursive relationships within an entity, one that offers potentially great savings on software maintenance.
- *Provide generic ultimate-ancestor/ultimate-child detection in bill-of-material-like structures*: Given any starting point in a bill-of-materials-like structure, the highest and lowest levels of the structure can readily be determined.
- *Provide automatic or semiautomatic adjustments when a level of a bill-of-material-like structure is moved up or down*: Components in the structure can be added or deleted at any level, and the parent and child relationships remain intact. Components can be moved from one branch to another.
- *Provide for enforcement of integrity rules*: This includes restrictions on cycles and ensures consistency of type hierarchies.
- *Determine an outcome based upon a complex interaction of multiple parameters*: This can take multiple forms, two of which are explored in detail: dynamic condition search and general-purpose evaluation.

An essential message is that developers should think about worst-case scenarios and, within reasonable limits, design for them. Another message is that software developers should get away from designs that address every business requirement as unique. Just as we recommend careful analysis of entities for common attributes and characteristics, we recommend analysis of processes to identify patterns of behavior. Good programmers already do this informally. When presented with an assignment, they typically look for a program that does something similar and clone it. With good design, business staff can manage much of that cloning process through maintenance of data.

2.3 Change or Die

Real-world systems must change or they die. However, most automated-world systems are so brittle that, when they are modified, they die or are crippled unless costly life-support measures are taken. To continue its life beyond the present, the automated-world system must ideally be as flexible as the real-world system it represents. A good example of such a flexible system was developed at the Investment Trust Bank in Vienna [Woolfolk et al., 1996]. During initial development in 1990, approximately 30 work processes were incorporated into an automated system. This development project consumed 140 person-months of effort.

During the early years of system operation, over 170 work processes were added to the system, requiring over 2700 modifications. Specially trained and designated system end users maintained the control data that defined the work processes. IT professionals did not make these modifications. The bank's original requirements were not detailed; instead, the systems development effort concentrated on achieving flexibility. Programs were designed to process elementary actions that could be added or modified independent of existing code by manipulating the control data. Due in large part to this adaptability, the bank has enjoyed an enviable record of rapid response to challenges, market opportunities, and changing regulatory demands.

These 2700 modifications required only 24 person-months of effort over three years. This is a remarkably low level of effort in comparison with nonflexible systems. Applying Keen's [1995] cost dynamics, one would expect these modifications to require roughly 168 person-months (more than the original development effort). Initial development would result in 40 percent maintenance for each of these three years, or 56 person-months per year. The 2700 modifications made at the Investment Trust Bank included much more than routine maintenance, and they were accomplished at 14 percent of the typical effort.

The bank's experience illustrates that automated-world systems can be designed to facilitate their resynchronization with unanticipated changes in the real-world systems they represent. Such systems thereby enable the enterprise to break out of the fatal economic embrace that erodes development resources, pushes IT budgets ever higher, and inhibits change in the enterprise itself.

2.4 Evolution of Flexibility

Since the dawn of computer programming and computer systems, there have been efforts to make systems easier to modify and to reduce the side effects from such modifications. Three clear examples are:

1. More flexible handling of "constants"
2. Adoption of structured programming techniques
3. Introduction of database management systems

2.4.1 More Flexible Handling of "Constants"

Early on, values for elements such as "tax rate" were implemented as literals and embedded in the procedural code. Although values may be relatively stable, they do change over the course of time. Later, they were moved out of procedural code into a "constant section" or "data division," where they could more easily and more reliably be found and modified. Eventually, some of these "constants" were moved to files where they could be modified without changing and recompiling affected programs. Refer to Exhibit 2.2 for an illustration of this progression. A flexibility progression can easily be seen here. In the first case, the entire program had to be searched for occurrences of values such as "BJ," whose meanings were not always clear. Then the program had to be modified, recompiled, and tested. In the second case, only the data portion of the program had to be searched. With luck, the value was contained in a meaningful data name such as SALESPERSON. But the program still had to be modified, recompiled, and tested. In the third case, no programs needed to be changed or compiled, and only the external file had to be changed. And, of course, the changes still needed to be tested, but the chances of side effects were reduced and, if the logic and procedure were done right, could be eliminated.

We introduce a tabular notation in Exhibit 2.2 that is used throughout the book. The tabular notation is a convenient way to define various sample relations:

Label: | A-ID | B-ID || Attribute 1 | Attribute 2 | . . . | Attribute n |

with identifier data items to the left of the | | and attribute data items to the right. The order of attribute data items is immaterial.

For example:

Person: | Person-ID | | Last-Name | Birth-Date | Address |

A sample instantiated relation is made by extending the bars (|) downward to form columns and filling in data values:

```
Person: | Person-ID | | Last-Name | Birth-Date | Address         |
        | 123       | | Adams     | 19410420   | 234 Straight St. |
        | 234       | | Smith     | 19580606   | 5555 Dolphin Ave |
```

2.4.2 Structured Programming

The adoption of structured programming techniques increased programmer productivity by almost ten times and fostered easier program maintenance. In 1960, a professional programmer would code in the neighborhood of 12 lines of tested code per day.

Structured programming is defined as a method of developing program logic using only three control structures. The three are: the sequence, if-then-else, and looping. Structured programming was designed to avoid the jumps in logic that were embodied in the "GO TO" statement that was in popular use and tended to create "spaghetti code."

Edsger W. Dijkstra of the Netherlands wrote a letter to the editor of the *Communications of the ACM* in March 1968 entitled "GO TO Statement Considered Harmful." His conclusions were based upon work presented by Bohm and Jacopini at an international conference in Israel in 1964 and published in 1966 in *Communications of the ACM*. Dijkstra stated that the quality of a program was inversely proportional to the number of GO TOs. (Particularly programmers trained in FORTRAN, a heavy user of GO TOs, had difficulty visualizing programs without GO TOs.) But remember, it is not the absence of the GO TO that makes a structured program; it is the proper utilization of the three basic control structures.

Yet, like so many things in the history of computing in the United States, the concept was not taken seriously until IBM took an interest. Two IBM employees, Harlan Mills and F. Terry Baker, were able to demonstrate the practical aspects of the technique while working on a *New York Times* project [Baker, 1972]. The structured programming technique became widely accepted and dramatically increased the lines of tested code produced per day. While the increase in productivity from structured programming and the like is important, as well as considerable, its value to flexibility lies primarily in the readability of the code. It is simply easier for a programmer to follow the logic of structured programming.

2.4.3 Database Management Systems

In the early days of batch-process-driven systems, electronic record keeping mirrored paper record keeping. The business rules were maintained in the heads of the staff. Design of the sequential files was typically based on input and output used to support traditional paper processes, i.e., lists sorted in a specified order. Interpretation of the data was done in the programs that did the processing. Exhibit 2.3 illustrates such a batch process.

Data input was a batch process, often very complex, involving sorting and matching records. Output could be relatively simple to produce if it came from a single file. If multiple files were required to produce the output, the programming became increasingly complex. For example, from the "class" file shown in Exhibit 2.3, you could produce the following lists by varying the sort order.

1. Instructor's list of students in the class, with students in alphabetical order
2. List of classes a specified instructor is teaching
3. List of classes a specified student is taking

If you wanted to add the student's major and phone number to the instructor's list (list 1), you would need to add programming to retrieve that information from the "student" file.

At that time, processing time and machine efficiency drove most design decisions. The design goal was to make processes as efficient as possible. Logical data design was not necessarily a high priority and data redundancy was common. For example, in the above design, if the student's name changes, you would need to change it in the student file and in all class records where it occurs.

The introduction of database management systems and the processing capacity of modern computers have combined to give developers the tools to eliminate data redundancy. The elimination or reduction of redundancy, among other things, reduces the number of potential side effects. For example, making a name change to most — but not all — records. Or, again, changing the class or instructor in some records but not all. Having to make the change in only one place makes it easier and faster to modify the system, making it more flexible.

Even with flexibility improvements such as these, systems still are not very flexible. The goals of greater processing efficiency, and more recently

Process = Enroll in a Class

Three chief characteristics:
· Class
· Instructor
· Student

Simple paper record keeping, and early electronic record keeping, may have looked something like this.

CLASS

Class:	Engl 101
Term:	Fall 2004
Location:	Smith, MWF 10:00 to 10:50
Instructor ID:	567-89-0123
Instructor Name:	Jones, Horace
Credit Hours:	3.0

ID	Student	Grade
123-45-6789	Johnson, Ann	C
234-56-7890	Knox, Richard	B
345-67-8980	Wilson, Jane	A

The data would have been stored in a sequential format, something like this:

Engl 101 Fall2004 Smith MWF10001050 567890123Jones, Horace 3.0 123456789Wilson, Jane A
Engl 101 Fall2004 Smith MWF10001050 567890123Jones, Horace 3.0 234567890Knox, Richard B
Engl 101 Fall2004 Smith MWF10001050 567890123Jones, Horace 3.0 345678901Johnson, Ann C

INSTRUCTOR

Instructor ID:	567-89-0123
Instructor Name:	Jones, Horace
Department:	English
Office Location:	Fulbright 203
Office Telephone:	6245
Home Address:	123 Easy Street
	Salem OR
Home Telephone:	451-2323

In sequential format:

567890123Jones, Horace English Fulbright 203 6245 123 Easy Street Salem OR 451-2323

STUDENT

Student ID:	345678901
Student Name:	Wilson, Jane
Major:	History
Home Address:	16 Parkside Lane
	Salem OR
Home Telephone:	451-8383

In sequential format:

345678901Wilson, Jane History 16 Parkside Lane Salem OR 451-8383

Exhibit 2.3.   Batch Processing

greater development speed, continue to drive design, and redundancy continues to be a fact of system life. Data redundancy represents a desire to make a specific business process execute faster. It also represents a gamble that data needs will not change or that changes in data needs can be accommodated effectively and efficiently.

Interestingly, in these days of instant access and online processing, the payoff for data redundancy is likely to occur in batch processing. A fraction of a second of response time when processing an individual's record is not noticeable. A reduction of an hour in batch processing of a million records may seem significant.

The examples above illustrate three advancements that have significantly increased the speed of development and have increased flexibility slightly. Exhibit 2.4 summarizes computing developments throughout history and highlights resulting contributions to flexibility from several perspectives:

- Developments over time
- Programming language progression
- Progression of software flexibility techniques

Again, while Exhibit 2.4 shows a great deal of progress in computing power and systems development capabilities, it shows limited progress toward flexibility. Software systems still have far to go before they are truly responsive to the ever-changing needs of organizations.

Date	Development	Significance	Flexibility Enhancement
Developments Over Time			
3000 years ago	Abacus	Portable computing	
1642	First attempt to add by machine Blaise Pascal	Mechanical adding	
1671 1694	First mechanical calculator Gottfreid Leibniz	Mechanical computing	
1801 1804	Automatic pattern loom Joseph Jacquard	Precursor to the punched card	
1820	Analytical engine Charles Babbage	More advanced computing	
1888	Punched card	Data storage and input/output	
1930	Turing machine Alan Turing	Developed theory of automated computing	
1940s	Stored program John von Neumann EDVAC		From wires to internal storage Enabled program modification without rewiring
1944	Mark I — First electromechanical digital computer Dr. Admiral Grace Hopper	Increasing computer power	Subroutines facilitated modular programming
1945	Magnetic tape	First medium to allow searching	
1946	ENIAC — First electronic digital computer (vacuum tubes)	No longer mechanical	
1951	UNIVAC I — First "mass" produced computer	Led to new industry	
1954 1957	FORTRAN — Scientific language First third-generation language	Writing scientific programs faster—adds to maintenance backlog	Enabled scientific programs to be easier to write and understand—and therefore modify
1958	FLOWMATIC Commercial language	Writing commercial programs faster—adds to maintenance backlog	Enabled commercial programs to be easier to write and understand and therefore modify
1960	First generalized database management systems (DBMS)		Enabled the separation of data from processing. Reduced data redundancy = easier to modify system
1961	COBOL Common business-oriented language		Promoted standardization, readability COPYlib modularity
1964	IBM 360 family	Hardware architecture compatability	
1964	Structured programming Boehm and Jacopini Edsger Dijkstra		Enabled modular programs using three basic control structures; easier to read, understand, and modify

Exhibit 2.4. Computing Developments and Flexibility

Date	Development	Significance	Flexibility Enhancement
1972	Chief programmer teams Harlan Mills	Technique for improving programmer productivity	
1975	*The Mythical Man Month* Fred Brooks	Demonstrated difficulty of estimating time and cost of computer projects	
1970s	Rapid DBMS growth IMS, TOTAL, CODAYSL, SQL Codd, Chen	Can make programs harder to change and understand	Further separated data from procedure
1970s	Enterprise Resource Planning (ERP)	Maintenance difficult and unwieldy	Early "integrated" off-the-shelf software system
1979	First spreadsheet VisiCalc	Complicated management of corporate computing	Facilitated user programming — mixed effect for flexibility
1975	Microprocessor Noyce and Hoff MITS Altair	Vastly increased number of computers and programs	
1980s	Microcomputer DBMS DBASE II, RBASE, Paradox, Access	Complicated management of corporate computing	Facilitated user programming — mixed effect for flexibility
Second Half 1980s	CASE computer-aided software engineering	Assumed that software could be developed as a physical engineered product was developed	Promoted "if we only got the requirements right the first time" approach to methodological emphasis
1987	"No Silver Bullet: The Essence and Accidents of Software Engineering" Fred Brooks	Showed how complicated the human activity of programming digital computers actually is	
1990s	Commercial Distributed DBMS	Facilitated distributed processing	Complicated maintenance
1990s	Information superhighway Bitnet, Internet, WWW	Even wider spread of distributed processing	
1990s	Client server demise of the mainframe?		Beginning of n-tiered architecture
1990s	Business-driven approaches The business rule approach	Codifying business policies and operations in a standard form	Beginning of separation of rules from processing; thus easier to change rules and triggered processing
1995	Java Sun Microsystems	Difficult language to learn Program once Run "anywhere"	
2000s	Commercial rules technology	Off-the-shelf software for managing business rules	Flexibility is beginning to be mentioned as a benefit of the business rule approach

Exhibit 2.4.   (continued)

Date	Development	Significance	Flexibility Enhancement
	Programming Language Progression		
	1st-generation machine: bit no bit	Used hardware operation codes and memory addressees	Procedural—coding could only be done by "real engineers"
	2nd-generation symbolic: one for one assembler	Symbolic names substituted for operations and for data rather than machine addresses	Procedural—coding could be done by a larger number of persons
	3rd-generation macro: many for one	One symbolic macro instruction could generate many symbolic machine instructions	Procedural – further increased number of persons who could develop programs
	3rd-generation High-level syntactical	Syntactical analysis leads to variable number of macro or machine language instructions per higher level language instruction	Procedural – even further increased number of persons who could develop programs
	4th-generation	Tell the computer what to do, not how to do it	Nonprocedural Nonprogrammers can now produce "programs" or develop their own "software"
	5th-generation	Expert systems Artificial intelligence	Non procedural Borders on one of the latest buzzwords "business rule approach"
	Progression of Software Flexibility Techniques		
	High(er) level programming languages		Easier to write and modify; Nonprocedural
	Parameterization		External versus internal parameters (table files)
	Job control language		
	Reuse		macros, COPYlibs
	Object orientation		Modular approach

Exhibit 2.4. (continued)

2.5 IT Misconceptions and Flexibility Concepts

When developing flexible systems, mind-set and understanding are just as important as — if not more important than — tools and techniques. This section presents a series of pervasive and persistent misconceptions about IT that have led to such problems as failed and runaway projects and the severe maintenance burdens noted previously. These IT misconceptions have acquired the status of industry myths, in line with Roget's [Roget's II, 2003] definition of a myth:

1. A traditional story or tale that has no proven factual basis: fable, legend
2. A body of traditional beliefs and notions that has accumulated about a particular subject: folklore, legend, lore
3. Any idea of a fictitious nature that is accepted as part of an ideology by a group that is uncritical; a received idea: creation, fantasy, fiction, figment, or invention

Exhibit 2.5 presents 11 myths and contrasts them with their ultimately more manageable realities. With each myth, a flexibility concept is introduced to counteract the myth. These myths and their related flexibility concepts are discussed in more detail in later chapters.

IT Misconception	Flexibility Concept
The myth of perfect knowledge	
Myth: With enough effort, we can attain essentially perfect knowledge of a system's requirements. **Reality:** The real world changes, so knowledge of a system's requirements is necessarily imperfect, as significant parts of the requirements lie in the future and are not available at the time the automated system is developed. This myth has led to the industrywide focus on improving requirements determination methods and the corollary *myth of methodology.*	Accuracy today has virtually no effect on synchronization with change tomorrow.
The myth of methodology	
Myth: Good methods will produce good systems. **Reality:** Good methods can and do produce bad systems, when the system perfectly fitted to current requirements cannot be efficiently adapted to unanticipated future requirements.	Systems developed with such great precision can be ruinously expensive to maintain.
The myth of rapid application development (RAD)	
Myth: The race against change is won by going faster — rapid application development. **Reality:** Rapid application development may simply lead to faster development of inflexible systems if adaptability to future requirements has not been considered.	Rapid application development cannot be applied to the 60 to 100 percent that is maintenance – where the real leverage is.
The myth of the isolated system	
Myth: We'll develop the new project control system initially for the engineering department. Then as we get requirements from the other departments, we'll evolve the system and roll it out across the company. This evolutionary approach will be cost effective and will not commit us to too big a development piece at any one time. We can develop systems one at a time and fit them together into an integrated whole as we go along. **Reality:** We can build an organization's systems one at a time, but the underlying information structure for all the systems must be *analyzed and designed* first if integrated systems are to result.	Establish a single coherent stable data structure and then fit (sub)systems into that stable foundation.
The myth of the successful system	
Myth: Successful computer systems usually generate few, if any, modification requests. **Reality:** Successful computer systems generally generate continuous demands for modification.	Often the unsuccessful system is mistaken for a successful one and vice versa. Establish a system "success metric" that includes the level of usage and modification requests by system customers.

Exhibit 2.5. IT Misconceptions (*Source*: Adapted from Johnson, B., Woolfolk, W.W., and Ligezinski, P., *Business Horizons*, Mar.-Apr., 42:2, 29–36, 1999. With permission.)

IT Misconception	Flexibility Concept
The myth of the naïve customer	
Myth: Customer perceptions of what it should take to implement systems modifications are grossly unrealistic; they do not appreciate how complex automated systems are. Thus, IT needs to educate customers in this matter. **Reality:** Customer perceptions of what ought to be the case are realistic. What they do not perceive correctly is the inflexibility and fragility of current systems. IT must learn how to develop flexible and stable systems.	Build systems consistent with the customers' accurate sense that modifying the automated system should be no harder than changing the real-world system.
The myth of retroactive documentation	
Myth: The most important step in developing a replacement system is to "document the existing software system." **Reality:** The existing real-world system is usually distorted by the presence of its entrenched automated component.	Where an automated-world system has been in place for some time, it usually represents past versions of the real-world system — it is literally an accident of history.
The myth of the solution	
Myth: Information systems are solutions to business problems. **Reality:** Information systems simply offer fast, cheap, and accurate automated assistance with business functions.	Substitute the concept of "automated assistance" whenever the term "solution" is used when considering systems investments.
The myth of comparative evaluation	
Myth: The best product is chosen by comparing candidate products to *each other*. **Reality:** The best product is chosen by comparing candidate products to *requirements*.	Compare the candidate system to your requirements.
The myth of outsourcing	
Myth: We can hire an outside firm with the appropriate expertise that will manage our information technology cheaper and better, and we won't have the management headaches. **Reality:** It's your business — you must manage it — including the IT component.	The transformation processes leading to successful IT systems require diligent effort, proper project management, and just plain hard work by management, system customers, and IT professionals alike.
The myth of parallel perceptions	
Myth: Managers, customers, and IT professionals have shared perceptions of the business, technology, and their interactions. **Reality:** Managers, customers, and IT professionals speak widely different languages and have different views of both automated-world systems and the real-world systems they are derived from.	We talk as if we understand that there are serious communications problems between managers, customers, and IT professionals. But we do not walk the talk during the chaos of daily business.

Exhibit 2.5. (continued)

2.6 Summary

Over the life of an information system, it is maintenance, not development, that is the main work. And within maintenance, it is resynchronization, not error correction ("debugging"), that is the dominant activity.

- Because knowledge of a system's requirements is imperfect, the objectives of system design must include adaptability to change as well as functional accuracy.
- Our software systems can be viewed as automated representations of the real world. Systems development is therefore a series of transformations accomplished through the steps of analysis, design, and build.
- Maintenance repeats the transformation steps of development starting with a changed real-world system and ending up with a modification to the automated-world system.
- Systems must be built so that they can be synchronized with the real world, not just mirror today's business world.
- A flexible system is one that can be resynchronized with changes in the real-world system almost entirely through user-controlled data-value modifications with minimal or no program code modification or information restructuring.
- Flexible computer software requires stable information structures.
- To be truly flexible, software requires both stable data structures and stable, reliable processes that effectively utilize those structures.
- Automated-world systems must change or they die.
- Software systems capability has increased exponentially over the years, and most of these improvements have occurred in the area of computing power and development. While some of these improvements, often as a side effect, added to system flexibility, overall the advances in flexible design have not kept pace with the advances in technology.
- The IT world has misconceptions, many of which impede flexibility. These myths must be exposed and counteracted by their reality if flexibility is to progress at a more rapid rate.

It is a common IT management myth that systems development holds primacy in IT success. Over the life of an information system, however, it is maintenance, not development, that is the main work. And within maintenance, it is resynchronization, not error correction ("debugging"), that is the dominant activity.

You cannot reduce or eliminate the potential maintenance backlog of the future unless you think about it during the development phase. It is possible to design with greater flexibility than developers typically do. But you have to ask the questions: What can change? How will it affect the design? How can I design to accommodate such change? And so on. It does not seem revolutionary. It is just a minor triumph of practical thinking over wishful thinking!

Chapter 3

Outcome, Not Methodology

In their 1996 paper, "The Problem of the Dynamic Organization and the Static System: Principles and Techniques for Achieving Flexibility," Woolfolk, Ligezinski, and Johnson emphasized that development of a flexible information system requires a shift in thinking. The design objective is no longer functional accuracy with regard to current business requirements, but rather adaptability to changes so that current and future requirements can be met.

3.1 Mired in Methodology

> *The design objective is no longer functional accuracy with regard to current business requirements, but rather adaptability to changes so that current and future requirements can be met.*

Many software development methodologies already exist, and new ones are introduced almost daily. The history of these methodologies includes the waterfall method, object-oriented (OO) design, and rapid application development (RAD). More recently introduced methodologies include the rational unified process (RUP), adaptive software development (ASD), and the many agile development methods.

There are many ways to build systems. What really counts is how they perform their intended support of the business, both now and in the future. Some methodologies lend themselves to flexibility more than others. Exhibit 3.1 shows how many of the methods enhance or detract from flexibility (methods are presented in no specific order). In general, the methodologies listed here address one or more of the following:

- Building a more complete system
- Building a system faster
- Incorporating changes in requirements that are uncovered during development
- Providing better systems documentation
- Making the system easier to change during development

But none of them, with the possible exception of the business-rules approach, address directly the issue of ease of maintenance after the system is placed into operation, i.e., flexibility. Remember, built-in or planned flexibility is a characteristic of the system itself. We must first determine the nature of that characteristic and the forms it can take in the system itself, and then secondarily and derivatively determine how to achieve that outcome. See Exhibit 3.2 for an example from civil engineering of the method-versus-outcome issue.

Generally, the methodologies shown in Exhibit 3.1 provide the discipline needed to develop systems faster and with more initial functional accuracy. While this is important, it does not specifically help with the maintenance burden.

A humorous story tells of the inventor whose successful design goes against all conventional wisdom. The inventor, baffled by seeing the results of his invention, expresses his exasperation by saying, "That's fine in practice, but what about theory." The message is that developers should judge the effectiveness of methodologies by the results achieved. This brings to mind the story about a boss who kept saying, "But, Bruce, you keep getting the right answers for the wrong reasons!"

Highsmith, who is an outcome person, chronicles some of the history of what he calls "monumental methodologies":

> At the pinnacle of this approach were the Monumental methodologies of the 1980's in which fourteen volumes of detailed tasks, documents, and forms defined every aspect of development. The practice led to the development of the silver-bullet solution called computer-aided software engineering (CASE). In the 1990's the mantle of Monumental Development was taken up by the Software Engineering Institute (SEI) and given a new name — process improvement [Highsmith, 2000, p. 6].

Methodology	Summary	Flexibility Impact
Object-Oriented Design	Treats data and processes as objects with polymorphism, inheritance, data hiding, and other generality and stability-oriented features.	Mixes structure and process in the same modules. Modules can be quite large (objects). Modular approach facilitates programmer-performed maintenance but does not address flexibility directly.
Rapid Application Development (RAD)	Addresses issues of rapid iterative development and reaction to requirements changes that occur during development.	Can allow systems to be developed faster, but does not address flexible quality of outcome directly. If not pursued carefully, may actually increase the maintenance burden.
Computer-Aided Software Engineering (CASE)	Treats software development as an engineering discipline	Assumes that requirements are fully known and understood at manufacturing time. Focuses on current requirements.
Adaptive Software Design (ASD)	Specifically for larger more complex projects where collaboration is required.	Includes iterative nature that reacts to requirements changes that are encountered during development—but not necessarily after the system is in production.
Extreme Methodologies (Agile Programming)	Generally geared to more rapid development and to capturing requirements changes that surface during development. Agile Programming calls for not wasting development time on providing for any potential future requirement that may not materialize.	Does not address issue of requirements that surface after initial implementation. Defines flexibility in methodological terms as a continuous refactoring of software to changing requirements.
Joint Application Development (JAD)	Includes (all) stakeholders in the development effort.	Focuses on capture of requirements identified during development but not on potential requirement changes
Business Process Reengineering (BPR)	Not specifically a system development method—but IT is considered an enabler.	Emphasis is on process—not outcome.
The Business-Rules Approach	Aims to separate data, processing, and business rules into three tracks —each handled co-dependently.	Material on the The Business Rules web site http://www.businessrulesgroup.org says very little about flexibility and system change-oriented topics. But several of their contributors' [von Halle 2002, Ross 2003] works are heavy on the topic of flexibility—ease of system change since the rules are managed separately.
Total Quality Management (TQM)	Not specifically a system development method but IT often involved.	Emphasis is on process—not outcome.
Capability Maturity Model (CMM)	Deals only with the processes that are "believed to produce" good/better software.	Does not address outcome at all.
Rational Unified Process (RUP)	A graphical notation-based method for capturing requirements during development and documenting their implementation	Documents requirements encountered during development—not during operation.

Exhibit 3.1.   Flexibility Impact of Various Software Development Methodologies

One author investigated a system for a Fortune 500 paper company that was claiming to follow a "monumental methodology," although he remembers it as "only" 12 volumes. In any case, the development of the system did not survive the method.

At one time, civil engineers specified exactly how the contractor was to build a highway. The contractor was told what method to use: the type of machinery, how many passes to make with the roller, how many layers of fill, etc. Eventually, contractors and engineers agreed that this approach was not achieving the desired results and was stifling innovation and creativity at considerable cost to the industry. For a time debate raged between proponents of the "new way," and the "old way," but the debate is long since over. Civil engineers now specify the characteristics of a good highway, and contractors determine the best ways to produce the desired outcome. Continuous improvements are now made independently in both construction methods and design. By contrast, the software world is still in the pre-debate stage over method versus outcome.

Exhibit 3.2. Civil Software Engineering (From Johnson, B., *IEEE Software*, Nov. 1995. With permission. © 2004 IEEE)

Highsmith, who equates methodology with process and workflow, and outcome with results, goes on to say:

> In product development, indeed in any endeavor in which a degree of creativity and innovation are involved, we must abandon the workflow mentality and apply increasing rigor to managing the results.... The process workflow mentality is so engrained in our business culture that we experience a latent feeling of immaturity if we are not process-oriented [Highsmith, 2000, p. 21].

He is right. This emphasis on methods at the expense of outcome may have come about for good reasons. But whatever those reasons were, it is time to question conventional wisdom and focus on outcome — the system itself.

3.1.1 Myth of Methodology

The industrywide focus on improving methods has led to the myth of methodology:

> Myth: Good methods produce good systems.
> Reality: Good methods can and do produce bad systems, especially when the system perfectly fitted to current requirements cannot be efficiently adapted to unanticipated future requirements.

Organizations rely increasingly on system development methods to improve the precision with which requirements are elicited and implemented.

There has also been a corresponding emphasis on the automation of methods, referred to as computer-assisted systems engineering (CASE), to improve the speed with which requirements are recorded and transformed into computerized systems. Both improved system-development methods and improved development tools are good things. The reality, however, is that methods produce what they produce, and good methods simply do so more efficiently or reliably. The systems developed with such great precision and efficiency can still be ruinously costly to maintain. The focus on accuracy today has virtually no effect on synchronization with change tomorrow. The problem is not precision; the problem is change.

IT professionals must make and keep this distinction clear: first, determine *what* functionality the system must provide, and only then, secondarily and derivatively, determine *how* that functionality is to be achieved (see Exhibit 3.2).

3.1.2 Myth of Rapid Application Development

As the pace of change in the real world increases, organizations have reacted by finding ways to speed up the pace of computer systems development. That it is better to go faster is the myth of rapid application development (RAD).

> Myth: The race against change is won by going faster — rapid application development.
> Reality: Rapid application development may simply lead to faster development of inflexible systems if adaptability to future requirements has not been considered.

Treating software development as a race rather than as the dance that it really is leads to this myth. It results in application of method-oriented solutions to an outcome-based problem. RAD tools and methods are valuable additions to the developer's toolkit, but they are not magic. The result of rapid, streamlined development of new systems (or more often replacements for old systems) can simply be inflexible systems that are built faster. The erosion of development capacity by maintenance is accelerated as inflexible development is accelerated. Because techniques of rapid application development may not be transferable to maintenance work, the maintenance backlog may increase more rapidly. The point of decreasing return on IT resource investment arrives much sooner, and attention is diverted from solving the real problem — the maintenance burden created by inflexible systems. An existing inflexible automated-world system is not a green field amenable to fast footwork but more like a minefield requiring extreme care in moving about. Rapid application development, assuming it truly speeds up development or reduces its cost, can be applied only to the 40 percent (or less) of IT that is development. Rapid application development cannot be applied to the 60 to 100 percent that is maintenance [Keen, 1995], where the real leverage is.

We must stop paying homage to rapid application development. RAD is flashy and it can speed development significantly, but it does not automatically provide real payoff in terms of the development/maintenance cost ratio. So rather than focus on methodologies, developers and customers alike must focus on outcomes.

3.2 Software Engineering Shifts

The specific outcome that we are looking for is low maintenance, because it allows organizations to respond to business needs as they develop and change over time.

The popularly recognized methodologies address issues associated with the initial system development, including requirements uncovered during the development process itself, but they do not address, in any serious or detailed way, the key postinstallation issue: maintenance. So exactly what outcomes should we be looking for? Obviously, all of the traditional development project outcomes addressed by one of more of the mentioned methodologies — meeting specifications, being on time and on budget, customer satisfaction, and the like — are required outcomes. But these are not enough when months or even years after the system is installed it becomes too cumbersome to modify to meet ongoing business needs.

Proponents of methodologies may recognize that postinstallation issues do exist. The following quote comes from a book on an object-oriented analysis and design approach.

> But the real measure of goodness may not be apparent for several years after a system has been put into operation. Software lasts forever; many large organizations around the world are now maintaining application systems that are older than the programmers who maintain them! From this perspective, a good design is one that balances a series of tradeoffs in order to minimize the *total cost* of the system over its entire productive life span. Obviously, we want a system that is reasonably efficient, and we want it to be elegant, user-friendly, portable and so forth. But we also want it to be reasonably easy to test, modify, and maintain. At least half of the total cost of the system — and often as much as 90%! — will be incurred *after*

the system has been put into operation. It may not be glamorous or politically expedient, but that's where we should be focusing our attention [Yourdon et al., 1995, p. 301].

Unfortunately, Yourdon et al. have nothing more to say on this topic. The quote appears in the final chapter of the book, and the authors provide no specific information about how we should be focusing our attention except to say, "The development approach should cover the whole project life-cycle from project planning to application support during the operation phase of the life cycle" [Yourdon et al., 1995, p. 312]. The flexible approach described in this book will provide specific advice to help the reader focus attention on this issue.

The importance of outcome is often misunderstood, as shown in the following myths.

3.2.1 Myth of the Successful System

A flexible system is supposed to be modified.

Managers are often uncomfortable with change, because it tends to upset both people and information systems. This yields the myth of the successful system.

> Myth: Successful computer systems usually generate few, if any, modification requests.
>
> Reality: Successful computer systems generally generate continuous demands for modification.

Often the unsuccessful system is mistaken for a successful one, and vice versa. The system that is unused does not generate requests for the system to do more. On the other hand, the system that is really being used effectively is subjected to high levels of customer demand. "If you can produce my design report, why can't you also calculate shop times?" And once that has been done, "Why can't you make materials order lists by supplier?" Because such systems are "never finished," they are often looked upon as failures. The truth is, "Use it or lose it." Successful computer systems generally generate continuous demands for modification. Thus, it is a counterintuitive managerial truth that being bugged for money and resources for modifications is really a sign of a successful, not a failed, system. Inability to keep up with demand for modifications is a sign of an inflexible "successful system."

A system "success metric" that includes the level of usage and modification requests by system customers would be a useful indicator of inflexibility in successful systems. What we are really saying here is that a flexible system is supposed to be modified.

3.2.2 Myth of the Naïve Customer

The cost of adding tollbooths to a bridge should be independent of the length of the bridge.

System customers generally perceive that the level of effort needed to make systems modifications is out of proportion to the change requested: "All I wanted was for the system to reflect that now one person often holds two jobs. What's the big deal? How can it take six people six months? What do you mean you have to modify the information structure? And what's to test? You keep talking about all the testing that will be needed; it's just a simple request!" This common scene from the experience of IT managers has led to the myth of the naïve customer.

> Myth: Customer perceptions of what it should take to implement systems modifications are grossly unrealistic; they do not appreciate how complex automated systems are. Thus, IT needs to educate customers in this matter.
>
> Reality: Customer perceptions of what ought to be the case are realistic. What they do not perceive correctly is the inflexibility and fragility of current systems. IT must learn how to develop flexible and stable systems.

In one sense, the customer's feeling for the size of a modification is not realistic. IT customers generally do not appreciate the internal complexity of their computer applications. And when a large estimate is made for what seems to the customer to be a small modification, the estimate more or less accurately reflects the size of the work, not the size of the request. But despite the efforts to educate the customer about system complexity, the discrepancy between the customer's intuition and the current reality persists. After all, the customer deals with the real-world system and is an integral part of it, while the computer application is only a representation of the real-world system. Consequently, there is an almost inescapable expectation on the customer's part that the effort required to modify the computer system should be approximately the same size as, if not smaller than, the effort expended on the real-world system to implement the same change. In this sense, the customer's intuition should be right, particularly when the modification seems unrelated to the size of the system. Like adding tollbooths to a bridge, the cost of adding tollbooths to a bridge should be independent of the length of the bridge.

IT professionals must stop trying to educate customers and instead must make customer perceptions correct by focusing on building systems consistent with the customers' accurate perception that modifying the automated system should be no harder than changing the real-world system.

3.2.3 CRUDmudgeons: Information Structure Is the Critical Foundation

On the surface, the IT world appears to be moving very fast. Yet, in reality, the underlying foundation does not change all that rapidly or perhaps at all. Data still must be collected, validated, organized, stored, updated, deleted, and disseminated as, hopefully, useful information from which timely and enlightened decisions can be made. The most critical aspect of this underlying foundational technology is the organizing and storing of data — the database in some form.

By far the majority of systems analysis and design activity is centered on process. This is not necessarily surprising, as most users of IT systems are engulfed in their processes, i.e., what these systems do. This process orientation turns out to be unfortunate for system flexibility. When the data exists, is accurate, is properly and flexibly organized, and is properly maintained, the vast majority, if not all, of the processes can be supported both in its current form and as the business inevitably changes. It is easier and less disruptive to modify process than it is to modify data structures. With flexible information structures, even process code often requires little or no modification at all.

We focus much of our effort, therefore, on the analysis and design of the CRUD (create, read, update, destroy) portions of the systems. In effect, we are old CRUDmudgeons. The fact is that with well-analyzed and well-designed flexible databases, virtually any processes/techniques are not only eminently possible, but they are fully supported, and systems developed using them will be orders of magnitude more flexible.

We do understand that processes are important. We would apply to processes the same standards regarding quality of outcomes that we apply to information structures.

3.2.4 Object-Oriented Approach — Another Cautionary Tale

Inflexibility is its own punishment.

In doing the programming, developers of flexible system generally use an iterative prototyping approach. The assumption is that business experts are satisfied only when they have a chance to test-drive a product — the

A mid-sized insurance company decided to build a completely new and very modern computer system. A well-known software house was awarded the development contract and promised to build an advanced OO-based system. The software house interviewed employees of the insurance company and taught them how to describe their work processes in object-oriented terms. Total project expenses reached nearly $4 million. Design documents describing methods, work processes, functionalities, etc. consumed 36 feet of shelf space! Finally the first programs to maintain the partners' (client) database were presented to a client review team. Immediately flaws were discovered, including a failure to disallow incorrect combinations of title and gender (Mr., Ms., male, female, company, etc.), failure to allow multiple gender values for one title (e.g., Dr.), and failure to allow couples (Mr. and Ms.) to have a common insurance policy.

The seemingly trivial nature of the errors prompted the designers to demonstrate the virtues of OO, specifically inheritance, by offering to rectify the problem while the reviewers went to lunch. Two hours later it was apparent that the errors were merely symptoms of basic flaws involving gender-determined rate calculations and over-constrained relationships among policyholders and policies. Additional serious problems were discovered. It was determined that, although the design probably satisfied the stated original requirements, it did not meet current requirements. The enhancements would not be done free of charge, the project was scrapped, and the software house lost the contract.

Exhibit 3.3. A Mid-Sized Insurance Company (From Woolfolk, W.W., Ligezinski, P., and Johnson, B., "The Problem of the Dynamic Organization and the Static System: Principles and Techniques for Achieving Flexibility," in *Proc. 29th Annual Hawaii International Conference on System Sciences*, HICSS-29, Vol. 3, 1996, pp. 482–491. With permission. © 2004 IEEE)

outcome. The number of iterations can vary, depending on the process and the customers. The iterative approach is, of course, not unique to flexible development. Both the object-oriented (OO) approach and rapid application development (RAD) methodologies, for example, make use of iterative prototyping. We have no quarrel with either OO or RAD. There is no question that both can increase programmer productivity, in that an outcome can be achieved more quickly. By all means, use these tools. However, bear in mind that the use of an approach, technology, or set of tools does not guarantee flexibility of design, as illustrated in Exhibit 3.3.

The moral of the tale in Exhibit 3.3 is that the OO approach does not address flexibility in the sense that we have been discussing. Indeed, violations of structural and procedural stability are as easily committed with the OO approach as with any of the traditional approaches.

Similarly, rapid achievement of outcome is not enough. What is the quality of the outcome and what happens when a hole is discovered? In an information system project, the emphasis is often placed on getting results at any cost, and the perceived delay of starting over is considered unacceptable. This attitude is often counterproductive in the long run. How many of you readers have at some point regretted taking a quick-and-dirty approach to save a few hours of programming time as the long-term cost of that decision revealed itself? Bad design is its own punishment. Inflexibility is also its own punishment.

Discovery of holes may mean that the system design is not flexible. If the overarching consideration is design for flexibility, repairing the hole may mean taking the design back to square one, not simply "patching" the hole. Before alarm bells go off, let us emphasize that we are not proposing that developers throw away their program code whenever they discover a missed requirement.

In software composed of small modules, going back to square one is likely to mean reviewing and modifying an individual module. The modifications will involve changes to program code and may or may not involve changes to information structures. Nevertheless, the design team must overcome its fear of tearing things up and starting over. One of our authors repeatedly says, "I am proudest of the designs that I threw away. I would still be maintaining them and would have been unable to retire and write."

James Martin [Software AG, 1994] defines application quality as "meeting the true business requirements at the time the system comes into operation." His definition is only partially correct. Application quality also includes ease of maintenance to accommodate changes in those business requirements over the life of the software.

3.3 Summary

Development of a flexible information system requires a shift in thinking. The design objective is no longer functional accuracy with regard to current business requirements, but rather adaptability to future changes in business requirements.

- While we must be "methodical" in our system-development efforts we must not become mired in methodology.
- Recognized, popular software engineering methodologies address issues associated with the initial system development, including requirements uncovered during the development process itself. They do not address postinstallation issues such as low maintenance and the ability to easily respond to changing business needs.
- The "myth of methodology" shows that bad outcomes can proceed from "good" methods. Methods are not the answer.
- The "myth of rapid application development" tells us that without attention to flexibility, inflexible systems are just made faster while the maintenance burden increases.

- The "myth of the successful system" says that the unsuccessful system is mistaken for a successful one and vice versa. The truth is that successful computer systems generate continuous demands for modification.
- The "myth of the naïve customer" tells us that our IT systems frequently do not mirror the flexibility inherent in the business systems that they claim to support.

Rather than focus on methodologies, developers and customers alike must focus on outcomes. Traditional development-project outcomes such as meeting specifications, being on time and on budget, and customer satisfaction are important outcomes. But these are not enough when months or even years after the system is installed it becomes too cumbersome to modify to meet ongoing business needs.

The specific outcome we are looking for is ease of maintenance. Systems that are easy to maintain permit organizations to respond to changing business conditions and requirements quickly and easily.

Chapter 4

Realignment of Roles

The development and support of an information system is a complex undertaking, involving many individuals. The development and support of a *flexible* information system adds additional responsibilities for the participants, but it also provides benefits to the business and technical staff, to individual business units, and to the organization as a whole.

Flexibility brings additional responsibilities for business and technical staff, including, but not limited to, the following:

- Business staff must fully participate in the development, testing, and subsequent operation of a flexible system. They cannot distance themselves from any of these phases. They will ultimately maintain the software system, so they must understand how it meets their needs today and in the future.
- Technical staff must design and develop the software system so that, once it is in operation, they can step back and be assured that the business staff can continue to maintain the software.

The benefits of flexible systems to the business and its staff include, but are not limited to, the following:

- Enabling business people to do their jobs more effectively without having to develop work-arounds for systems that are unable to respond to their business needs.
- The ability to respond to business opportunities and threats without waiting for the maintenance logjam to clear.

■ The availability of the company's technical resources to go on to the next software system opportunity rather than being mired in maintenance.

■ Increased job satisfaction of business and technical staff. Business staff is freed to do their jobs without interference from their software systems. Technical staff are freed from the everyday fire fighting that maintenance often involves and thus receive much more professional satisfaction from their endeavors. Both camps enjoy increased mobility to move outward or upward, as they are not stuck as the only ones who can make the system work today or maintain it for tomorrow.

4.1 Roles and Responsibilities in Traditional and Flexible Development

No one person can provide all the knowledge, expertise, or time required either to develop a large formal system or to evaluate vendor-developed software products. Many individuals are typically involved. Participants fall into three major groups, or roles:

1. *Managers*: those who set direction and manage the business and IT resources
2. *Customers*: those who use a system to do their business
3. *Developers*: those who do the technical work of building and maintaining a system

Unfortunately, these three groups are frequently at odds with each other. For example, developers often believe that customers do not know what they want, either because requirements are vague or because they keep changing. Customers often believe that developers speak a foreign language and that it takes them much too long to do everything. Fingers are often pointed in blame when a system-related business failure occurs. The failure may be that the system did not perform as expected. That type of failure may result from incorrect programming, or poor communication about the business requirements, or inadequate testing, or the overlooking of possible scenarios in defining the requirements, or other reasons. Another type of failure is that system-related work was simply not completed, often due to lack of technical resources. All of these issues reflect a "myth of parallel perceptions" that must be understood and overcome if flexible software systems are to be developed.

4.1.1 Myth of Parallel Perceptions

In the daily pressure to get things done, we often fall victim to the myth of parallel perceptions.

> Myth: Managers, customers, and technical staff have shared perceptions of the business, the technology, and their interaction.
> Reality: Managers, customers, and technical staff speak widely different languages and have different views of both real-world and automated-world systems.

This myth is different from the others that we examine throughout the book. We *say* that we do not really believe the myth, but we *act* as if we *do* believe it. Furthermore, although we say that we understand that there are serious communication difficulties among managers, customers, and technical staff, we often do not try hard enough to overcome them.

Business staff must learn and understand flexible software system development as they work with the technical staff. Technical staff must obtain sufficient knowledge of the business to be able to effectively communicate the nature of flexible software systems and their development to the business staff. This requires dedication to the process as well as time and patience.

All persons/roles involved in system development have professional responsibility, responsibility to the organization as a whole, and responsibility to their individual business units or specialties. Role responsibilities exist in both traditional and flexible development, but they expand when flexibility is the goal. The primary expansion can be thought of in terms of each camp spending time in the other camp to fully understand the partnership required for flexible software development.

Exhibit 4.1 and the following discussions present traditional roles in system development as well as the added responsibilities for the flexible approach. The additional responsibilities are not trivial. They require understanding of the business, dedication to the organization, and most importantly, a focus on the future. That is, they require focus on what can happen after initial implementation, when things change.

We have assumed that customers *want* to be in control of their business, free of the need for IT intervention. Similarly, we have assumed that developers *want* to design creative and flexible approaches that free them from routine maintenance activities. If, for a given project, these two assumptions are invalid, a flexible design is not likely to emerge because it is not important to the participants.

Role • Typical titles	Traditional Responsibility	Added Responsibility to Achieve Flexibility
Manager • Executive • Business manager • IT manager	• Establish vision, strategies, and broad goals • Allocate/manage business and IT resources to support these strategies and goals	• Make sure that the accomplishment of the vision, strategies, and broad goals are not impeded by the software system developed to support them
Customer • Business staff • Business supervisors • Business owner • "Business experts"	• Identify business objectives • Define business requirements • Test system to verify that it meets business requirements	• Test against potential future business requirements and determine what types of system modification, if any, are needed to accommodate such change • After a flexible system is in place, customers make most system modifications without developer involvement
Developer • System analyst • System architect • Programmer • Software engineers • Developer • Designer	• Translate business requirements into technical design that will support those requirements • Develop system from technical design	• Understand the technical characteristics of flexible systems • Anticipate changing business requirements and develop a system that minimizes the need for IT intervention as those changes occur • Design for such change, specifically, design to place control over change in the hands of business staff • Recognize process patterns and use the same approaches when two or more processes follow the same pattern • Write programs that work indirectly (contain the logic to look up the business rules) • After implementation, serve as expert consultant for both customers and developers regarding the best way to eliminate or reduce system modification through use, or reuse, of existing system features or components

Exhibit 4.1. Roles and Responsibilities in Traditional and Flexible Development

4.1.2 Manager

The role of manager includes executive management, business management, and IT management. Managers clearly have a stake in successful system development. Typically, executives establish the vision and strategies of the organization, and departmental management identifies the broad goals and objectives to support the vision. Individuals in this role also allocate and manage the financial and human resources needed to execute against these goals.

Management, in general, views an information system as a tool for achieving business objectives quickly and effectively, for both the short term and the long term. Managers need to see that flexible systems allow faster and less expensive reaction to change.

To achieve flexibility, executives must anticipate and plan for change. Good questions to ask are: "What if strategies succeed and goals are achieved? What next? Is the system ready for quick reaction to success? To failure?" Executives must provide resources to develop or purchase the system that is ready for change.

Business managers must recognize and support the goals and strategies of the entire organization, not just of their individual business units. They must recognize that it is not a zero-sum game. These managers must advocate analysis of how success or failure of organizational goals will affect business units, interaction between units, communication among units, and requirements for system support. They must imagine what can change. Business managers need to communicate these ideas to their executives.

IT managers must advocate analysis of potential change as it may affect such areas as technical environment, system design, and IT staffing. The IT managers must also:

■ Guard against independent-minded programmers who would rather do things their own way, presenting a significant barrier to the success of a flexible system
■ Take an active role in establishing and enforcing adherence to standards, including the concept of reuse
■ Communicate their ideas to their executives

All managers must ensure that staff members — both technical and business — consider the organization as a whole and that they follow standard procedures.

4.1.3 Customers

Flexible systems offer the best possibility to achieve "new, improved good old days."

Customers are individuals who use a system to do their work. They include front-line business staff, business supervisors, and what we call "business experts." Customers must participate in both development and maintenance. They provide the business requirements and then validate the resulting system work that is done by the developers. Because communication between business and technical people is often a challenge, it may take several iterations before a system matches the business requirements. However long it takes, responsibility ultimately lies with the customers. They define the requirements and verify that the developers have met them.

Customers, as the only ones who are truly inside their system, must be responsible for: (a) conveying to developers the objectives, needs, and requirements of their systems, (b) controlling their systems, and (c) justifying their systems [Johnson, 1984]. Customers are focused on using the information system to do their job. Frustration results when inflexible design requires intervention by the IT staff for every change in business requirements. The need for such intervention leads to backlog and more frustration. Flexible systems put control over change in the hands of the business staff.

In some respects, the "good old days" before computer information systems may seem attractive to the customers. In those days they had control. When they needed to add something new to their business processes, make changes to existing processes, or record new information, they did it. There were no developers to intervene. It seems unlikely that today's customers would want to go back to quill pens and paper ledgers. As with most things, they want the best of both worlds. We believe that flexible systems offer the best possibility to achieve "new, improved good old days."

Front-line clerical staff tend to be the individuals who use the existing system most. They are all too aware of its flaws and weaknesses. Clerical staff, however, are typically oriented to the processes of their daily work, and system enhancements are viewed in terms of their effect on those processes. They have a valuable role to play in the development and modification processes, especially in the area of testing. However, the front-line staff are not likely to be the key customers in a flexible software development or redevelopment project. Key customers know that the data and flexible software depend heavily on stable data structures.

Essential to good system design is an understanding of the business and of the business requirements of the system that will support it. Such understanding starts with data. The essential data kept by an organization of today is very similar to data kept by a similar organization of a hundred years ago. The most critical customers are those who know the data elements and their relationship to each other. They typically know the processes that act on that data. Perhaps most importantly, they understand the business well enough to be able to answer the "why" question. Understanding why certain data is stored and why certain processes behave as they do, such customers are in the position to consider different approaches. They can disengage themselves from "the way we've always done it." These key customers are often found in middle management, often supervising the front-line staff, and they tend to be the people the organization turns to on a regular basis to get things done. The term "business expert" is sometimes used to classify these individuals. The use of such a term sets the right tone for a development or maintenance project. It acknowledges that the customer knows more about the business than the developer. It also acknowledges that serving the needs of the business is the point of the project. Indirectly, it also places boundaries on the customer's area of expertise. The customer is not the technical expert. The developer plays that role.

Analyzing business requirements generally involves significant role change for business experts. We will have much more to say about this in Chapter 12 on requirements. Testing a flexible system imposes additional responsibilities. Because changes to business rules ideally do not involve changes in program code, the customers must test potential future business requirements and determine what types of system modification, if any, are needed to accommodate such change. Thus testing both during and after installation becomes an important customer function with flexible software systems. We will also have much more to say about this in Chapter 15 on testing.

4.1.4 Developer

Developers are the individuals who do the technical work of building systems, both traditional and flexible. They are also generally involved in the maintenance of traditional systems. Typical job titles include developer, programmer, system analyst, system architect, software engineer, and designer.

It is critical for developers to understand that an information system is a means to a business end. It is not an end in itself. The following item from a project mission statement identifies criteria for success that apply to any information system project: "Services and systems will be driven by client needs and will exceed client expectations."

Developer responsibilities include:

■ Translating business requirements into a technical design that will support those requirements
■ Developing system from technical design
■ Anticipating potential changes in business requirements and developing a system that minimizes the need for IT intervention as those changes occur

With the flexible approach, the change for the developer's staff can be as significant as it is for the customer's. Just as the front-line business staff typically concern themselves with individual processes, the programming staff have typically concerned themselves with coding programs to support those individual processes. In building a flexible system, however, the technical staff cannot view each process independently. They must recognize process patterns and devise approaches that fit those patterns. Two or more processes that follow the same pattern should be able to use the same approach. Rather than coding programs that do their work directly, programmers have to be oriented to writing programs that work more indirectly. Programs often do not contain the actual business rules. Instead, they contain the logic to look up the rules wherever they are stored. Furthermore, because the developers have isolated many reusable pieces of complex logic, programs are often assemblies of references to other specialized programs. This approach takes some getting used to. It also requires good communication and documentation. Independent-minded programmers who would rather do things their own way present a significant barrier to the success of such an approach.

> Software engineers have not been trained to design for change.... It is necessary to stop thinking of systems in term of components that correspond to steps in processing [Parnas, 1979].

4.1.4.1 Great Designers

> *"Software construction is a **creative** process," and "great designs come from great designers."*

Because this is a book on flexible software design, we need to recognize the importance of the designer's role. According to Brooks [1987, p. 18], in his seminal work *The Mythical Man Month*, "Software construction is a creative process," and "great designs come from great designers." He further says that "whereas the difference between poor conceptual designs and good ones may lie in the soundness of design method, the difference between good designs and great ones surely does not." He also says that "sound methodology can empower and liberate the creative mind; it cannot inspire the drudge." But examples of great design, of principles, practices, and techniques that lead to well-designed computerized information systems can only help to make great designers greater, and the near greats great! Remember, however, great designers can only create great designs in a supportive, empowered environment where there are sufficient resources and time to do the job right. Developers, along with managers and customers, must work to eliminate the developer's maintenance jobs so that they can concentrate on the more creative and professional work of developing flexible software systems.

4.1.4.2 System Analyst Role Critical to Flexible Development

We believe that the system analyst role is most critical to flexible development. This role involves translating business requirements, expressed in the language of the business, into technical specifications that the programmers or software engineers can work from. This individual must work closely with the customers to verify that their requirements have been met and that potential areas of change have been identified. The analyst must also work closely with the other developers to verify that the design meets current requirements and is flexible enough to accommodate change.

The system analyst must have an understanding of both business and technology. Typically, someone filling this role needs to have significant development experience. At the same time, the systems analyst needs to know a great deal about the workings of the business, either through past experience working on the business side or through having worked frequently with customers. Sometimes a programmer may serve as both analyst and programmer. The title programmer/analyst reflects the combination of roles. Frequently, the analyst also serves as the system designer. Thus programmer, analyst, and designer may be one, two, or three persons.

Analysts must anticipate that business requirements will change and design to accommodate such change. Specifically, analysts must ensure that a proposed design places control over change in the hands of business staff whenever possible. The responsibility and value of the system analyst do not end when system implementation occurs. Very often, those in both the developer and customer camps, unaccustomed to system flexibility, assume that a new business requirement inevitably requires system modification. In a system designed with flexibility in mind, this is not true. But if the system is large, individuals may not be aware of certain or specific flexibility features of the design. A system analyst who is familiar with all areas of the system serves as an expert consultant for both customers and developers regarding the best way to eliminate or reduce system modification through use, or reuse, of existing system features or components.

In designing a flexible system, the developer knows that he will be placing control in the hands of the customers. Once the flexible design is in place, he will not typically be called on to take care of routine maintenance.

One of the best and best-known analyses of roles with regard to the development and maintenance of software systems is Zachman's [1987, 1993] framework. A representation of Zachman's framework, adapted from Hay [2000], is shown in Exhibit 4.2. The rows represent the points of view of different roles in the systems development process. The columns represent aspects of the development and maintenance process.

Exhibit 4.2 addresses various roles/stakeholders involved in the transformation from the real-world system to the automated-world system including planner, business owner, architect, designer, and programmer. Note that the names given to the various roles do not exactly correspond to the ones we have used above, but the connections are clear.

For each role, the exhibit examines the following aspects of the systems development effort: data (what), function (how), and motivation (why). To solidify our thoughts on roles and responsibilities for flexible software development, we have expanded Zachman's framework to include the added considerations required for flexibility — column eight. The flexible approach focuses on logical analysis and design, not on specific physical implementation. We believe that the flexible approach adds value to discussion of columns two, three, and seven of the Zachman model: data, function, and motivation. Columns four through six — network, people, and time — have no specific flexibility impact and have been removed from the exhibit. See Zachman [1987, 1993] and Hay [2000] for descriptions and analysis of the columns that we have removed.

4.1.4.2.1 Data (Column Two)

Each of the rows in the data column addresses understanding of and dealing with an enterprise's data. This begins in row two with a list of the things that concern the company and affect its direction and purpose. Row three is a model of the things as seen by the participants in the business. Many-to-many and *n*-ary relationships may be present, reflecting the way the business views them. Also, relationships may be shown that themselves have attributes. Row four provides more of an information-based perspective, resolving many-to-many and *n*-ary relationships, along with relationships containing their own attributes.

Attributes are more exhaustively defined. Entities are generalized to more closely reflect the underlying structure of the business and its relationships. In row five, entities are converted to table definitions, object classes, hierarchy segments, or whatever is appropriate for the type of database management system (DBMS) to be used. This is tantamount to creating the data definition language statements. In row six, the tables are actually implemented on physical media, using the underlying organization of the database management system. This is where, for example, table spaces are defined and files are allocated. The actual database itself is created, and initial data is converted and loaded for row seven.

4.1.4.2.2 Function (Column Three)

The rows in the function column describe the process of translating the mission of the enterprise into successively more detailed definitions of its operations. Row two is a list of the kinds of activities the enterprise conducts. Row three describes these activities in a business process model. Row four portrays them in terms of data-transforming processes described exclusively in terms of the conversion of input data into output data. The technology model in row five then converts these data-conversion processes into the definition of program modules and how they interact with each other. Pseudocode may be produced here. Row six then converts these into source and object code. Row seven is where the code is linked and converted to executable programs. Note that in the object-oriented approach, functions and data tend to be addressed together.

4.1.4.2.3 Motivation (Column Seven)

The motivation column is concerned with the translation of business goals and strategies into specific ends and means. This column can be expanded to include the entire set of constraints that apply to an enterprise's efforts. In row two, the enterprise identifies its goals and strategies in general, common-language terms. In row three, these are translated into the specific rules and constraints that apply to an enterprise's operation. In row four, business rules may be expressed in terms of information that is and is not permitted to exist. This includes constraints on the creation of rows in a database as well as on the updating of specific values. In row five, these business rules are converted to program design elements. In row six, they become specific programs. In row seven, business rules are enforced.

4.1.4.2.4 Flexibility Considerations (Column Eight)

In row two, the planner contemplates likely changes in goals, strategies, and anything of importance to the enterprise. In row three, the business model considers how these changes are likely to be reflected as business rules changes. In row four, the architect considers stable information structures and business rule declaration. In the fifth row, the designer

Row 1	1. Role	2. Data (What)	3. Function (How)	4-6 *	7. Motivation (Why)	8. Flexibility Considerations
Row 2	Planner • View = objectives / scope • Defines enterprise's direction and business purpose to establish the context for system development effort • Sees system as a tool for implementing strategies and achieving goals	Things important to the enterprise Entity = class of business things	Processes the enterprise performs Function = class of business processes		List of business goals / strategies	Likely changes in goals / strategies – things of importance What has changed in the past?
Row 3	Business owner • View = business model • Defines the nature of the business, including its structure, functions, organization, etc. • Sees the system as a tool for carrying out the activities that support the business strategies and goals • Business manager and IT manager must communicate the plan to the Business staff and system analyst • Business manager and IT manager must develop the plan to implement the strategies and identify the resources required	Entity relationship diagram (including $m:m$, n-ary, attributed relationships) Entity = Business Entity Relation = business constraint	Business process model (physical data flow diagram) Function = business process Argument = business resources		Business rules	How business rules are likely to change
Row 4	Architect • View = Model of the Information System • Defines the business in more rigorous information terms (e.g., describes business functions specifically as transformations of data) • Describes those things about which the organization wishes to collect and maintain information, and begins to describe that information	Data model (converged entities, fully normalized) Entity = data entity Relation = data	Essential data flow diagram; application architecture Function = application function Argument = customer view		Business rule model	Stable information structures Business rule declarations

Exhibit 4.2. Zachman Framework with Flexibility Considered (*Sources:* Zachman, J.A., *IBM Syst. J.*, 26, 3, 1987; Zachman, J.A., The Zachman Framework and Its Implications for Methods and Tools, in *Proc. Second International Conference on Software Methods*, Orlando, FL, Mar. 23, 1993; Hay, D.C., The Zachman Framework, 2000, available online at http://www.essentialstrategies.com/publications/methodology/zachman.htm. With permission.)

Row 1	1. Role	2. Data (What)	3. Function (How)	4-6 *	7. Motivation (Why)	8. Flexibility Considerations
Row 5	Designer ○ View = technology model ○ Describes how technology may be used to address the information processing needs identified in the previous rows ○ For example, relational databases are chosen over network ones (or vice versa), kinds of languages are selected and program structures are defined, user interfaces are described	Data architecture (tables and columns); map to legacy data Data design Entity = segment/row Relation = pointer/key	System design: structure chart, pseudocode Function = computer function Argument = Screen/device formats		Business rule design	Stable information structures Business rule storage and processing
Row 6	Programmer ○ View = detailed representations ○ Here particular language is chosen, and deliverables such as program listings, database specifications, network, are produced.	Data design (denormalized), physical storage design Entity = field Relation = address	Detailed program design Function = language statements Arguments = control blocks		Rule specification in program logic	Manipulating stable information structures Processing of stored rules with general purpose programs
Row 7	Functioning system ○ Is the automated world system ○ Finally, a system is implemented and made part of an organization	Data Converted data	Function Executable programs		Enforced rules	Changing business rules without modifying information structure or programs

Exhibit 4.2. (continued) *Rows 4–6 (Network, People, and Time) have no specific role in flexibility and have been removed from the exhibit.

considers flexible information structure and business rule storage. In row six, the programmer works with manipulating stable information structures and processing the stored business rules. Row seven represents an operating flexible system with a highly flexible regulation capability in which business rules changes can be made without modifying information structures or programs.

As you might expect, we consider column eight to be the most important from the flexibility consideration, but columns two, three, and seven must also be attended to in a proper manner.

This representation of Zachman's framework can help to ensure that the fidelity of the requirements model is sustained as it passes from one conceptual realm to another in the systems development or acquisition process. It also guides all parties to perform their roles with regard to ensuring that the system exhibits the maximum feasible degree of flexibility.

4.2 Flexibility Attitudes

Everyone must be committed to the goal of flexibility.

It is our firm belief that customers, technical staff, and, for that matter, all actors involved in the development of flexible systems must adopt the following attitudes:

- *Commitment*: Everyone, from the project sponsors to the technical staff and business staff, must be committed to the goal of flexibility. They must all take the vow of flexibility. Developers and customers must always ask the question, "Might this change in the future?"
- *Patience*: It may take longer to develop a flexible implementation than a specific implementation, at least until you get used to doing it.
- *Persistence*: Under pressure, developers and customers may be tempted to go with a quick-and-dirty (i.e., rigid) design, with the intention of going back later to do it right. Unfortunately, going back to it is difficult to justify when other work needs to be done. "If it ain't broke, don't fix it" becomes the justification for leaving the rigid solution in place. Eventually, the time saved with the quick-and-dirty specific implementation is lost many times over to the effort required to maintain it. No one ever goes back and does it over.
- *Creativity*: By this we mean simply thinking in new ways. This is essential and rewarding at the same time for customers and developers as they free themselves from "the way we've always done it."

4.3 Summary

- All participants in the development and operation of flexible systems acquire added responsibilities as well as added benefits.
- Customers must fully participate in all phases of development and operation. In turn, they are freed from many job limitations brought on by their inflexible software systems.
- Developers, managers, and customers must work to eliminate the developer's maintenance jobs so that they can concentrate on the more creative and professional work of developing flexible software systems.
- With flexibility, the organization gains the ability to adapt to changing business requirements and to compete more effectively. Flexibility frees up the resources of business experts who no longer need to spend time circumventing systems that impede the conduct of their jobs.
- All parties must overcome the myth of parallel perceptions and recognize the need to work together to understand both the business requirements and the process of developing flexible software system.
- Above all, all parties to the development of flexible systems must adopt the attitudes of commitment to the process, patience with the process, persistence with and at the process, and creativity. Think in new ways.

When compared with traditional systems, flexible systems represent a paradigm shift in the roles of those who are involved in its development, operation, and maintenance. Customers must be more involved in the development and maintenance of their software systems as well as the operation. Developers must design and build so as to eliminate the developer's role in maintenance. Managers at all levels are responsible for seeing that this happens.

Chapter 5

UniverSIS: A Flexible System

This chapter introduces an information system that was developed with flexibility as the guiding principle. One of the authors implemented this system, University Student Information System (UniverSIS), in the late 1990s at the University of Cincinnati (UC) and has monitored the system's evolution up to the present day. As will be seen, in that time the system has undergone frequent and even major enhancements with minimal professional IT intervention.

We present a few success stories and then explore two system features in detail from a business perspective, focusing on the benefits to the university and its business units. Chapter 17 examines these and other features in more detail, focusing on the technical design. We do not attempt to cover all aspects of the business of university administration. For our illustrations, we have selected features that have applicability to businesses other than a university. Our point is to illustrate how the flexible features save time and effort. Think flexibly as you read this chapter.

5.1 Background

The University of Cincinnati (UC) is the second-largest public institution in the state of Ohio, with approximately 34,000 students, and the largest employer in the Cincinnati area. The university has 17 colleges and offers over 300 academic programs of study ranging from associate degree to doctoral, medical, and law degrees. The scope of UC's business require-ments for a student information system covers recruitment of potential students through the completion of a student's academic program. Com-prehensive student-information-system suites offered by vendors were investigated and found to meet only 60 to 70 percent of the university's business requirements.

The UniverSIS developers divided the system into the following busi-ness modules: demographics, curriculum, admissions, registration/records, student accounts, financial aid, and degree progress audit. Of these seven modules, two were purchased — financial aid and degree progress audit — because vendor products for those modules satisfied all essential business requirements, including the ability to accommodate change easily. More detail about the business requirements for the seven modules can be found in Exhibit 5.1. The developers implemented interfaces to the vendor products and to the university's financial records and human-resource systems. The rest of the system was developed in-house.

5.2 Success Stories

Several brief anecdotes illustrate the positive impact of the flexible design of UniverSIS. In an inflexible system, the modification necessitated by the changes in requirements described in these anecdotes could be any or all of the following: costly, time-consuming, disruptive, or, most likely, not done at all. Some of the features described in these success stories are covered in more detail in Chapter 17.

5.2.1 On-Campus Transfer

Although the central admissions office used UniverSIS to process applica-tions for admission to the university, students who wished to transfer from one college to another within UC (on-campus transfer) were required to fill out paper forms. All on-campus transfer processing continued to be done manually. The situation occurred because the developers designed the admissions module based on specifications provided by the central office and were told nothing about the on-campus transfer process. Some time after the admissions module was in place, a clerical staff member from the central admissions office took a position in one of the colleges, where she was responsible for processing on-campus transfers. She recognized that the process was nearly identical to the process of the central office and asked, "Can't we do this in UniverSIS somehow?" Adding a single code

The following lists provide a flavor of the business requirements of each of the modules in UniverSIS.

Demographics
· Information about the Person, independent of relationship with the university
· ID number independent of SSN
· Multiple relationships with the university
· Relationships with other individuals
· History of name changes and reasons for change
· Personalized name format
· Multiple types of address: Residence, Business, Campus, Telecommunication
· Multiple addresses of each type, with history
· Support for e-mail addresses
· Support for international addresses

Curriculum
· Inventory of academic awards and programs
· Inventory of colleges and with history of names and deans
· Inventory of departments and department heads
· Inventory of academic disciplines
· Inventory of course subjects
· Distributed maintenance of course master catalog
· Electronic course approval with option to delegate authority
· Schedule of classes
· Distributed class ordering
· Maintenance of all instructional facilities and management of classroom space
· Multiple grading systems
· Flexible control over publication of the schedule of classes
· Rollover of classes from term to term
· Support for multiple term formats and dates
· Management of prime time slot allocations for class scheduling
· Support for both general purpose and private classrooms
· Support for multiple campuses and multiple scheduling areas within a campus

Admissions, Graduate and Undergraduate
· Business-maintained control over size of incoming class per program
· Comprehensive prospect management
· Application processing for undergraduate and graduate programs
· Automated management of required admissions credentials
· Automated admission decision option
· Recommendations for alternative programs
· Coordination of admission decisions with decision letters
· Complete history of interactions with student/applicant
· Automated assignment of admissions counselors to applications
· Transfer credit management with automated evaluation
· Applications and inquiries via World Wide Web
· Contact management
· Complete correspondence management system.
· Correspondence tracks, i.e., predefined set of mailings with personalized schedule
· Maintenance of standardized tests, e.g., SAT, ACT, GRE
· Maintenance of college and high school transcripts, optional specific courses

Exhibit 5.1. UniverSIS Business Requirements

to a business staff-controlled table, for "on-campus transfer application," allowed the UniverSIS admissions module to be used for this new purpose. Business staff performed all necessary system modifications by modifying data. The paper process for on-campus transfers was eliminated.

Records/Registration
· Support for prerequirements, co-requirements, preconditions and permissions
· Academic "fresh start"
· Registration via mainframe or Web
· Complete audit of registration activity
· Free-form comments with access security
· Support for program-related academic committees
· Maintain record of student's co-curricular activities
· Support for batch priority-based preregistration and demand analysis
· Faculty grading via the Web
· Complete audit of grade-change activity
· Student access to grades via the Web

Student Accounts
· Business-maintained account transactions
· Business-maintained charging groups
· Business-maintained billing rates and assessment rules
· Business-maintained refund schedules
· Business-maintained waiver rules
· Student waivers with authorizing person identified
· Posting of individual transactions
· Adjustment of individual transactions
· Mass posting of transactions of the same type
· Force posting of individual transactions
· Browsing of individual student account by date or term
· Online display of student bill
· Browsing of student charges
· Service blocks
· Sponsor contracts
· Mass student contract authorization
· Browse sponsor bill summary
· Browse sponsor contract students
· Integration with admissions, registration, financial aid
· Contact management
· Support for collections for delinquent accounts
· Student access to bill and loan information via the Web

Financial Aid
· Live interface with vendor-supplied financial aid package
· Support for electronic transfer of loan funds
· Support for automated determination of loan eligibility
· Student access to financial aid information via the Web

Degree Audit
· Interface with vendor-supplied degree audit package
· Online maintenance of student's program completion status
· Standard credit feature to establish course equivalencies

Exhibit 5.1. (continued)

5.2.2 Correspondence Control

UniverSIS provides a correspondence-management feature that can be used to generate personalized letters. The feature was initially developed to produce offer letters for the admissions office. Without any changes to program code, the collections office was able to utilize the same feature to generate personalized letters to students who have delinquent accounts.

Business staff performed all correspondence-related work by modifying UniverSIS data values. The only change that involved technical staff was setting up a new batch job.

5.2.3 Financial Oversight for Athletes

UC, like other large universities, is frequently under scrutiny by the NCAA to make sure that athletes are not receiving money they should not be receiving. The athletic director ordered that the system be modified, immediately, to block financial aid checks for athletes until financial aid award requirements had been verified. Only 12 hours of programmer time were required to develop the required modification, which includes automated block of the checks and automated e-mail notification to the athletics department when a change in an athlete's enrollment or financial aid status occurs. The developers were able to adapt and reuse existing features, reducing significantly the need for custom coding. In this instance, UniverSIS already had a mechanism called the "service block," a general-purpose feature used to record administrative blocks of specified services such as transcripts and grade reports. Adding a service block for financial aid checks for athletes required very minor modification to programs and no changes to data structures. The modular, flexible design proved its value.

5.2.4 Tuition and Fees

The university was faced with a sudden and unexpected midyear drop in financial support from the state. In the middle of autumn quarter, a decision was made to increase all tuition and fees as of winter quarter, five weeks away. One business staff member made all rate adjustments in less than two business days. No IT intervention was required.

The ability to change rates through adjustment of data values is of course unremarkable. In addition, however, the business staff member was also able to make any necessary adjustments to the business rules that determine which students are assessed each charge. Such rules are typically embedded in program code:

```
IF the student is registered for 12 to 18 credit hours
AND the student is enrolled in the College of Arts &
Sciences
AND the student is an out-of-state resident
AND the student does not live in a Kentucky county
with which the university has a reciprocity agreement
THEN assess Charge #1
```

5.2.5 A New College

In 1996, prior to implementation of UniverSIS, UC added a new college. By estimates of the IT department, it took approximately 5000 person-hours to make the necessary changes in the legacy student information system. Subsequently, another college was added, this time after UniverSIS was in place. As part of this change, some current students migrated to programs in the new college but were allowed to retain the tuition rates of their previous college. Those responsible for planning the addition of the new college and these special charging rules did not consider the impact on the student information system until quite late in the process. Just a few weeks before implementation of this business plan was to occur, a discussion of the system-related changes finally took place. Much to everyone's relief, business staff were able to establish the new college, its academic programs, its courses, its tuition and fees, special rules for students migrating to the new college, etc. by entering data values in existing data structures. No IT intervention was required. This was possible because the answer to the question, "What can change?" was, "We could add a new college," and UniverSIS was designed to accommodate such an occurrence.

5.2.6 Telecounseling

The admissions office decided to initiate a telecounseling effort, i.e., phone banks for recruitment of prospective students. Some of the admissions staff had seen a telecounseling software package at a conference and were anxious to buy it. One of the authors asked to see a demonstration, which was conducted over the Web. After seeing it, he pointed out that UniverSIS already had essentially all the features of the package. These existing features simply needed be combined in a new way. With approximately two days of effort, one programmer was able to provide the required functionality without any file changes or any modifications to core data maintenance logic.

5.2.7 Success Stories Summary

What these anecdotes have in common is a need to provide system support for modest changes in business requirements and to provide it quickly. The value of the flexible design is reflected in the absence of impact on the IT department. In some cases, no IT intervention was required. In the other cases, it was limited to a few days of programming effort. There was no need to realign priorities, pull programmers off ongoing projects for an extended period, hire consultants, outsource work, purchase software, or point fingers. The point of these anecdotes, and of the book, is that flexible design pays off not necessarily at the time of initial implementation, but later, when small changes in business requirements can be accommodated without a large amount of system support effort.

5.3 Two System Features

We will now look at two flexible features of UniverSIS in more detail. In Chapter 17, we provide a more extensive list of such features. The first feature, generic code and code-to-code is presented here because it is probably the easiest to understand. The second feature, locators, is presented because we often use it as an example of flexible design in later sections.

5.3.1 Generic Code and Code-to-Code

The developers of UniverSIS identified two types of regulatory data: simple entities and complex entities. These are discussed further in Chapter 8 on regulation. All records for simple regulatory entities are maintained in a single physical data structure called a "generic code table." Each simple regulatory record is composed of an entity identifier, a code, a description, an active/inactive indicator, and a default indicator. Simple regulatory records for the same entity make up a (logical) simple table. Typical examples are state, gender, and ethnic category. Exhibit 5.2 illustrates such a generic code table for state records.

When a simple regulatory entity is added to the system, no programs need to change. A new simple table is added to the generic code table, and table owners are designated. The table owners determine who has access to the table. Those who have access to the table maintain its contents. The data dictionary enforces the correct length of values stored in the code field. The instant a value is added to a simple table by a

Entity	Code	Description	Inactive	Default
STATE	AL	Alabama	N	N
STATE	AR	Arkansas	N	N

Exhibit 5.2.   Generic Code Table

Entity	Code	Description	Inactive	Default
UCACADINT	BIOL	Biology	N	N
UCACADINT	ZOOL	Zoology	N	N

Entity	Code	Description	Inactive	Default
ACADINFO	BIOL-1	Biology brochure	N	N
ACADINFO	BIOL-2	Zoology brochure	N	N

Exhibit 5.3. Code Tables for UC's Academic Interest Areas and Academic Information

business staff member, the value is available for use in any of the functions that validate a field or fields against that table. Once added to a simple table, values are never deleted; instead, they are simply deactivated. This prevents codes from ever being "orphaned." Two examples from the admissions module are illustrated in Exhibit 5.3. These simple tables identify academic interest areas and preprinted informational brochures.

Values within simple tables are often related to each other. For example, the university might wish to send the brochures for both biology and zoology to prospective students who express an interest in either biology or zoology. To provide system support for such relationships, UniverSIS has a mechanism called a code-to-code structure. It is a simple one-directional translation table. The argument is composed of a "from" table-ID and code plus a "to" table-ID. The result is a code from the "to" table. Given the three components of the argument, a translation module can return the result code or codes. The code-to-code mechanism allows the system to serve as a virtual business expert. Exhibit 5.4 illustrates the code-to-code mechanism for UC's academic interest areas and academic information.

This tool has had a significant impact in the admissions office. Before UniverSIS, there was no consistent relationship between the prospect's academic interest and the materials actually sent. Student employees prepare most of the mailings, and their training and attention to detail varies. Now UniverSIS does the analysis and provides the student employee with a list of specific materials to be sent to the prospect. It knows the rules and follows them consistently.

The admissions office was able to extend this functionality. UC receives ACT and SAT scores in electronic form. Included in the individual's record is a list of academic interests, coded with the testing-service values. Using the generic code and code-to-code mechanisms, business staff matched

```
(Argument)                                      (Result)
|----------------------------------------------| |-------------|
            From        To
UCACADINT    BIOL    ACADINFO          BIOL-1
UCACADINT    BIOL    ACADINFO          BIOL-2
UCACADINT    ZOOL    ACADINFO          BIOL-1
UCACADINT    ZOO     ACADINFO          BIOL-2
```

Exhibit 5.4. Code-to-Code Mechanism for UC's Academic Interest Areas and Academic Information

Entity	Code	Description	Inactive	Default
ACTACAD	001	Biology	N	N
ACTACAD	002	Zoology	N	N

Entity	Code	Description	Inactive	Default
SATACAD	441	Biology	N	N
SATACAD	442	Zoology	N	N

Exhibit 5.5. Code Tables for Academic Interest Areas Used by ACT and SAT

the ACT/SAT academic interests to the university's information brochures automatically.

First, the admissions office established simple tables for the academic interest areas used by the testing services—one for ACT (American college test) and one for SAT (scholastic aptitude test) — as shown in Exhibit 5.5. Then the admissions office established a set of code-to-code records for each testing service's academic interest codes, translating them into their UC equivalents. From the sample tables in Exhibit 5.6, we see that ACT interest codes of 001 and 002 will be translated to UC codes of BIOL and ZOOL. For the SAT, interest codes of 441 and 442 will also be translated to BIOL and ZOOL.

A chain of relationships is now established. An ACT interest of 001 translates into a UC interest of BIOL, which in turn translates into both a

From	To	
ACTACAD 001	UCACADINT	BIOL
ACTACAD 002	UCACADINT	ZOOL
SATACAD 441	UCACADINT	BIOL
SATACAD 442	UCACADINT	ZOOL

Exhibit 5.6.   Code-to-Code Mechanism for Academic Interest Areas Used by ACT and SAT

Biology brochure and a Zoology brochure, as shown earlier. ACT interest of 002 and SAT interests of 441 and 442 follow the same pattern.

5.3.2 Generic Code and Code-to-Code: Discussion

The data structures of the simple tables and the code-to-code mechanism are very stable, yet UC continues to find new ways to use the features. Control of the contents is in the hands of the business staff. When coding must make use of the simple tables or code-to-code relationships, the programmer needs to know only which tables and code-to-code relationships are needed to support a given process. A program is coded to pass parameters identifying the tables and relationships to a standard, reusable routine that returns the desired results.

5.3.3 Locators

To generalize the concept of addresses, the developers coined the term "locator," the idea being that the point of an address was to have a means of locating an individual. Since the ways of locating an individual have expanded beyond physical location, it was necessary to accommodate both addresses and nonphysical locations, e.g., cell phones, e-mail addresses, and World Wide Web addresses.

The developers identified four categories of locator:

1. Residence
2. Business
3. Campus
4. Telecommunication

Residence	Permanent
Residence	Local
Residence	Co-op
Residence	Parent
Residence	Billing
Residence	Temporary
Business	Employer
Campus	Department Office
Campus	Residence Hall
Telecommunication	Personal (e-mail)
Telecommunication	University (e-mail)

Exhibit 5.7. Locator Types

Each category can have one or more locator types. Within each locator category, business staff can define locator types, as shown in Exhibit 5.7. For each locator category, predefined data elements are available, as illustrated in Exhibit 5.8.

As the need for additional types arises, business staff can add them without the need for software modification. The Telecommunication-Personal locator illustrates how changes in the real world can have an effect on a system. When the UniverSIS project began, all students received a University e-mail account and almost no students had another e-mail account. Today, approximately 70 percent of incoming freshmen have a Web-based e-mail account when they arrive at UC. In addition, students increasingly have their own Web sites. UniverSIS can accommodate Web address without any system changes with the addition of a new locator type.

The locator feature provides for both domestic and international addresses. Locators are effective for specified date ranges. This feature has proved useful for students who will live at a temporary location for a specific period of time. For example, UC has a number of co-op programs that require students to obtain work experience in their fields. The co-op address can be defined for the specific ten-week co-op period. The system maintains a history of locator changes.

A Web interface to UniverSIS allows students to make modifications to their address information directly. Students change local address frequently, making it a challenge to keep local addresses accurate on the system. Because the Web has become the students' preferred method of registration for classes, students now get an active reminder to verify their address information each term as they register for classes. The locator

LOCRES - Maintain Residence Locator

*ID: 000 99 9365
Jane Student

*Locator Code....: __
Street..........: _____
_____
City............: _____
*State...........: __   Zip Code....: _____ ____
Telephone Number: ___ ___ ____ Extension: ____ Unlisted?...: N (Y/N)
Fax Number......: ___ ___ ____

Province........: _____
*Country.........: __
Postal Code.....: _____
Internat'l Phone: _____ Extension: ____ Unlisted?...: N (Y/N)
Internat'l Fax..: _____

Begin Date.: __ __ ____ End Date.: __ __ ____

LOCBUS - Maintain Business Locator

*ID: 000 99 9365
Jane Student

*Locator Code....: __
Company Name....: _____
Company Position: _____
In Care of......: _____
Street..........: _____
City............: _____
*State...........: __   Zip Code: _____ ____
Province........: _____
*Country.........: __
Postal Code.....: _____
Internat'l Phone: _____ Extension: ____
Internat'l Fax..: _____

Telephone Number: ___ ___ ____   Extension: ____
Fax Number......: ___ ___ ____

Begin Date: __ __ ____ End Date: __ __ ____

Exhibit 5.8. Predefined Data Elements for Each Locator Category

```
                    LOCCAMP - Maintain Campus Locator

                              *ID: 000 99 9365
                               Jane Student

        *Locator Code..........: __
        Campus Mail Location..: ____
        *Building..............: _____
        Room Number...........: _____
        Telephone Number......: ___ ___ ____
        Fax Number............: ___ ___ ____

        Begin Date: __ __ ____ End Date: __ __ ____ Bad Locator? N (Y/N)
```

```
                    LOCTELE - Maintain Telecontact Locator

                              *ID: 000 99 9365
                               Jane Student

        *Locator Code..........: __

        Telephone Number......: ___ ___ ____
        Fax Number............: ___ ___ ____
        E-Mail................: _____

        International
        *Country Code..........: __
        Telephone Number......: _____
        Fax Number............: _____

        Begin Date.: __ __ ____ End Date.: __ __ ____ Bad Locator?.: N (Y/N)
```

Exhibit 5.8. (continued)

feature has improved the quality of data while reducing the workload of the staff maintaining that data.

5.3.4 Locator: Discussion

Like those of the generic code and code-to-code features, the data structures of the locator mechanism are very stable. There is no limit to the number of locators that can be recorded for an individual. This provides a great deal of flexibility, but it presents some difficulties as well. Within UniverSIS, it is not enough to ask what a student's address is. You have to ask, "Which address" and "On what date?" As with generic code and code-to-code, the developers built a single, reusable module for retrieval of locator information. Given the individual's ID, locator type, and date, it returns the appropriate information.

5.3.5 Two System Features: Summary

The two features presented here convey the nature of flexible software design. Neither is especially complex. For those at UC, it may even seem obvious that such features should be part of the system design. In fact, though the value of these features is now obvious, their design was not.

5.4 Summary

- UniverSIS is an example of a successful flexible system with a multiyear track record of maintenance changes and enhancements performed largely by business staff.
- The primary success of UniverSIS is that it helps the business staff do their jobs better and with less effort. Its success can also be judged by how well it accommodates current and future business requirements and by how business staff have taken ownership of the system.
- The value of UniverSIS's flexible design is further reflected in the absence of impact on the IT department.
- Generic code tables and code-to-code mechanisms — examples of flexible features used in UniverSIS — allow the system to serve as a virtual business expert. These data structures are very stable. UC continues to find new ways to use the features.
- The locator feature shows that an apparently simple thing, an address, can be quite complex. Designing a flexible feature to accommodate that complexity positioned the organization well for real-world changes of the future.

The UniverSIS developers found that some of the UC's business staff enjoyed the process of developing a system more than others, but in the end they all judged the system by the results. Success was measured by whether the system helped them to do their jobs better and with less effort. The developers found it worthwhile to emphasize to the business staff that they were designing UniverSIS with future modification in mind.

Initially, this emphasis was met with skepticism, since it appeared to slow development. Over time, however, as the inevitable modifications were accommodated easily by the design, the benefits of flexibility became clear. As new business requirements emerge, users recognize how much direct control they have. Furthermore, they recognize the value of reuse and consistency. The authors believe that the success of any system can be judged by how well it accommodates current and future business requirements and by how business staff takes ownership of the system. By those standards, UniverSIS can be judged a success.

WHAT IS REQUIRED TO ACHIEVE FLEXIBILITY

The specific system development outcome we are looking for is ease of maintenance. Systems that are easy to maintain permit organizations to respond to changing business conditions and requirements quickly and easily. Our definition of a flexible, easily maintained system is one that can accommodate change with little or no program modification.

The potential maintenance backlog of the future cannot be reduced or eliminated unless you think about it during the development phase. But what are the essential ingredients for flexible software design? And how are flexible systems designed and developed?

The five chapters in Part II present the key ingredients, or techniques, for achieving flexibility:

- The discussion of what to do to achieve flexibility starts in Chapter 6 with a set of guidelines for flexible design. These design guidelines provide a solid foundation upon which the flexibility techniques in the subsequent chapters build.
- Chapter 7 emphasizes the importance of stable identifiers in flexible software design. It presents key characteristics of stable identifiers, lists what is wrong with many of today's identifiers from a flexibility standpoint, and shows the errors to avoid in designing and assigning identifiers.
- Chapter 8 presents the concept of regulation, which is used to manage a system's artificial limits or business rules. Two types of

regulation are covered: general business rules regulation and cardinality regulation. Business staff can use regulation to adjust system behavior without IT intervention.

■ Flexible systems require stable information structures, and Chapter 9 addresses the issue of how to stabilize the information structure. We separate structure from process through the use of generic entities, generic relationships, recursion, and variable typing, all of which make the system more flexible. These generic information structures support a wide variety of processing, and processing changes, without the need for structure modification.

■ Chapter 10 introduces the Generic Entity Cloud (GEC) — a flexible, generic information structure that supports all of the above techniques with regard to stable data structures and flexible software systems. The GEC provides an automatic way to implement highly stable data structures. The information structure of a GEC consists of generic entities formed into logical rings with a cloudlike appearance, thus giving the GEC its name. Part IV presents several applications of the GEC as well as a number of extensions that show its versatility in designing and developing flexible systems.

Part II tells you "what" to do. Part III explains "how" to apply these techniques in the development of flexible systems.

Chapter 6

Guidelines for Flexible Software Design

Done well, software systems can serve an organization for many decades over multiple technological generations. If the attributes of flexible software systems are recognized, and if the guidelines and techniques are understood and practiced, then fewer inflexible software systems will be created. The schedule and cost trade-offs that today often result in seriously compromised design quality can be shifted in favor of preserving designs that will pay for themselves, if not quickly, then repeatedly, by extending the cost-effective life of the system.

System flexibility does not occur serendipitously; it is the result of focused efforts. In learning what to do to achieve flexibility, start by following the guidelines presented in this chapter:

- Treat "design" as a noun
- Design for the long haul
- Observe consistent standards
- Use N-tiered architecture
- Employ individual data objects
- Take advantage of reusable logic
- Code general-purpose routines
- Recognize the limits of flexibility

6.1 Treat "Design" as a Noun

Design is typically treated as a process — as part of software development. This again puts the emphasis on the process rather than the outcome. Treat "design" as a noun so that it describes what flexible software systems are, do, and look like.

6.2 Design for the Long Haul

Flexibility is about the system being functional for the long haul. The top executive or sponsor must be involved in the identification of broad long-term objectives of the organization and of the system that is to support it. A mission statement for a specific software development project is helpful in providing a long-term focus. System development is hard work, often over an extended period of time, and participants in a project must be able to step back periodically and recall the long-term purpose of their efforts. The long-term purpose is never simply to "get the system implemented."

In flexible development, when the design proves inadequate because the original design is too rigid, it must be revisited and revised where necessary. Though this can be painful, the effort to correct the design and make it more flexible will be worthwhile in the long run. Remember, we are not designing just for current requirements, but also for business needs that will surface in the future. New requirements may emerge even during the development process. If you discovered during development that a new requirement necessitated changes to data structures and program code, you can be nearly certain that this pattern will be repeated in the future after the system is in production.

6.3 Observe Consistent Standards

All the members of the development team must follow a consistent approach. This means that consistent technical and user interface standards must be defined and enforced. Effective software tools can facilitate establishment of standards. A data dictionary can be used to define standard fields and data relationships. Use of program models and templates facilitates coding. A code generator, in conjunction with the active data dictionary, reduces significantly the amount of manual coding that must be done. Technical managers must ensure that standards are documented and must enforce their use.

We have found absence of standards to be one of the greatest impediments to quality designs. It appears that very few programming managers enforce standards, even when standards are in place. Obviously, unenforced standards are not standards at all. We therefore make the following strong recommendations about standards:

■ Consistent standards must be defined, recorded, and understood by all involved.
■ Standards must be rigorously enforced.
■ Standards must be subject to review and modification.

Like the real world in general, the world of system development changes. Members of the development team should be encouraged to submit proposed changes through a review process. Once accepted, proposed changes become part of the standard and must be enforced.

The following excerpt is a preamble to a set of standards that are to be followed to the "spirit", not just the letter.

> In all instances, the standards, which follow, have grown from proven need, stem from actual experience, and are based on common sense. It is intended that they be interpreted according to the "spirit of the law" as well as the "letter of the law." Once the situation which causes such standards to be recommended is recognized and the common sense upon which they are based is appreciated, then they should become an almost "second nature" coding technique. Standards can be made to work by continuing awareness of the spirit in which they are intended and by keeping them current with the personnel, applications, hardware, software, and practice of the industry [Johnson and Ruwe, 1991].

6.4 Use N-Tiered Architecture

While it can be a good thing, N-tiered architecture does not guarantee flexibility.

The term "N-tiered architecture" is used widely in IT today. Even when a traditional development approach is used, incorporating N-tiered architecture into system design provides flexibility by separating the user interface, business logic, and data storage. This approach allows various interface media, such as touch-tone, cell-phone, World Wide Web (WWW), or personal digital assistant (PDA), to be utilized without change to business logic or data storage. For example, when the UniverSIS project began, the World Wide Web was in its infancy. The developers were able to include a Web interface without any change to core business processes. It is not just the business that may change. The world is also changing.

The N-tier concept has more to do with physical separation of the tiers than with the application design, which is our primary concern. The database can be on one machine, programs running on one or more machines, and the user interface on the Web. This provides flexibility of a kind different from the topic of this book. It is possible to have an inflexible Java application with a Web interface running on an N-tiered architecture on multiple platforms. Conversely it is possible to have a flexible COBOL application with green screens running completely on a mainframe. While it can be a good thing, N-tiered architecture does not guarantee flexibility.

6.5 Employ Individual Data Objects

Identify logical data entities, and entity types, and maintain them as individual objects — generic entities and generic-entity clouds (GECs, presented in Chapter 10). Like N-tiered architecture, object-oriented (OO) design is consistent with, though not synonymous with, flexible design. In UniverSIS, each object has its own maintenance program. The object maintenance program performs all maintenance of object records. All business rules are enforced through that object, ensuring that those rules are applied consistently. It is essential that generic entity types be considered in the design.

We have more to say on this topic in Chapter 9 on stable data structures and Chapter 10 on generic-entity clouds (GECs).

6.6 Take Advantage of Reusable Logic

Code reusable logic in callable routines. Use of such routines falls under the heading of "standards." Documenting such routines and requiring uniform use of the routines is an essential aspect of technical management. This is an area where communication and supervision of technical staff are critical.

There generally is more than one logical way to solve a problem, and it is critical that the review process ensure that an effective logical solution is used. A colleague [Scheuer, 2004] recently reported this situation to us.

> I remember a very specific situation where an individual who reported to me complained that his "very logical approach" to modifying a program didn't work. I pointed out to him that

while I agreed with his approach, it did not follow the same logical pattern used by the original program developer.

Another colleague [Murphy, 2004] reported,

> Reusable logic is one of the most useful ideas in modern programming, but also one of the hardest to achieve. It takes careful thought on what functions are necessary at the beginning, and good cataloging tools to allow programmers to find the function they are looking for. There have been many instances over the years where functions were duplicated because a programmer couldn't find the one he wanted. There is just so much code a programmer is willing to pore through to find the right function when on a deadline.

We have observed that programmers typically take pride in their work and try to write the best code possible. This is a good thing. However, it is often possible to improve the effectiveness and efficiency of code. Let us say that there is a standard routine to calculate a customer discount. Programmer X, while working on an assignment that makes use of the standard routine, may determine that there is a better way to calculate the discount.

The wrong approach, one unfortunately taken all too often, is for Programmer X to write his own "improved" routine. This is bad for several reasons. The two routines may not produce identical results in all cases. Even if the logic is identical, changes in the logic will need to be made to both programs and both must then be tested. Other programmers may not be aware of the existence of two routines and may, when making modifications, apply the modifications only to one. And so on.

The right approach would be for Programmer X to propose changes to the existing routine through an established review process. The result may be agreement that the changes do in fact improve the processing of the program. The result may be that Programmer X is made aware of a critical factor that led to the existing design. The result may be that the proposed changes improve processing only for a special situation, the one Programmer X is working on, but is likely to degrade performance in the majority of situations.

The point is that there was a standard routine for a reason, and changes to a standard routine need to be reviewed thoroughly. Programmers must not exercise the option to write their own code because they "can do it better." At one time, the term "ego-less programming" was in favor. While the term is not often heard these days, the idea is still applicable. Program code is not about the programmer. It is about its contribution to the system. Exhibit 6.1 demonstrates the value of shared logic routines. It is

Way back when, one of our authors was in a system software development group for a Fortune 500 company that utilized a second-generation computer with a powerful macroinstruction language. The programmers in this little group loved writing powerful macros that with one instruction could generate literally hundreds of lines of one-for-one symbolic machine code, which could vary significantly depending on the nature of the operands. Given this, the programmers decided among themselves that whenever any kind of logic or programming was done for the third time, it would be made into a macro, written up, and placed in the library for all to use. Subsequent changes or additions would be made to this very same macro and the documentation updated and redistributed. As a result significant programs requiring very little testing could be written quickly in very few instructions.

Exhibit 6.1. Don't Reinvent the Wheel

echoed today in the "agile methodology" approach to computer programming, which calls for diligent adherence to reuse of computer code (see Chapter 12).

6.7 Code General-Purpose Routines

Develop general-purpose, reusable business processes whenever possible. Separate business processes often follow the same pattern. In such cases, a general-purpose processing tool should be developed, rather than purpose-specific processing tools. We provide examples throughout the book. For example, the UniverSIS developers generalized the process of producing admission decision letters, the result being the correspondence-management feature identified in Chapter 5.

6.8 Recognize the Limits of Flexibility

Recognize that there are limits to flexible design. We emphasize the importance of letting business staff control system behavior through maintenance of data. There will be times when this is simply not possible. For example, in the UniverSIS admissions module, a status is recorded for each application: denied, accepted, confirmed. Each status triggers a predefined process that results in creation of other records. The developers could not give users the capability of adding new status values because they had no way of simultaneously giving them control over which processes were triggered by those values. New processes, i.e., programming, may be needed when a new value is added.

In a human-resource system, there may be two types of employee, hourly and salaried. Certain information would be recorded for each type. Let us say that a new type, contractor, was introduced. Simply adding a new value to the list of employee types may not be sufficient. It is possible that new information specific to contractors would need to be recorded. Modification of information structure and programs may be required.

6.9 Summary

- Design is typically treated as a process — as part of software development. This puts the emphasis on the process rather than the outcome. Treat "design" as a noun so that it describes what flexible software systems are, do, and look like.
- Flexibility is about the system being functional for the long haul. The top executive or sponsor must be involved in the identification of broad, long-term objectives of the organization and of the system that is to support it.
- System development is hard work, often over an extended period of time, and participants in a project must be able to step back periodically and recall the long-term purpose of their efforts.
- All the members of the development team must follow a consistent approach. This means that consistent technical and user interface standards must be defined and enforced. Technical managers must ensure that standards are documented and must enforce their use.
- Incorporating N-tiered architecture into system design provides flexibility by separating the user interface, business logic, and data storage. This approach allows various interface media, such as touch-tone, cell-phone, World Wide Web, or personal digital assistant (PDA), to be utilized without change to business logic or data storage.
- Identify logical data entities, and entity types, and maintain them as individual objects — generic entities and generic-entity clouds (GECs, presented in Chapter 10).
- Code reusable logic in callable routines. Use of such routines falls under the heading of "standards." Documenting such routines and requiring uniform use of the routines is an essential aspect of technical management.
- Develop general-purpose, reusable business processes whenever possible. Separate business processes often follow the same pattern. In such cases, a general-purpose processing tool should be developed, rather than purpose-specific processing tools.
- Recognize that there are limits to flexible design. There will be times when it is simply not possible or affordable to have business staff control system behavior through maintenance of data.

These design guidelines provide a solid foundation upon which to build the flexibility techniques presented in the subsequent chapters.

Chapter 7

The Importance of Stable Identifiers

Unstable identifiers are responsible for a significant share of the maintenance burden. Identifiers are unstable when they contain information, because virtually any information about the thing identified is subject to change. In contrast, stable identifiers are information-free, conforming to the principle of strict uniqueness discussed below. Stable identifiers are an essential component of a stable information structure, and they play an important part in reducing the maintenance burden. It is essential that the identifiers (primary keys) used in a system not be subject to modification as the requirements of the system change.

7.1 Information-Free Stable Identifiers

> The key to identifier stability is the exclusion of meaning from the identifier. That really is the beginning and end of this subject: descriptive IDs, no; indicative-only IDs, yes.

Identifiers are the names we give to things, and naming conventions are the rules devised to assign names to things. Identifiers are artifacts of serious convenience. The ability and inclination to name things is so convenient that it is probably wired into our brains. This chapter highlights serious mistakes that are frequently made in the design of identifiers.

When checking in at a resort we were told that we were assigned to cabin 58 and were given keys with 5602 stamped on them.

When we checked the map that we were given to see where cabin 58 was—no cabin 58 was shown. We saw that all cabins had names. But, fortunately, the map included a table for conversion between numbers and names. However, it was in no particular order—so after a serial search we found that cabin 58 was named Snowdrift. And the location of Snowdrift was shown on the map.

Upon arriving at a cabin with the sign Snowdrift, we discovered that it also had another number 1251 posted on its side. The last inconsistency in naming and numbering was that the phone extension was 1492!

Exhibit 7.1. Where Are We?

Chapter 14, "Implementing Stable Identifiers," shows how to do it right. The importance of identification, for both human and software systems, cannot be overemphasized, as demonstrated in Exhibit 7.1.

The terms "identifier" and "name" are used informally and interchangeably. Certainly distinctions exist among these and other similar terms, such as "primary key," "label," "tag," "handle," and "functional determinant." However, virtually everything presented here will apply to all these terms, and where there are differences, the context should be apparent and easily supplied by the reader. For example, where we use the term "identifier," the reader may mentally supply the term "primary key" when it is clear we are speaking at the level of files and fields as distinct from entities and attributes. We will use the term "identifier" generically to mean that which picks out a single instance of a thing, regardless of whether we are speaking of the real-world system or the automated system, and regardless of whether the thing so picked out is a simple thing (entity) or an associative thing (relationship). We will later explicitly make a distinction between internal and external identifiers relative to the automated system.

Identifiers are a core part of the information structure, and a stable structure is essential to flexibility. There are two basic types of information-structure modifications that can be performed on a system, both of which are to be avoided:

1. Moving a property (attribute) from one thing (entity) to another
2. Changing the semantic characteristics of a property's identifier

This chapter assumes that the information structure has been designed so that all attributes are aggregated with their correct entities and focuses only on the second issue: identifier stabilization.

The key to identifier stability is the exclusion of meaning from the identifier. That really is the beginning and end of this subject: descriptive IDs, no; indicative-only IDs, yes. The reason an entire chapter is devoted to this subject is twofold. First, the potentially severe consequences of using unstable IDs are usually not adequately appreciated. Second, innumerable texts, manuals, articles, and classes have for years provided intuitively appealing but incorrect advice on how to form IDs, to the point where it is commonly assumed to be a closed subject. Identifier stability has had many proponents over the years, but for some reason the voices of those proponents are rarely heard. Von Halle [2002] reminds us that Whitener [1989] documented the core characteristics of sound identifier design many years ago, and, of course, they have been independently invented and reinvented many times both before and since.

7.1.1 Uniqueness and Invariance

Uniqueness is a necessary condition, but it is not a sufficient condition. The other fundamental requirement is invariance.

A fundamental requirement that identifiers must satisfy is, of course, uniqueness. Without uniqueness you have ambiguity (Exhibit 7.2). Specifically, a naming convention must assign unique identifier values on a one-to-one basis to each distinct thing to which the convention applies. Here are a few names that satisfy this condition; they are each unique within their appropriate contexts: Zooey, Slartybartfast, Chingachgook, Gilgamesh, THX1130, Heliogabalus, Albuquerque, Poodpah, and 3944865. In contrast, we have not only the fictitious Bruces, but the 2300 Zhang Lis in Tianjin, China; the 4000 Hansens of Oslo, including 50 Hans Hansens; and the Danes' reaction to ambiguity with tombstone inscriptions such as Mr. Managing Director Jensen and Mr. Unskilled Worker Jensen [Kaplan and Bernays, 1997].

Uniqueness is a necessary condition, but it is not a sufficient condition. The other fundamental requirement is invariance. Stability of an identifier under changing conditions is as essential as uniqueness if we want stability in the information structure. The names given above also satisfy this condition: they are unchanging by virtue of being meaningless, and they convey nothing about the things to which they have been assigned — not color, gender, age, political persuasion, or even type. We may know, with the exception of the last two names, that these refer to people and places only because they are famous, not because of any information in the names themselves (Exhibit 7.3).

Second Bruce	Goodday, Bruce.
First Bruce	Oh, hello, Bruce.
Third Bruce	How are yer?
First Bruce	Bit crook, Bruce.
Second Bruce	Where's Bruce?
First Bruce	He's not here, Bruce.
Second Bruce	Ah, here comes the Bossfella now — how are yer Bruce?
Fourth Bruce	Goodday Bruce, hello Bruce, how are yer Bruce? Gentlemen, I'd like to introduce a Chap from pommie land …who'll be joining us this year here in the Philosophy Department at the University of Woolamaloo.
All	Goodday.
Fourth Bruce	Michael Baldwin Michael Baldwin — this is Bruce. Michael Baldwin — this is Bruce.
First Bruce	Is your name not Bruce, then?
Michael	No, it's Michael.
Second Bruce	That's going to cause a little confusion.
Third Bruce	Yeah. Mind if we call you Bruce, just to keep it clear?

Exhibit 7.2.   The Four Bruces and Michael [Chapman, 1989]

7.1.2 Strict Uniqueness

The frequent failure in systems design to engineer static names has serious and costly consequences and takes many forms.

We introduce a term, strict uniqueness, at this point, which we define in contrast to simple uniqueness as follows.

- *Simple uniqueness*: An identifier must be at least unique.
- *Strict uniqueness*: A stable identifier must be at least unique and at most unique.

MOYERS:	Did you name the quark?
GELL-MANN:	Oh yes, I chose the name.
MOYERS:	Does a scientist get that privilege: If you discover something new in the universe, you can name it?
GELL-MANN:	I guess that's right.
MOYERS:	Why "quark"?
GELL-MANN:	Well, I could easily have invented some pompous name, derived very carefully from some apparently appropriate root. But names like that often turn out to have been derived from something inappropriate, as you understand more about the phenomenon. With a meaningless name like "quark," that could never happen. I had the sound first; I didn't know how I would spell it. And then while I was paging through James Joyce's Finnegans Wake, I came upon the line, "Three quarks for Muster Mark."

Exhibit 7.3.   Naming of the Quark [Moyers, 1990]

For example, the ABC Company uniquely identifies one of its products as P6DHL225, which is encoded with information about the product:

P6 = production plant = Peoria
DH = product type = heavy-duty detergent
L = material type = liquid
225 = sequence number within product type

This identification convention satisfies the requirements for simple uniqueness, but not for strict uniqueness. If the production of the item were moved to the Kansas City plant, the product ID would be subject to change. If the product were uniquely identified as, say, 273758, with no encoded information, then nothing could change that would require the ID to be changed. This identification convention satisfies the requirements for strict uniqueness. The "missing" information can, of course, be maintained as attribute data elements of the product entity instance determined by the ID 273758, so no information is lost.

The main objection to meaningless identifiers is that it is convenient to have the information easily available to hand, so to speak. Embedding it in the ID saves the effort of looking it up. It is argued here that the disadvantages of meaningful IDs far outweigh the advantages. Identifiers should serve only one purpose: to indicate the instance. The identifier should not be used to describe, sequence, or categorize the instance or to relate the instance to anything. Invariance is the issue. The frequent failure in systems design to engineer static names has serious and costly consequences and takes many forms.

7.1.3 Name Changes

How serious is the problem of name changes? The systems that interest us here are just those systems that deal with many instances of the same kind of thing and many different kinds of things — multiple orders, customers, assets, etc. — and with multiple objects of any sort and of many sorts. When references are made to those instances within a system, they are recorded in the system's current files, in history files, in archived files, in reports, forms, drawings, charts, etc., on paper, on microfiche, in catalogs, in people's memories, and so on. This is not a consequence of "uncontrolled" redundancy, it is a normal outcome in even a fully normalized database system. If the value of the ID is changed, the many references to it must also be located and changed accordingly. While changing an ID value or the size of an ID is not intellectually demanding, even in a large system or set of systems, it can be laborious and painstaking. All the uses must be located (hopefully, with the help of an accurate data dictionary), changed, recompiled, and tested. Files must be reloaded, and screens and reports must be reformatted, sometimes necessitating some clever and irritating work to fit in the (usually) larger name.

Changing the internal structure of a name, which is the equivalent of changing its semantic content or meaning, is much worse, involving value changes and often size changes, as above, plus program logic changes. For example, consider the identifier of an organization unit as shown in Exhibit 7.4. If the organization structure changes and the ID must be modified to, say, insert a Group ID between division and department, then any programs that access inventory records must also be modified to assemble or interpret the primary key differently. Most database management systems (DBMS) today provide a "view" facility that enables a program's view of its data records to be restricted to only those data fields it needs. However, because every view of any record must include at a minimum the record's primary-key field, view facilities cannot insulate programs from name-definition changes. As organization IDs are typically used in multiple files and even multiple systems, the modifications multiply.

What happened in the aluminum plant discussed in Exhibit 1.2? Why were the automated-world systems modifications far more costly than the corresponding real-world systems changes? The answer is not that the IT function was inefficient or had inadequate tools or used expensive

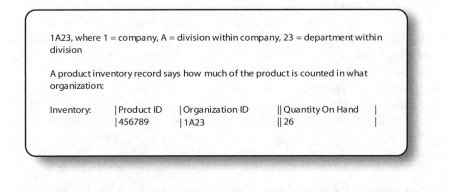

1A23, where 1 = company, A = division within company, 23 = department within division

A product inventory record says how much of the product is counted in what organization:

Inventory:		Product ID		Organization ID	|| Quantity On Hand	
		456789		1A23	|| 26	

Exhibit 7.4.   Identifier with Embedded Information

resources. The usual method-oriented answers do not apply. The answer is that to implement the desired behavioral outcome (that is, to resynchronize the automated-world systems with the changed real-world systems), a core structural component of the automated-world systems complex had to be modified. And this was because what had been treated as a static characteristic, the plant's organization scheme, and embedded in the structure, was in reality a variable whose time had come to vary! The final irony of this true tale is that after all the costly systems work was done, the newly designed identifier number now contained the new organizational information, which lay waiting in the system like a time bomb for the next organizational change. Identifiers are structural, so they had better be static.

Johnston [2000] points out a hidden problem that greatly affects the cost of reengineering primary keys, which is that a primary-key modification cannot be done as an atomic transaction. The key's presence as a foreign key in multiple files would result in failed joins for instances not yet modified. Cross-referencing of old to new keys can be used as an interim measure to prevent failed joins, but this requires modification of queries to include an intermediate join to the cross-reference table. It quickly gets very costly, even without logic changes to reflect restructuring of keys.

7.1.4 Shared Identifiers versus Hidden Surrogates

Before proceeding further, we should briefly mention surrogates. The term surrogate normally refers to an identifier that is primarily intended for the internal use of a DBMS (or DBMS/operating-system ensemble). Typically these are very large floating-point format DBMS-assigned numbers, usually information-free, by which every record can be distinguished. In some cases, surrogates are made available to applications and in other cases not, being completely transparent to any system outside the DBMS itself. As Haughey [2004] explains, surrogates do not work well for identifying association entities in application systems. Henceforth, when using the term "identifier," we will mean only those entity identifiers subject to design by the application system designer. Later, we will make an important distinction between what we will call internal and external identifiers, but we are then still referring to two types of designable identifiers used by the application system and not to surrogates.

7.2 Types of Unstable Identifiers

There are five primary types of information found in traditional identifiers:

1. Qualification information
2. Embedded information
3. Abbreviation information
4. Sequence information
5. Function-selection information, check digits, and delimiters

The principle problem, of course, is change, but other problems also accrue to the use of unstable identifiers. There are problems of:

- Scope
- Existence
- Inclusiveness
- Redundancy
- Error proneness
- Reliability

7.2.1 Qualification Information

When multiple things have the same name, there is potential ambiguity unless a context is given within which the name is unique. A common technique for resolving this ambiguity is to use qualification. Qualification is a single or nested set of context names appended to the object's otherwise nonunique name to achieve uniqueness. Context names can be explicit or implicit; implicit naming is referred to as partial qualification. A simple example is city (Columbus) qualified by state (Indiana, or Ohio, or Georgia, etc.). Qualifications can be nested, such as a complete street address number, street, city, and state. The zip code, of course, is not part of the nested qualification; the zip code is a separate, independent ID for the mailing location. It also requires a higher-level qualification (country) for uniqueness.

Kent [1978], in his classic *Data and Reality*, uses the example of the naming of employees' dependents to illustrate the problems that can arise with qualification information. In this case, qualification can be thought of as being based on the relationship between the object and some other object, where "the scope (of qualification) becomes the set of things having a particular relationship to a particular object." Suppose the employee's ID number plus the dependent's first name identified dependents. What are some of the problems with this scheme?

First, the *scope* of uniqueness may change. The employee with dependent John (husband) may acquire another dependent John (son), or even a third John (grandfather). Remarriage may either add another dependent of the same name or shift a dependent's parent from one employee to another. Divorced parents may change who claims the dependent for tax purposes. So while the dependent has not changed (John is still John), his ID and all references to it will need to be changed because it contains descriptive information about his relationship to another person, which is subject to change.

A second problem concerns the *existence* of the qualifying thing. In Kent's example, because the dependent must have a related employee, the system cannot cope with an extension of benefits to those who are unrelated to employees. Both of these scope and existence limitations point out a more general problem with qualification as a means to achieve uniqueness. Qualification is inherently hierarchical, with each of the instances of the higher (more inclusive) level of qualification standing in a one-to-many relationship to the instances of the next lower level. Qualification is an overly constrained relationship that can break down as circumstances change, particularly as the relationship becomes many-to-many. We can recognize the unstable identifier in the aluminum plant example as a victim of a change in qualification information.

7.2.2 Embedded Information

Excessive length is a clue to the existence of embedded information and, hence, of instability.

Qualification information is a special case of embedded information. There is no limit to the information that ID designers include. Indeed, any or all of a thing's properties and relationships are candidates for embedded information. In computer file IDs, for example, it is common practice to

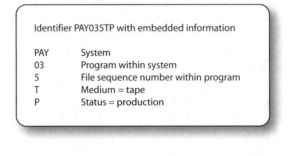

Identifier PAY035TP with embedded information

PAY	System
03	Program within system
5	File sequence number within program
T	Medium = tape
P	Status = production

Exhibit 7.5. Information Embedded in a File Name

include the file type, file status, as well as qualifying the file by program within system. A typical file ID might look like the file shown in Exhibit 7.5.

Obvious problems arise when any of this information changes. Files must be re-referenced in directories, programs, etc. Such identification schemes are also usually misleading to the maintenance programmer, because often more than one program (and system) accesses the file and more than one may update the file. The device type could change, and although the status of a file does not usually change, the P versus T coding is a notoriously poor technique for ensuring that a test file is not used on a production system and vice versa.

Paradoxically, the embedded-information ID is both more and less inclusive than necessary. The file ID example above is eight characters long, which, if the embedded information were ignored, is sufficient to identify 100 million things using just numeric digits. This is too much. But it can only name ten files per program if the embedded information is retained. This is not enough. Embedded information uses up available character positions and, of course, information embedded in the high-order positions of an ID uses up available character values exponentially.

In the universal product code (UPC), administered by the UPC Council in Dayton, Ohio, the five high-order positions of the basic ten-digit UPC identify the manufacturer or vendor, and the five lower-order positions identify the product supplied by that vendor (Exhibit 7.6). The council issues a vendor ID to each vendor, and the vendor assigns product IDs within its block of 100,000 available values that are unique within its vendor number. This means that vendor 00123 gets to identify 100,000 items and vendor 00124 also gets to identify 100,000 items, never mind that 00123 is a Procter & Gamble with over 300,000 items and 00124 is a Celestial Seasonings with a few dozen items! So the numbers get used up too fast. If the ten-digit UPC were single purpose, it could identify 10 billion items, but the supply of values for the current multipurpose

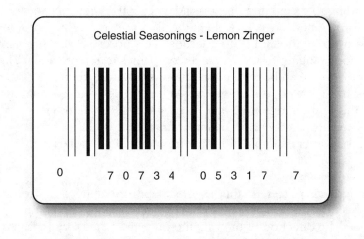

Celestial Seasonings - Lemon Zinger

0   7 0 7 3 4   0 5 3 1 7   7

Exhibit 7.6.   UPC Code

UPC will be quickly exhausted. A number of extensions to the basic UPC have been devised to cope with this problem. However, the root problem of embedded information remains.

Some companies maintain large databases of product sales information keyed on the UPC. Market research companies in particular have very large databases covering years of demographically related product information and thousands of vendors. In addition to the prospects of UPC size increases as available numbers are used up, there are three other serious consequences of the use of this embedded information scheme. First, UPC values for existing products are subject to change as a result of mergers and divestments. The products have not changed, but the vendor has, so new UPC values need to be assigned to all affected items. Second, vendors that use up their 100,000 values can request and receive additional vendor numbers and a new block of 100,000 values; then one vendor is identified by more than one identifier value. Third, some vendors reuse IDs from discontinued products; then the same identifier value picks out more than one product. Technically, this last problem is not a consequence of the embedded information ID per se, as it is a procedural matter to disallow reuse of UPC values. But it is a related problem because the practice of reusing old numbers is used to circumvent the inconvenience of having multiple vendor IDs.

Many other examples of embedded-information IDs are familiar to all of us, such as credit card account numbers — typically from 16 to 24 characters long and sufficient to identify many times more than all the people who have ever lived. Excessive length is a clue to the existence of embedded information and, hence, of instability.

According to recent news reports [Mayne, 2004], the 17-character codes of the North American vehicle identification number (VIN) are expected to be used up by the end of the decade. This poses serious problems for organizations ranging from insurance companies to repair shops. The VIN contains extensive embedded information, which, regardless of its stability, exhausts the allowed values rapidly. If the VIN were information free, then at the current reported rate of usage of 60 million VINs per year, 17 digits would provide 1.67 billion years worth of VINs.

Here is another example, this time from one of our colleagues [Scheuer, 2004].

> I might also refer to this as the inappropriateness of "sense codes." While we were working at a Fortune 100 company under the direction of the CIO the personnel director presented a tongue-in-cheek White Paper to a meeting of the Grocery Manufacturer's Association in which he described a 99 character code that would encompass all of the information needed to define a product — manufacturer, date of manufacturing, size, shelf life, etc. Supposedly after he returned to his office, he received six e-mails telling of something he had left out!

Lastly, the embedded information ID conveys *redundant* information each time it is used. Most IDs, just because they are IDs, are used repeatedly in a variety of circumstances. For example, every time a UPC value is keyed or read into a system, it is providing information that the system already knows. We are entering over and over that this can of chicken soup is made by xyz, this can of chicken soup is made by xyz, thus wasting effort, energy, and resources.

7.2.3 Abbreviation Information

The example above of the embedded and qualified file ID also illustrates another ploy for using an ID as a vehicle for information: the abbreviation, as in PAYroll system. Abbreviations (and acronyms) are a little less stable than the names they represent. If we abbreviate an identifier that in itself is stable, the abbreviation should also be stable. The difficulty is that, being shorter, the abbreviation is more susceptible to duplicate values arising. For example, the word processor used to compose this sentence lists 12 subfunctions under the File menu, only five of which use the initial letter of the function. When duplicates arise, the designer of an abbreviation ID lengthens the abbreviation to retain the characteristic of being a meaningful short substitute for the full name, or permits departures from the abbreviation scheme to ensure uniqueness.

While waiting for their wedding day to arrive, Susan Simpson and Hank Thompson contemplated their options: Simpson-Thompson or Thompson-Simpson. A coin-flip made it Thompson-Simpson, and no hard feelings.

After the honeymoon Susan returned to classes at Zanier University where she was in her last quarter of studies toward her MBA in Information Technology. On her first day back on campus, Susan went directly to the registrar's office to have her name changed on the school records. She came away not knowing what to do. She discovered that the university records were kept by a student ID with a dual purpose. It was used to alphabetize students as well as to uniquely identify them. In order to change her name she would have to be assigned a new student number and have all her records transferred to the new number.

She knew from experience, as well as from her IT classes, that this violated Professor Johnson's single-purpose entity identifier rule. She also knew that having her records transferred from one student number to another using the school's antiquated computer system was risky. If this did not go well it would jeopardize her ability to graduate and the chance to manage the Information Center at the Resolution Notrust Corporation. She wanted to use her new name, but she did not want to jeopardize her graduation and her fabulous job opportunity.

Questions:
1. If you were Susan, what would you do?
2. Why do system designers continue to make entity identifiers serve purposes other than identification?

Exhibit 7.7. The Multipurpose Identifier Strikes Again

7.2.4 Sequence Information

Sequencing, or collating, information is used to keep records in a convenient order and, of course, is subject to change (Exhibit 7.7).

7.2.5 Function Selection, Check Digits, and Delimiters

It should be noted that not everything that is attached to or embedded in an identifier necessarily destabilizes it. Function-selection information specifies a function to be performed on the ID to which it is attached. A familiar example is found in North American telephone numbers. The digits 0, 1, 800, etc. tell the phone system what to do with the phone number. The long-distance function code embedded, until recently, in the area code part of the phone number has not destabilized phone numbers but has merely limited the quantity of available numbers. The area code prefix is qualification information, which is what has caused many existing phone numbers to be changed. Of course, now that cell phones are so prevalent and one can keep the number when moving, area codes are becoming less associated with place and the 10-digit phone number is becoming more of a stable identifier.

When a check digit is used, it becomes, necessarily, an intimate part of the ID because it must accompany the ID to serve its error-detection function. But a check digit does not contribute to identification or description, and it can be removed without affecting the ID's uniqueness or stability.

Delimiters in an ID are not a problem. An example of a delimited ID is the U.S. Social Security number (SSN): nnn-nn-nnnn. It is interesting that the SSNs of different countries or political units generally have different delimiting formats. A Canadian citizen and a U.S. citizen with the same numeric value for their SSNs nevertheless have unique SSNs due to the different placement of delimiters. The SSN is also an example of an embedded information ID. However, the information is so irrelevant to anything about the individual identified by the SSN as to be essentially immune to change, and so we ignore it here. Way back when, a colleague discovered just as he was on the verge of discarding some seemingly incorrect SSNs from a shareholder record system, that the H and W suffixes that occurred in them had meaning during the Second World War. They were used to extend a person's SSN to their husband or wife — a bad idea, mercifully short-lived.

If delimiters are delimiting embedded information, then you have the problems associated with embedded information, and you have them whether delimiters are used or not. Delimiters can make it easier to remember or transcribe an ID. Whether they are treated as a permanent part of the ID (even if they are blanks) is at the discretion of the designer.

7.3 Identifiers and the Relational Data Model

> Identifiers are not attributes; they are identifiers, a distinct component of information structure.

This section assumes that the reader is familiar with the relational model, normalization, and referential and existence integrity; readers who are not may wish to skip this section.

It is important to establish that the information-free identifier is not only consistent with, but specifically supports the relational data model, normalization, and the maintenance of referential and existence integrity in a system. The relational model provides for relations and their attributes as a form of representation of information about things and their properties. But despite the existence of the relational model as a guide to good information structure design, identifiers continue to be incorrectly designed.

This occurs because the identifier of a thing is tacitly assumed to be an inherent attribute of the thing itself. For example, it is common to see instructions like the following given for analysis and design using the relational model:

1. Relations consist of attributes, some of which serve to uniquely identify the entity the relation represents and some of which do not; these are key attributes and non-key attributes, respectively.
2. Examine the attributes. Any attribute or collection of attributes that uniquely identifies the entity is a candidate key for the relation.
3. Choose one from among the candidate keys to be the primary key of the relation.

These instructions seem to make sense when the example entity has at least one convenient identifying attribute such as a product number for a product. But the product number is not an inherent property of the product. Rather, it is an artifact, assigned to the product as an alternative to referring to it by the set of inherent properties that collectively identify it, of which there may be several required to guarantee uniqueness, e.g., color, size, weight, functions, features, etc.

Things in the real world are identifiable because the values of some of their inherent properties distinguish one instance of a thing from another. These are correctly referred to as the thing's *identifying properties*. They can collectively serve as the identifier, but it is impractical to be constantly referring to, say, a specific product as the "red, heavy-duty liquid, formula NACNO3, with bleach concentration of 1.75x, in the 150-oz. size product." Instead, our naming brain kicks in, and IDs are invented and associated with things through naming conventions (Exhibit 7.8).

Product numbers are a matter of agreement among people and are not *attributable* to the product alone. In an important and underappreciated statement about keyness, Dadashzedah [1990, p. 251] wrote,

> The important thing to note is that keyness is an intentional property and must be true for every extension of the relation. It cannot be inferred by inspection of existing extensions.

Extension in this context means the data values that populate the relation — e.g., the values in actual filled data records — i.e., you can guess what the key of a relation is by looking at the data, but you cannot really know without having access to the definition of the relation that specifies which key is intended.

A properly designed primary key is not chosen from among the candidate keys of an entity, just as the ID is not chosen from among the

The binomial naming convention for organisms was published by Linnaeus in 1758 and has been in use ever since. Each species receives a two-word name, the first word for its genus and the second for its species within that genus. For example, Canis familiaris for dogs and Canis lupus for wolves. Linnaeus developed the scheme from the current tradition of naming an organism with a series of Latin words that supposedly described its essential characteristics, and at one point Linnaeus' system included up to twelve words in a name. As Stephen J. Gould [1995] explains,

At first he regretted giving up the key idea that a word string should accurately describe the species' key features … But Linnaeus later realized that he had accomplished something enormously useful … The Linnean species name is not a description but a placeholder – a legal device to keep track and to confer a distinctive name upon each natural entity. Any comprehensive system based on millions of unique items must use such a mechanism … he had brought a necessary and fundamental principle of naming through the back door of a search for modes of epitomized description.

The terseness of the system promotes the placeholder function and discourages taking the Latin terms literally. The system does include hierarchically qualified information, but what is greatly to the credit of the two international bodies that administer the rules for naming animals and plants is their diligent enforcement of a fundamental objective to preserve "… maximal stability as new knowledge demands revision." As Gould said, *"If we had to change names every time our ideas about a species altered, taxonomy would devolve into chaos."*

Exhibit 7.8. Identifiers as Placeholders

identifying properties of a thing. The ID is defined intentionally, and the assignment of ID values takes the form of an agreed mapping. IDs are not givens in a relational design; they are themselves designable. It is a simple matter then, in applying the relational approach, to assert that, in both the real-world and automated-world models, there is an identifier for any thing. The product thing, for example, is correctly modeled as being identified by a strictly unique ID — the product ID — without regard to any product attributes.

Identifier stabilization and normalization are closely related. Suppose an ID with embedded information can also, by virtue of the information it contains, be considered a relation. This is debatable, of course, for if the system ignores the information content, then the ID is de facto informationless. We contend, however, that virtually all systems that employ IDs with embedded information do in fact exploit their information content, and that all information recognized by the system must be accounted for in any relational treatment of the system's data.

For example, the computer file ID PAY035TP shown in Exhibit 7.5 and containing embedded information would be represented by the relation:

File: | System Code | Prog No. | File No. |Type Code | Status Code| |

Let us say that the real-world functional dependencies for computer files are:

> File <<—> File Type
> File <<—> File Status
> System <<—>> Program
> Program <<—>> File

where <<—> means many-to-one, and <<—>> means many-to-many. Then the relation is unnormalized, does not accurately represent the real world, and creates an integrity issue, as follows:

■ *Domain key normal form (DKNF)*: In the relation, the File <<—> File Type and File <<—> File Status constraints are not a logical consequence of the key of the relation or of any domains that can be defined on the elements of the relation. Hence the relation is not in DKNF.

■ *Boyce-code normal form (BCNF)*: Neither Program, File, File Type, nor File Status is determined by only the whole key. Hence, the relation is not in BCNF. Of course the fact that it is not in BCNF automatically means that it is not in DKNF, but it is instructive to see the degree to which this embedded information file ID, as a relation, is unnormalized.

■ *Real-world system to real-world model mapping*: The relation is not just unnormalized; it is also incorrect. In the relation, the qualification of file by program and program by system each specifies a one-to-many association, but the inherent real-world constraints are many-to-many. The processes of the artifact-world system will be overconstrained by the structure that contains this relation.

■ *Referential and existence integrity*: There are also potential difficulties in the maintenance of database integrity when IDs contain embedded information. In our File ID example, the ID is normally treated as a single data element, and the embedded system, program, type, and status codes are unknown to a DBMS's conventional referential integrity mechanism. The deletion of a file-type code, for example, would fail to trigger an integrity check on the existence of a reference to that file-type code value embedded in the File IDs in the system's records. Similarly, the insertion of a new file ID value would fail to trigger checks on the validity of the embedded code values. A more complex referential integrity maintenance facility would be required to accept declarations of the embedded information and act accordingly.

Some conventional referential integrity facilities are not capable of distinguishing between the single components of a complex identifier and the components taken in specific combinations and declared to be identifiers of specific foreign entities. (This capability is desirable regardless of whether strictly unique IDs are used or not.)

7.4 Summary

- Unstable identifiers are responsible for a significant share of the maintenance burden.
- Identifiers are unstable when they contain information, because virtually any information about the thing identified is subject to change.
- Stable identifiers are information-free, conforming to the principle of strict uniqueness. As an essential component of a stable information structure, they contribute to reducing the maintenance burden.

The chapters on stable information structures (Chapter 9) and the generic-entity cloud (Chapter 10) assume stable identifiers that are designed according to the chapter on implementation of stable identifiers (Chapter 14). We cannot overemphasize the importance of strictly unique identifiers!

Chapter 8

Regulation: Managing Artificial Limits

The behavior of any real-world system is constrained by both natural limits (the laws of physics and logic) and artificial limits (business rules established or observed by an organization). In a flexible system, the natural limits are represented in stable information structures that are acted upon by stable processes. The artificial limits, or business rules, are represented in a way that does not affect the information structures or processes. The interpretation of artificial limits, or business rules, can be changed as the business changes. We use the term "regulation" to describe the management of artificial limits within a system.

Flexibility in an automated system is the characteristic of allowing resynchronization with its changed real-world system at low cost. A flexible system can be resynchronized through business-staff-controlled data-value modification and without the need to modify program code or information structures. This no-programming approach brings the benefits of reduced maintenance but may result in additional development costs. We will discuss the benefit/cost trade-offs.

8.1 Business Rules as Artificial Limits

A user-controlled resynchronization process is accomplished through regulation or management of the system's artificial limits.

The Business Rules Group (BRG) has explored the concepts of business rules in depth. Its charter is to formulate statements and supporting standards about the nature and structure of business rules, the relationship of business rules to the way an enterprise is organized, and the relationship of business rules to systems' architectures. The group's Business Rules Manifesto is presented in Appendix 8B.

According to BRG, "A business rule is a statement that defines or constrains some aspect of the business. It is intended to assert business structure or to control or influence the behavior of the business" [Hay and Healy, 2000, p. 10; Ross and Healy, 2000]. BRG's business rules come in two flavors or assertions: structural and action. Structural assertions identify the composition of the system, the set of things, and their relationships to each other. Action assertions identify the processes or behavior of the system.

In contrast to BRG's assumption that structural assertions are static, we recognize that changing business requirements can result in changes to the cardinality of relationships. Data structures can be designed to accommodate cardinality changes without modification. In general, however, the concepts we promote for achieving the flexibility of regulatory mechanisms are consistent with the principles espoused by the BRG.

8.1.1 Maintaining Business Rules

A guiding principle in designing flexible systems is that business staff, through the alteration of data values, should manage the maintenance of business rules.

Changes in business rules are the most likely trigger of system modifications. A guiding principle in designing flexible systems is that business staff, through the alteration of data values, should manage the maintenance of business rules. In the past, the current interpretations of business rules were typically coded in programs. A rule could involve something as straightforward as validating a value against a list of values, such as lists of valid states, genders, and countries. A rule could also involve something much more complicated, such as evaluating an individual's profile against a set of conditions that control some aspect of the business process. Over time, developers have adopted some forms of flexibility. They have recognized the advantage of storing lists of valid values as data, maintained by business staff. This is now standard practice in systems development. We believe that developers can push this concept even further. One way is with rules engines; Babcock [2004] says, "Rules engines let companies adapt offerings without lots of programming."

Our perspective on maintenance of business rules differs significantly from that of other advocates of the business rules approach. We focus on design that permits business staff to maintain the business rules, because we believe that is where the greatest reductions in system maintenance will be realized. C. J. Date, a strong proponent of the business-rules approach, stresses the importance of compiling business rules. He proposes that business rules be converted into executable code: "It's important for performance reasons that the rules in fact be compiled, not interpreted" [Date, 2000, p. 37]. While recognizing that performance is always a factor, we strongly caution that implementations of business rules not foreclose on business staff maintaining the rules directly.

Remember that information systems are developed or redeveloped (maintained) via a series of transformations (Exhibit 2.1). First comes analysis, transforming the real-world system to a model of the real-world system. Then comes design, transforming the real-world model to an automated-world model. Last comes construction, transforming the automated-world model into the automated-world system. The real-world system is constrained by the laws of physics. The real-world model is constrained not only by the laws of physics, but by business rules and policies. In the real-world model, business rules and policies can be changed relatively easily to reflect changing business needs and opportunities. But at any given time, the model reflects only the current state of these business rules and policies, whereas the real-world system allows the entire range (or at least a significant portion) of states of these business rules. It is here where much of the problem with system development lies. When building a system, the developer typically assumes that the automated-world system need do no more than the current real-world model dictates. In fact, the developer should be thinking in terms of the real-world system. The real-world model does not limit the potential of the real-world system any more than a model airplane limits innovation in real airplane design. Neither should the real-world model limit the capabilities of the automated-world system. Things change. Though the automated-world system is permanently constrained by the laws of physics, constraints of business rule and policies should be adjustable as the current state of the automated world changes.

In our flexible approach, regulation comes in two flavors:

1. *General regulation of business rules*: allows adjustment of business processing
2. *Cardinality regulation*: allows adjustment of the underlying information structures

Both types of regulation can be accomplished without program or database modifications.

8.2 General Regulation of Business Rules

By general regulation we mean those aspects of regulation that have to do with processing-oriented business rules — what the BRG calls action assertions. General regulation is "on top of" the BRG structural assertions; these structural assertions are, in essence, our cardinality regulation.

8.2.1 Identifying Entities and Rules

The following simple example of a business process helps us to identify potential system entities and business rules.

When asked about the admissions process at a university, the director of admissions said something like this:

> An <u>applicant</u> submits an <u>application</u>, indicating the <u>term</u> and <u>major</u>. We review the applicant's <u>test scores</u>, <u>high school tran-script</u>, etc. If the applicant meets the <u>criteria</u> for that major, we send an <u>offer letter</u>. If not, we send a <u>denial letter</u>, suggesting <u>alternatives</u>.

In a discussion of business requirements, any noun is a potential entity. The nouns (and adjectives) in the above passage are underscored. Further investigation of each of these entities will identify other entities, the need to record more information about each of these entities, and so on. Eventually, we will reach a point where we have identified all the entities and all the attributes about those entities that are of interest to the system.

Where adjectives are encountered, the potential for entity types exists. We explore entity typing in Chapter 9, but the description provided by the director of admissions includes a few possibilities. Note that the description differentiates <u>offer</u> letters from <u>denial</u> letters. We should there-fore explore the possibility of a generic data structure for letters, providing for different types of letters. The term "<u>high school</u> transcript" was spec-ified, which should lead us to investigate what other type of transcript might exist.

Wherever the description specifies a condition of some kind, we have the potential for a business-staff-maintained business rule. Such rules can be very simple. For example, the description indicates that a term and major must be specified. The fact that they must be specified constitutes a simple rule. Presumably, there are some business rules that determine which term and major values are valid, another form of simple rule. Designers should provide a mechanism to allow business staff to maintain those rules as data.

Any statement involving the word "if" identifies a business rule. In the admissions example, there are apparently conditions under which individuals are admitted and conditions under which they are not. The logic of such conditions has traditionally been coded in programs. Migrating such logic to data structures maintained by business staff offers great potential for improving system stability and flexibility and reducing system maintenance by the IT staff.

8.2.2 Validation Rules

The developer of a flexible system should think in terms of a design that allows a new logical table to be added to the system without a change in information structure.

The term "validation rule" can be used to describe a basic form of business rule, which is to verify that the value entered into a field is valid. Such rules range from validation of a single value against a single file to validation of complex combinations of values and multiple files and operators. For simple validation of a value against a list of values, a generic logical table facility works well. One of the most common modifications to a system's information structure is the addition of a table for storing valid values for a new data element. Knowing that, the developer of a flexible system should think in terms of a design that allows a new logical table to be added to the system without modifications to the information structure. This can be accomplished by adding an element to the information structure that identifies the logical table. Where an inflexible design would contain separate physical validation tables for ethnicity, state, and country, a flexible design would contain a single physical validation table separated into logical tables by type. Ethnicity, state, and country would be types. Addition of a new data element to the system requires only a new record type to be accommodated in the information structure. This approach works for simple regulatory entities in which each logical table type requires the same data elements. We use the term "regulatory" to indicate that its purpose is to support the business rules.

UniverSIS makes use of this approach, as illustrated by several examples in Exhibit 8.1. In UniverSIS, when a simple regulatory entity is added to the system, no programs need to change. A new simple table is added to the code table. The table owners determine who should have access to it. Those who have access to the table maintain its contents. The data dictionary determines the correct length of the code field and prevents values for that table from exceeding the correct length. The instant a value

Case 1: Country

Entity	Code	Description	Inactive	Default
COUNTRY	YU	Yugoslavia	Y	N
COUNTRY	ZM	Zambia	N	N

Case 2: Academic Awards

ACAD-AWARDS - Maintain Academic Awards

Award: AA_____

Abbreviation.........: A.A._____
Description..........: Associate of Arts_____
_____

*External Report Level: 03 Associate degree
*External Degree Code.: 2.3 Associate Degree

Case 3: Academic Program

ACADPGM - Maintain Academic Program

Academic Program: 15BA_____

Description: Bachelor of Arts - 15_____

*Award	*Study Level	*Required For
BA_____ Bachelor of Arts	MAJ_____ Major	A
_____	_____	_
_____	_____	_
_____	_____	_
_____	_____	_

*Admin Unit: ∧ 1 15__ Arts and Sciences
            ‖ 2 ____
            ∨ 3 ____   1 used of 10

*Student Classification Group: BNORM_ BACCALAUREATE NON-COOP NORMAL

*Program Category...: ENRL Enrollment

*Program Load Level.: F Full Time   Credit Hour Threshold: 12.00
                      H Half Time   _6.00
                      P Part Time   _1.00

*Program Time Period: D_ Day
                      E_ Evening

*Credit Level Code..: U Undergraduate
Program Number of Years: _4 Overload Credit Hour Threshold: 19.00

Exhibit 8.1.   Validation Rules in UniverSIS

Case 4: Maintain Course
COURSE – Maintain Course
 Course Id: 15FREN104___
 *Effective Term: 72A_____   *Through:_____

 *Standard Credit ID: 15FREN104___ ELEMENTARY FRENCH
 *College......: 15__ Arts and Sciences   *Dept.: RLL_ Romance Lang
 *Discipline...: FREN French
 Full Title...: Elementary French_____
 Abbrev Title.: ELEMENTARY FRENCH__   Alternate Title Allowed? N (Y/N)
 *Credit Level.....: U Undergraduate _   _
 *Grading System...: U Undergraduate _   _
 Honors Status....: N/A
 Credit Hours Unit: Q Variable Credit: F (F,C,S) Fixed
 Minimum Hours....: _5.00 Maximum: _5.00
 Status...........: Ready to Offer   As of 01 29 1998

 Description.:
        1 An intensive course for beginning students;_____
   /\ 2 reading, writing, speaking, listening; grammar;___
   || 3 culture. Not open to native speakers of French.___
   \/ 4 _____
 3 used of 25

 *Instruction Method:
        1 LE Lecture (formalized instruction)
   /\ 2 SE Seminar (small,less formal than lect/discussion)
   || 3 SP Self-paced (include independent learning)
   \/ 4 __
                        3 used of 10
 *Pre-Requisite Courses *Type
   /\ 1 _____ _
   \/ 2 _____ _   0 used of 5

 *Co-Requisite Courses
   /\ 1 _____ Required? N (Y/N)
   \/ 2 _____   N   0 used of 7

 *Pre-Conditions..: FREN 104_____ 12 10 2002 French 104 Registration Requirements
                    _____

 Publication Note: _____
                   _____

 First Offered: 99A   Last Offered: 04S

 Load Hours..... ..: __5.00 Load Type.. : F (F-Fixed/E-Enrollment)
 Financial Hours..: __5.00 Charge Type: F (F-Fixed/E-Enrollment)

 *External Classification: 160901 French Language and Literature
 External Classification Notes
 _____
 _____

Exhibit 8.1.   (continued)

is added to a simple table by a business staff member, the value is available for use in any of the functions that validate a field or fields against that table. Once added to a simple table, values are never deleted, simply deactivated. This prevents codes from ever being "orphaned." The developers of UniverSIS took this approach to allow historical data to remain valid. For example, "country" is a simple regulatory entity (see Case 1 in Exhibit 8.1). A code is used to identify each country. At some point, some countries cease to exist, e.g., Yugoslavia. Yet records on the system may still contain the code for Yugoslavia. Marking Yugoslavia's code as inactive prevents it from being entered as a new value but allows it to be retained as a historical value.

Complex regulatory entities fall along a continuum of complexity. "Academic Awards" (Case 2 in Exhibit 8.1) provides an example of a complex entity that is actually no more complex than a simple entity. It is classified as complex because the combination of data elements for "academic award" is unique to that entity. From the names of two of the elements, you see that the university provides information to external agencies about its academic awards.

For developers who are already in the habit of providing business-maintained lists of valid values, a regulatory entity such as academic awards is not a great leap in flexibility. However, there are situations where data such as this is maintained in program code. The thinking, such as it was, probably went as far as determining that the university had offered the same awards for NNN years and that designing a data structure for business maintenance was not worth the effort. When things change, you may find out that it was not worth the potential risk of having to fix it later.

"Academic Program" (Case 3 in Exhibit 8.1) provides an example of a complex entity having more elements. The design of the data structure provides the flexibility to handle the unusual program as well as the routine program. Normally a student earns a single academic award upon completion of a program. However, there are special dual-award programs. Similarly, two colleges may offer a dual-award program jointly. The college of business and the college of law might, for example, offer a combination MBA and law program. UC's legacy system was not programmed to support such programs. Colleges had to keep track of them with paper records.

Anticipating even greater complexity in the future, the designers of UniverSIS provided for expansion beyond dual-awards and joint programs offered by two colleges, with necessary modifications performed by business staff. Carefully designed data elements give business staff the ability to establish and modify all characteristics of the program without IT intervention.

The possibility of multiple awards illustrates a point we make about cardinality throughout the book. Consider the possibility that an attribute or related set of attributes will occur more than once for an entity. If the potential for multiple occurrences exists — even it if does not exist today — design for that possibility. In the case of academic programs, there would have been no need for paper records of dual-award programs if the legacy system designers had considered that possibility.

The relationship between "program load level" and "credit hour threshold" illustrates how coded logic can be stored as data. In the legacy system, the rules for full-time/half-time/part-time were in fact coded in a program with a series of logic branches based on the undergraduate/graduate level of the program. The logic was very stable over the years, but introduction of undergraduate or graduate programs that did not follow the rules required modification to the logic. In addition, the rules were hidden. To see the rules, a programmer had to look at the code and interpret it for the business staff.

"Maintain Course" (Case 4 in Exhibit 8.1) provides an extreme example of a regulatory entity in a student information system. The elements shown here comprise only part of the full set of elements associated with a course. What the developers of UniverSIS did was identify essentially every attribute of a course that was maintained via program logic in the legacy system and provide the business staff with the tools to maintain it themselves. For that analysis, veteran business staff were the key team members. As with the "academic programs," the new design of "course" allowed business rules to be moved out of the code and into the data structures, making the rules visible to all.

The "maintain course" example also illustrates another point that we stress throughout the book — meaningless identifiers. The name of the course 15FREN104 used by the business staff is in fact meaningless to the software system. For the comfort of students and business staff, the designers of UniverSIS allowed the business staff to develop a naming convention for Courses, but the system derives no meaning from the name 15FREN104. The college and department that offer the course and the subject matter of the course are maintained as separate data elements. If the course name were changed to "123456" and that change rippled through the system today, it would have no effect on system processing.

Ironically, a national organization developing XML standards for exchange of information between universities has not adopted this principle of meaningless identifiers, despite prodding from one of the authors. The group rejected the idea of a separate data element for "course identifier." Their assumption is that combining the subject code and a number can derive a course identifier. Many universities do in fact follow such a naming convention, but it is not universal, and the University of

Cincinnati is an institution that does not follow that convention. This means that UC will have to work around the standards, and those institutions receiving information from UC will need to know how UC worked around the standards.

8.2.3 Business Rules and Logic

Another level of regulation involves determining whether an action is valid. Conditional logic, generally in the form of IF/THEN/ELSE program statements, is used to determine what action should occur. The validity of the action is typically determined by characteristics of an instance of an entity. For example, looking at a student entity, we might see that Mary may register for a calculus class but John may not. The decision regarding who may register will be based on data values on the students' records. In a traditional system design, program logic would be coded to retrieve the data and execute conditional logic to arrive at the decision. If a change of logic is needed because additional data values must be considered, a programmer must change the code. Multiply that scenario by the number of processes in a system and you have the makings of a maintenance backlog.

It is best to design system components to allow business staff some control over conditional logic as well as valid values. In other words, allow business staff to write the business rules without IT intervention. An example from UniverSIS is the tool called the Evaluator, described in Chapter 18. It is a general-purpose tool that permits business staff to construct complex conditional statements from predefined elements and associated data-retrieval routines. It is independent of specific business processes. The elements can be combined in any set of logical statements that the business staff find useful. The tool is used in several different modules, e.g., charging, registration restrictions, assignment to correspondence tracks, etc.

8.2.4 Regulation and New Processes

Another type of business rule involves determining which action the system should take. Implicit in this type of regulation is the addition of new actions and new processes. Modification of a system to accommodate a new business process typically requires new programming, as illustrated in Exhibit 8.2.

Exhibit 8.2 illustrates a university admissions process. The original system shown in Case 1 is designed with two valid values: admitted and denied. If the applicant is admitted, an offer letter is sent and the

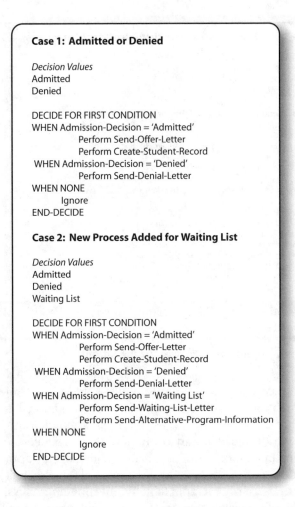

Case 1: Admitted or Denied

Decision Values
Admitted
Denied

DECIDE FOR FIRST CONDITION
WHEN Admission-Decision = 'Admitted'
          Perform Send-Offer-Letter
          Perform Create-Student-Record
WHEN Admission-Decision = 'Denied'
          Perform Send-Denial-Letter
WHEN NONE
     Ignore
END-DECIDE

Case 2: New Process Added for Waiting List

Decision Values
Admitted
Denied
Waiting List

DECIDE FOR FIRST CONDITION
WHEN Admission-Decision = 'Admitted'
          Perform Send-Offer-Letter
          Perform Create-Student-Record
WHEN Admission-Decision = 'Denied'
          Perform Send-Denial-Letter
WHEN Admission-Decision = 'Waiting List'
          Perform Send-Waiting-List-Letter
          Perform Send-Alternative-Program-Information
WHEN NONE
          Ignore
END-DECIDE

Exhibit 8.2.   New Admissions Process: Programmer-Controlled

applicant's student-related records are established in the system. For a denial, only a letter is sent. The valid values (admitted and denied) are established in a programmer-controlled rather than a business-controlled table because they are associated with specific system actions. The pseudocode shown in Exhibit 8.2 describes the processing. This processing logic resides in a program.

In Case 2, the university has established a new process: "waiting list." To make the necessary adjustments to the system, a programmer must add the new value to the list. He writes whatever programs are needed to do the appropriate processing for someone on the waiting list. In this example,

---

Case 1: Simple Table Connecting a Decision Value to IDs of Specialized Programming Modules

Decision	Module
Admitted	Send-Offer-Letter
Admitted	Create-Student-Record
Denied	Send-Denial-Letter

Case 2: Generic Module that Changes Behavior Based on Parameters

Decision	Module
Admitted	Send-Admission-Letter (Parameter: Admitted)
Admitted	Create-Student-Record
Denied	Send-Admission-Letter (Parameter: Denied)

Case 3: Result of Adding Waiting List Decision Value to Case 2 Design

Decision	Module
Admitted	Send-Admission-Letter (Parameter: Admitted)
Admitted	Create-Student-Record
Denied	Send-Admission-Letter (Parameter: Denied)
Waiting List	Send-Admission-Letter (Parameter: Waiting List)
Waiting List	Send-Alternative-Program-Information

Exhibit 8.3.　New Admissions Process: Business-Controlled

the processing consists of send-waiting-list-letter and send-alternative-program-information. Finally, he modifies the conditional logic shown above to add "waiting list" to the list of possible conditions.

How can we design this part of the system to reduce the amount of programmer maintenance? Exhibit 8.3 illustrates several approaches and examines trade-offs in achieving increasing levels of flexibility.

First we can establish a simple table connecting an admission decision value to the IDs of specialized programming modules (Case 1 of Exhibit 8.3). Like stored lists of valid values, modular design of programs is a well-established practice in system development. Instead of the simple decision structure in Case 1 of Exhibit 8.2, the programmer could write logic to look up the applicant's decision value in the table and execute the related module or modules (Case 1 of Exhibit 8.3). This example does not indicate that the order of module execution is significant, although order could be accommodated by the addition of a sequence number. The logic controlling the actual processing for an "admitted" applicant would reside in those modules.

In Case 2 of Exhibit 8.3 we see that send-offer-letter and send-denial-letter offer opportunities for flexible design. Case 2 shows the design of a generic module called send-admission-letter that changes its behavior depending on parameters sent to it, in this case the admission decision.

UniverSIS has just such a feature. It allows business staff to construct letters, including personalized data inserts, without programmer intervention.

Case 3 of Exhibit 8.3 shows the impact of adding the new waiting-list value, which requires a completely new form of output in addition to a variation on the admission letter. What has been saved by the design of Case 3? The only significant programming required when "waiting list" is added to the list of valid values is that of send-alternative-program-information. That same logic would need to be written with the original design as well. In the best case, that logic involves execution of existing programs and passing parameters, i.e., no real new logic. With the new design, two new values will be added to the decision/module table. With the original design, the DECIDE logic would need to be modified, but that would involve only a few minutes of a programmer's time.

The design presented in Case 3 of Exhibit 8.3 is perhaps slightly more flexible than that in Exhibit 8.2, but is it worth the effort? To evaluate this, we would need to think about potential future changes. Is it likely that other decision values will be added in the future? Will the actions associated with those new values require new programming? If the decision values rarely change and a new value always requires additional programming, the added complexity of the slightly more flexible solution may not be worthwhile. If the values are very dynamic and the actions allow reuse of existing modules in every case, the more flexible solution is probably worthwhile because IT intervention and testing of programming changes can be eliminated. If a more flexible solution simplifies the work of the IT staff but does not eliminate it for every case, a cost/benefit analysis is called for. How often will a new decision value be added? How much time/effort will be required to implement and test the modification? Does the more-flexible solution involve significantly more processing time than the less-flexible solution?

We are not necessarily advocating the ultimately flexible design in every case. But we do urge the reader to think about the ultimately flexible design and make a conscious decision about its value.

8.2.5 No Retroactive Regulation

Business rules should have effective periods, but regulation must not be retroactive. In other words, if a specific regulatory rule was in effect when the action was taken, a subsequent change in that rule can affect only actions taken in the future, not actions taken in the past. Retroactive regulation is not permitted because it would cause the system to violate its own rules.

For example, if order 6629 were taken when there was insufficient inventory and back orders and if partial shipments were not allowed, the order would have been rejected. A subsequent change to allow back orders or partial shipments would not change the fact that order 6629 had been rejected. To create a back order for what was order 6629, the data would have to be reentered, and now order 7651 would become a back order.

The caution against allowing internal rules violations should not be taken to mean that you cannot use effective period dating to support what-if processing. That is, one of the advantages of effective dates as part of the primary key of an association is that different sets of data can be maintained that represent different hypothetical conditions. For example, a properly designed database will permit multiple organization schemes or product structure schemes or cost accounting schemes, etc. to be maintained concurrently but separated by different effective dates. With this capability, extensive what-if scenarios can be explored using the normal production processing routines.

8.2.6 Summary of General Regulation

Regulatory processes should be content-free programs that "know" where to retrieve information about rules and how to enforce the rules.

Careful analysis and design of regulatory features is one of the key requirements of a flexible system. Regulatory processes should be content-free programs that "know" where to retrieve information about rules and how to enforce the rules. Changes in the content of the rules should not affect the regulatory process unless a new factor is introduced. However, even when a new factor is introduced, most of the time a flexible design should limit the impact to minor program code modifications and rarely to file-structure modifications.

Appendix 8A (Using Regulation to Make a Flexible System) is presented for readers desiring to study regulation in greater detail. It walks through two examples — one with regulation and one without — illustrating the use of decision tables to determine shipments in an order-processing system.

8.3 Cardinality Regulation: Variable Cardinality, Many-to-Many Associations

In many ways, cardinality regulation is "adjustable" structure. We have stated that a key objective of flexible design is a stable data structure.

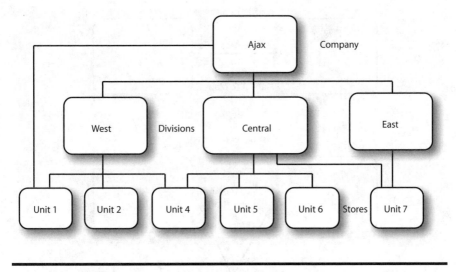

Exhibit 8.4. Example of a Networked Organization

The flexibility available in a stable structure is realized through cardinality regulation. Cardinality regulation provides a mechanism for enforcing current enterprise-specific entity-relationship constraints within a least-constrained database schema. Such a mechanism allows constraints on the system to vary without modification of the system's structure or processes. Associations among entities are stable if they represent the general case, i.e., many-to-many. One-to-one and one-to-many are considered special cases of the general many-to-many association. (Whenever we refer to the many-to-many association in general, it is understood that it is a many-to-many-to … -many association, and that "many" means 0, 1, or more than 1.) For example, specific data entered by the end users may well describe a hierarchical organization, whereas the database could actually accept data that describes a more complex, networked organization (Exhibit 8.4).

For the information structure to remain unmodified while the organization changes from hierarchical to network or vice versa, the information structure must always represent the more general case, which in this instance is the network (many-to-many) organization. If enforcement of the hierarchical (one-to-many) organization is a current requirement or the system, then that enforcement must be implemented *outside* the information structure by means of cardinality regulation.

A mechanism for cardinality regulation provides for the dynamic setting (within database integrity rules) of the minimum and maximum number of children entities that the parent entity in a relationship can have. For

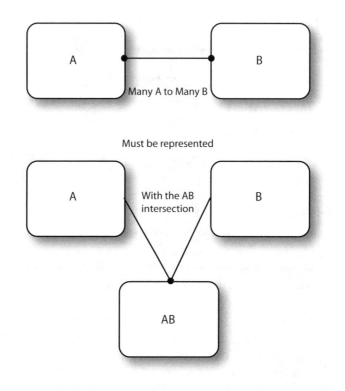

Exhibit 8.5. Representing Many-to-Many with an Intersection File

example, the cardinality regulation table for the general many-to-many case (i.e., where the relationship between A and B is many-to-many (A <<—>> B), which of course must be represented as A <— >> AB <<— > B) is presented in Exhibit 8.5.

Exhibit 8.6 shows a constant schema whose interpretation is varied through cardinality regulation:

- In Case 1, a Person can have many Person-types, and a Person-type can be assigned to many Persons. Note also that a Person must have a Person-type but that a specific Person-type need not be assigned to a Person.
- In Case 2, a Person can have only one Person-type, and a Person-type can be assigned to many Persons. Note also that a Person must have a Person-type but that a specific Person-type need not be assigned to a Person. If, instead of a Person-type, the assignment

Relationship	Parent	Child	Parent		Child		
			Min	Max	Min	Max	Actual
1	A	AB	1	1	0	n	x
2	B	AB	1	1	0	n	x

Since referential integrity requires that the parent side of the relationship always be 1, the parent min/max columns can be omitted:

Relationship	Parent	Child	Child		
			Min	Max	Actual
1	A	AB	0	n	x
2	B	AB	0	n	x

It would look like this for a case in which the relationship enforced between A and B is one A to many B. (A < —>>B):

Relationship	Parent	Child	Child		
			Min	Max	Actual
1	A	AB	1	1	x
2	B	AB	0	n	x

Exhibit 8.5. (continued)

were to be, say, "job," then this would be a case where job sharing was not allowed; a given job would be assigned to only one Person.

■ In Case 3, a Person can have many Person-types, but a Person-type can only be assigned to a maximum of one Person but need not be assigned at all. Case 3 is certainly not a likely real-world scenario!

How cardinality regulation is implemented will depend upon the tools used to develop the system, but the concept is essential. Both general and cardinality regulation are used to avoid implementing artificial limits in a system's structure or procedures.

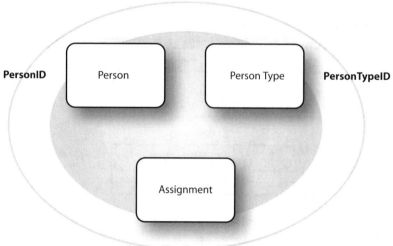

PersonID   Person   Person Type   **PersonTypeID**

Assignment

Person ID + PersonTypeID

CASE 1			Child		
Relationship	Parent	Child	Min	Max	Actual
1	Person	Assignment	1	n	x
2	Person-type	Assignment	0	n	x

CASE 2			Child		
Relationship	Parent	Child	Min	Max	Actual
1	Person	Assignment	1	1	x
2	Person-type	Assignment	0	n	x

CASE 3			Child		
Relationship	Parent	Child	Min	Max	Actual
1	Person	Assignment	1	n	x
2	Person-type	Assignment	0	1	x

Exhibit 8.6.   Cardinality Regulation Example

8.4 Summary

- The behavior of any real-world system is constrained by both natural and artificial limits. Artificial limits are business rules established or observed by an organization.
- User-controlled resynchronization of the automated system with its changed real-world system is accomplished through regulation or management of the system's artificial limits.
- Changes in business rules are the most likely trigger of system modifications. A guiding principle in designing flexible systems is that business staff, through the modification of data values, should manage all maintenance of business rules.
- The current interpretations of business rules are typically coded in programs. Migrating such logic to business-staff-maintained data structures offers great potential for improving system stability and flexibility and reducing system maintenance.
- The first principle of regulation is to store business rules as data.
- There are (at least) two types of regulation: (a) general business rules regulation and (b) cardinality regulation. General regulation of business rules allows adjustment of business processing; cardinality regulation allows adjustment of the underlying information structures.
- Regulatory processes should be content-free programs that "know" where to retrieve information about rules and how to enforce the rules. General business-rules regulation can accomplish the following without the need for program or database modifications:
  - Verifying, or validating, that the value entered into a field is valid
  - Determining whether an action is valid
  - Determining what action the system should take
  - Accommodating the addition of new actions/processes
- Regulation should have effective dates, and it cannot be retroactive. In other words, the setting of regulation values must not cause the system to violate its own rules.
- Cardinality regulation is one technique for varying constraints on the system without modifying the system's structure (or its processes).
- For an information structure to remain unmodified while the cardinality requirements change (e.g., from hierarchical to network organization or vice versa), the information structure must always represent the more general case (in this instance, the network or many-to-many organization). If enforcement of one-to-many (the hierarchical organization) is a current requirement of the system, then that enforcement must be implemented outside the information structure by means of cardinality rules.

While many of today's authors and gurus recognize the value of reducing the maintenance burden, their efforts and thoughts generally tend toward practices that make it easier to modify programs and information structures — active flexibility. Our goal is built-in or planned flexibility, enabling maintenance of software systems *without* modifications to programs or information structures.

Appendix 8A: Using Regulation to Make a Flexible System

This appendix is for those inclined to work through examples, as it requires the reader to study the details. The two examples, one with and one without regulation, use decision tables to determine shipments in an order-processing system. Knowledge of decision tables is assumed.

The entities and decision table in Exhibit 8.7 show an order entry/shipment subsystem that does not provide for business-staff regulation of rules, specifically rules governing back orders and shipping of partial orders. There is no way to change parameters without modifying data structures or program code. Partial shipments and back orders are not allowed under current business policies. Programming modifications would be required to reflect changes in these policies to allow either back orders or partial shipments or both. In Exhibit 8.7, columns 2, 5, and 6 and rows C and F are included as placeholders. They are left blank because they are not active. Note also that the pseudocode includes only operational data.

The decision table in Exhibit 8.7 represents logic that is managed via program code. It might be an internal table in a program implemented with constants in the "data division," or it might be IF/THEN/ELSE statements with embedded literals. The point here is that it is under programmer control and not business staff control. Throughout the book, we have planted the idea that business staff should maintain values in tables. Here is what happens when the IT staff, rather than the business staff, maintain the business rules.

As seen in Exhibit 8.7, when management decides to allow back orders, an IT professional, via program modifications, can activate columns 2 and 6 and deactivate columns 3 and 4. Should management decide to allow partial shipments, an IT professional, via program modification, can activate column 5. If both partial shipments and back orders are allowed, program modifications can activate columns 2, 5, and 6 and deactivate columns 3 and 4. Any or all of these changes would then require regression testing to ensure that (a) the program modifications allowed orders to be processed correctly and (b) the modifications did not create side effects.

OPERATIONAL
    CUSTOMERS
    ORDERS
        ORDER-TYPE (Regular/Backordered/Partial)
    ORDER-LINE
        ORDER-QUANTITY (OQ)

    INVENTORY-ITEM
        ONHAND-QUANTITY (OHQ)

	Condition/Rule	1	2	3	4	5	6
A	OnHand Quantity Compared to OrderQuantity	>=		<	<		
B	OnHandQuantity Compared to Zero	*		<=	>		
C	BackOrders Allowed						
D	Partial Ship Allowed						

	Action/Rule	1	2	3	4	5	6
E	Ship	OQ					
F	BackOrder						
G	Reject Entire Order			Y	Y		

Explanation of Decisions and Processing:

Condition/Rule A1: OnHand Quantity greater than or equal to Order Quantity.
Condition/Rule B1: Actual OnHand quantity doesn't matter
Action/Rule E1: Ship Order Quantity.

The system compares the OnHand quantity to the Order Quantity and determines that the (entire) order can be shipped.

Column 2 is not operational in this Exhibit

Condition/Rule A3: OnHand Quantity less than Order Quantity
Condition/Rule B3: OnHand Quantity less than or equal to zero

Action/Rule E3: No shipment

Action/Rule G3: Reject entire order
 Because there is no inventory, nothing can be shipped, so the entire order is rejected.

Condition/Rule A4: OnHand Quantity less than Order Quantity
Condition/Rule B4: OnHand Quantity greater than zero

Action/Rule E4: No shipment

Action/Rule G4: Reject entire order

  There is insufficient inventory to ship the (entire) order, so the order is rejected.

Columns 5 and 6 are not operational in this Exhibit

Exhibit 8.7. Decision Table of Order-Entry Process (without Regulation)

In Exhibit 8.8, with the addition of the regulating entity ORDER-POLICY and its BACK-ORDER- and PARTIAL-SHIP-RULE attributes, to change the back-order constraints to activate rules 2, 5, and 6 and the partial ship in

```
OPERATIONAL
        CUSTOMERS
        ORDERS
                ORDER-TYPE (Regular/Backordered/Partial)
        ORDER-LINE
                ORDER-QUANTITY (OQ)

        INVENTORY-ITEM
                ONHAND-QUANTITY (OHQ)

REGULATION
        ORDER-POLICY
                BACK-ORDER-RULE (Yes/No)
                PARTIAL-SHIP-RULE (Yes/No)
```

	Condition/Rule	1	2	3	4	5	6
A	OnHand Quantity Compared to OrderQuantity	>=	<	<	<	<	<
B	OnHandQuantity Compared to Zero	*	<=	<=	>	>	>
C	BackOrders Allowed	*	Y	N	N	Y	Y
D	Partial Ship Allowed	*	*	*	*	Y	N

	Action/Rule	1	2	3	4	5	6
E	Ship	OQ	0			OHQ	
F	BackOrder		OQ			OQ-OHQ	OQ
G	Reject Entire Order			Y	Y		

Explanation of Decisions and Processing:

Condition/Rule A1: OnHand Quantity greater than or equal to Order Quantity.
Condition/Rule B1: Actual OnHand quantity doesn't matter
Condition/Rule C1: BackOrdersAllowed doesn't matter
Condition/Rule D1: PartialShipAllowed doesn't matter

Action/Rule E1: Ship Order Quantity.

The system compares the OnHand quantity to the Order Quantity and determines that the entire order can be shipped. Back orders and Partial Shipments are not a consideration.

Condition/Rule A2	: OnHand Quantity less than Order Quantity
Condition/Rule B2	: OnHand Quantity less than or equal to zero
Condition/Rule C2	: BackOrders are allowed
Condition/Rule D2	: PartialShipAllowed doesn't matter

Action/Rule E2: Ship Quantity of zero
Action/Rule F2: BackOrder OrderQuantity

Exhibit 8.8. Decision Table of Order-Entry Process (with Regulation)

rules 5 or 6 requires only that the actual value of the rule variable be changed by the regulating procedure. In Exhibit 8.8, all columns and rows are active, and regulatory data has been added to the pseudocode.

The point of Exhibit 8.8 is that users maintain the values. The condition/rule table is essentially a complex logical IF statement. The action/rule is essentially a logical THEN. Thus the condition results in rows A and B

Because there is no inventory nothing can be shipped regardless of partial ship policy, and because back orders are allowed, the entire order is back ordered.

Condition/Rule A3: OnHand Quantity less than Order Quantity
Condition/Rule B3: OnHand Quantity less than or equal to zero
Condition/Rule C3: BackOrders are not allowed
Condition/Rule D3: PartialShipAllowed doesn't matter

Action/Rule E3: No shipment
Action/Rule F3: No back order
Action/Rule G3: Reject entire order

Because there is no inventory, nothing can be shipped regardless of partial ship policy, and because back orders are not allowed—the entire order is, in essence, rejected.

Condition/Rule A4: OnHand Quantity less than Order Quantity
Condition/Rule B4: OnHand Quantity greater than zero
Condition/Rule C4: BackOrders are not allowed
Condition/Rule D4: PartialShipAllowed doesn't matter

Action/Rule E4: No shipment
Action/Rule F4: No back order
Action/Rule G4: Reject entire order

There is insufficient inventory to ship it all, and because back order is not allowed to ship the rest, no shipment is made.

Condition/Rule A5: OnHand Quantity less than Order Quantity
Condition/Rule B5: OnHand Quantity greater than zero
Condition/Rule C5: BackOrders are allowed
Condition/Rule D5: PartialShip is allowed

Action/Rule E5: Ship on-hand quantity
Action/Rule F5: Back order the rest

Partial ship and back orders are both allowed, and because there is insufficient inventory to ship it all the on-hand quantity is shipped and the rest back ordered.

Condition/Rule A6: OnHand Quantity less than Order Quantity
Condition/Rule B6: OnHand Quantity greater than zero
Condition/Rule C6: BackOrders are allowed
Condition/Rule D6: PartialShip is not allowed

Action/Rule E6: No shipment
Action/Rule F6: Back order the entire order

Exhibit 8.8. (continued)

are facts and are not subject to evaluation or interpretation: "If the order quantity is greater than the order inventory, the result is <."

Rows C and D are a little different. For example, cell C2 is saying, "If we allow back orders," then some result occurs. It is not saying whether back orders are allowed. That determination is made elsewhere. The determination could be universal company policy, i.e., we allow back orders or we do not. Or it could depend on the customer. This is the ideal spot for business staff-controlled business rules. The rules can change, but the data structures, and even the values, represented by the tables do not have to change.

In Exhibit 8.8, no programming modifications are necessary, and there is no need for an IT professional to intervene. Of course, testing by the business personnel has not been eliminated. Tests must be run to ensure that regulatory variables have been set properly, but given proper initial testing of the system's regulatory capabilities, no testing for side effects should be needed.

As new business requirements emerge, such as safety stock or special treatment, support for those features should be designed for user maintenance as well. Having established the flexible design, do not corrupt it later by adding inflexible features.

Appendix 8B: Business Rules Manifesto

See Exhibit 8.9.

Business Rules Manifesto
The Principles of Rule Independence
by Business Rules Group

Article 1. Primary Requirements, Not Secondary

1.1. Rules are a first-class citizen of the requirements world.

1.2. Rules are essential for, and a discrete part of, business models and technology models.

Article 2. Separate From Processes, Not Contained In Them

2.1. Rules are explicit constraints on behavior and/or provide support to behavior.

2.2. Rules are not process and not procedure. They should not be contained in either of these.

2.3. Rules apply across processes and procedures. There should be one cohesive body of rules, enforced consistently across all relevant areas of business activity.

Article 3. Deliberate Knowledge, Not A By-Product

3.1. Rules build on facts, and facts build on concepts as expressed by terms.

3.2. Terms express business concepts; facts make assertions about these concepts; rules constrain and support these facts.

3.3. Rules must be explicit. No rule is ever assumed about any concept or fact.

3.4. Rules are basic to what the business knows about itself — that is, to basic business knowledge.

3.5. Rules need to be nurtured, protected, and managed.

Article 4. Declarative, Not Procedural

4.1. Rules should be expressed declaratively in natural-language sentences for the business audience.

4.2. If something cannot be expressed, then it is not a rule.

4.3. A set of statements is declarative only if the set has no implicit sequencing.

4.4. Any statements of rules that require constructs other than terms and facts imply assumptions about a system implementation.

4.5. A rule is distinct from any enforcement defined for it. A rule and its enforcement are separate concerns.

4.6. Rules should be defined independently of responsibility for the who, where, when, or how of their enforcement.

4.7. Exceptions to rules are expressed by other rules.

Article 5. Well-Formed Expression, Not Ad Hoc

5.1. Business rules should be expressed in such a way that they can be validated for correctness by business people.

5.2. Business rules should be expressed in such a way that they can be verified against each other for consistency.

5.3. Formal logics, such as predicate logic, are fundamental to well-formed expression of rules in business terms, as well as to the technologies that implement business rules.

continued…

Copyright, 2003. Business Rules Group. Version 2.0, November 1, 2003. Edited by Ronald G. Ross. www.BusinessRulesGroup.org
Permission is granted for unlimited reproduction and distribution of this document under the following conditions: (a) The copyright and this permission notice are clearly included. (b) The work is clearly credited to the Business Rules Group. (c) No part of the document, including title, content, copyright, and permission notice, is altered, abridged or extended in any manner.

Exhibit 8.9. Business Rules Manifesto

Article 6. Rule-Based Architecture, Not Indirect Implementation

6.1. A business rules application is intentionally built to accommodate continuous change in business rules. The platform on which the application runs should support such continuous change.

6.2. Executing rules directly – for example in a rules engine – is a better implementation strategy than transcribing the rules into some procedural form.

6.3. A business rule system must always be able to explain the reasoning by which it arrives at conclusions or takes action.

6.4. Rules are based on truth values. How a rule's truth value is determined or maintained is hidden from users.

6.5. The relationship between events and rules is generally many-to-many.

Article 7. Rule-Guided Processes, Not Exception-Based Programming

7.1. Rules define the boundary between acceptable and unacceptable business activity.

7.2. Rules often require special or selective handling of detected violations. Such rule violation activity is activity like any other activity.

7.3. To ensure maximum consistency and reusability, the handling of unacceptable business activity should be separable from the handling of acceptable business activity.

Article 8. For the Sake of the Business, Not Technology

8.1. Rules are about business practice and guidance; therefore, rules are motivated by business goals and objectives and are shaped by various influences.

8.2. Rules always cost the business something.

8.3. The cost of rule enforcement must be balanced against business risks, and against business opportunities that might otherwise be lost.

8.4. 'More rules' is not better. Usually fewer 'good rules' is better.

8.5. An effective system can be based on a small number of rules. Additional, more discriminating rules can be subsequently added, so that over time the system becomes smarter.

Article 9. Of, By and For Business People, Not IT People

9.1. Rules should arise from knowledgeable business people.

9.2. Business people should have tools available to help them formulate, validate and manage rules.

9.3. Business people should have tools available to help them verify business rules against each other for consistency.

Article 10. Managing Business Logic, Not Hardware/Software Platforms

10.1. Business rules are a vital business asset.

10.2. In the long run, rules are more important to the business than hardware/software platforms.

10.3. Business rules should be organized and stored in such a way that they can be readily redeployed to new hardware/software platforms.

10.4. Rules, and the ability to change them effectively, are fundamental to improving business adaptability.

Exhibit 8.9. (continued)

Chapter 9

Stable Information Structures

The differentiation between structure and process in a system — between, roughly speaking, the fixed and the variable parts of the system — is generally recognized [Wand and Weber, 1990, pp. 125–126; Weinberg and Weinberg, 1979, pp. 122–135]. The relationship between structure and process is that *structure constrains process*. Changes made to a system that are limited to its process components tend to be low in cost because the changes remain local. Changes to a system's structure tend to be high in cost because they alter the constraints on all the system's processes that access the changed portion of the structure.

This provides an important part of the explanation for why a conceptually simple and inexpensive change in a real-world (RW) system is often accompanied by a complex and costly modification to its supporting automated-world (AW) system. This happens when the RW system change is limited to process components, but the corresponding AW system modification requires alteration to structural components. This in turn has nonlocal effects on the system's processes. High costs are incurred when a chain reaction of compensatory modifications is triggered by the need to adjust many other components of the system to the new constraints.

This constraint relationship between structure and process presents us with a fundamental design problem: how to keep the structural part of a system stable while supporting a wide procedural repertoire that can accommodate future changes. We want changes to be enacted with few or no program code modifications, and we want those that are required to be limited to local-only modifications. We want change to take the form of data-value manipulations rather than coding and declaration manipulations.

This chapter addresses how to stabilize the information structure and some of the procedural factors in exploiting that structure. The following items are key to stable information structures:

- Invariant, unique identifiers
- Externally enforced cardinality
- Generic entities
- Generic relationships
- Recursive and nested recursive relationships
- Variable subtyping versus static subtyping
- Explicit typing-integrity maintenance

Identifiers were addressed in Chapter 7. The current chapter discusses generic entities, relationships, recursion, and typing. It assumes the existence of an external cardinality facility, the details of which were discussed in Chapter 8. It begins by relating stability to generality.

9.1 Structure/Process Differentiation: Generic Structures

> *The essence of adaptability to change lies in structure/process differentiation, which is essentially the exclusion of what is variable from what is constant.*

The static, structural part of a system is referred to as the "composition" of the system — the set of "things," their properties, and their interrelationships [Wand and Weber, 1990]. Agents that implement value changes within this framework constitute the variable, i.e., the process, part of the system. The essence of adaptability to change lies in structure/process differentiation, which is essentially the exclusion of that which is variable from that which is constant. The implied methodological principle is that, in proceeding through the transformations: RW system → RW model → AW model → AW system, the distinction between structure and process must be discerned in the RW system, then be preserved in the model of the RW system, and in the specification and construction of the AW system. Differentiation of structure and process can also be viewed as an increase in the level of generality of the composition of a system. So we can say that flexible systems have stable structures and that stable structures exhibit a high degree of generality. Two of the forms that generality can take in an information structure are generic entities and generic relationships [Woolfolk et al., 1996].

9.1.1 Generic Entities

Because an entity is a person, place, thing, concept, etc., the idea of a generic entity recognizes that such things come in subtypes. For example, a Person entity can have subtypes of employee, student, dependent, client, etc. The generic entity "organizational unit" can be used to represent an organization's divisions, sections, departments, etc. Subtypes of a generic entity necessarily have some attributes in common and some that differ. The flexibility to be gained from generic treatment far outweighs the problem of unshared attributes.

Consider an enterprise organized into companies, divisions, and stores as shown in Exhibit 9.1. Exhibit 9.2 shows the traditional structure model representing this organization scheme along with a simple example of a sales entity in which the store sales amount is determined by the key of

Co-ID + Div-ID + Store-ID

If a new type of organization is added to the enterprise, e.g., if strategic business units (SBU) are created to manage groups of divisions, then the model and its corresponding database representation would have to be modified as shown in Exhibit 9.3. What is most important, however, is

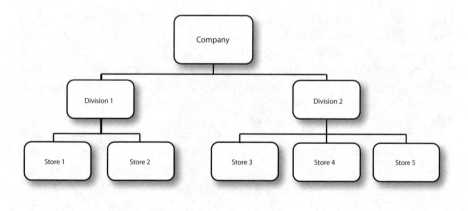

Exhibit 9.1. Example of Enterprise Organization

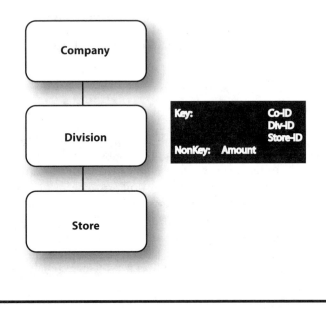

Exhibit 9.2. Traditional Model

that processes that access division and store data also have to be modified to take into account the new organization scheme. The difficulty of modification is compounded if traditional nested qualification identifiers are also used, as shown in Exhibit 9.3.

In contrast, Exhibit 9.4 shows a generic representation of the same organization, with the "organization unit" entity representing any organization subtype (e.g., company, division, etc.) according to the "organization type" specified for any specific instance of organization unit. The relationships between organization units are represented by the recursive Org Unit–Org Unit relationship. This structure absorbs the addition of the SBU, or any other hierarchically related organization subtype, without itself needing to be modified. The recursive Org Type–Org Type relationship supports maintenance of a consistent (sub)typing. That is, any Org Type scheme that is implemented becomes the rule for how Org Units can be related [Business Rules Group, 2004].

Notice that this basic generic-entity concept confers significantly increased stability on the information structure in which it is used, provided that (a) the RW organization is not changed from hierarchical to network and (b) only one organization scheme at a time needs to be represented. Additional generic enhancements can be made, as in Exhibit 9.5, that allow the organization to depart from its single hierarchical scheme to accommodate multiple complex networked relationships, all without the

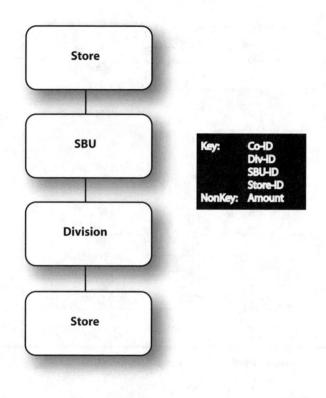

Exhibit 9.3. Modification to Incorporate SBU

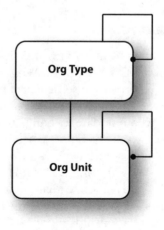

Exhibit 9.4. Generic Model

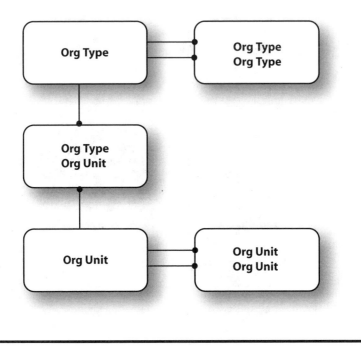

Exhibit 9.5. Generic Model of Network Organization

need to change the structure itself [Business Rules Group, 2004]. This brings us to generic relationships.

9.1.2 Generic Relationships

The one-to-one (1:1) and one-to-many (1:n) relationships are special cases of the many-to-many (m:n) relationship. Wherever we have an m:n relationship in an information structure, it is clear that it can represent a corresponding m:n or 1:n or 1:1 RW relationship, depending on what data fills it. Thus, it can accommodate a change to the cardinality requirement at any time without itself needing to be modified. If we desire to enforce a specific cardinality requirement, say 1:m, then such enforcement needs to be provided outside the information structure. At this point in the discussion, we will simply assume that such an external cardinality enforcement facility exists, as was discussed in Chapter 8.

It is clear that generic relationships along with generic entities confer additional stability on the information structure. As noted previously, generic entities employ recursive relationships.

9.2 Recursive Relationships

Recursive relationships are a direct consequence of generalization. When an entity, such as organization unit, is a generalization of more specialized entities, such as company, division, and store, and when instances of those specialized entities can be related to each other, then those relationships are necessarily represented at the level of the generic entity by a relationship of the generic entity to itself — a recursive relationship. Another way to look at this is to consider that generalization of a set of specialized entities is a sensible concept simply because those entities do stand in one or more relationships to each other. Therefore, the generic entity will necessarily stand in one or more relationships to itself. (The phrase "or more" in the previous sentence will be taken up later in the discussion of roles in Chapter 10, Section 4.)

The combination of the generic entity with a recursive relationship to itself provides the structure for the familiar bill of material (BOM) that relates products to assemblies to parts, etc., from which the traditional indented materials list is produced, as seen in Exhibit 9.6. Of course, the recursions in such a structure must not be endless. The mechanism used

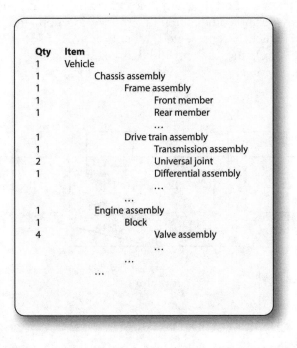

Qty	Item
1	Vehicle
1	Chassis assembly
1	Frame assembly
1	Front member
1	Rear member
	...
1	Drive train assembly
1	Transmission assembly
2	Universal joint
1	Differential assembly
	...
	...
1	Engine assembly
1	Block
4	Valve assembly
	...
	...
	...

Exhibit 9.6. Example of Indented Bill of Material

to support the recursions must enforce the rule that cycles are not allowed. For example, if part A is an assembly component of part B directly or indirectly, then part B may not be an assembly component of part A directly or indirectly.

Clearly, organization charts, charts of accounts, complex documents, etc. can be expressed as this same bill-of-materials type of recursive generic structure. Hay and Healy [2000] argue for business rules to support this form as opposed to the traditional approach. Increased usage of this powerful concept awaits only the alert designer to discover many more applications.

9.2.1 Nested Recursive Relationships

The existence of recursive relationships in an information structure has significant implications for processing. It requires reusable routines that can cope with recursive relationships. These, of course, have been built many times for the bill-of-materials structure. What is less common is processing of related BOM-like structures. Information structures that contain generic entities will necessarily also contain relationships among different generic entities. For example, consider an on-hand inventory quantity for a specific combination of product, location, and organization unit, each of which is represented generically in Exhibit 9.7. That is, at the database level, the quantity field is an attribute of an association relation with a primary key of product ID + location ID + organization unit ID.

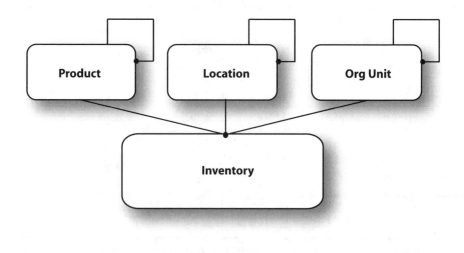

Exhibit 9.7. Related Generic Entities

This is straightforward information-structure modeling and database design. The difference between this and a traditional structure is that each of the foreign keys of the inventory entity participates in a recursive relationship that defines the corresponding current product, location, or organization scheme. This means the processing of this structure is more complex than for a traditional structure. For example, rolling up the inventory quantity to totals for various combinations of product, location, and organization means processing through what is essentially a set of nested recursive relationships. While the algorithm is more complex to design and implement and is possibly, but not necessarily, slower to execute, the resulting inventory processing is thereafter immune to structural changes in the product, location, or organization schemes. And such schemes, of course, do change.

9.3 Typing and Generic Entities

We use the term *m:n* relationship and association entity interchangeably. We prefer the term association entity in recognition that it has attributes just as a simple entity does. Attributes, independent of the type of entity, can be single valued, such as a person's birth date, or multivalued, such as a person's hobbies. A permanently single-valued attribute can appropriately be represented "within" the entity it describes, as an attribute functionally determined by the entity's identifier, as shown in Exhibit 9.8. Assuming we disallow repeating attributes in an entity as required by

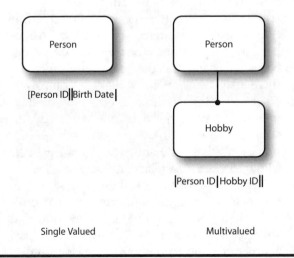

Single Valued   Multivalued

Exhibit 9.8. Single-Valued and Multivalued Attributes

normalization, a multivalued attribute, such as hobby, necessarily must be represented "outside" the entity it describes, as shown in Exhibit 9.8.

9.3.1 Control Types and Consistent Typing

A generic entity will typically have at least one typing that characterizes the entity as generic. We call this a control type.

There are two distinct ways of grouping entities: "selection" and "typing." Any dynamic combination of attribute or relationship values of an entity can be used to select the entity for a transient purpose such as production of a report. Generalized query and report-writer tools are designed to do selection to a greater degree than most specialized code. And the larger the set of attribute values, relationship values, and comparisons among these values that such a tool can simultaneously accommodate, the stronger is the tool. Typing refers to classifying an entity for an ongoing business purpose. It is typing that concerns us here, not selection.

Typing of a generic entity is accomplished through proper design of the information structure and population of the structure with data values. One or more attributes of a generic entity can be used to type the generic entity. We call such an attribute a control type.

In Exhibit 9.9, recognizing that the business may need to view an organizational unit differently for different purposes, we establish an Org-Type control-type attribute with potential values of company, division, and store. The exhibit shows several instances of organizational units, their types, and the relationships between them.

In Chapter 10, we introduce the generic-entity cloud and show how control types can be used to manage data-related business rules. They can be used to control the number of type values an entity can have. They can also be used to define relationships between control-type values. For example, there may be a need to allow a company to be directly responsible for a division but disallow direct responsibility for a store.

A generic entity can have more than one control type. For example, a generic organization unit might have the usual organization control type (e.g., company, division, store, etc.) and also, say, a legal control type (e.g., incorporated, wholly owned subsidiary, holding, etc.).

The relationship rules imposed by these types may legitimately be inconsistent with each other. This simply means that organization units participate in more than one organization scheme and that the different schemes have different relationship roles. In Chapter 10 we also demonstrate how data structures and values can be used to reflect and manage these inconsistent concurrent types and relationships.

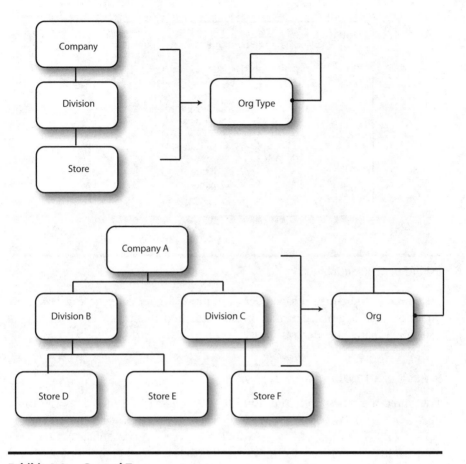

Exhibit 9.9. Control Type

9.3.2 *Variable versus Fixed Typing*

> *If there is anything in the real world that is variable, it is the groupings that we use.*

Those involved in exploration of database design methods have focused much of their attention on capturing more meaning in the database schema. An approach that appeared promising was that of declaring sub-/supertyping distinctions [Hammer and McLeod, 1981]. However, because such typing is static, this method presents significant limitations. Professional IT intervention is required when typing is to be altered. Such alterations are necessarily modifications of the information structure.

If there is anything in the real world that is variable, it is the groupings that we use. A flexible system needs to reflect these groupings used by

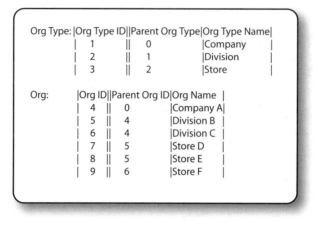

```
Org Type: |Org Type ID||Parent Org Type|Org Type Name|
          |    1      ||      0         |Company       |
          |    2      ||      1         |Division      |
          |    3      ||      2         |Store         |

Org:        |Org ID||Parent Org ID|Org Name  |
            |  4   ||      0       |Company A|
            |  5   ||      4       |Division B |
            |  6   ||      4       |Division C |
            |  7   ||      5       |Store D    |
            |  8   ||      5       |Store E    |
            |  9   ||      6       |Store F    |
```

Exhibit 9.9. (continued)

people and their institutions. The argument for variable typing is simply an argument for no structurally imposed typing at all. Let us look at some examples using the Person entity.

9.3.2.1 Example: Fixed Typing

The implementation shown in Exhibit 9.10, Case 1, has the following three files, one for each of the *current* Person-Types: employee, manager, and contractor. Adding a new Person-Type (e.g., representative) requires another file as in Case 2. Besides inflexibility, another ugly part of this design is the data redundancy if an individual has multiple roles, Bruce Johnson being the example. As we all know from experience, when the "same" data is in multiple places, it does not always stay the same.

9.3.2.2 Example: Limited Variable Typing

The implementation shown in Exhibit 9.11 has only one file and will always have one file regardless of how many Person-Types there are. This also eliminates the duplication of recorded data seen in Exhibit 9.10. A limitation on this scheme is that a person can be only one Person-Type at a time.

Case 1: Original Inflexible-Nongeneric Implementation

Case 2: Modified Inflexible-Nongeneric Implementation

Employee

Identification	Name	Address	Extension	E-mail	Rate
1	Bruce Johnson	Here	1234	Here@isp	100.00
2	Sam Smith	Elsewhere	2345	Else@isp	10.00
.....					

Manager

Identification	Name	Address	Extension	E-mail	Rate
1	Walt W. Woolfolk	There	3456	There@isp	33.33
2	Bruce Johnson	Here	1234	Else@isp	100.00
.....					

Contractor

Identification	Name	Address	Extension	E-mail	Rate
1	Sarah Jones	Upthere	5678	Upthere@isp	75.25
2	Jimmy Jimson	Where	1492	Where@isp	44.44
3	Bruce Johnson	Here	1234	Here@isp	100.00
...					

Exhibit 9.10. Example of Fixed Typing

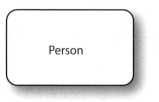

Person

ID	Name	Address	Extension	E-mail	Rate	Type
1	Bruce Johnson	Here	1234	Here@isp	100.00	Employee
2	Sam Smith	Elsewhere	2345	Else@isp	10.00	Employee
11	Walt W. Woolfolk	There	3456	There@isp	33.33	Manager
21	Sarah Jones	Upthere	5678	Upthere@isp	75.25	Contractor
12	Jimmy Jimson	Where	1492	Where@isp	44.44	Contractor
.....						

Exhibit 9.11. Example of Limited Variable Typing (One Type per Person)

9.3.2.3 Example: Expanded Variable Typing

Exhibit 9.12 has three files and will always have three files regardless of how many Person-Types are required. The advantages of this implementation are as follows:

- No new files are required to identify additional Person-Types.
- Data about a person occurs only once regardless of how many Person-Types that person may be.
- A person has one unique identifier rather than an identifier per Person-Type.
- Data about persons is persistent, even if they currently have no Person-Type.
- A person can be multiple Person-Types at the same time.
- A person cannot be of a Person-Type that is not recorded. Referential integrity is ensured.

This implementation could be improved further by moving the rate from the person file to the Person/Person-Type file, thus allowing a different rate depending upon the Person-Type.

We see from the examples how small changes in system data organization can have major impacts upon the flexibility of the system.

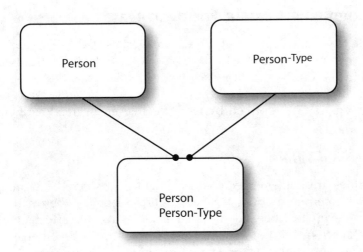

Persons

ID	Name	Address	Extension	E-mail	Rate
1	Bruce Johnson	Here	1234	Here@isp	100.00
17	Sam Smith	Elsewhere	2345	Else@isp	10.00
3	Walt W. Woolfolk	There	3456	There@isp	33.33
43	Sarah Jones	Upthere	5678	Upthere@isp	75.25
5	Jimmy Jimson	Where	1492	Where@isp	44.44
.....					

Person Type

ID	Descriptions	Other Information
37	Employee	
47	Manager	
63	Contractor	

Person/Person Type

Person-ID	Person-Type-ID	Start-Date
1	37	2000-11-17
1	47	2001-01-12
1	63	2000-10-23
17	37	2000-11-13
3	47	2000-10-23
43	63	2001-01-12
5	63	2000-11-17
....		

Exhibit 9.12. Example of Flexible Generic Implementation with Variable Typing

9.4 Recognizing Certain Forms of Data

Developers often find a need to store dates, times, flags, and derived values for system performance reasons. We offer additional flexibility-oriented thinking on these data forms. Derived values need to be in the right place in the data structure. Date and time data may serve two purposes. Flags can be replaced by more flexible multivalued attributes.

9.4.1 Derived Values

Derived values are implemented for performance reasons. For example, an individual's current account balance might be stored rather than calculated whenever it is needed. Derived values have no effect on the flexibility characteristics of a system. However, it should be emphasized that when derived values are identified during analysis or design, they must be correctly located in the information-structure model. Derived values, regardless of their nature, have functional determinants that establish their correct placement in the information structure. While it may seem obvious that they must be placed correctly, their seemingly informal nature can cause this fact to be ignored. If you find it advisable to maintain derived data elements, recognize that they, just like any other attributes, require adherence to sound information-structure design.

9.4.2 Date and Time

Date and time can be both attributes and (parts of) identifiers. Generally they serve as attributes. However, when an entity is an event or when an effective period is required, date and time values are used to ensure identifier uniqueness. Dates/times subject to change must always be treated as attributes. If a date or time is part of an identifier (such as effective date), then — because identifiers must be stable and unchangeable — the date in this ID cannot be changed. If the date or time is the expected ship date or time, then it is subject to change and may be changed as the information changes. Any field that is changeable must be an attribute and not (part of) an identifier.

Effective dates and effective periods come into play when it is desirable to track versions of an entity. In analyzing what aspects of a system can change, consider the possibility of versions. When business rules are stored as data, as we strongly recommend, considering that rules change over time, they should have effective dates. If a rule (or any entity for that matter) can have multiple effective dates, then you have a requirement

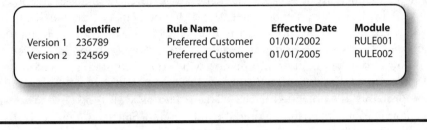

	Identifier	Rule Name	Effective Date	Module
Version 1	236789	Preferred Customer	01/01/2002	RULE001
Version 2	324569	Preferred Customer	01/01/2005	RULE002

Exhibit 9.13.   Preferred-Customer Rule

for an association entity that includes the date as part of the identifier. In Exhibit 9.13, we show two versions of the "preferred customer" rule.

During the period when Version 1 is effective, a module called RULE001 executes the logic to enforce the rules. When Version 2 becomes effective, RULE002 takes over. Note that this approach allows the business staff to set up and test Version 2 in advance of its implementation without affecting existing processing. They can perform comparative analyses about the potential effect on the number of preferred customers when the new rules take effect. Similarly, after Version 2 is in effect, they can perform a backward analysis of what would have occurred had Version 1 remained in effect. This is an example of the management of business rules to reflect changes in business policy. The implementation of business rules themselves is covered in Chapter 8 on regulation.

9.4.3 Flag

> *Avoid a physical design that includes data elements that are themselves single-purpose flags.*

There may appear to be good reasons to include flags in the design of a system, but when designing a flexible system, one must think carefully. For example, in the following cases, the answers to the yes/no questions may provide enough information for certain business processes.

Account Active flag (Is the account active?)	Y/N
Tuition Remission Eligibility flag (Is the person eligible?)	Y/N
Child of Alumnus flag (Is this person the child of an alumnus?)	Y/N
Employee Child flag (Is this person the child of an employee?)	Y/N
U.S. Citizen flag (Is this person a U.S. citizen?)	Y/N
Deceased flag (Has the person died?)	Y/N

For certain current business activities, you might contact a customer only if the U.S. Citizen flag is set to No. If your current business needs to know nothing more about an individual's citizenship, a simple flag is sufficient for your current needs. However, for an organization intending to employ a noncitizen, other information will be needed, such as the country of citizenship or visa status. If you are storing the country of citizenship, you probably do not need a U.S. Citizen flag as well. For U.S. citizens, the country of citizenship would be the United States. For noncitizens, the country will be something else.

Even if it is necessary to store information that simply answers yes/no questions, adding a new flag every time a new question arises requires IT intervention to add a new field to a record. An alternative might be to define a table/file to record valid attribute values for an entity. Instead of a series of questions, each having a yes or no answer, you have a series of attribute values. The presence of the value indicates that the answer to the equivalent yes/no question is yes. For example, using the attribute approach, the following information is equivalent to that stored in the flag approach above.

Identifier	Mnemonic	Description
985421	CALUM	Child of Alumnus
776597	CEMPL	Child of Employee

The presence of an attribute pertaining to the flag item is equivalent to a flag value of Y. Its absence is equivalent to a flag value of N. We know the individual <u>is</u> a child of an alumnus because the attribute for Child of Alumnus is present on the individual's record. We know that the individual's account <u>is not</u> active because we do not see the attribute for Account Active on the individual's record. Similarly, the attributes on the individual's record tell that he <u>is</u> a Child of Employee and that he <u>is not</u> eligible for tuition remission, and so on.

Using the various techniques we have described, maintenance of valid attribute values can be placed under business staff control with no IT intervention required. Adding a new flag element, however, requires changes to both information structures and program code. The attribute approach is clearly more flexible.

The concept of a flag may be legitimate, but in the interests of flexibility, we strongly recommend that you avoid a physical design that includes data elements that are single-purpose flags. There are better alternatives. Always consider what can change.

9.5 Bottom-Up Derivation of Generic Entities

Significant overlap of attributes between two specific entities provides a clue that it may make sense to declare the two as subtypes of a single generic entity.

As discussed previously, attributes contain descriptive information (e.g., name, street address, and social security number) about the entity, but an attribute can serve an additional purpose: to distinguish one entity from another. Sometimes, careful analysis reveals that two apparently different entities have a significant number of attributes in common. However, one or more data elements or attributes typically differentiate one entity from the other.

Significant overlap of attributes between two specific entities provides a clue that it may make sense to declare the two as subtypes of a single generic entity. We believe that a thorough analysis of the necessary data structures requires the analyst to combine both a top-down approach and a bottom-up approach. The top-down approach typically works well when gathering business requirements. When describing an organization's business, a member of the business staff might, for example, use terms such as customer, employee, clerk, representative, salesman, etc. Taking a top-down approach might lead the analyst to identify an entity in the system for each of those terms. Taking a bottom-up approach, which works well when designing the actual information structures, is likely to lead to the discovery that these terms have many common attributes and that having one entity — Person — with multiple types provides greater system flexibility.

9.6 Summary

- The differentiation between structure and process in a system — between, roughly speaking, the fixed and the variable parts of the system — is accepted wisdom.
- Flexible systems are characterized as stable information structures with wide behavioral repertoires.
- Flexible systems require stable information structures.
- Separating structure from process raises the generality of the system and makes it more flexible.
- Stable information structures are characterized by: invariant, unique identifiers; variable cardinality; generic entities; generic-entity relationships; recursive-entity relationships; consistent typing; and variable typing.

- Variable typing rather than fixed typing confers stability.
- Control types govern generic entities' recursive relationships.
- Care must be taken to ensure that derived values, when used, are stored in the correct place in the information structure.
- Date and time can be both attributes and (parts of) identifiers. When they are part of an identifier, they must not change.
- A flag is a special type of two-valued code, with the values generally consisting of Y and N or on and off. Flags present flexibility problems, and the data that they represent is often handled more flexibly by codes or attributes. Additional study of the impetus for flags often leads to a better understanding of the application and a more flexible treatment.
- The bottom-up derivation of entities and attributes may lead to the observation that several entities have attributes in common and thus should be considered for inclusion as subtypes of a more generic entity.

A stable information structure built upon stable identifiers is one of the most important considerations when developing a flexible computer system. Designing stable information structures, as set forth in this chapter; will go a long way in ensuring that your system is flexible. The generic-entity cloud (GEC) presented in the next chapter does all of this automatically.

Chapter 10

The Generic-Entity Cloud

This chapter introduces the generic-entity cloud (GEC) approach, an analysis/design technique that is particularly effective for developing flexible information systems. The GEC is a stable information structure. The following sections show how the GEC is developed step by step, utilizing the characteristics of stable information structures: invariant and unique identifiers, variable cardinality, generic entities, generic-entity relationships, recursive-entity relationships, consistent typing, and variable typing.

The GEC approach utilizes a cardinality-regulation mechanism to define and enforce relationships between and within GECs, as well as broader regulatory mechanisms that eliminate artificial limits from the structural and procedural parts of the software system. The GEC approach provides a pattern for analysis of information system requirements and design of a flexible system that satisfies those requirements. Analyses that follow the GEC pattern will lead to sound and flexible designs. That is, developers will build information systems that support current business requirements and accommodate changes to those requirements with a minimum of intervention from IT staff.

10.1 What Is a Generic-Entity Cloud?

We want to identify entities in a generic way because things will change.

The generic-entity cloud (GEC) provides an automatic way to implement highly stable data structures. The information structure of a GEC consists of generic entities formed into logical rings, as illustrated in Exhibit 10.1. The GEC is named for its cloudlike appearance.

To build a GEC, we start by identifying entities. An entity is something in the real world about which we want to record information. Having identified an entity, we determine the information we wish to record about that entity, i.e., its attributes as well as its relationship to other entities.

Essential to the GEC analysis is reduction in the number of entities. Where a more traditional approach would identify many specific entities, the GEC approach identifies a reduced number of *generic* entities. Entities should not be so specific that they limit flexibility and not be so generic that they are useless. As in all systems design, judgment is required.

To explain the GEC approach, we will start by examining general principles to clarify the design result we want to achieve. We will use specific examples to focus our thinking. After that, we will address the issue of how to achieve the desired result.

Let us look at a large business organization. For example, a company may have divisions. Each division may have stores. Company, division, and store might typically be considered specific entities. However, in the GEC approach, each is considered a "type" of a more generic entity called "organizational unit" (Exhibit 10.2).

We want to identify entities in a generic way because things will change. The company may reorganize or be acquired by a corporation that has a different structure, e.g., region, area, and center instead of, or in addition to, company, division, and store. We want to be able to accommodate such change without changing file structures or programs.

We design the system using GECs. The GECs can be connected with externals (explained below) to represent generic-entity relationships between the GECs. Internally, the information structure of a GEC consists of a six-node ring that accommodates maximum complexity. Each node represents a component of the GEC as well as a logical file in the system. To avoid overwhelming the reader, we will develop the GEC step by step, starting with a three-node GEC to represent a simple case.

10.2 Three-Node Generic-Entity Cloud

The GEC must support relationships between instances of a generic entity (recursion). This is shown in the general sense in Exhibit 10.3. In the GEC, the generic entity, type, and entity-entity nodes fall within the cloud.

Exhibit 10.3 (and many of the exhibits that follow) is a variation on the typical entity-relationship diagram. The presence of a dot on the line indicates "many." The absence of a dot indicates "one." For example, tracing the relationship from "type" to "generic entity," we see that a given

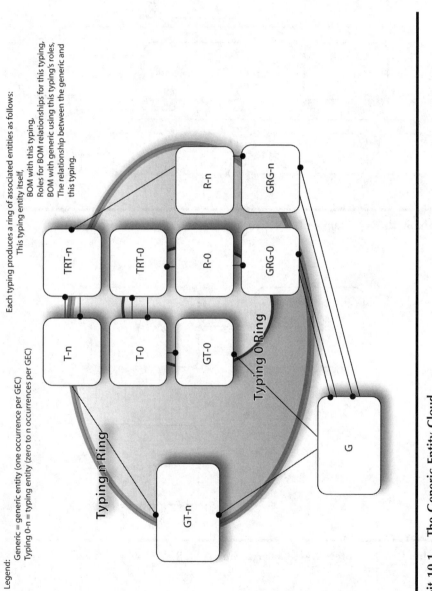

Legend:

Generic = generic entity (one occurrence per GEC)
Typing 0-n = typing entity (zero to n occurrences per GEC)

Each typing produces a ring of associated entities as follows:
This typing entity itself,
BOM with this typing.
Roles for BOM relationships for this typing.
BOM with generic using this typing's roles,
The relationship between the generic and this typing.

Exhibit 10.1. The Generic-Entity Cloud

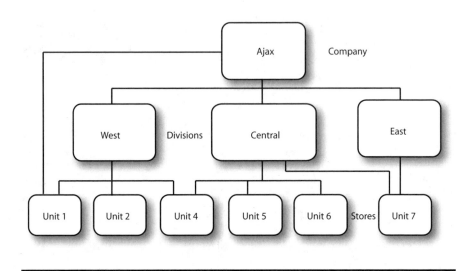

Exhibit 10.2.   Example of a Networked Organization: Ajax Company

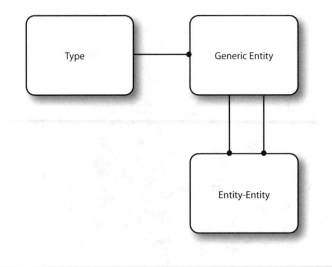

Exhibit 10.3.   Three-Node Generic-Entity Cloud

type can be used on many generic-entity records. Tracing the relationship from generic entity to type, we see that only one value for type is stored for a specific generic entity. The entity-entity record references exactly two generic-entity values, hence the two lines.

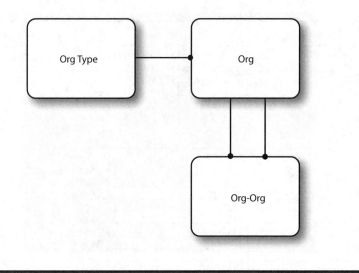

Exhibit 10.4. Organizational Database as a Three-Node GEC

In our organization example, the GEC must allow for expression of the relationship between company and division, division and store, etc. They are given the generic-entity type Org for organization unit. A simple schema for this general association is given in Exhibit 10.4.

The tabular notation in Exhibit 10.5 shows the networked organization in Exhibit 10.2 represented as a three-node GEC according to the schemas in Exhibit 10.3 and Exhibit 10.4. This is an example of the bill of materials (BOM) structure. Identifiers are simply (sequentially assigned) numbers that have no inherent meaning. Entities with identifiers of 1 and 13 have been deleted from the system, and Unit 3 does not exist any more, if it ever did. In Exhibit 10.5, the names in parentheses ( ) are not actually in the database; they are given here for ease of understanding.

The organizational database represented above and in Exhibit 10.2 and Exhibit 10.3 shows that each organizational unit has one control-type value (e.g., company, store, department, etc.) and can have zero or more organizational units reporting to it or that it may report to. The result is that, unlike in the case of the aluminum processing plant in Exhibit 1.2, the organizational unit types and their relationships can be changed at any time by simply manipulating data.

Let us examine what happens when things change. Let us say that the Ajax Company is acquired by Megalith Corporation and is now one of its many companies. For simplicity, let us assume that the structure within Ajax remains the same. Assuming that Megalith has the same GEC-based information-system design as Ajax, the change can be accommodated with a few entries to the tables shown earlier. New entries are in gray in Exhibit 10.6.

Org Type

Org-Type-ID	Org-Type-Name
0	Company
2	Division
3	Store

Org

Org-ID	Org-Name	Org-Type-ID
4	Ajax	0 (Company)
5	West	2 (Division)
6	Central	2 (Division)
7	East	2 (Division)
8	Unit 1	3 (Store)
9	Unit 2	3 (Store)
10	Unit 4	3 (Store)
11	Unit 5	3 (Store)
12	Unit 6	3 (Store)
14	Unit 7	3 (Store)

Org-Org

Parent Org-ID	Child Org-ID
4 (Ajax)	5 (West)
4 (Ajax)	6 (Central)
4 (Ajax)	7 (East)
4 (Ajax)	8 (Unit 1)
5 (West)	8 (Unit1)
5 (West)	9 (Unit 2)
5 (West)	10 (Unit 4)
6 (Central)	10 (Unit 4)
6 (Central)	11 (Unit 5)
6 (Central)	12 (Unit 6)
6 (Central)	14 (Unit 7)
7 (East)	14 (Unit 7)
8 (Unit1)	9 (Unit 2)

Exhibit 10.5. Tabular Notation: Ajax Company Organizational Database as a Three-Node GEC

Org Type

Org-Type-ID	Org-Type-Name
0	Company
2	Division
3	Store
15	Corporation

Org

Org-ID	Org-Name	Org-Type-ID
4	Ajax	0 (Company)
5	West	2 (Division)
6	Central	2 (Division)
7	East	2 (Division)
8	Unit 1	3 (Store)
9	Unit 2	3 (Store)
10	Unit 4	3 (Store)
11	Unit 5	3 (Store)
12	Unit 6	3 (Store)
14	Unit 7	3 (Store)
16	Megalith	15 (Corporation)

Org-Org

Parent Org-ID	Child Org-ID
4 (Ajax)	5 (West)
4 (Ajax)	6 (Central)
4 (Ajax)	7 (East)
4 (Ajax)	8 (Unit 1)
5 (West)	8 (Unit1)
5 (West)	9 (Unit 2)
5 (West)	10 (Unit 4)
6 (Central)	10 (Unit 4)
6 (Central)	11 (Unit 5)
6 (Central)	12 (Unit 6)
6 (Central)	14 (Unit 7)
7 (East)	14 (Unit 7)
8 (Unit1)	9 (Unit 2)
16 (Megalith)	4 (Ajax)

Exhibit 10.6.   Changes Required When Megalith Corporation Acquires Ajax

Looking at employment positions within the organization, we find a similar opportunity to define a new generic entity: position. Exhibit 10.7 represents the relationships graphically. Exhibit 10.8 provides a simple tabular representation showing a position structure having three values for its control type.

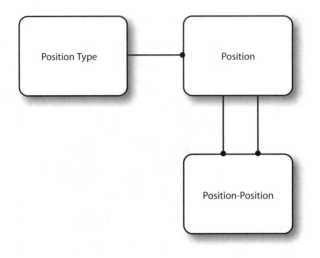

Exhibit 10.7. Position Database as a Three-Node GEC

Position Type

Pos-Type-ID	Pos-Type-Name
17	Executive
18	Management
19	Staff

Position

Pos-ID	Pos-Name	Pos-Type-ID
20	HR Director	17 (Executive)
21	Dept Manager	18 (Management)
22	Worker	19 (Staff)

Position-Position

Parent Pos-ID	Child Pos-ID
20 (HR Director)	21 (Dept Manager)
21 (Dept Manager)	22 (Worker)
20 (HR Director)	22 (Worker)

Exhibit 10.8. Tabular Notation: Position Database as a Three-Node GEC

Position Type

Pos-Type-ID	Pos-Type-Name
17	Executive
18	Management
19	Staff
23	Supervisor

Position

Pos-ID	Pos-Name	Pos-Type-ID
20	HR Director	17 (Executive)
21	Dept Manager	18 (Management)
22	Worker	19 (Staff)
24	Shift Leader	23 (Supervisor)

Position-Position

Parent Pos-ID	Child Pos-ID
20 (HR Director)	21 (Dept Manager)
21 (Dept Manager)	22 (Worker)
20 (HR Director)	22 (Worker)
24 (Shift Leader)	22 (Worker
21 (Dept Manager)	24 (Shift Leader)

Exhibit 10.9. Changes Required to Add New Position between Management and Staff

Exhibit 10.9 illustrates what happens when things change and a new position level is required between management and staff. Note that with the three-node GEC there is no notion of hierarchy within position type. However, the six-node GEC does provide for position-type hierarchy, which then supports disciplined position-position reporting based upon position type — what we have called the consistent subtype rule.

Again, the change can be accommodated with a few entries to the tables. New entity instances are shown in gray. New entities (control types) need not be defined for the new position value "supervisor" and the new position value "shift leader." Both can be accommodated within the existing GEC structure.

10.3 Externals

In addition to the recursive relationships within a generic entity, the GEC approach must support relationships between GECs. This is the typical relationship depicted in an entity-relationship diagram (ERD).

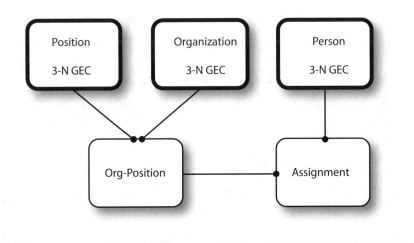

Exhibit 10.10. **Example Schema of Connected Three-Node GECs**

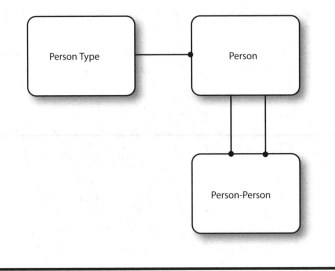

Exhibit 10.11. **Person Database as a Three-Node GEC**

Exhibit 10.10 illustrates this concept using what the GEC approach calls "externals." Note that we have introduced a Person GEC, as illustrated in Exhibit 10.11. In a situation where a many-to-many relationship exists between two entities (GECs in this case), it is generally shown as two separate one-to-many relationships, with a separate relationship node that is "external" to the GECs themselves. In Exhibit 10.10, the heavy-bordered single boxes designate the GECs. In the GEC approach, many-to-many relationships between entities are possible, even if current reality indicates otherwise. Therefore, any relationship between GECs produces an "external" generic-entity relationship (association) file.

We see that we have a generic-entity relationship between organizational units and positions (Exhibit 10.10), which we have called Org-Position. In addition, we have a relationship between the Person and the Org-Position, which we have called an "assignment." The instances of this data structure are represented in tabular format in Exhibit 10.12. Note that only one instance of the Person control type has been defined.

Person Type (part of Person GEC)

Per-Type ID	Per-Type-Name
25	Employee

Person

Per-ID	Per-Name	Per-Type-ID
26	Mary Smith	25 (Employee)
27	William Jones	25 (Employee)
28	Lynn Anderson	25 (Employee)
34	Chris Johnson	25 (Employee)
35	Kim Kimberly	25 (Employee)
... and so on		

Person-Person (part of Person GEC, Shown in Exhibit 10-11). This node is empty. The person-person cardinality for both parents and children has been set to zero.

Org-Position

Org-ID	Pos-ID
16 (Megalith)	20 (HR Director)
16 (Megalith)	22 (Worker)
4 (Ajax)	21 (Dept Manager)
4 (Ajax)	22 (Worker)
5 (West)	21 (Dept Manager)

Assignment

Org-ID	Pos-ID	Per-ID
16 (Megalith)	20 (HR Director)	26 (Mary Smith)
16 (Megalith)	22 (Worker)	27 (William Jones)
4 (Ajax)	21 (Dept Manager)	28 (Lynn Anderson)
4 (Ajax)	22 (Worker)	34 (Chris Johnson)
5 (West)	21 (Dept Manager)	35 (Kim Kimberly)

Exhibit 10.12. Tabular Notation: Connected Three-Node GECs

10.4 Six-Node Generic-Entity Cloud

The schema in Exhibit 10.3 and Exhibit 10.4 allowed the entity to be typed, but only one value of the typing attribute was allowed because the type value was stored with the entity. Similarly, only one association was allowed between entities. For example, two persons could not have multiple relationships, e.g., father/daughter, supervisor/worker, etc. Such limitations do not reflect the real world, where multiple type values and multiple associations are possible. Remember from Chapter 9, control types are what set apart generic entities. The entity itself becomes the generic node in the GEC.

The six-node GEC, by using additional building blocks, facilitates recognition that multiple control-type values may exist and that associations are often qualified with "roles." The six-node GEC shown in Exhibit 10.13 is not restricted to a mutually exclusive control typing, and the (relationship) role adds a dimension to the entity-entity association. An example of multiple control-type values and role-qualified associations would be an organization scheme where some organization units are of more than one control type. This could occur in a single-store division or where the relationships among organization units can take on one or more roles, such as direct, line, staff, dotted line, etc., as shown earlier in Exhibit 10.2. The *role file supports adherence to the type-control mechanism (Chapter 9)

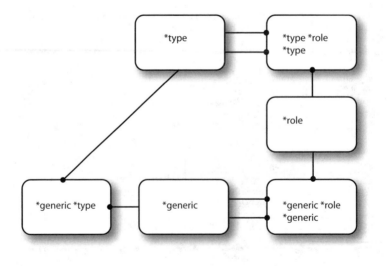

Exhibit 10.13. Six-Node Generic-Entity Cloud

in the *type*role*type and *entity*role*entity files. For a specific application, the * is replaced with the name of the generic entity.

The six-node GEC depends on the cardinality-regulation facility presented in the regulation section (as did the three-node GEC). When the typing is mutually exclusive (i.e., when an entity can only have one type value), for example, it is so designated in the cardinality table for that relationship, and not in the information structure. All GEC relationships are many-to-many associations, constrained as needed by cardinality regulation.

Again looking at organizational units, we could have a situation like the one represented in Exhibit 10.14 as a tabular notation of a six-node position GEC. Any position-role-position relationship must respect the rules encoded in the other nodes of the GEC — the type-control mechanism. For example, if current reality (in type-role-type) does not allow staff (Child-ID = 19) to directly report (Role ID = 47) to a supervisor (Parent-ID = 23), then no position whose control-type value is staff can report to a position whose control-type value is supervisor. Thus in the example above, no worker (who in this instance is defined as type "staff") can report directly to a shift leader (who in this instance is defined as a supervisor). Due to the type-control mechanism, the only role that can connect worker and shift leader is "dotted line report."

With the six-node GEC, even more changes in how business operates can be reflected in the information structure without an analyst, programmer, or database administrator modifying the software's underlying information structure or process.

10.4.1 The Final-Form GEC

As Exhibit 10.14 shows, for a given entity control type, the GEC requires a ring of six supporting information structures. For each control type, the supporting information structures form a ring shape, as illustrated in Exhibit 10.15 (identical to Exhibit 10.1). A series of such rings superimposed on a single diagram yield a cloudlike appearance, hence the term "generic-entity cloud" or GEC.

The six-node GEC is designed to accommodate the most complex situation. For simpler, more typical situations, cardinality regulation effectively masks this complexity. For example, if the generic entity, as currently used in the enterprise, does not have a bill-of-materials relationship, the number of child occurrences is simply set to zero. If an organization currently has multiple control-type values, the number of child occurrences is set to many. If only one is allowed, then the maximum number of children is set to one, and so on. The same logic applies to roles. In a

6-Node Position GEC		
Type		
Pos-Type-ID	**Pos-Type-Name**	
17	Executive	
18	Management	
19	Staff	
23	Supervisor	
Position		
Pos-ID	**Pos-Name**	
20	HR Director	
21	Dept Manager	
22	Clerk	
24	Shift Leader	
49	Secretary	
50	Store Manager	
51	Night Supervisor	
Pos-Type		
Pos-ID	**Pos-Type-ID**	
20 (HR Director)	17 (Executive)	
21 (Dept Manager)	18 (Management)	
22 (Worker)	19 (Staff)	
24 (Shift Leader)	23 (Supervisor)	

Role		
Role-ID		**Role-Name**
47		Direct Report
48		Dotted Line Report
Type-Role-Type		
Type-ID	**Role-ID**	**Child-ID**
17 (Executive)	47 (Direct Report)	17 (Executive)
17 (Executive)	47 (Direct Report)	18 (Management)
17 (Executive)	47 (Direct Report)	19 (Staff)
18 (Management)	47 (Direct Report)	23 (Supervisor)
18 (Management)	47 (Direct Report)	19 (Staff)
23 (Supervisor)	48 (Dotted Line Report)	19 (Staff)
Position-Role-Position		
Parent-ID	**Role-ID**	**Child-ID**
20 (HR Director)	47 (Direct Report)	20 (HR Director)
20 (HR Director)	47 (Direct Report)	21 (Dept Manager)
21 (Dept Manager)	47 (Direct Report)	22 (Worker)
20 (HR Director)	48 (Dotted Line Report)	22 (Worker)
24 (Shift Leader)	48 (Dotted Line Report)	22 (Worker)
21 (Dept Manager)	48 (DottedLine Report)	24 (Shift Leader)

Exhibit 10.14.   Tabular Notation: Six-Node Generic-Entity Cloud

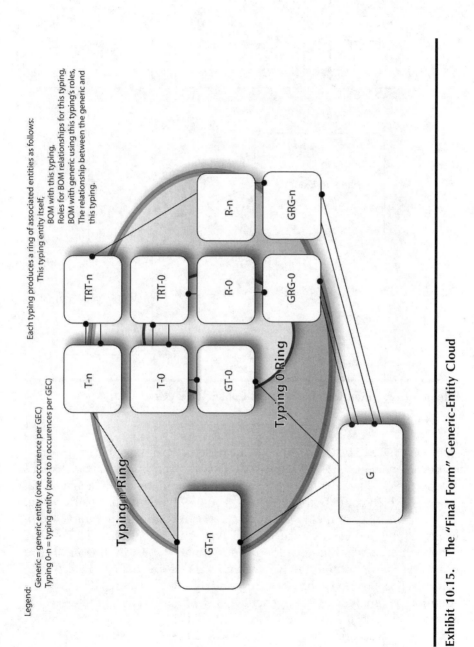

Legend:

Generic = generic entity (one occurence per GEC)
Typing 0-n = typing entity (zero to n occurences per GEC)

Each typing produces a ring of associated entities as follows:
This typing entity itself,
BOM with this typing,
Roles for BOM relationships for this typing,
BOM with generic using this typing's roles,
The relationship between the generic and
this typing.

Exhibit 10.15.   The "Final Form" Generic-Entity Cloud

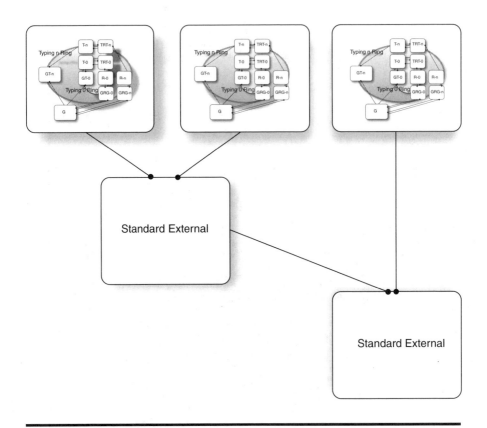

Exhibit 10.16. Example of Schema of Connected GECs

six-node GEC, one control type is provided. We know that in the real world, an entity may have multiple control types. For example, an admissions prospect might have multiple academic interests and multiple extracurricular interests, which could both be treated as control types, each causing a ring.

The possibility of multiple control types is recognized in Exhibit 10.16, where a ring represents each control type and its associated files. The generic entity anchoring the cloud has N control types. Each control type has a ring going through the generic entity that corresponds to a six-node GEC. Each control type has a corresponding bill of materials for both its control-type entity and the generic entity. It also has an intersection relationship with the generic entity itself, which implements the control type. GECs are connected with external entities (see Exhibit 10.16) and are always parents in their relationships with externals. Again, all relationships are many-to-many.

10.5 GECs, Attributes, and Flexibility

In the GEC, the T node represents a control type, but it too is characterized by flexibility. The T node represents a multivalued element (MVE). In its most basic form, the MVE simply represents a multivalued attribute (MVA). In its more powerful form, it represents a control type (CT) that generates rings, as we have shown above.

In Chapter 9, we indicated that attribute values provided more flexibility than flags. The GEC structure supports this approach. Exhibit 10.17 gives an example of a system that maintains data about admission prospects who have multiple academic interests and multiple extracurricular interests, all represented as attribute values.

Each of these attributes would be represented as a T node in the GEC. Because a T node always represents a multivalued element (MVE), one or more values can be defined for each attribute, the number being governed by regulation. If the T node is to be considered a control type (CT), rather than simply a multivalued attribute (MVA), the GEC provides for declaration of a typing ring, which includes role (R), type-role-type (TRT), and generic-role-generic (GRG) nodes. R, TRT, and GRG node creation are controlled through cardinality and record-count regulation. To add new attribute values to an existing T node is a simple data-entry job. To add a new T node, another ring must be generated. That automatically builds the files and their identifiers. Attribute values can then be added as needed, but no existing data structures need to change.

An MVA-type T node can be converted into a CT-type T node. When this occurs, the declaration of the T node must be modified. This allows the regulatory data for R, TRT, and GRG nodes to be modified. Together, these data modifications result in changes to the operational behavior of the system. Where a T node of type MVA does not permit R, TRT, and GRG nodes, a T node of type CT does. The system modification is purely automatic and safe, without changes to data structure and program code and therefore without the normal maintenance repercussions.

For purposes of data-entry convenience, a system designer might wish to implement a mechanism that allows business staff to enter abbreviations or codes rather than full attribute values. An obvious example would be the entry of well-known codes for states, e.g., entry of the code "MA" requires much less time than entry of "Massachusetts." The code also requires less space for data storage. This approach is neither required nor precluded by the generic-entity cloud. A code by its very nature requires a decoding mechanism. System designers should implement such a mechanism via the generic-entity cloud in a way that provides business control over maintenance of code values. Of course, logic to translate the code into its full equivalent must be developed and implemented in appropriate business processes.

Person (Generic Entity) who is an Admission Prospect

ID	Name	Other data
23	Sue	...
54	Mohammad	...
49	Joe	....

Academic Interest (Type Ring 0)

ID	Description	Other Data
11	Engineering	...
32	Information Technology	....
41	Basket Weaving	.....

Extracurricular Activity (Type Ring 1)

ID	Description	Other Data
14	Bowling	...
59	Macramé	....
29	Bridge	.....

Person-Academic Interest (Entity-Type Ring 0)

PersonID	Academic Interest ID (TypeID Ring 0)	Other Data
23 (Sue)	11 (Engineering)	...
54 (Mohammad)	11 (Engineering)	....
54 (Mohammad)	32 (Information Technology)	....
49 (Joe)	41 (Basket Weaving)	

Person-Extracurricular Activity (Entity-Type Ring 1)

PersonID	Extracurricular ID (TypeID Ring 1)	Other Data
49 (Joe)	29 (Bridge)	...
49 (Joe)	14 (Bowling)	...
23 (Sue)	59 (Macramé)	...
54 (Mohammad)	14 (Bowling)	....
54 (Mohammad)	29 (Bridge)	

Exhibit 10.17. Handling Admission Prospects' Interests as Attributes in a GEC

10.6 Externals Connected to Generic-Type Node

For simplicity of presentation in the previous examples, we have shown externals with a connection between IDs from the generic nodes of the associated GECs. In fact, the connection is made between the external and the *generic*type nodes of the GECs. This means that specific control types of generic entities can be connected, providing additional flexibility. The design of the GEC supports this approach by providing as ring 0 a default control type that carries the name of the GEC.

Default control type has only one value, which matches the name of the generic entity and the control type. The default cardinality of the *generic*type node is set to allow minimum = maximum = 1 from both the generic and the type nodes. For example, the Person GEC has a default control-type value of Person for the control-type Person. This means that if a *generic Person record exists with a value of "Jane," a *generic*type record with a value of |Jane|Person|| will also exist.

Exhibit 10.18 shows that Locator and Class only have one ring — the default ring — with name and one value of Locator and Class. Person has two rings, one for Person and one for Student, both with one value the same as the name of the control type. Exhibit 10.18 shows that Jane and Tom's connection to their various locator possibilities is made through their control type of Person. Their connection to enrollment is made through their control type of Student. The |Jane|Person|| *entity*type association record within the GEC may have attributes dealing with Jane as a person, whereas the *entity*type dealing with Jane as a student may have different attributes. Taking this approach allows us to specify that all persons can have locators, but only students can register for classes, exactly the flexibility that the business requires.

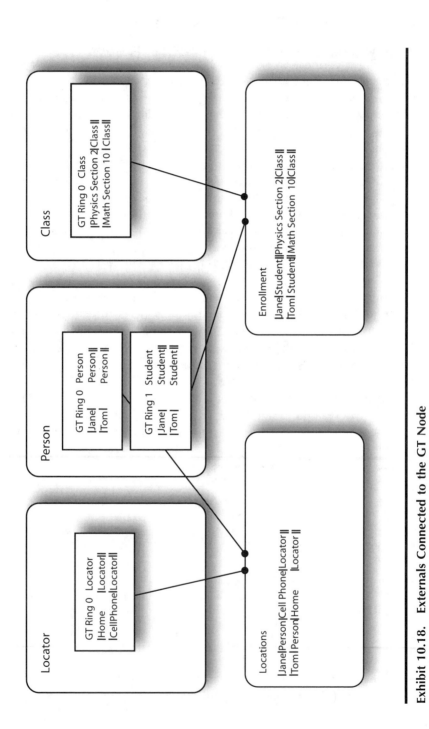

Exhibit 10.18.   Externals Connected to the GT Node

10.7 Summary

- The generic-entity cloud (GEC) provides an automatic way to implement highly stable data structures utilizing invariant, unique identifiers; variable cardinality; generic entities; generic-entity relationships; recursive-entity relationships; consistent typing; and variable typing.
- Essential to GEC development is reduction in the number of entities. Where a more traditional approach would identify many specific entities, the GEC approach identifies a reduced number of *generic* entities.
- The fully developed GEC has one or more control types, each of which causes a ring of six nodes, all anchored by the common generic entity itself. The generic-entity cloud is named for its cloudlike appearance.
- GEC systems do not require reprogramming or database reorganization to reflect changes. Rather, the change can be accommodated with a few entries to the nodes.
- Where a many-to-many relationship exists between two GECs, it is generally shown as two separate one-to-many relationships with a separate relationship node that is external to the GECs themselves. This external general-entity relationship (association) is referred to as an "external."
- The six-node GEC facilitates recognition that multiple control-type values may exist and that associations are often qualified with "roles."
- All GEC relationships are inherently many-to-many associations, which are required for a flexible system.

Part IV presents more detail on the GEC, including several applications of the GEC as well as a number of extensions that show its versatility in designing and developing flexible software.

HOW TO DESIGN FLEXIBLE SOFTWARE SYSTEMS

III

Part I introduced the concept of software flexibility and made a case for its necessity. Part II clarified the key ingredients of flexible design, with emphasis on stability of data structures and how stability facilitates business control over change. The six chapters in Part III provide guidance on how to apply the techniques presented in Part II to develop flexible software.

- Chapter 11 addresses strategic systems planning as an ideal opportunity to gain access to the diversity of requirements needed for designing flexible software systems. We clarify the importance of both flexibility and application integration and show how the two are mutually reinforcing.
- Chapter 12 presents requirements-determination methods for flexible software systems. These methods are based on a fundamental reorientation to software design, in which the focus is no longer primarily on functional accuracy, but rather on achieving flexibility. The emphasis of requirements gathering thus shifts to identifying dynamic requirements, especially eliciting and modeling information *structure* requirements.
- Chapter 13 covers two general techniques for flexible software design: structure-oriented and process-oriented. Structure-oriented techniques take the form of information structures composed of generic-entity types and many-to-many relationships that identify and exploit common data characteristics and common patterns of relationships between and within entities. Process-oriented techniques

identify and exploit common logic patterns, supported by common information structure.

- Chapter 14 presents the "how to" of implementing stable identifiers, starting with the basic rule for assigning identifiers. Identifiers that support stable data structures are essential to flexible software systems.

- Chapter 15 addresses testing and maintenance of flexible software. With a flexible system, not only do business staff test the system during initial development, but they also make the modifications during ongoing operation and do the testing

- Chapter 16 addresses topics associated with identifying, managing, and acquiring flexible software. It provides a checklist of characteristics to help readers evaluate products for flexibility and ask the right questions. The positive connection between flexibility and quality improvements is highlighted, and guidelines are presented to help project managers effectively champion flexibility. Interestingly, the biggest payoff for flexibility may be for vendors of packaged systems, where flexible features can be utilized by thousands of customers without requiring custom coding. The fact that vendors have multiple customers to satisfy with the same product provides a powerful incentive for flexible systems. There is evidence that vendors are paying attention to flexibility, and as more customers require flexibility features, vendors will continue to respond.

Chapter 11

Flexibility and Strategic Systems Planning

The more diverse the current requirements supported by an information structure, the more that structure will be able to support future requirements without needing modification. In effect, designing a single database to support multiple application systems is like looking into the future. One does not actually see future requirements per se, of course, but the need to support a broad variety of requirements confers a concurrent need to increase the generality of the database. It is a way to partially offset the reality of imperfect knowledge caused by the impossibility of knowing future requirements.

A good example of this "future now" effect occurred as a result of a strategic systems planning study at a major retailer. Their financial account structure was routinely used for reporting to senior management, shareholders, and the Securities and Exchange Commission (SEC). The enterprisewide planning study recognized that many of the same accounts were also used for tax reporting but employed a different set of interaccount relationships required by the tax rules. To accommodate the different but related requirements, the database design was generalized to be capable of representing multiple sets of account relationships concurrently. This allowed the integration of general-ledger and financial reporting with tax reporting and the elimination of the previously intractable problems of reports that did not agree with each other. It also made it easy to do what-if processing to explore the financial effects of alternative accounting

177

scenarios and to set up new accounts and account relationships in advance of their effective date.

The enterprisewide nature of strategic systems planning, with its emphasis on developing a comprehensive multibusiness-function enterprise model, provides a unique opportunity to gain access to the diversity of requirements needed to design a stable information structure. In return, the orientation of flexible systems toward structural stability can substantially improve long-range planning results. Software flexibility and application integration are not competing concepts; they reinforce each other.

Achieving a reasonably high degree of interoperability of applications across an enterprise is often one of the objectives of strategic systems planning. Interoperability can take two basic forms:

1. *Integration* uses a common semantic framework via a single database schema shared among multiple applications.
2. *Interfacing* uses conversion protocols to translate data from one semantic framework to another as needed for each application, passing data via extract files, event files, or messages.

An enterprise can, of course, operate with a mixture of both forms. In either case, as the degree of integration/interfacing increases, so does the exposure to changes in the underlying information structure, whether it consists of a common schema or disjoint schemas. That is, as information sharing is increased through applications integration or interfacing, exposure to disruptive changes in the shared data structures is also increased. Thus, a stable information structure is needed to achieve sustainable application interoperability.

11.1 The Myth of the Isolated System

It is common for organizations to develop systems in isolation.

It is common for organizations to develop systems in isolation. Typical thinking goes something like this: "We'll develop the new project control system initially for the engineering department. Then, as we get requirements from other departments, we'll evolve the system and roll it out across the company. This evolutionary approach will be cost-effective and will not commit us to too big a development piece at any one time." This thinking is based on the myth of the isolated system:

Myth: We can develop systems one at a time and fit them together into an integrated whole as we go along.

> Reality: We can build an organization's systems one at a time, but the underlying information structure for all the systems must be analyzed, designed, and built first if integrated systems are to result.

Information processing can be evolved, but the underlying information structure cannot. The information structure must be worked out in advance and held constant. For flexibility, it is critical to establish a single coherent stable data structure and then fit systems and subsystems onto that stable foundation.

11.2 Traditional Planning Approach

Entire books have been written on the subject of strategic systems planning [e.g., Martin, 1982; Ward and Peppard, 2002], but not many. Enterprisewide systems planning has tended to be the purview of the larger information technology consulting organizations with their proprietary methods. In spite of some distinguishing differences, the usual approaches follow more or less the same steps and apply the same techniques. The basic idea is to develop a blueprint for long-term IT direction and investment. There are at least three planning dimensions:

1. Technology
2. Organization/management
3. Applications

Traditional strategic systems planning steps, which are related to the enterprise's application portfolio, are usually as follows:

- Obtain the backing of top management for the planning study.
- Identify critical success factors within each major management area.
- Obtain the organization chart.
- Break down the enterprise functionally into understandable pieces (functional decomposition).
- Assess current automation coverage by function and identify new automation opportunities.
- Construct a high-level data flow model, e.g., data flow diagram (DFD).
- Construct a high-level information-structure model, e.g., entity-relationship diagram (ERD).
- Assemble an information-precedence matrix.
- Identify development projects and development sequences suggested by the precedence matrix.
- Apply business priorities to projects.
- Prepare a development projects schedule and cost/benefit analysis.

An enterprisewide IS planning study was undertaken at a major telecommunications services company in response to general agreement that systems effort there for many years had been merely reactive in the face of an increasingly unmanageable backlog of work on aging systems.

They had other motivations for the study as well. As one analyst reported, their "portfolio" included:
· 54 automated business systems, of which 37 were stand-alone. The remainder interfaced
  in twos and threes, including multiple unintegrated systems purchased from the same vendor
· 5 project control systems
· 5 inventory tracking systems
· Several incompatible e-mail systems
· Dozens of redundant personnel/organization files
· More than 1500 Lotus Notes "databases"
· And loosely speaking, one each of just about every piece of hardware and software going.

The plan was prepared by a team of some of the company's best and brightest who conscientiously followed the recommended planning methods and techniques then (and still) current. A year later the team had been disbanded, its leader had found "more appropriate work," the plan was shelved, and only a few copies of the planning document remained as souvenirs of what had been the occasion of much esprit de corps and hope for finally developing a sensible IT strategy.

Exhibit 11.1.   The Plan Not Followed

Most planning studies follow the outline above, whether with the aid of a planning consultant or through the efforts of in-house staff. Usually, strategic systems planning is undertaken in response to a perception of some broad problem in the IT area. Examples would be lack of manageability, uncontrolled technology disparities, maintenance overload, and a lack of applications integration. While the planning effort may be motivated by practical business-related concerns, the ostensibly long-range plan often turns out to have only short-term utility or no utility at all. In fact, most planning study results find themselves on the dusty shelf within a few months of completion. Exhibit 11.1, Exhibit 11.2, and Exhibit 11.3 provide some examples of failed strategic plans.

What happened with the plans not followed? The reasons given were invariably that business priorities had changed in ways that preempted following any long-term plan, however swiftly it could be revised. That is, the plan, had it been maintained, would have been simply an ever-changing list of projects to be done — a schedule intended to meet current demands. The speakers at the conference (Exhibit 11.3) were saying, in effect, that "yes, planning is a good thing and here's how to do it, but right now is not a good time."

"Not a good time" is a familiar expression. But in these cases, there was a clear perception on the part of all concerned of a real need for the guidance that a strategic information system plan should provide. Both

The systems and programming (S&P) manager for a large publishing house, along with his staff, were continually bombarded with conflicting and overlapping requests from the vice president of sales in New York who was his boss's boss. Fire fighting was rampant, systems and support morale and effectiveness were going downhill fast, and it had been a long time since the job was fun. With considerable effort, the S&P manager prevailed on the vice president to grant a multiday "strategic planning" session, which was held off-site at a downtown hotel. The vice president of sales and other key executives were there so that a strategic direction and schedule could be established, thus eliminating the conflicting interruptions to the staff.

When the meeting ended, the S&P manager left with his list of priorities and a great sense of relief. The next day, back in the office, he called his staff together to lay out their schedules and to show them that their jobs should now be more professional and rewarding. As he was speaking to them, the secretary interrupted and said that the vice president of sales was on the phone. He picked up the phone and was informed that influential individuals (squeaky wheels) had gotten priorities changed. They were back to fire fighting. Eventually the S&P manager protested once too often and was fired. (The good news is that he was hired back as a consultant, at a considerably higher rate of pay, to update several antiquated systems.)

Exhibit 11.2. Another Failed Strategic Plan

Some years ago, an analyst attended a major national convention devoted entirely to the subject of strategic systems planning. A number of the speakers presented the planning efforts with which they had been involved at their companies or on behalf of their clients. Each of the presentations described in detail both the method used and the resulting plan. The roster included the analyst's boss, who provided an entertaining recap of what had been learned at his company about the don'ts of successful planning. Questions taken at the end of each presentation included the usual requests for information about systems-and-technology projects in which the speaker's company was currently engaged. Each speaker responded with variations on "We're working on such-and-such systems and installing this-and-that equipment." In not one case were these activities part of the strategic plans that were presented.

Exhibit 11.3. Strategic Planning Disconnect

IT management and senior management wanted viable long-range plans and had authorized their preparation at considerable expense. It was not changing priorities that undid the plans. The plans themselves were inherently deficient because they failed to provide a stable foundation upon which to construct systems and exploit computing technology over a long term. Incidentally, the fired systems and programming manager (Exhibit 11.2) illustrates another fallout of failed planning: IT management is a risky job.

11.3 Stable Enterprise Model

Pant and Hsu (1995) reviewed the six top planning methods, all of which were developed in the early 1980s with evolutionary refinements accruing through the 1990s. Their overall assessment is that most companies found that "planning is unnecessarily detailed and takes a long time," with notable deficiencies being lack of adequate information-structure models and lack of connection of planning results to subsequent development. Our observation is that the enterprise model that results from traditional planning emphasizes the procedural and variable aspects of a business. In contrast, an enterprise model that emphasizes the structural and stable aspects — those characteristics of an enterprise upon which long-term decisions about its automation resources can be based — provides the foundation for successful strategic planning. Its core deliverable is a reasonably accurate model of the structural components of the enterprise. (The term "model" here does not refer to a simulation model. In a simulation model, the time-varying activities of a process are simulated to recreate or predict the process's behavior by altering input parameters and iterating over successive units of time. Rather, we are referring here to an analytic model, in which a system (enterprise) is statically described; a change in the system's structure or processes will require that the model itself be changed.) It is vital to be able to express automation plans in terms of the real and permanent functions the enterprise performs and the equally real and permanent entities about which it keeps information.

The traditional enterprise model, as a real-world model, is a collection of specialized submodels, some of which are stable and some of which are subject to change. The submodels that are relevant to the application-planning dimension and that are relatively technology-independent include the following:

- Organization model (variable)
- Business-function model (stable)
- Information-process model (variable)
- Information-structure model (stable)
- Information-precedence model (stable)

11.4 Strategic Systems Planning for Flexibility

Exhibit 11.4 combines the planning steps and the enterprise submodels to which they apply. The long-term utility of each planning step is assessed in terms of its contribution to the stability of the submodel. Step 8, normally missing from conventional planning methods, has been added as essential for effective planning.

Long-Term Utility	Planning Step	Contributes to Submodel	Contribution's Stability
	1. Obtain top management approval	- -	- -
	2. Identify critical success factors	- -	- -
	3. Obtain organization chart	Organization	Variable
	4. Perform functional decomposition	Business function	Stable
	5. Assess automation coverage	Business function	Stable
	6. Construct data flow diagram	Information process	Variable
	7. Construct high-level entity-relationship diagram	Information structure	Stable
	8. Construct detailed data-element-level information structure schematic (Note: Not normally included in traditional planning)	Information structure	Stable
	9. Identify subject databases	Information structure	Variable
	10. Assemble precedence matrix	Information precedence	Stable
	11. Identify development projects	- -	- -
	12. Apply business priorities	- -	- -
	13. Prepare projects schedule and cost/benefit analysis	- -	- -

Exhibit 11.4. Long-Term Utility of Planning Steps

In the interests of promoting planning that results in a durable enterprise model and materially aids the development of flexible systems, we will discuss the effectiveness of each of the steps/models listed in Exhibit 11.4. The motive here is to maximize the genuinely useful and minimize the marginal or cosmetic. These observations are based on experience with multiple planning efforts at different enterprises over two decades.

11.4.1 Obtain Top Management Approval (Step 1) ↓ ↑

We begin with an equivocal step. This step does not get a full thumbs-up rating to draw attention to some cautions. Obtaining top management approval is always the recommended first step in any systems planning method, invariably strongly recommended by any consultancy involved. This insistence on access and continued visibility to senior management is, of course, a lucrative posture for a consultancy to adopt. The fact is that strategic systems planning and its enterprise model building process entail a great deal of detailed analytical work in which top management typically has little interest. Large portions of the study can be accomplished through a grassroots effort requiring virtually no top-level involvement other than sponsorship. The materials needed to perform the really essential analyses are plentiful at low levels in an organization. The focus of top management approval should, after all, be on the planning study's recommendations and results, not on the study itself. Indeed, senior management might expect strategic systems planning to be a normal, ongoing function within MIS (management information system) rather than an extraordinary one. Regarding top management — approval, yes; heavy involvement, no.

Moreover, the process of obtaining a high-level go-ahead usually means overselling the program and proposing to deliver too much in less than the minimum time required. Done properly, a planning study takes time. In an organization characterized by a senior-sponsorship approach to major initiatives, the duration of the effort required will usually exhaust the brief tenure of one sponsor, and the attempted transition to a second often kills the study. Similarly, in the many organizations where IT is itself traditionally under a business manager who is "passing through," the program becomes associated with the IT head at the time and rarely survives the next change in leadership. In summary, a great deal can be accomplished at a low expense rate over an extended time without major senior management involvement and without the compromises and risks to an effective outcome that go along with high-level visibility.

11.4.2 Identify Critical Success Factors (Step 2) ↓

The point of this step, like the first, is to get buy-in. Identification of critical success factors typically focuses on the performance goals of senior managers whose cooperation is sought. Thus this step can be omitted without loss of essential planning data.

11.4.3 Obtain Organization Chart (Step 3) ↓ ↑

A typical product of the early stages of a planning study is a model of the company's organization. This is simply an organization chart, showing the organizational components (divisions, departments, etc.), their relationships to each other, and the principal personnel responsible for each unit. A current organization chart is certainly useful during the study itself. For example, as part of the enterprise model, it serves as input to the assessment of organization and management controls. Of course, it helps identify whom to interview for what. But the organization chart models a characteristic of the enterprise that changes. If the organization chart becomes a permanent part of the enterprise model, then procedures must be put in place for keeping it up to date. It is a tactical element, not a strategic one.

11.4.4 *Perform Functional Decomposition (Step 4)* ↑

In contrast to the organization chart, the function model is stable. It identifies the enterprise's business functions through the well-known process of functional decomposition. The result is a hierarchical structure describing, in a top-down fashion, the most fundamental functions, their subfunctions, and their subfunction's subfunctions (Exhibit 11.5). The set of functions of an enterprise is one of its most stable characteristics. That

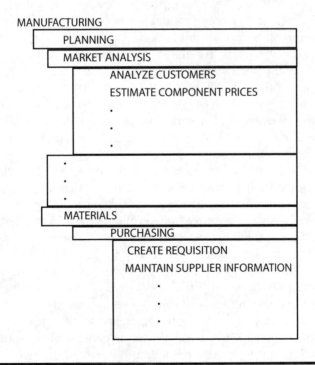

Exhibit 11.5. Part of a Business Function Model

a manufacturing business needs to do materials planning and inventory control is a fact that will not change so long as it remains a manufacturing business. *How* these functions are performed may vary considerably over time and circumstance, but the set of basic functions remains. When changes to functions do occur, their representation takes the form of additions to or deletions from the existing model. For example, a bank may acquire a real estate role, or an insurance company may divest itself of a mortgage loan facility. But if the model is done well, you will not see changes such as the management development subfunction some day shifting from the human resources function to the product engineering function. As James Martin [1982] said, "The (function) model should survive reorganizations."

Strictly speaking, the process of functional decomposition does not bear directly on the characteristics of flexible systems. But it does provide a useful tool in the organization of subsequent development work and also results in identification of important structural components of the enterprise model. It should be done early in the planning process. The technique is intuitive and well understood, entailing identification of the highest-level (most inclusive) functions of the enterprise, such as business strategy management, financial management, product/service production and delivery, etc., then identifying the highest-level functions in each of these, and so on, until a useful model has been achieved. What is a useful degree of decomposition, without taking it down to the minutest activity? The theoretical answer is that the model is not detailed enough if there are "loops" in the information-precedence model, as will be discussed later. The practical answer is simply three to four levels, not counting the enterprise itself. As will be seen below, this provides a function model adequate for assessment of automation coverage, determination of information precedence, establishment of system boundaries, and charting of development direction and progress.

It is important not to confuse functional components with organizational components. It is well understood that function and organization unit are distinct things with a many-to-many relationship between them. For example, a human resources department may handle payroll, recruiting, and training functions, but functions like budgeting, project control, or purchasing may be common to many organizational units in an enterprise. The distinction is clear enough in the abstract, but in practice keeping it clear in the minds of all concerned can be surprisingly difficult. Organization names are often similar or even identical to function names. Purchasing does purchasing. Cash management manages cash reserves. There is also an inclination to think that a general one-to-one mapping of organization unit to function is a sensible way to arrange things in an enterprise. These tendencies combine so that the process of eliciting the function model from management can generate political maneuvering and may result in a spurious functional decomposition. That is, if the function model is seen to imply a certain organization, then some individuals will be motivated to bend the function model to accommodate their ambitions. Planners have found that maintaining an up-to-date matrix relating organization components to business functions is a good way to keep things clear.

Finally, do not overlook the information-systems function and the strategic systems planning subfunction themselves as components of the function model. They are key functions of the enterprise. They have important information exchanges with other business functions, and their inclusion will have a significant effect on the information-structure and information-precedence models.

11.4.5 Assess Automation Coverage (Step 5) ↑

Obviously, we need to know the current state of the organization's automation efforts. Taking an inventory of current application systems and their health, age, technology employed, maintenance level, degree of integration/interfacing, etc. is useful in itself. It also provides the opportunity to establish a clear and simple correspondence between application systems and enterprise functions. The functional decomposition step (Step 4) produces a stable set of hierarchically related functions, any or all of which are candidates for automation assistance. We recommend establishing a one-to-one correspondence between a function/subfunction and its supporting automated system/subsystem (Exhibit 11.6).

This allows the entire application portfolio to be identified, both existing and future, and provides a stable reference for years of planning and implementation. System boundaries are, after all, arbitrary — we can draw them where we want to — so why not make them coincide with the functions they are to automate? Purchased systems can also be fitted into this scheme. Even if their components are scattered noncontiguously over the function model, the correspondence with specific functions/subfunctions is perfectly valid. The degree of automation can be graphically represented and updated over time without destabilizing the business function submodel. Hence, although the degree of automation changes over time, the assessment step is making an essentially stable contribution.

This assessment of automation coverage is a good time to ensure that the enterprise has a technology obsolescence/application retirement plan in place. Without such a plan (one that is followed), the enterprise faces an ever-enlarging application portfolio with its ever-increasing maintenance burden — unless, of course, all the applications are flexible.

Function	System
MANUFACTURING	Manufacturing System
PLANNING	Planning Subsystem
MARKET ANALYSIS	
ANALYZE CUSTOMERS	
ESTIMATE COMPONENT PRICES	
•	
•	
•	
•	
•	
•	
MATERIALS	Materials subsystem
PURCHASING	
CREATE REQUISITION	
MAINTAIN SUPPLIER INFORMATION	
•	
•	
•	
FINANCE	Finance system
RECEIVABLES	Receivable subsystem
PAYABLES	Payables subsystem
GENERAL LEDGER	General ledger Subsystem
•	
•	
•	

Exhibit 11.6. Aligning Business Functions and Business Systems

11.4.6 Construct a Data Flow Diagram (Step 6) ↓

Counter to expectations, the flow of information actually tells us nothing about the internal structure of that information.

A data flow diagram (DFD) is a picture of how things are done *now*. It is a model of the flow of information within the enterprise and between the enterprise and its environment. It includes descriptions of the processes that originate, change, calculate, store, discard, etc. that information. Producing a data flow diagram for an enterprise, even at a high level, involves time-consuming and painstaking work. The diagram is subject to constant revision as the day-to-day activities of the enterprise evolve. It

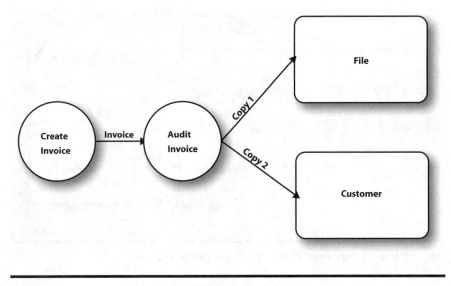

Exhibit 11.7.   Data Flow Diagram (DFD) Example

is usually out of date the day it is finished (and often within a day or two of the day it was started). The flow of information actually tells us nothing about the internal structure of that information.

For example, Exhibit 11.7 illustrates the following flow of information: billing creates an invoice, which is forwarded to billing audit for checking. The content of the invoice, specifically the data items and their relationships to each other, is not captured in a DFD. But the content is what is needed to understand how to represent the invoice in a database. DFDs are popular, and with good reason. Programmers and analysts have for decades used them for understanding and documenting information *processing* requirements. It appears that DFDs are enlisted in strategic enterprise modeling efforts simply because they are familiar to the modelers, many of whom probably rose through the programmer ranks. The DFD is helpful with process analysis in systems development, but not with systems planning. Process analysis is extremely time consuming. Its omission from the planning process provides a secondary benefit of considerable time savings.

11.4.7 Construct High-Level Entity Relationship Diagram (Step 7) ↓ ↑

The entity relationship diagram (ERD) shown in Exhibit 11.8 can be a useful tool but, by itself, is not adequate for producing a fully developed information-structure model of the enterprise, as provided for in Step 8

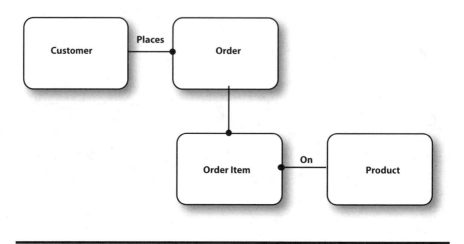

Exhibit 11.8.   Entity Relationship Diagram (ERD) Example

below. ERDs have two proper uses in planning, but only in the context of a detailed data-element-level model:

1. *As a heuristic aid in developing the data-element-level information-structure model*: A series of ERDs can function as useful preliminary organizations and guides during iterative detailed analysis of information requirements. The ERD process, used in this way, is properly an integral part of Step 8.
2. *As a final high-level abstraction from the detailed model for use for communication or promotional purposes*: An ERD has value as an abstraction of, but not as a substitute for, the detailed information-structure model. The high-level ERD, used in this way, comes after Step 8.

11.4.8 *Construct Detailed Data-Element-Level Information-Structure Schematic (Step 8)* ↑

*It is precisely for lack of a **detailed** information-structure model, upon which an enterprise's application portfolio can be based, that traditional planning efforts fail.*

Of the planning steps that have significant planning value, this is the most difficult and time-consuming. But it is a vital step if we are concerned with obtaining something strategically useful over the long term. Although information-structure schematics (in traditional strategic plans) are usually high-level constructs, in this case it is necessary to produce a detailed diagram at the data-element level of most, if not all, of the enterprise's information. In contrast to a DFD, it has the virtue of being stable and the product of a one-time effort. And it is precisely for lack of a *detailed* information-structure model, upon which an enterprise's application portfolio can be based, that traditional planning efforts fail.

All the other recommended planning tasks together may take, say, eight weeks to complete. This task may take several months or longer, depending on available resources and the scope of the enterprise. Basically this work involves:

- Gathering samples of the information packets that exist throughout the enterprise — invoices, orders, product specification sheets, marketing plans, commission tables, etc. — much of which is available at low to mid levels in the organization
- Analyzing this material to identify data elements and their aggregations into entities
- Ensuring a high degree of generalization to stabilize the model

It also necessitates numerous interviews, both to identify and collect samples and to confirm interpretations of the data they contain, particularly with regard to identification of entities. The elicitation of information structure and structure stabilization are discussed in Chapter 12. For now, a fragment of an example model in Exhibit 11.9 shows that it serves two essential purposes:

1. It accurately identifies the (basic and association) entities of the enterprise. This is input to the information-precedence matrix below.
2. It can be mapped directly into a database schema.

This comprehensive and stable information structure goes by various names: normative data model, global data model, data architecture model, and generic data structure model. Many automated tools exist that can be adapted to this task. Once a stable structure is captured in sufficient detail in the tool's repository, most such tools can then automatically generate the corresponding data definition statements for most commercial database management systems. At this point, we have both a logical and a physical schema, and the physical schema is capable of supporting virtually the entire applications portfolio with a high degree of structural stability.

Again, why is this level of detail needed in a strategic model? It is because this is the only way to identify all the essential entities of the enterprise, particularly those that exist as association entities. Products, locations, accounts, and persons are basic entities essential for planning

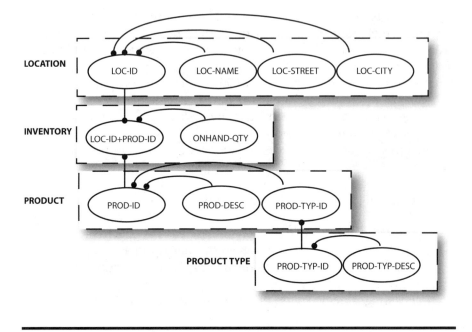

Exhibit 11.9.   Information-Structure Diagram at Data-Element Level

purposes. Inventories, charts of accounts, and employments are association entities, equally real and essential for planning purposes, but often missed in the traditional top-down analysis that starts with a high-level entity-relationship diagram and then goes no further.

11.4.9 Identify Subject Databases (Step 9) ↓

Faced with the task of designing a large system, the analyst may be tempted to break the database into separate subject areas. It might appear sensible, for example, to divide the database along the lines of business unit responsibility and design the pieces separately. While dividing a large task into smaller, more manageable tasks makes sense in some contexts, it does not make sense in the context of designing a database. An examination of the information-structure model for any enterprise will show that there are virtually no isolated entities or collections of entities.

Attempts to partition the logical database usually reflect current political, demographic, or business priority factors, and the long-term result is therefore likely to be unsatisfactory. Virtually all the entities in an enterprise's information structure participate in chains of associations, and the functions that access them are subject to changing processing requirements. While there are often technical reasons for physical database partitioning, there really is no reason for logically partitioning the information-structure model into subject databases.

11.4.10 Assemble Precedence Matrix (Step 10) ↑

The information-precedence matrix combines the function model from the functional decomposition step (Step 4) with the data entities identified in the information-structure model (Step 8). It simply defines the optimum order for systems implementation based on which information is used by which business functions.

The appropriate access requirement, which we will limit to "create" (C) and "use" (U), is recorded at the intersections for the lowest-level functions. Exhibit 11.10 shows the initial stage of a portion of the matrix. Exhibit 11.11 shows the final stage after shifting entities right to left and functions bottom to top until all necessary data creation is accounted for prior to (i.e., above) corresponding data use.

The following examples explain how the matrix is interpreted (see Exhibit 11.11).

- *Organization data maintenance*: To perform this function, one must be able to create (C) an organization unit and create (C) an organization structure.
- *Cash management*: To perform this function, one must be able to update (U) an organization unit, update (U) an organization structure, and create (C) a bank account.

Exhibit 11.11 also shows that the matrix was examined for "loops" in which data is both created and used by the same function and for entities used but never created. These conditions are resolved by adding specific entity-creation functions, in this case "organization data maintenance." Such functions are currently performed within the enterprise but are embedded within other functions, and they need to be identified explicitly (other examples might be "customer data maintenance," "rate data maintenance," etc.).

We can now extract from the matrix one or more optimum development sequences, such that functions that supply data are developed before those that use that data. Automation support for those functions that fall below the gray line in Exhibit 11.11 can be done in any order. When business priorities require development of a system or portion of a system out of the optimum sequence (and they will), the matrix can be used to identify the portions of other systems/subsystems that will need to be at least partially constructed to supply needed data. This is essential information for properly sizing a development project. The information-precedence

Business Function	BANK ACCOUNT	COMMERCIAL PAPER	TAX AUTHORITY	ITEM	ITEM INVENTORY	ITEM STRUCTURE	EXTERNAL ORGANIZATION	EMPLOYMENT	PERSON	POSITION	JOB	BENEFIT PLAN	FIXED ASSET	LEDGER ACCOUNT	LEDGER ACCOUNT CHART	ORGANIZATION UNIT	ORGANIZATION STRUCTURE
Strategic planning		U			U		U	U					U			U	U
Financial																	
Cash management	C															U	U
Investments		C														U	U
Acquisitions	U														U	U	U
Legal																	
Copyright			U														
Liability	U																
Compensation							U	U	U	U						U	U
Acquisition/divestment							U							U		U	U
Tax management																	
Sales			C		U	U								U	U	U	U
Income			C		U	U		U						U	U	U	U
Capital		U	U										U	U	U		
Marketing																	
Product selection				U	U	U	U									U	U
Market research				U	U	U	U									U	U
Sales																	
Product stocking				U	U	U	U							U	U	U	U
Advertising				U			U									U	U
Purchasing																	
Vendor management							C										
Retail finished goods				C	C	C								U	U	U	U
Services							U									U	U
Raw materials				U	U	U	U									U	U
Supplies				U	U	U	U									U	U
Public relations																	
Charitable foundation admin.	U						U		U					U	U	U	U
Communications							U		U		U					U	U
Human resources																	
Payroll																	
Executive								C					U	U	U	U	U
Salaried								C					U	U	U	U	U
Hourly								C					U	U	U	U	U
Contract													U	U	U	U	U
Personnel admin.																	
Recruitment								U	C	C	C	U				U	U
Training									U	U	U					U	U
Succession planning								U	U	U	U	U				U	U
Benefits admin.																	
Program evaluation								U				C				U	U
Program admin.								U	U			U				U	U
Real estate													C				
Receivables							U							U	U		
Payables							U							U	U		
Financial reporting																	
General ledger admin.														C	C		
Internal	U	U		U			U							U	U	U	U
External	U	U		U		U	U							U	U	U	U

Exhibit 11.10. Information-Precedence Matrix — Initial

Business Function	ORGANIZATION UNIT	ORGANIZATION STRUCTURE	BANK ACCOUNT	COMMERCIAL PAPER	LEDGER ACCOUNT	LEDGER ACCOUNT CHART	EXTERNAL ORGANIZATION	ITEM	ITEM INVENTORY	ITEM STRUCTURE	BENEFIT PLAN	EMPLOYMENT	PERSON	POSITION	JOB	TAX AUTHORITY	TAX RETURN	FIXED ASSET
Organization data maintenance	C	C																
Financial																		
Cash management	U	U	C															
Investments	U	U		C														
Financial reporting																		
General ledger admin.					C	C												
Purchasing																		
Vendor management							C											
Retail finished goods	U	U			U	U		C	C	C								
Human resources																		
Benefits admin.																		
Program evaluation	U	U									C	U						
Payroll																		
Executive	U	U			U	U						U	C					
Salaried	U	U			U	U						U	C					
Hourly	U	U			U	U						U	C					
Personnel admin.																		
Recruitment	U	U									U	U	C	C	C			
Tax management																		
Sales	U	U			U	U		U	U							C	C	
Income	U	U			U	U		U	U				U			C	C	
Real estate																		C
Human resources																		
Personnel admin.																		
Training	U	U											U	U	U			
Succession planning	U	U									U	U	U	U	U			
Benefits admin.																		
Program admin.	U	U									U	U	U					
Receivables					U	U	U											
Payables					U	U	U											
Financial reporting																		
Internal	U	U	U	U	U	U			U				U					U
External	U	U	U	U	U	U	U		U				U					U
Strategic planning	U	U		U			U		U				U					U
Financial																		
Acquisitions	U	U	U															U
Legal																		
Copyright							U											
Liability				U														
Compensation	U	U									U	U	U	U				
Acquisition/divestment	U	U					U											U
Tax management																		
Capital					U	U	U									U	C	U
Marketing																		
Product selection	U	U					U	U	U	U								
Market research	U	U					U	U	U	U								
Sales																		
Product stocking	U	U			U	U	U	U	U	U								
Advertising	U	U					U	U										
Purchasing																		
Raw materials	U	U					U	U	U	U								
Supplies	U	U					U	U	U	U								
Services	U	U					U											
Public relations																		
Charitable foundation admin.	U	U	U		U	U	U						U					
Communications	U	U					U					U	U					

Exhibit 11.11.   Information-Precedence Matrix — Final

matrix is a stable component of the enterprise model and will be useful throughout many projects.

There can be confusion regarding precedence considerations and the use of a flexibility technique discussed later and referred to as "object subprograms." Object subprograms isolate the activities of add/update/delete for an object, and anytime a process needs to maintain an object, it does so through the object subprogram. Object subprograms tend to be as stable as the data structures they maintain. The object subprograms can be developed as soon as the database schema is in place and before any processes are automated that will make use of them, and so they are independent of precedence considerations. The precedence matrix is a planning tool at the system/subsystem level, whereas the object-subprogram approach is a design consideration at the information object/entity level.

11.4.11 Getting to Projects (Steps 11 to 13) ↑

The last three steps are normal IT project-management practices commonly performed iteratively whether strategic planning has been done or not:

- Step 11: Identify development projects.
- Step 12: Apply business priorities to projects.
- Step 13: Prepare projects schedule and cost/benefit analysis.

As such, they require no expansion here. What is important to emphasize, however, is the acceleration effect that comes with working within an information framework that is already well developed. As each development project is begun in turn, more of the data is found to be already present and being maintained in production. Making use of previously developed information structures works well when business priorities allow approximating the optimum development sequence. When this is not the case, at least it can be determined when additional steps must be taken.

11.5 Summary

- The more diverse the current requirements supported by an information structure, the more that structure will be able to support future requirements without needing modification. Strategic systems planning can provide that diversity. As a result, the stable information structure needed to achieve the planning goal of sustainable applications interoperability can emerge.
- Achieving interoperability of applications (via integration or interfacing) across an enterprise is often one of the objectives of strategic

systems planning. A stable information structure is needed to achieve sustainable application interoperability.

■ The "myth of the isolated system" tells us that we can build an organization's systems one at a time, but the underlying information structure for all the systems must be analyzed, designed, and built first if integrated systems are to result. For flexibility, it is critical to establish a single coherent stable data structure and then fit systems and subsystems into that stable foundation.

■ The results of strategic planning studies are rarely followed. But it is not changing priorities that undo the plans. The plans themselves are inherently deficient because they fail to provide a stable foundation upon which to construct systems and exploit computing technology over a long term.

■ The enterprise model that results from traditional planning emphasizes the procedural and variable aspects of a business. In contrast, an enterprise model that emphasizes the structural and stable aspects — those characteristics of an enterprise upon which long-term decisions about its automation resources can be based — provides the foundation for successful strategic planning. Its core deliverable is a reasonably accurate model of the structural components of the enterprise.

■ It is vital to be able to express automation plans in terms of the real and permanent functions that the enterprise performs and the equally real and permanent entities about which it keeps information.

■ The recommended, useful steps in strategic systems planning for flexibility are:

    Step 1. Obtain top management backing

    Step 3. Obtain organization chart

    Step 4. Perform functional decomposition

    Step 5. Perform automation assessment

    Step 7. Construct a high-level entity-relationship diagram

    Step 8. Construct data-element-level information-structure schematic

    Step 10. Assemble an information-precedence matrix

    Step 11. Identify development projects and development sequences suggested by the precedence matrix

    Step 12. Apply business priorities to projects

    Step 13. Prepare a development projects schedule and cost/benefit analysis

■ A stable enterprise model is the foundation of a workable plan that remains effective for the long term. The data-element-level information-structure schematic, usually omitted from strategic planning studies, confers a great deal of long-term strategic value.

Enterprise strategic systems planning, with an emphasis on developing a comprehensive multibusiness-function enterprise model, provides a unique opportunity to gain access to the diversity of requirements needed for designing a stable information structure. In return, the orientation of flexible systems toward structural stability can substantially improve long-range planning results. Application integration and flexibility — mutually reinforcing objectives — are both essential to a well-designed enterprise system. Analysis techniques for eliciting information structure are explored in Chapter 12.

Chapter 12

Requirements Determination for Flexible Systems

The software development process is driven by requirements. Typically, the focus is on defining precise requirements and then implementing exactly those requirements. However, once delivered, virtually every major software product produces major disappointments for its customers as new requirements emerge. Experts agree that it is unrealistic to specify precise requirements:

> Detailed specification writing is often wasted effort because rapid changes occur during the project, making the specifications obsolete [McConnell, 1996].

> Sometimes, our technically oriented analytical personalities would have us specify every detail up front, but it is difficult to do so for two simple reasons. First, the requirements constantly change in extreme environments and second, even when the requirements are known, they can too easily be misinterpreted, in part because of the ambiguity of language [Gause and Weinberg, 1989, pp. 14–33].

> It is impossible to precisely specify software requirements.... Since complex projects are nonlinear and can be unpredictable,

the belief that one can accomplish precise, complete requirements definition at the beginning of a project is a myth [Highsmith, 2000, p. 159].

The drive to define precise requirements is embodied in the "myth of perfect knowledge," presented in the following section.

12.1 Myth of Perfect Knowledge

It is widely accepted that the cost of system modification increases over the course of the development cycle. Clearly, it is more costly to modify a software system at the back end of the development process than at the front end. It takes more effort to modify computer programs and file structures than to modify design specifications, and it takes more effort to modify design specifications than to modify a requirements model. From these facts, a fundamental misconception has emerged: that high system maintenance costs are largely due to imprecise requirements determination (analysis) at the front end of the process. Business staff and managers often say, "We're spending a lot of money changing this system because we didn't get all the requirements right at the beginning. We need more exact requirements analysis in our systems development method." This is the myth of perfect knowledge at work:

> Myth: With enough effort, we can attain perfect knowledge of a system's requirements.
> Reality: The real world changes, so knowledge of a system's requirements is necessarily imperfect because a significant part of the requirements lies in the future and is not available at the time the automated system is developed.

Given this myth, arriving future requirements are viewed as "missed requirements," whose incorporation into existing software is disruptive. This means that we must rely on techniques other than mere determination of improved requirements. As Brooks [1987] stated long ago in his famous essay, "No Silver Bullet: Essence and Accidents in Software Engineering," the assumption that a satisfactory software system can be specified in advance is basically wrong. The fact that knowledge of requirements is necessarily imperfect alters the development objective fundamentally — from achieving functional accuracy to providing adaptability to functional change. We must remember that most of the system's life is in tomorrow and that accuracy today has virtually no effect on flexibility, which is needed to synchronize change with tomorrow's reality.

Another way of expressing this myth goes way back to the 1960s, when a CIO (for whom one of the authors worked) said:

> We design and develop the third best system. The perfect system requires knowledge of all aspects of world economics and future changes, which we can't acquire. The second best system requires knowledge of all the things that our competitors now do and will be doing. We therefore develop the third best system [Scheuer, 2004].

12.2 Definition of Effective Requirements

A fundamental reorientation to software design is required, one in which the focus is no longer primarily on functional accuracy but rather on achieving flexibility.

Inadequate definition of requirements often bears the brunt of the blame for systems problems:

> Requirements champions can point to millions of dollars that are written off each year in failed software projects; as often as not, they contend, sloppy initial requirements were at the root of the problem [Seeley, 2003, p. 31].

The analytical approach discussed in this chapter can both limit the amount of detail and expand the effectiveness of requirements definitions. One of the driving forces behind the techniques for eliciting flexible-systems requirements is that the more generic the requirements model, the less detailed it needs to be. Think of it: we are getting more (a less costly system to maintain) for a less costly analysis effort. A core concept in getting more for less concerns achieving a better balance between process- and structure-requirements analysis.

12.2.1 Structure/Process Differentiation

The structure of information, as we perceive it, affects both our process design and our design process.

The imbalance of attention between processing requirements and structural requirements is a major cause of our current legacy of inflexible systems. This imbalance developed, in part, because computerized information systems have their roots in computer science rather than in business. Even though the first use of computers in business was called "data processing" (and not "information systems") the main emphasis was on the processing rather than on the data.

Computer scientists have concerned themselves with algorithms since the very beginning of computers. Even their apparent concern for data, when examined closely, deals with the development and understanding of data structures such as stacks, queues, trees, etc., structures that support efficient processing algorithms. Emphasis has been on the physical aspects of data as opposed to its semantic characteristics. The subsequent development of information systems necessarily required attention to information structures that support the business requirements as well as to data structures that support processing efficiency. It is unclear why the historical development of the information-systems profession — including methods, training, database design, and programming practices — perpetuated the imbalance that favors data-processing concerns over information-structuring concerns, but it remains a factor to this day. It affects our thinking as analysts and designers. The importance of information structure is borne out by Exhibit 12.1.

Years ago, one the authors discovered that a given information structure not only can constrain the computing processes that operate on it, but that it also can constrain one's thinking. One might say that the structure of information, as we perceive it, affects both our process design and our

As I sat alone at my desk, I tried to concentrate on my programming project. Yet the fear and worries continued to cross my mind. The company was in a slump, my project was crucial to meeting the payroll, and there was no one available to help me. All the programmers were committed to other projects. I had to get it done on my own.

As I studied the specifications, I was stymied—just plain stumped. I did not know how to proceed. After several false starts, I interrupted myself and got up to get a cup of coffee. While wandering around the office it came to me. I visualized a solution based upon a specific data arrangement; if the data only looked like this I could solve the problem. But, the data did not look like "this." No matter. I had no choice given the deadline, my state of mind, and the lack of available help. I sat down again and began to code the solution based upon the nonexistent data arrangement.

Over the next few days as I developed code, I was still concerned about the conditions within the company, my project in general, and the fact that the data did not "look like this." As I approached the end of the development process I became more and more concerned about my imaginary data. But literally as I finished the last line of code, a vision came to me. It was an algorithm by which the data could be made to "look like this." And, voilá, with just a page or two of code, I developed a front-end conversion routine that completed the system.

From this point, things flowed. The testing and implementation must have gone smoothly, as I barely remember it. But the lesson learned is real. Data constrains procedure. If I had waited to code the procedure until I understood how to do it in the original format, I would not have made it.

Exhibit 12.1.   If the Data Only Looked Like This...

design process. With this in mind, this chapter emphasizes the need for a fruitful collaboration between process thinking and structure thinking.

12.3 Identifying Dynamic Requirements

The development of flexible systems shifts the emphasis to identifying dynamic requirements.

The search for the perfect set of static requirements is never ending. The development of flexible systems shifts the emphasis to identifying dynamic requirements. The approach to eliciting requirements for flexible systems builds on standard analytical practice. It adds emphasis to eliciting and modeling information-structure requirements, and it is consistent with various guides on the subject of data modeling.

Our approach has the following primary characteristics:

- It discovers both the structure and the processes that govern the behavior of the real-world system.
- It clearly differentiates between the structure and the process in its analytical model.
- It requires that the physical design observe the analytical model's structure/process differentiation.

These characteristics are achieved through the following analytical tasks:

1. Gathering current requirements, both structural and procedural
2. Representing the current structural and procedural requirements in an analytical model
3. Identifying past, and probable future, variations from current structural and procedural requirements
4. Questioning cardinality assumptions
5. Identifying candidates for generic entities
6. Identifying conditional logic patterns
7. Iterative analysis and design

12.1.1 Gathering Current Requirements, Both Structural and Procedural (Task 1)

The analyst needs to guide discussions back and forth between business data and business processes to identify what is essential and what is simply an adaptation to a limitation in the current automated system. The analyst who has the benefit of working within an organization that has followed the strategic systems planning prescription (Chapter 11) and has already developed a comprehensive and stable information structure (Chapter 11, Step 8) can focus on current process requirements and expect to rapidly fit new development onto that foundation. In reality, of course, our analyst is not likely to be so fortunate, so we will be looking at both structural and procedural requirements analysis. Although the structure design must be put in place prior to the process design, it is efficient to gather both sets of requirements in parallel.

Much of the physical material gathered for process modeling is the same as that needed for structure modeling. Specifically forms, reports, displays, and responses to interviews provide information that aids in understanding both processing requirements and data requirements. Given, however, that analysis of information requirements and interview results often miss important data structure-related information, what kinds of questions should be added to the requirement-gathering effort and how should the answers be represented in the analytical model?

Imagine two analysts interviewing a user, one for the purpose of eliciting process information, and the other for the purpose of eliciting structure information.

The "process interviewer" asks questions regarding:

- What is done?
- How it is done?
- What is the input to each process and where does it comes from?
- What is the output from each process and where does it go?
- How much input/output is there?
- With what frequency is it processed?

The "structure interviewer" asks questions regarding:

- What entities are being acted upon?
- How are they identified (distinguished from each other)?
- What are the cardinalities of the relationships among them (e.g., whether in relationship to x there can be more than one y)?
- What synonymous entities might exist (e.g., whether an x recognized by one organizational component is the same as the y recognized by another part of the enterprise)?
- What generalization schemes are there (e.g., is entity x a subtype of entity y)?

Of course, the analyst uses business language. Rather than "What entities do you work with?" the analyst asks, "What is the difference between a job and a position?" Rather than "What are the cardinalities for position and job?" the analyst asks, "Can there be more than one position per job?"

Analyzing structural business requirements generally involves a significant role change for business experts. Even while expressing our preference for starting with data, we acknowledge that business experts are often more comfortable starting with existing business processes. The focus of daily activity for many of them is processing. The analyst needs to guide discussions back and forth between business data and business processes to identify what is essential and what is simply an adaptation to a limitation in the current automated system.

Focusing on data even when discussing a business process helps to separate the essential from the nonessential. For example, a customer's description of a process of recording personal information about an employee might be as follows:

> The individual fills out a three-part form. The yellow copy goes in our files. The blue copy is sent to Personnel. The pink copy is sent to Research, where it is stamped and filed alphabetically within zip code.

This description has focused entirely on the process, saying nothing about the personnel information itself. A good analyst will direct attention alternately between the process and the information structure of, in this case, the three-part form (and will ensure that Personnel's and Research's requirements are also examined). Interestingly, developer questions about data do not seem to elicit emotional responses from customers the way questions about processes sometimes do.

12.3.2 Representing the Current Requirements in an Analytical Model (Task 2)

After initial requirements are gathered, the next task involves representing these current requirements in an analytical model or real-world model. We show two diagramming conventions, one for representing processes (Exhibit 12.2) and one for representing information structures (Exhibit 12.3), each at different levels of detail.

Process-oriented models are commonly used at this stage in requirements definition. Exhibit 12.2 presents a traditional information-flow diagram (generally referred to as a data flow diagram, DFD) with labeled symbols: circles representing processes, boxes representing data stores and arrows representing the flow of information. (Sometimes distinctions are also made between information-flow arrows and control-flow arrows.)

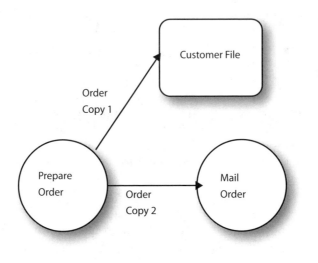

Exhibit 12.2. Process-Oriented Information-Flow Diagram

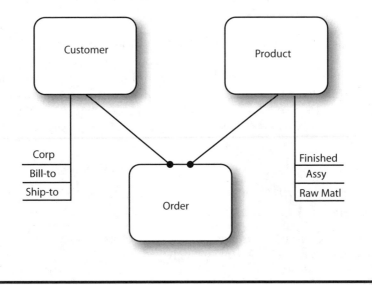

Exhibit 12.3. Information-Structure Diagram: Entity Level

12.3.2.1 Structural Modeling at Entity and Data-Element Levels

For flexible software design, we shift the emphasis from modeling process-oriented requirements to modeling structural requirements. Structural requirements are represented analytically in data structure diagrams at

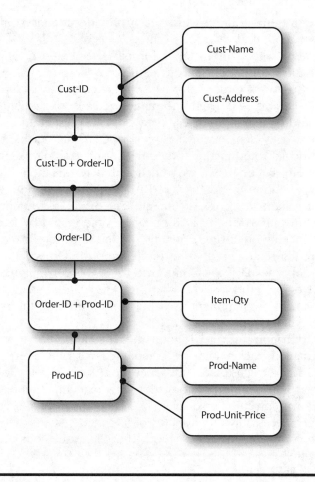

Exhibit 12.4. Information-Structure Diagram: Data-Element Level

both the entity level and the data-element level. An important point about information-structure diagrams is that, as discussed in Chapter 11 (Flexibility and Strategic Systems Planning), they are properly the product of a heuristic (learn as you go) approach. The analyst makes preliminary high-level identifications of data entities, such as "customer" or "product," followed by detailed analysis of data elements and their relationships to each other. Exhibit 12.3 provides an example of an information-structure diagram representing the entity level. It shows labeled symbols, with boxes representing data entities and directed lines representing the static cardinality relationships among the entities. Entity generalization schemes (showing generic entities and their included types) may also be suitably represented and included in the diagram. Exhibit 12.4 shows the same information at the data-element level. As the analyst iterates between the top-down and the bottom-up views, each provides a context in which to investigate, extend, and refine the other.

The primary source of material for data-element-level analysis and modeling is the information packet. Exhibit 12.4 represents, greatly simplified, the Customer Order information packet that was shown being processed in Exhibit 12.2. Each information packet is examined in detail, identifying and documenting every data element present and its relationships to other data elements, including data elements outside the packet itself. In particular, the functional determinant of each data element must be determined. To establish the functional determinant for each data element, the question to be answered is: "What must be known to pick out a single value for this data element?" For example, the unit price on Customer Order information packet may be determined by knowing the product ID. Picking out a single quantity on the same information requirement may require knowing the Product ID and the Order ID, or perhaps also the Order Line ID if the same product can occur multiple times on one order. Notice in this last case that the Order Line ID may not appear on the information requirement itself but is inferred from the presence of other data elements.

In the information-structure diagram, the data elements that comprise the Order information packet may be components of one or more entities: customer name from customer, unit price from product, etc. So the information packet in a high-level information-flow diagram is represented in a low-level information-structure diagram by a set of interrelated data elements, which are not necessarily all attributes of a single entity. As the structures of multiple information packets are worked out, they are combined into the total information-structure diagram on the basis of common data elements.

This analysis also includes identification of derived data elements (e.g., extended amount, 30- to 60-day amount past due, total amount, etc.). While any particular derived data element may or may not eventually be stored in the database, depending on a variety of design and performance factors, it should be properly located in the information-structure model according to its functional determinant.

The information-structure diagrams (both entity level and data-element level) developed during this task are preliminary, requiring elaboration subsequently, specifically during Task 7.

12.3.2.2 Keep Structure/Process Models Distinct

One might consider combining into one diagram the information-process and the information-structure requirements. We see no useful purpose in making such a diagram. But it is useful to recognize the *conceptual* connection while keeping the models distinct. The traditional view of

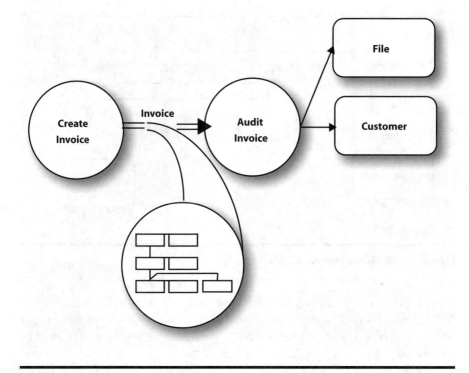

Exhibit 12.5. Information Structure as a Cross-Section of a Logical-Process Diagram

combining the two diagrams is that each data store (box) on a flow diagram corresponds to some subset of the structure diagram. The data stores that appear in a process diagram such as a DFD either correspond to existing physical files (automated or manual) in the current systems, or are put in to avoid branching flow arrows. In either case, they are nonlogical artifacts in a logical model. We saw above that it is the information packet, represented by the arrow in a flow diagram, that has an internal structure whose dependencies among data elements are modeled in a structure diagram. That is, the structure diagram corresponds to the static cross section of the flow arrow on the process diagram (Exhibit 12.5), and the total structure diagram corresponds to the collective static cross sections of the flow arrows on the total process diagram. Practicality clearly precludes a consolidated process/structure diagram.

12.3.2.3 Natural and Artificial Limits

The real-world system has natural and artificial limits imposed on its information structure. For example, Exhibit 12.6 attempts to show that some

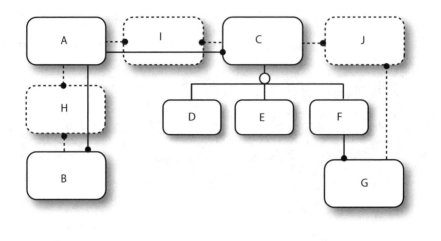

Exhibit 12.6. Natural and Artificial Limits

relationships (e.g., between A and B) are currently required to be 1:*m*, but that the natural limit is many-to-many. It also attempts to show that only a specific subtype (F) of a generic entity (C) is currently in 1:*m* relationship to another entity (G) but that the natural limit is that any of C's subtypes may be in many-to-many relationship to G. Furthermore, the exhibit needs to represent all of C's potential subtypes, not just those currently defined.

Now imagine Exhibit 12.6 extended to include all the natural and artificial structural aspects of even a small application; the result would obscure rather than illuminate the requirements. At the detailed data-item level, the result would be even more difficult to comprehend. Because the constraints appear at the entity level, not at the data-element level, it is possible to maintain a single model of current artificial constraints and perpetual natural constraints, as in Exhibit 12.6. But, admittedly, it is cumbersome. Alternatively, it is entirely appropriate to model them separately. The natural-constraint model serves as input to database design. The model of current artificial limits serves as input to initial loading of the cardinality-regulation data if that facility is employed. It also is input to the design of process components or database triggers that enforce integrity within the automated system.

An alternative is to simply take natural constraints into account at design time, rather than at analysis time. In a very real sense, there is only one natural set of limits on any given set of real-world application entities. It is modeled by a normalized representation of entities in many-to-many relationships with each other and with generic entities that are also in recursive many-to-many relationships (see Chapter 9). This model is just as available to analysts and designers, mentally, as it would be if drawn out on a (very large) piece of paper. As a representation of natural limits among real-world entities, it can serve as the backdrop for the model of the artificial limits imposed by current practice. If one expects that the natural constraints will be taken into account at design time, then they need not be represented explicitly in the analytical model.

Either alternative is viable; they are simply different views of our perception of generic information structures. In one view they are discovered during analysis of the real-world system, and in the other view they are imposed during design of the automated-world system. This "view alternation" is also compatible with the recommendation given later (Section 12.3.8) for overlapping and iterating analysis and design.

12.3.2.4 *The Data Dictionary*

The tool of choice for the analysis task of recording process and structural models is an automated data-dictionary facility. There are two reasons. First, it is specifically designed and intended for recording in human- and machine-readable form metadata on information structure down to the data-element level. Second, it enables application-processing programs to exploit that metadata. As described in Chapter 13, access to the metadata of the applications information structure enables the design of programs that can perform generic processing without needing to have elements of the information structure declared within or to the programs, because they obtain them dynamically from the dictionary.

For example, in the UniverSIS Generic Code feature, standard validation tables are defined through reference to elements defined in the data dictionary. When a new data element is defined, an entry is made in the dictionary, and the logical validation table can be established to support that element without changes to data structures or programs. The metadata in the dictionary enforces the correct format and length of the data. Standard logic makes use of the tables to validate values entered by the user and to provide "help" lists of valid values. A programmer makes use of the standard logic by simply identifying the applicable data element at the appropriate place in the program. In the UniverSIS project, the code generator was adapted to use the dictionary to recognize the connection between a data element and its corresponding validation table and to generate the necessary logic automatically.

12.3.3 *Identifying Past and Probable Future Variations from Current Structural Requirements (Task 3)*

When an automated system has been in place for a long time, business staff may have difficulty imagining that business could be done any other way. As discussed in Task 1 above, focusing on the data that is to be recorded helps customers, and developers for that matter, to recognize that the current process does not represent the only way of doing things. The key to eliciting potential variations to current structural requirements lies in asking the "Why?" questions and the "Change?" questions.

12.3.3.1 Why? What Is the Basic Cause?

This question is often met with puzzlement, particularly when no one is sure about the answer. If the answer is "because we've always done it that way," then more analysis is required to answer the question, which might be phrased in this general form: "If it were not for what basic cause, would we be doing this?" For example, "If it were not for the fact that we've always done it this way, would we be doing this?" Why is the "why" important? It is important because it helps distinguish between the essential and the nonessential.

Business experts understand the business well enough to be able to answer the "why" questions. Understanding why certain data is stored and why certain processes are as they are, such individuals are in the position to consider different approaches. They can disengage themselves from "the way we've always done it."

There is, of course, no need to automate something for which the purpose is obsolete (Exhibit 12.7). But knowing what is essential can often substantially reduce the quantity of detail that needs to be considered in defining requirements, and it can provide opportunities for designing in flexibility.

One of our authors recalls a story from his days at a major manufacturer. When cartons of goods were sealed, a piece of wax paper was placed

A familiar story, having several variations, tells of grandmother's recipe for baked zucchini, which involves cutting off the end of the zucchini before placing it in the pan. The recipe was passed along from grandmother to her daughter and granddaughter. After following the recipe for several years, the granddaughter finally asked why it is necessary to cut off the end of the zucchini. As it turns out, the original reason was that grandmother didn't have a pan long enough to hold the entire zucchini. Yet every aspect of the recipe had become enshrined, not just the essential aspects. In other words, generations of zucchini bakers had focused only on the "How" question without ever asking "Why." The recipe had achieved the revered status of "we've always done it that way."

Exhibit 12.7. Baked Zucchini

between the product and the folded carton ends. This had been done literally millions of times when a bright new employee (not the author) asked the IF question "If it were not for what basic cause, would we place this wax paper here?" In other words: "Why?" No one knew right off, but when the answer was researched it was found that long ago the machine that sealed the carton spilled glue on the product. The wax paper was used to protect the product from the spill. With the new machine, this had been an unnecessary operation and expense for many years.

12.3.3.2 Change?

Systems include both frequently and infrequently changing variables, Haughey's [2004] "fast-changing variables" and "slow-changing variables." Fast-changing variables are generally obvious in the most casual inspection of requirements. Examples include inventory quantities, prices, customers, and employees. Slowly changing variables, on the other hand, are not typically obvious. Examples include inventory control policies, employment practices, and organization schemes.

To elicit the slowly changing variables, ask questions like "Does it ever change?" or "Has it ever changed in the past?" Here the collective institutional memory of long-time employees can be invaluable. They will know what has changed and, often, what the impact has been. Most of the future is uncertain and thus does not provide much to work with, but much is known about the past, and it provides a source for identifying slowly changing variables.

Just because something changes infrequently does not mean that it can be overlooked. The astute analyst will give priority to discovering everything that can change, regardless of the time frame of the change. It is the determination that x is a variable that is important. When designing systems, consider asking the following questions regarding the "finished" designs: "What will be the next three changes that will affect the system? And how will they be implemented?" Having answers does not necessarily guarantee a flexible system. Not having considered the questions essentially guarantees an inflexible system

12.3.3.3 Myth of Retroactive Documentation

Highsmith [2000] argues that rather than facing the difficulties of operating with partial information, the emphasis in serial development on obtaining complete requirements is a futile attempt to increase the developers' comfort level. This is particularly true when an old automated system is to be replaced with a new one. The mantra of system replacement work has been, "First, document the old system."

The "myth of retroactive documentation" is an important myth to understand and to keep in mind as we seek to uncover changes from the past and probable changes of the future.

> Myth: The most important step in developing a replacement system is to document the existing automated system.
> Reality: The existing real-world system is usually distorted by the presence of its entrenched automated component.

Where an automated system has been in place for some time, it usually represents past versions of the real-world system; it is literally an accident of history. More importantly, as it has fallen farther out of synchronization over time, it has increasingly overconstrained the current real-world system, which must be bent in various ways to circumvent the limitations of the automated system. When coupled with frequent breakdowns of the automated system during modifications, the resulting lack of predictability leads to fear of the system and an understandable reaction to counter this by completely understanding the old system before attempting to replace it. This may be understandable, but it is not very useful.

Although documenting the existing system can perpetuate the distortions into the next generation, examining the existing system has value, provided this caution is kept in mind. Business staff can be quite ingenious in working around the limitations of the system, typically by recording "special" values in data elements designed for different purposes. Identifying such situations can bring data requirements to light.

Analysts who design flexible systems tend to get impatient with people who want to tell them how "the old system" worked. While tapping their feet impatiently, they want to shout, "Who cares about how the old system worked? How was it supposed to work?" They want to get on to their most effective tool: the simple "why" question. "Why did you put an asterisk in that field?" Specific tools and techniques for the analyst are covered in Chapters 9 and 13 and throughout the book.

12.3.4 Questioning Cardinality Assumptions (Task 4)

Structural information elicited in the first task included cardinality information. Questions asked during this initial task included: "What are the cardinalities of the relationships among entities (in relationship to x can there be more than one y,...)?" As the flexibility requirements are further explored through analytical modeling (Task 2) and asking "why" and "change" questions to identify variability (Task 3), the analyst should cultivate an attitude of questioning every cardinality assumption, and particularly those that are one-to-many. In most cases, the usual assumption is correct, e.g., a person has one birth date. But we urge you to err on the side of flexibility by seriously examining every attribute of an entity for a possible many-to-many relationship.

For example, UniverSIS allows students (persons) to have multiple addresses or locations. This is not traditionally considered a requirement of most personnel systems, but this relatively simple recognition has contributed to UniverSIS's demonstrated ability to adapt to unforeseen needs. Indeed, by also recognizing that one person can function in multiple roles within the university community, e.g., student, employee, instructor, etc., the system's information structure easily handles the location requirements pertinent to each such role.

One of our colleagues, who has twin sons, reported a situation that drives home the need to question cardinality.

> My son Glenn was once denied insurance coverage because (from the agent), "That medical situation has already been covered during a visit on a given date." After researching the circumstances, I discovered that Mark, Glenn's twin brother, had indeed been treated for the specific situation. The insurance company, however, had a patient file that recorded the insured based on last name plus date of birth! [Scheuer, 2004].

12.3.5 Identifying Candidates for Generic Entities (Task 5)

A basic entity is a person, place, or thing in the real world about which we want to record information. Almost any basic, nonassociation entity is a candidate for generic treatment. They may be more common than one realizes at first; generic entities can be obscured by the use of different terms. Often different parts of the organization call the same thing — the same entity — by different names, such as material, item, assembly, part, component, product, packaging, finished good, etc. When the analyst has a set of terms that are generally recognized as merely synonymous, then it is only necessary to ensure that a standard term is adopted in the information-structure model. The difficulty arises when there is not general agreement.

For example, at an aluminum company, materials management and operations personnel were organized separately from the manufacturing management and operations personnel, who in turn were organizationally separate from the finished-goods people. There were three distinct sub-cultures within just the production stream, with their own terms and proprietary attitudes about "their" items. It took analysts several iterations to see that they were all working with a common entity. With the identification of a generic "item" entity, multiple entities were reduced to one. A single bill-of-material structure worked for all three areas. With unit-of-measure conversions, a common file structure accounted for inventories for all three areas.

Generic entities can mean fewer total entities needed in the information structure. Where a more traditional approach would identify many specific entities, the flexible approach identifies a reduced number of generic entities. At a large retail organization analysts had employed a generic account entity to support extensive multidivision financial reporting requirements. When they looked at the "tax management" function, they found that a slight increase in the generality of the presentation of the financial account relationship readily accommodated tax accounting requirements. The same was found for "general ledger" maintenance and reporting.

The generic account, along with other key basic generic entities, reduced the number of basic entities to be represented by files in the corporate database and also the number of relationships to be represented. It also reduces the analytical effort, as we saw in Chapter 11. Of course, entities should not be so specific that they limit flexibility and not so generic that they are useless. As in all software design, judgment is required.

12.3.6 Identifying Conditional Logic Patterns — Business Rules (Task 6)

As the analyst asks the process questions — "What is done?" "How is it done?" — some of the answers identify conditional logic patterns. These patterns constitute rules for order shipment when inventory is short, credit terms, sales commissions, billing algorithms, wire sizing, overtime and bonus calculations, and the like. Today, these are generally called business rules. Consider some of the "requirements" uncovered by an analyst during a sales automation project, as shown in Exhibit 12.8.

It should not take much of this for the alert analyst from Exhibit 12.8 to discern that she has essentially a set of varying selection conditions that is a candidate for a generic condition selection process. At that point it is necessary only to document the factors (e.g., product type, price, customer, etc.) and not the details or specific combinations. Elaborate modeling of rules is often not necessary if the essence of a rule set is understood and if the intention is to design a facility that provides maintenance of rules through data manipulation during the operation of the system. For another example, see the Investment Trust Bank project discussed in Chapter 2.

An analyst developing an order processing system is obtaining requirements related to sales force commissions:
· The first user interviewed explains that "we generally apply only one commission rate of 0.80% to all our business."
· The second user says that principally this is right, "but some of our sales force get a higher rate for selling big ticket products to corporate customers."
· A third user says, " When I had the difficult Conos account in '98, I negotiated a special rate for myself for the winter quarter, usually our slow time in sales."
· A fourth user reports, "Don't forget that in the past the sales people for a new territory have gotten a higher rate initially, except in soft goods, of course."
· The *n*th user says, "Yes, but ."

Exhibit 12.8. Order-Processing System

12.3.7 Iterative Analysis and Design (Task 7)

The traditional waterfall or serial development method can be characterized as "first you do this, then you do that, then you're done." While a certain degree of analysis must necessarily precede design, there is much to be gained from iterating the two steps in a cycle and intentionally overlapping design with analysis.

In the case of UniverSIS, the work began with a careful analysis of the business data requirements followed by design of the supporting information structure. On those occasions when design work indicated that essential details had been missed, further analysis was undertaken. When analysis showed the design to be inadequate, the developers reworked the design. More often than not, the redesign was necessary because the original design was too rigid. Though it was painful, the effort of correcting the design to make it more flexible was worthwhile in the long run.

12.3.7.1 Prototyping — a Strong Note of Caution

We recommend use of prototyping only with a stable information structure and only where it will elicit better, faster, or more flexible requirements.

It is a short step from analysis/design iteration to analysis/design/build iteration, which, when done in small increments, is prototyping. Prototyping is a way to both elicit and confirm understanding of requirements.

Frequently, an end user does not know exactly what is needed until some working model is available:

> The primary vehicle for confirming requirements is most likely to be interactive versions of the application itself [Highsmith, 2000, p. 160].

Yes, but. A very real potential problem with attempting to achieve flexible systems through prototyping is that, as von Halle [2002] points out, the incremental development can make it difficult to grasp the comprehensive information structure needed to support the finished software or system ensemble. It is important to avoid frequent or substantial redesign of the underlying information structure, otherwise the result will be time-consuming chain reactions of modifications to existing code. Incremental development can become massive redevelopment. A stable information structure best results from a broadly comprehensive view, preferably one that considers multiple applications and organization components across an enterprise. (See Chapter 11, Flexibility and Strategic Systems Planning.) Indeed, the University of Cincinnati's initial intent was to market UniverSIS to other universities. Although this has not happened, the thought processes involved in considering the potential requirements of other institutions proved valuable in the design effort. In fact, we recommend adding a similar exercise to any software development project. In analyzing business requirements, ask yourself the following question: "This is how we do it, but how might it be done elsewhere?"

Prototyping is not a good way to develop a stable and comprehensive information structure. But it is an excellent way to elicit processing requirements from business staff once a stable structure is in place. Our strong caution to the developer is to ensure that the system actually developed exploits and does not circumvent the stable nature of the structure.

12.4 Agile Methodologies

Lying in the same methodological direction, but beyond prototyping, are more "extreme" approaches to programming referred to collectively as *agile methodologies*. From the perspective of systems flexibility, what is most significant about these methodologies is, first, their recognition of the primacy of change and, second, the direction taken in reaction to this recognition.

> The perceived expense of the initial development process and the even higher perceived expense of making adjustments after

release has made scalability and control along many dimensions (number of users, time, rate of use) a very high priority. Proponents of agile methodologies have (accurately) claimed that such scalability requires perfect knowledge of requirements. Given that the only reliable rule about the real world is *things change*, true scalability is impossible. Agile developers, understanding the challenge of constant change, have responded with a manifesto predicated on acceptance of change and the necessity of constant refactoring: in system requirements, system tools, and the social systems that surround the development process [Dent, 2004].

As the Agile Manifesto states, "We welcome changing requirements, even late in development. Agile processes harness change for the customer's competitive advantage." While many agile techniques have been applied successfully, we are primarily concerned here with only a few of them, as they appear to directly contradict the flexibility program we espouse.

John Waters summarized the essence of extreme programming (XP) as,

> Do The Simplest Thing That Could Possibly Work. This is XP's prime directive, a fundamental principle considered the most important contributor to the rapid progress of XP projects. It is a mandate to implement a new capability in the simplest way you possibly can, as long as it works. This idea infuses everything XPers do [Waters, 2000].

Closely related to this is,

> ... to implement only what they [end users] really need, not what they might need — no speculative side trips [Waters, 2000].

So, starting from a common recognition of the problem of change, two apparently opposite directions are proposed. Our program locates flexibility in the system itself, and agile methods locates it in the development process, echoing Boogard's [1994] passive (built in)/active (fast maintenance) flexibility dichotomy (Chapter 2). While this dichotomy is a valid and astute categorization of flexibility approaches, it does not imply fundamental incompatibility between these two approaches. For example, insofar as they are an efficient means to program a new capability, extreme methods may well be appropriate for the development of passively flexible software, provided that the new capability is the user-maintained business rule.

Similarly, the second directive does not necessarily preclude built-in flexibility. There is an important difference between intentionally not implementing a specific known function because its need has not yet occurred, and not implementing a generic or rule-mediated function in a user-maintainable manner against known general but unknown specific future requirements. To take a simple example, not implementing a specific additional tax deduction in a payroll system, say for one's pet's medical expenses, because it has not yet been legislated, is quite different from not implementing a generic means of user-defined tax deductions against a future requirement of unknowable specific tax deductions. Indeed, the C3 Project at Daimler-Chrysler in 1996 [Waters, 2000], often considered the genesis of agile methods, was about consolidating 12 or 13 payroll systems into 1. From our perspective, this was an ideal candidate for the application of built-in flexibility; rarely does one have such a diversity of consistent requirements for one application from which generic rules and patterns might be abstracted.

Another thread in the agile tapestry is Weinberger's concept of "many small pieces loosely joined" [Weinberger, 2002]. While he was referring to components of the Web, this architectural concept has been adopted as a general guideline by the agile-development community. While applicable to many components of a system, the concept breaks down when applied to the relationship between procedural or algorithmic elements and the information structure. Von Halle's [2002] argument and ours is that changes in information structure *necessarily* have drastic effects on programs; programs cannot be loosely coupled to the information they operate upon. Our caveat regarding prototyping applies to agile methodologies as well. The information structure needs to be stabilized in advance of prototyping iterations or, in this case, "extreme" refactoring.

Finally, Shirky [2004] reminds us that the attitude embodied in "situated software," which factors in the social environment of a system, "refuses to embrace scale, generality, or completeness as unqualified virtues." We have had little to say of scale but much to say about generality as an antidote to the impossibility of completeness. So already between the agile methods and the flexible systems agenda we have neutrality, disagreement, and agreement regarding the factors of scale, generality, and completeness, respectively. This is hardly a clear-cut dichotomy.

Shirky's comment is also a mature caution we might all take to heart (and mind). There are different situations in the real world and different strategies appropriate to them in providing automation assistance. In an earlier life, one of the authors had an unpleasant experience with a 4GL development tool applied to a large, multibank, wholesale banking system. This tool had a pretty good track record, but it was limited, as it later became clear, to relatively small stand-alone applications. When applied to an application with a large number of functions, multiple interfaces, and an extensive information structure, it failed. And it was not a matter of scale. The productivity leverage the product provided was automatic generation of data files based on the data needs of manually coded processing programs. Within a limited application, the product's attempt to violate the structure/process constraint relationship was not apparent. Within a larger one, it became very evident that every time someone touched the processing code and the product "adjusted" the information structure, there was a chain reaction of compensatory coding changes required, as we would expect. The project failure was not caused by the tool itself, but by use of the tool in an inappropriate situation caused by the assumption of an unqualified virtue.

We have strongly promoted flexibility as a desirable built-in characteristic of computer applications — to the point where it might appear that we consider it an unqualified virtue. Certainly it is not such. Ultimate flexibility is not always suitable. Cost/benefit and other factors have to come into play. There are many development situations in which the balance needs to be established closer to the XP end of the spectrum. Our objective has been to offer additions to the developer's toolkit in support of built-in system flexibility, while assuming the developer's environment demands judgment and appropriateness, even craft, in the application of those tools. It seems entirely workable for the power of agile methods to be brought to bear on the challenges of built-in system flexibility.

12.5 Summary

- A fundamental reorientation to software design is required, one in which the focus is no longer primarily on functional accuracy but rather on achieving flexibility.
- A key point behind the techniques of eliciting and presenting requirements in a flexible structure is that the more generic the requirements model is, the less detailed it needs to be.
- The development of flexible systems shifts the emphasis to identifying dynamic requirements. It builds on standard analytical practice, yet adds emphasis on eliciting and modeling information-structure requirements.
- The flexible approach has the following primary characteristics:
  1. It discovers both the structure and the processes that govern the behavior of the real-world system.
  2. It clearly differentiates between structure and process in its analytical model.
  3. It requires that the physical design observe the analytical model's structure/process differentiation.

- These characteristics are achieved through the following analytical tasks:
  1. Gathering current requirements, both structural and procedural
  2. Representing the current requirements in an analytical model
  3. Identifying past, and probable future, variations from current structural requirements
  4. Questioning cardinality assumptions
  5. Identifying candidates for generic entities
  6. Identifying conditional logic patterns
  7. Iterative analysis and design
- Adequate attention must be given to both structure and process requirements elicitation. They entail different kinds of questions, as shown in Exhibit 12.9.
- Structural requirements are represented analytically in data structure diagrams at both the entity level and the data-element level. Packets of information, such as invoice, order, inventory report, etc. that move among the processes of an enterprise, are the primary source material for data-element level analysis and modeling. The functional determinant must be identified for each data element.
- The "why" question helps separate the essential from the nonessential. The "change" question helps separate the variable from the constant and to identify the rate of change of the variable.
- Question every cardinality assumption, but particularly those that are one-to-many. Err on the side of flexibility by seriously examining every attribute of an entity for a possible many-to-many relationship.

Process Questions	Structure Questions
• What is done?	• What entities are being acted upon?
• How is it done?	• How are they are identified?
• What is the input to each process, and where does it come from?	• What are the cardinalities of the relationships among them?
• What is the output from each process, and where does it go to?	• What synonymous entities might exist?
• How much input/output is there?	• What generalization schemes are there?
• With what frequency is it processed?	

Exhibit 12.9. Process and Structure Questions Compared

- Because the real world changes, to be flexible, we must identify entities in a generic way so that the system accommodates change without changing the information structure or programs.
- Elaborate rules modeling is often unnecessary if the essence of a rule set is understood and if the intention is to design a facility that provides maintenance of rules through data manipulation.
- Tasks 3, 5, and 6, identifying variations, generic entities, and conditional logic patterns (business rules), respectively, can greatly reduce the amount of detail required in Task 1, requirements gathering.
- Iterating analysis and design can be effective, but exercise caution that it does not lead to prototyping of processes while missing the larger information-structure picture.
- Agile methods are compatible with certain aspects of planned or built-in flexibility when used with care and when the principles of flexibility are not violated.

The approach defined in this chapter can both limit the amount of detail and expand the effectiveness of requirement definitions before and during development. It also accommodates changes in requirements that occur after the software has been developed and placed into production. In fact, it is after the system is in production that the determination of flexible software requirements truly pays off.

Chapter 13

System Design with an Eye on Flexibility

To build flexible systems, programmers must orient their thinking to writing code that works indirectly rather than directly. This approach runs counter to the traditional approach of programmers, who take pride in finding ways to reduce processing time. In flexible systems, programs often contain the logic to look up the rules wherever they are stored rather than the logic of the actual business rules themselves. Furthermore, because the developers have isolated many reusable pieces of complex logic, programs are often assemblies of references to other specialized programs. This approach takes some getting used to. It also requires good communication, good documentation, and good project management. The independent-minded programmer who would rather do things his own way presents a significant barrier to the success of such an approach. It is critical that management take an active role in establishing and enforcing adherence to standards, including the concept of reuse.

This chapter covers two overall techniques for flexible software design:

1. Structure-oriented techniques
2. Process-oriented techniques

13.1 Structure-Oriented Techniques for Flexible Software Design

Structure-oriented techniques were introduced in Chapters 9 and 10. They take the form of information structures composed of generic entity types and many-to-many relationships that identify and exploit common data characteristics and common patterns of relationships between and within entities. Exhibit 13.1, which is a diagram of the basic generic components discussed in Chapter 9, shows least-specialized entities and least-constrained relationships used in combination. Exhibit 13.1 shows multiple generic things related to themselves recursively as well to other generic entities.

An order-processing system is used to illustrate what happens when a series of requirements changes are imposed on a system with overly constrained information structure (Exhibit 13.2) compared with the corresponding effect on a flexible schema (Exhibit 13.3) employing an external cardinality-enforcement mechanism.

13.1.1 Requirement A

The initial requirement is that there is only one customer per order and that all products are in one location. Exhibit 13.2 supports this requirement.

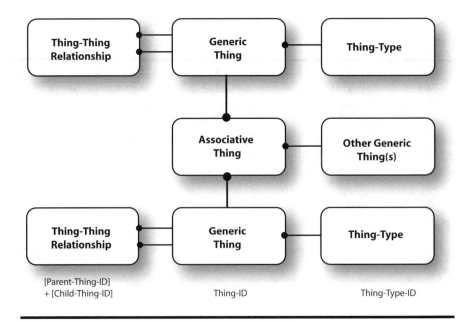

Exhibit 13.1. Basic Generic Components

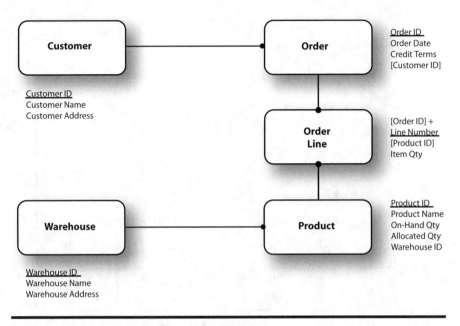

Exhibit 13.2. Overly Constrained Initial Design

Exhibit 13.3 also supports the requirement. It has an entity called Order Disposition that is not present in Exhibit 13.2. Because the initial requirement specifies one customer per order, the cardinality of Order Disposition would be set to one customer per order.

13.1.2 Requirement B

The company expands to multiple warehouses, with the possibility of each product being inventoried at multiple warehouses. Exhibit 13.2 runs into trouble here. The product record is linked to a specific warehouse. Recording the fact that a product can be inventoried at multiple locations will require modifications to information structures and program code.

The inventory entity of Exhibit 13.3 absorbs this change without modification. The initial requirement of a product being inventoried in only one location is managed with cardinality regulation. Adjustment to allow multiple inventory locations is accommodated with only a data value update in the cardinality facility.

13.1.3 Requirement C

Customers require additional discrimination: ordered-by, ship-to, bill-to, and sale-to customer. Again Exhibit 13.2 runs into trouble. The data

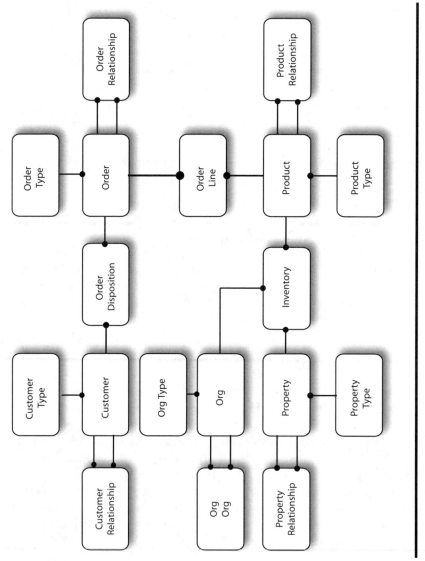

Exhibit 13.3. Flexible Design

structure design limits an order to one customer. To accommodate multiple customers per order, it will be necessary to modify data structures and program code.

Exhibit 13.3 makes use of the Order Disposition entity. With a record key composed of Order-ID+Customer-ID, it can accommodate multiple dispositions per order. That is, it is possible to identify ordered-by, ship-to, bill-to, and sale-to dispositions for the same order. The record for each can specify a different or the same customer. No modification of data structures or program code is needed.

13.1.4 Requirement D

Multiple ship-to customers and split commissions are required on the same order. For Exhibit 13.2, modifications to accommodate this new requirement build on its previous modifications, continuing to move it closer to the Exhibit 13.3 design.

In Exhibit 13.3, recording of multiple ship-to customers is just a matter of recording shipment action and Customer-ID along with Order-ID in the Order Disposition record. The customer record will be associated with the salesperson or persons (not shown) who is to receive the corresponding whole or fractional commission.

13.1.5 Requirement E

Different types of related organization components (corporate office, division, subsidiary, etc.) are required, as are different types of related orders, products (bills of material), and company properties. Modifications to the Exhibit 13.2 design would by now have brought it essentially into agreement with the Exhibit 13.3 design.

The generic structure in Exhibit 13.3 absorbed all the changes without modification. It is important to recognize that the specific changes identified in these scenarios need not have been known in advance for the designers to have adopted the flexible design at the outset. Also, the flexible schema and the cardinality-regulation facility provide independent benefits. That is, the schema can be used without a cardinality-regulation facility, in which case business staff must be relied upon to manually enforce current cardinality requirements. The addition of automated support for cardinality enforcement confers an extra benefit of improved reliability on top of an already substantial benefit of reduced IT maintenance.

13.2 Process-Oriented Techniques for Flexible Software Design

Process-oriented techniques identify and exploit common logic patterns supported by common information structures. The following are two specific examples of process-oriented flexibility techniques that have been successfully employed in commercial systems.

13.2.1 The Dynamic Condition Search

Consider a sales commission example based upon the order-processing system requirements presented in Exhibit 1.3 and Exhibit 12.8. Converted to a general, but still informal, description, the commission requirements could look like this:

> In our business practice we use a condition value called "commission." The value of this condition depends on a number of factors that are connected with products, salespersons, and customers, including product, salesperson, and customer classifications. The connection between the condition value and these factors is not fixed; it varies based on changing business situations.

Other values like discounts, fees, etc. often have similar complex and variable requirements.

The dynamic-condition-search approach represents this requirement with two files and a search program that operates on data provided by, in our example, a transaction file. The transaction file is shown in Exhibit 13.4 along with the transactions as a table with a header designating the fields in the transaction file. The two specific dynamic-condition-search files are:

1. The condition file along with its table, which is shown in Exhibit 13.5
2. The commission file along with its table, which is shown in Exhibit 13.6

In Exhibit 13.7 we show the results of running the dynamic-condition-search program using the data shown in Exhibits 13.4 through 13.6. The Java program that produced the output is shown in Appendix 13 at the end of the chapter.

For each transaction file record, the dynamic search program starts again with the first record in the condition file to build an argument with

```
TRA01PRG01PID01CUG01CID01SAG01SID01
TRA02PRG02PID01CUG02CID01SAG02SID01
TRA03PRG01PID02CUG01CID02SAG01SID02
TRA04PRG02PID02CUG02CID02SAG02SID02
EOF
```

ID	Product Group	Product ID	Customer Group	Customer ID	Sales Group	Sales-person ID
TRA01	PRG01	PID01	CUG01	CID01	SAG01	SID01
TRA02	PRG02	PID01	CUG02	CID01	SAG02	SID01
TRA03	PRG01	PID02	CUG01	CID02	SAG01	SID02
TRA04	PRG02	PID02	CUG02	CID02	SAG02	SID02
End of File						

Exhibit 13.4.   Transaction File and Table

```
CON01111111 All ones
CON02101010 one zero etc
CON03010101 zero one etc
CON99000000 All zeros
EOF
```

ID	Use Product Group	Use Product ID	Use Customer Group	Use Customer ID	Use Sales Group	Use Salesperson ID
CON01	1 (yes)	1 (yes)	1 (yes)	1 (yes)	1 (yes)	1 (yes)
CON02	1 (yes)	0 (no)	1 (yes)	0 (no)	1 (yes)	0 (no)
CON03	0 (no)	1 (yes)	0 (no)	1 (yes)	0 (no)	1 (yes)
CON99	0 (no)	0 (no)	0 (no)	0 (no)	0 (no)	0 (no)
End of File						

Exhibit 13.5.   Condition File and Table

which to search the commission file. If there is no match in the commission file, it then uses the second record, third record, etc. in the condition file until a match is found. Note that the last record of the condition file (all zeros) forces the default condition, which is the first record in the commission file.

```
COM01*****************************00.12
COM02*****PID01*****CID01*****SID0101.23
COM03PRG01PID01CUG01CID01SAG01SID0102.34
COM04PRG01*****CUG01*****SAG01*****03.45
EOF
```

ID	Product Group	Product ID	Customer Group	Customer ID	Sales Group	Salesperson ID	Commission
COM01	*****	*****	*****	*****	*****	*****	00.12 %
COM02	*****	PID01	*****	CID01	*****	SID01	01.23 %
COM03	PRG01	PID01	CUG01	CID01	SAG01	SID01	02.34 %
COM04	PRG01	*****	CUG01	*****	SAG01	*****	03.45 %
End of File							

Exhibit 13.6. Commission File and Table

```
Dynamic Condition Search

TRA01PRG01PID01CUG01CID01SAG01SID01
Commission for
  PRG01PID01CUG01CID01SAG01SID01 is 02.34%

TRA02PRG02PID01CUG02CID01SAG02SID01
Commission for
  *****PID01*****CID01*****SID01 is 01.23%

TRA03PRG01PID02CUG01CID02SAG01SID02
Commission for
  PRG01*****CUG01*****SAG01***** is 03.45%

TRA04PRG02PID02CUG02CID02SAG02SID02
Commission for
  ***************************** is 00.12%
End of Job
```

Exhibit 13.7. Program Output

Let us take the above step by step before we tackle the detailed example below. When the dynamic search module reads a transaction record, it then uses each condition record in turn to build a search argument until a match is encountered. The first condition record (shown in this example) directs that each field (because it has all 1s) in the transaction record be used for the search argument. The second condition record says to use only the odd-numbered (1,3,5) fields (which are the fields with 1s) in the transaction record when building the search argument; the even-numbered fields (which have 0s) are replaced with *****. The third transaction record is just the opposite, with the even-numbered fields used as they are and the odd-numbered replaced with *****. The fourth (and last) condition record has all 0s, which means that all transaction record fields are replaced with *****, which matches the default (first) record in the commission file.

The following numbered steps go through the sample files in great detail, keeping in mind the above summary presentation. We suggest that interested readers build their own arguments and follow along with this presentation.

1. The first transaction record

    TRA01PRG01PID01CUG01CID01SAG01SID01

    is read.
2. The first condition record CON01111111 (all 1s) is read.
3. As a result, all the fields in the record are used as the search argument.
4. This yields PRG01PID01CUG01CID01SAG01SID01.
5. Each commission file record is read until there is a match with this search argument or the end of file is reached. In this instance, there is a match on the third record, and the commission is 2.34 percent.
6. Then the second transaction record

    TRA01PRG02PID01CUG02CID01SAG02SID01

    is read.
7. The first search argument built is

    PRG02PID01CUG02CID01SAG02SID01.

    This again is based on using all the fields and is not found in any of the commission file records.
8. The next search argument built is

    PRG02*****CUG02*****SAG02*****

    using the next (second) condition record, which says use every other field. This again is not found.
9. The next search argument built is

    *****PID01*****CID01*****SID01

    using the third condition record. This is found at the second commission record, and the commission is 1.23 percent.
10. For the third transaction record, the arguments that are built are as follows:

```
PRG01PID02CUG01CID02SAG01SID02 not found
PRG01*****CUG01*****SAG01***** found at the
fourth commission record and the commission is
3.45%.
```

11. For the fourth transaction record, the augments that are built are as follows:

```
PRG02PID02CUG02CID02SAG02SID02 not found
PRG02*****CUG02*****SAG02***** not found
*****PID02*****CID02*****SID02 not found
************************** found at the first
commission record and the commission is 0.12%,
which is the default commission.
```

The last record in the condition file must have all zeros, and a record in the commission file must have all *s (or whatever symbol is used to indicate that a field is not used). This combination ensures that a commission (the default) is always "found," even when a specific combination of fields is not used.

Business staff use the condition file to adjust the dynamic-condition-search algorithm until the required condition value is found in the commission file. No program modifications are required to accommodate new rules so long as there are no more than (in this case) six factors determining a condition. The choice of factors, in the implemented solution, is linked by condition descriptors, which describe data about conditions (name, title, factors, computation rules, etc.). This permits the altering of labels, depending on the conditions used. The generalized algorithm is not affected because it handles any values passed to it.

As an example of the effect of a control-data change, suppose that it was decided to give a new salesman, Bruce, a special deal — a commission of 5.55 percent on all sales. All that would be required to do this could be to add the record CON04000001 to the condition file and the record COM05************************Bruce05.55 to the commission file. Then a transaction that had Bruce as the salesman identifier would yield a 5.55 percent commission.

The requirements informally described before are now formally defined and represented in such a way that business staff, manipulating the contents of the condition and the commission files, can maintain them. Of course a routine such as this, with its table searching and decision making, may take longer to develop and execute than a less flexible approach. However, given today's processing speeds and memory availability and the necessity to respond to changing business needs in near real time, this appears, in almost all cases, to be a worthwhile trade-off.

13.2.2 *The UniverSIS Evaluator*

This section introduces the UniverSIS Evaluator and describes its general operation. A much more detailed presentation with examples is included in Chapter 18.

The goal of flexibility often runs up against the reality of complex business requirements. In a university, examples include admission requirements, registration requirements, charging requirements, and eligibility requirements of various types. These requirements combine logic with valid values. Even in systems where developers have placed the lists of valid values under user control, the logic is typically coded in programs. Because change in business logic is a high-cost maintenance item, the UniverSIS developers analyzed how a system handles business logic. The goal was to place control of business logic in the hands of business staff for those processes in which the business rules are known to change.

One way of placing control of business logic in the hands of business staff is the process of selecting records based on specified criteria. Selection logic, often used in report processing, actually involves specifying business rules. Business staff want to select a group of students who fit a particular profile. They specify parameters. A program compares the parameter values with the values on the student's record. If the values match, the record is selected. The users control the valid values, but the programmer codes the logic directly in the program.

```
IF ACADEMIC-INTEREST EQ "parameter"
```

If the parameter value is HISTORY, the above statement becomes

```
IF ACADEMIC-INTEREST EQ HISTORY
```

In this example, the logic IF ACADEMIC-INTEREST EQ is coded in the program, and the parameter HISTORY is under business control. If the result of this statement is true, the student is selected. Note that the use of parameters rather than hard-coding HISTORY provides some flexibility. Programmers can add complexity and flexibility to this approach, allowing ranges of values and multiple input parameters, but the logic is tied to specific data elements.

The UniverSIS developers built something more flexible: a set of general-purpose tools that give users control over both the logic and the values. Business staff define and store criteria. The system evaluates those criteria and determines whether an individual meets them.

For example, the admissions office might wish to recruit students from a particular area who are interested in science. The criteria might look like the following.

IF		ACADEMIC-INTEREST	EQ	BIOLOGY
	or	ACADEMIC-INTEREST	EQ	CHEMISTRY
	or	ACADEMIC-INTEREST	EQ	PHYSICS
AND		ZIP-CODE	GE	12000
	and	ZIP-CODE	NE	13000
	and	ZIP-CODE	LE	14999

Selection elements (ACADEMIC-INTEREST, ZIP-CODE) are predefined. A separate selection-element module is coded to gather the data for each selection element. A selection element can be a derived field. It need not be a stored data element. For example, elements such as "highest test score," "grade point average," and "enrollment hours" have been defined.

In developing the module used to enter the conditions, the developers considered allowing the users to have complete control. That is, they considered giving the users control over all aspects of the condition, specifying AND and OR where appropriate. Given the difficulty even professional programmers have getting Boolean logic correct, the developers thought better of it. The module they developed allows the users to enter element, operator, and value, but the system controls the AND/OR logic. The key to defining the AND/OR logic correctly is sorting the statements by element and by value within element.

The evaluation module uses an algorithm for parsing a binary tree. The tool is designed to handle repeating fields and repeating groups. For example, if the criteria specified MAJOR EQ HISTORY and TERM EQ FALL2000, and if the student has multiple records, the tool will find a "true" condition only when a major of HISTORY and a term of FALL2000 occur on the same record. A module has been developed to allow business staff to test their conditions before putting them into production.

To summarize, the developers have built an evaluator mechanism in which criteria for business decisions are defined in the following hierarchy. The assumption is that all criteria can be expressed in the form of statements, or sets of statements, to which the answer is either true or false.

        And   Or   And

Business Decision < === >> Requirement < === >> Condition < === >> Subcondition

- All subconditions must be met for the parent condition to be met.
- At least one condition must be met for the parent requirement to be satisfied.
- All requirements must be satisfied for the business decision to be made.

The developers believe that they have taken this approach to the point where any logical business decision criteria based on data stored in the system can be defined in terms of these requirements, conditions, and subconditions. In other words, they have defined a general-purpose tool — a flexible tool — that can be used for much more than its original purpose of facilitating selection of records for reports.

This evaluator tool has been incorporated into the business logic of core administrative processes. For example, the student accounts office defines rules that allow the system to assess charges automatically. The admissions office defines rules that allow the system to make automatic admission decisions for a significant percentage of applicants. Other examples involve targeting of prospects for recruitment, analysis of student loan eligibility, and analysis of health insurance eligibility. The business staff and developers continue to find many other uses for the tool.

A mechanism such as the Evaluator is complex. Its development therefore involves a significant cost in money and time. Once completed, however, it is available for any business purpose that requires selection of records. Additional Evaluator programming occurs only when new selection elements are required. The selection element programs can typically be written and tested in two hours or less. For example, the registrar's office may have a process that selects students using the Evaluator and produces mailing labels for those students. If a new selection element is needed, e.g., ACADEMIC-PROGRAM, a programmer writes a specialized program that will retrieve that information for the Evaluator. ACADEMIC-PROGRAM is then added to the pool of selection elements. The rest is in the hands of the business staff. ACADEMIC-PROGRAM is now available for use by any business area, not just the registrar's office, and for any purpose, not just the production of mailing labels. The programmer does not need to be concerned with how or where the ACADEMIC-PROGRAM routine is being used. It is a tool in the user's toolbox. To cite a complex example, the student accounts office identified all the elements involved in assessing tuition and fees. Once the specialized modules for these elements were written, IT involvement in maintenance of the business rules ended. Business staff in the student accounts office maintain the rules without IT intervention.

Another cost of the Evaluator approach is the amount of processing time required. A program written for a specific purpose might well be more efficient than a general-purpose tool that must retrieve instructions stored as data. However, we believe that, over time, the benefits of flexible design will generally exceed the potential additional development and processing costs.

13.3 Summary

- Structure-oriented techniques for flexible software design take the form of information structures composed of generic entity types and many-to-many relationships that identify and exploit common data characteristics and common patterns of relationships between and within entities.
- Systems that follow structure-oriented techniques for flexible software design, through data value and cardinality changes, avoid information structure (and processing) modifications as the business develops and new requirements are encountered.
- Generic structures generally absorb business changes without modification, even when such changes are not known in advance.
- Process-oriented techniques identify and exploit common logic patterns, supported by common information structures.
- In a flexible system, business rule processing must not be buried in program code. Business rule processing must be under the control of business personnel, not IT personnel.
- The dynamic condition search and the UniverSIS Evaluator present two examples of business rule processing that meet the requirements for a flexible system.
- Although the approaches presented in this chapter may require more computing resources, given today's ever-increasing computer capabilities and their ever-decreasing costs, it seems more than prudent to reduce maintenance costs by enabling business personnel to make business rule changes without having to call upon IT to modify the program code.

As shown in this chapter, structure-oriented techniques for flexible software design go hand in hand with process-oriented techniques for flexible software design. Without generic stable information structures, it is difficult to produce stable flexible processes.

The application of the dynamic condition search and evaluator tools is limited only by the designer's imagination. More information on the UniverSIS Evaluator operation and implementation is provided in Chapter 18.

Appendix 13: Dynamic Condition Search Program Listing (in Java)

```java
import java.util.*;
import java.io.*;
import java.awt.*;
import java.lang.*;
public class DynamicConditionSearch
{   public static void buildArgument(String s)throws
IOException
    {    String t, c, argument = "", commission;
        int i, j,k, l;
        t = s;
        RandomAccessFile C = new RandomAccessFile
            ("C:\\java\\DynamicConditionSearch\\Data\\
            Condition.dat","r");
        if (C != null)
        {   c = C.readLine();
            commission = "00.00";
            while (!c.equals("EOF"))
            {    //System.out.println ("c = " + c );
                //EnterKey e1 = new EnterKey();
                argument = "";
                for (i = 0; i < 6; i++)
                { if (c.substring(i + 5,i + 6).equals("1"))
                    {     l = (i * 5 )+ 5;
                      k = l + 5;
                      argument = argument + t.substring(l,k);
                    } //if
                    else argument = argument + "*****";
                } //i loop
                commission = findCommission(argument);
                c = C.readLine();
                if (!commission.equals("00.00")) c = "EOF";
            } //while
```

```
    System.out.println ("Commission for \n    " +
    argument +
        " is " + commission + "%");
    }
}//method


public static String findCommission(String r)throws
IOException
    {       String s;
    s = r;
    String commission, comrec;
    commission = "00.00";
    RandomAccessFile Com = new RandomAccessFile
        ("C:\\java\\DynamicConditionSearch\\Data\\
        Commission.dat","r");
    if (Com != null)
    {   comrec = Com.readLine();
        String lookup = comrec.substring(5,35);

        while (!comrec.equals("EOF"))
        { //System.out.println("lookup  = " + lookup +
        //              "\nArgument = " + s);
        //EnterKey e1 = new EnterKey();
        if (s.equals(lookup))
            commission = comrec.substring(35,40);
        comrec = Com.readLine();
        //if (!commission.equals("00.00")) comrec =
        "EOF";
        if (!comrec.equals ("EOF")) lookup =
        comrec.substring(5,35);
    } //while

    return commission;
    }
```

```java
public static void main (String [] args) throws
IOException
   {   System.out.println("Dynamic Condition Search");

        String data;
        String argument;

        RandomAccessFile T = new RandomAccessFile
           ("c:\\java\\DynamicConditionSearch\\data\\
           Transaction.dat","r");
        if (T != null)
        {   data = T.readLine();
           while (!data.equals("EOF"))
           {   System.out.println("\n" + data);
              buildArgument(data);
              data = T.readLine();
           }
        }
        System.out.println ("End of Job");
        EnterKey ke = new EnterKey();
   }
}
```

Chapter 14

Implementing Stable Identifiers

Chapter 7 presented many types of unstable identifiers to be avoided when implementing a flexible software system. This chapter presents the "how to" of implementing stable identifiers in multiple contexts. We start with the basic rule and then discuss its various applications.

14.1 The Basic Rule

Our basic rule for generating stable identifiers (IDs) is as follows:

> A stable-entity identifier is assigned on a next-sequentially-available-number basis starting with 0 and incrementing by 1.

There should be no omissions or reservations of blocks of numbers. Each assigned value is unique and contains no explicit or implied information of any kind. A practical rule regarding the size of the identifier is that the number of digits in an identifier is that which accommodates ten times the highest of three informed estimates of the maximum number of instances of the entity likely to occur over the lifetime of the enterprise or for the next 20 years, whichever is longer. (This is equivalent to adding an extra digit to the estimated number.)

This rule forms IDs from numbers simply for convenience in assigning them, whether manually or automatically. Obviously, using numbers and letters in combination would give more bang for the byte, but they are not conveniently assigned sequentially. Sequential assignment itself is not essential; random assignment is also acceptable. The convenience comes in having an easily calculated next number, an algorithm that will never run out of numbers, and a result that will always give uniqueness on the first attempt. It has been suggested that ID numbering start with 1, because 0 means the absence of something and has no meaning. Zero serves us well, however, because that is what we want — no meaning. We know it is hard to look into the future 20 years hence, but we know of many systems that are over 20 years old. Try the life of the enterprise if that is easier.

Exhibit 14.1 presents an example where this basic rule is used to generate stable identifiers for a manufacturing resource planning (MRP) system.

14.2 Applying the Basic Rule

The following are factors in applying the basic rule:

- Internal and external identifiers
- Hidden versus exposed internal identifiers
- Global internal identifiers
- Identifier size
- Reuse of IDs assigned to deleted (obsolete) things
- Distributed ID assignment
- Codes
- Internet names

Most of the following material is oriented toward design considerations in implementing system-assigned identifiers.

14.2.1 Internal and External Identifiers

If an existing real-world ID is a fully stable ID, then it can be used as an ID in the automated-world system, and it is a simple matter to incorporate it by starting the automatic assignment with the next unused value. If it is not a stable ID — and most existing IDs are not — then it cannot be used as a primary identifier in the automated-world system. There are basically two options for resolving this:

1. Replace the old unstable ID with the new stable ID. This is the simplest solution if costs and preferences permit. However, the

Bruce: "We need to decide how many digits to include in the identifiers for our new manufacturing resource planning (MRP) software. "

Cindy: "Shouldn't six digits be enough? Six digits will handle a million unique entity instances."

Walt: "Wait a minute—remember the basic rule! We need to ask three experts how many unique entity instances there will be over the life of Flexible Manufacturing Enterprise (FME) or 20 years if we don't last that long—heaven forbid."

Bo: "I have already asked Joe over in the plant, and he said, 'What the h____ is an entity instance.' So I had to rephrase the question. Joe, I said, how may unique items, operations, jigs, machines, workers, suppliers, customers, etc. are you engaged with? He looked at me blankly and said 'Let me get back to you.' Well he did a few days later and said about 20,000."

Bruce: "That's good. I asked Joan, Joe's supervisor, pretty much the same question and received essentially the same response. She said that right now it's about 30,000 but, given FME's expansion plans, she expected the number to be almost 100,000 in three to five years."

Cindy: "Well that's two. Who else do we ask?"

Just then Alex stopped in to pay his respects. Alex, just retired, had been involved in the MRP system that FME acquired five years ago and was now being replaced, as it was not flexible enough to handle even today's requirements, much less those three to five years out.

Bo: "Hi Alex, glad that you stopped by."

A little chitchat followed, with Alex being welcomed and saying that he was glad to see us, and then Bruce asked, "Alex, you know that the identifiers in the current MRP system have caused us all sorts of problems. The new system will automatically assign them. Just how many 'things' do we handle over in the plant? We have heard 20,000, 30,000, and 100,000."

Alex: "Well I am not sure—but the main problem with the prior estimates is that we forgot that identifiers are assigned to work in process—and that really ups the number. How about 200,000 or so?"

Bruce: "Thanks Alex."

Cindy: "Well 200,000 appears to be the highest informed estimate and ten times that is 2 million, so it looks like seven digits will be required—and since even numbers seem to work best, lets make it eight digits."

Bruce and Bo: "OK, eight it will be."

Bruce: "Now we need to be assured that each time a new entity instance of any kind occurs it receives the next sequentially available number. The first one will be 0 and the next 1 on up to 99,999,999 if we or the system should live that long."

Bo: "How do we ensure that the next sequential number will always be used?"

Bruce: "We will use the routine I just wrote called 'Barber.' When you invoke Barber, it returns the next sequential number—just like a Barber says 'Next' and internally stores the next next."

Cindy: "OK, I hope that takes care of our MRP identifier, because I am already late for another meeting—designing the new general ledger system."

Bruce: "Well, make sure you get a handle on how many entity instances the general ledger system will have over 20 years or the FME's life, and make sure that eight digits will handle that and the 200,000 we have already identified"

Exhibit 14.1.   Basic Rule for Generating Stable IDs

costs of repopulating a large base of existing IDs may be unacceptable, and system users may object to adoption of a rational naming convention.

2. Use the new ID internally and the old ID externally. The stable ID is used for all internal identification and reference purposes without exception. The automated-world system maintains a cross-reference between the internal and external IDs. The end user has the option of using the external ID when communicating with the system.

Assume the second option is necessary, as shown in Exhibit 14.2. Once defined this way, the Product ID is then used for all subsequent references to product in the database, and the Product No. thereafter only exists internally in one place: the product record. This limits any instability effects that might occur with the Product Nos. by isolating them to one nonprimary key field.

An example for Product ID (internal ID) and Product No. (external ID) would be:

Product: | Product ID || Product No. | Product Desc. | Product Unit Price | ... |

Exhibit 14.2.   Internal and External Identifiers Together

For this approach to work, the external ID must be declared as both an indexed field, for performance reasons, and as an alternative primary key field, because it must remain in 1:1 correspondence with the internal ID. This is simply a matter of ensuring that the external ID is unique. This is easily accomplished if the database management system (DBMS) permits multiple fields to be declared as nonduplicate. Otherwise, special processing will have to be programmed to maintain the 1:1 correspondence. It is also essential that the information previously conveyed to the user by the external ID be broken out as separately maintainable attributes, as shown in Exhibit 14.3.

Note that this approach can also be used if it becomes necessary to integrate two or more systems that have independently employed strictly unique IDs. They almost certainly will have duplicate IDs among them. One of them gets chosen as the internal ID, and the others become external IDs.

14.2.2 Hidden versus Exposed Internal Identifiers

Others who have proposed the use of information-free IDs in automated-world systems tend to recommend restricting them to internal use only

Product No.: HDL0506R, where

HDL	Product Line (heavy duty liquid)
0506	Product Seq. No within Product Line
R	Special Use (R = refill, O = original, S = sample)

becomes:
Product: | Product ID|| Product No.| Product Line |Prod Seq |Special use| Product Desc. |
          | 00012378 || HDL0506R | HDL | 0506 | R| Dish Detergent|

Similarly, if the product has a UPC number:

Product UPC: 57000 02306, where

57000	UPC Vendor No.
02306	UPC Product No. within Vendor No.

becomes:

Product:| Product ID|| Product UPC | Vendor ID| UPC Product No. |Product Desc. |...|
        | 00012378|| 57000 02306 | 000046| 02306 | Dish Detergent |...|

Notice the value 000046 is an internal ID value for vendor. Thus we need a vendor relation, which includes the cross-reference between the internal vendor ID and the UPC vendor no.:
Vendor: | Vendor ID || Vendor Desc. | UPC Vendor No |...|
          | 000046 || Procter & Gamble | 57000 |...|

The Vendor ID is also six digits because it comes from the same pool of sequentially assigned identifiers.

But, because the UPC Council may assign more than one number to the same vendor, we need to move the UPC Vendor No from the vendor relation to a third relation:

UPC Vendor: | UPC Vendor No || Vendor ID |
             | 57000 || 000046 |
             | 60044 || 000046 |
             | 87301 || 000046 |

Note: In this presentation No has been used for the vendor designation assigned by the UPC Council and ID for our stable, internally assigned designation.

Exhibit 14.3. Keeping Old Information

and to make them transparent to the system user [Date, 1984; Kent, 1978]. The question being raised is whether the information-free internal identifier is also appropriate for external use in the real-world system. The authors' bias is that the end user would benefit from employing a stable ID in the real-world system. Such use does not preclude the use of external IDs. By exposing internal IDs to the end user, the best of both worlds is obtained.

At this point, it is appropriate to expand on the topic of surrogates that was briefly mentioned in Chapter 7. Some commercial DBMS products employ information-free IDs to permanently identify each database *record*. For this reason, we call them record sequence numbers (RSNs) rather than surrogates, as they are assigned on a next-sequential-number basis to each record in a file in the chronological order in which the records were

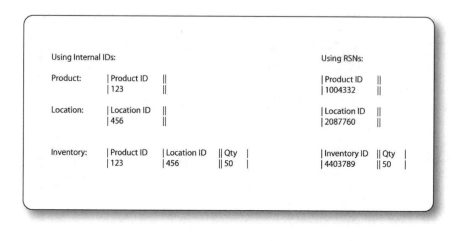

Exhibit 14.4. Loss of Information When Applying Record Sequence Numbers (RSNs) to Identify Association Entities

created. While RSNs are available to the application programmer, their use is limited to specialized utility functions such as supporting improved retrieval performance. That is, while they can be exploited to improve the physical response requirements of an application, they are not needed to support the logical requirements of the application.

The RSN should not be confused with the internal ID as we defined it above, and it should not be considered as a candidate for the internal ID role. In particular, there would be a loss of essential information when applied to identifying association entities. An association record's ID is formed by combining the IDs of its parents (referred to in the context of the association record as foreign keys). For example, in Exhibit 14.4, the record for a specific Product 123 has an RSN of 1004332, and the record for a specific Location 456 has an RSN of 2087760. It might appear that these RSNs could be used as internal IDs because they are permanent values. However, the record for the Inventory of Product 123 in Location 456 has an RSN of 4403789, which does not include the information that the inventory is for Product 123 in Location 456. That is, the RSNs of records representing association entities do not contain the foreign keys of the entities so associated.

So, regardless of whether our DBMS uses stable IDs internally, we are left, as before, with a need to design a proper internal ID assignment facility that delivers the next available ID (globally) upon request from an application system. The application system then can assemble association-entity IDs as needed to retain association information.

14.2.3 Global Internal Identifiers

Handling duplicate internal IDs that arise when systems are merged was discussed in Section 14.2.1. But there are two additional ways in which duplicate internal IDs can occur: through consolidator applications and through entity supertyping. Assigning internal identifiers globally, without regard to entity type, will prevent such duplicates from occurring.

What are sometimes termed "consolidator" applications can give rise to duplicate IDs. The accounts payable application is an example. At a food distributor company, the freight management system assigned IDs to shipment invoices and fed them to the accounts payable system. The warehouse management system also fed its independently identified invoices to the same payables system. Despite care taken to ensure that the IDs were assigned from different number ranges, the different rates of invoice generation resulted in duplicate IDs arriving at the payables system every few years. The ancient payables system did unspeakable things to records with duplicate IDs, and it typically took some weeks for the overlap to be recognized and corrected. This situation worsened with the addition of a new brokerage system and its independently (and manually) assigned invoice IDs. Of course, in a mixed environment of packaged and custom applications, it is unrealistic to expect all applications to use a common ID generator. In that case, one is forced to ensure that consolidator applications such as accounts receivable expect duplicates and handle them appropriately. This could range from simply raising an error condition to treating all inbound IDs as external IDs, as described in Section 14.2.1 The essential point is that, where possible and practical, one should assign internal IDs globally regardless of entity type to avoid possible future duplicates.

The ability to support changes in the classification of an entity is an essential element of the flexible system. The structures that support flexible subtyping were discussed in Chapter 9. It is important to recognize that supertyping as well as subtyping can occur. For example, suppose an existing real-estate entity and an existing equipment entity are subsumed under a more generic asset entity, as shown in Exhibit 14.5. A globally assigned internal ID would have avoided the duplicate Asset ID values. (The example in Exhibit 14.5 is only to illustrate duplicate IDs and does not reflect encoding of asset type or the possibility that an asset might be of more than one type.)

Another benefit of a global internal ID is that it supports an ultimate supertype entity. Supertyping cannot be done without IT intervention. Only subtyping can be done dynamically. Implementing the example of Exhibit 14.5, where a supertype entity replaced existing entities, would entail significant information-structure change and consequent reprogramming,

```
Real Estate:    |Real Estate ID       || Real Estate Desc.  |
                | 000001              || 4th and Main Bldg. |
                | 000002              || 7th St. Office      |

Equipment:      | Equipment ID        || Equipment Desc.    |
                | 000001              || Punch Press        |
                | 000002              || Rotary Kiln        |
                | 000003              || Cutter             |

The result will be duplicate Asset IDs:

Asset:          | Asset ID            || Asset Desc.        |
                | 000001              || 4th and Main Bldg. |
                | 000001              || Punch Press        |
                | 000002              || 7th St. Office     |
                | 000002              || Rotary Kiln        |
                | 000003              || Cutter             |
```

Exhibit 14.5. Nonglobally Assigned Identifiers Resulting in Duplicate Identifiers

whether a global ID is used or not. Plus, in the absence of a global ID, the asset type would need to be embedded in the Asset ID to ensure uniqueness. But if an ultimate supertype entity is defined such that all other entities are automatically subtypes of it, then subsequent supertyping of existing entities can take the form of intermediate subtypes, with the possibility of handling them dynamically.

14.2.4 Identifier Size

A practical consequence of global ID assignment is that the ID must be large enough to accommodate all instances of all types of things that can be expected to occur in the lifetime of the system while also allowing for multiple systems sharing a single ID-assignment facility. This is why, in Exhibit 14.1, Bruce suggested to Cindy that the potential instance counts in the proposed general-ledger software be added to the estimates just received for the MRP software.

This leads to two design issues: the response time of a shared ID-assignment function and the presentation of a large ID. The resource-contention problem has numerous solutions, including keeping the next available ID in memory or employing a resource-allocation algorithm. For presentation, display only significant digits. For IDs over ten digits, use delimiters to create groups of four to six digits to aid recall.

14.2.5 Reuse of IDs Assigned to Deleted (Obsolete) Things

Just do not do it.

14.2.6 Distributed ID Assignment

For various reasons, an ID-assignment facility must sometimes be physically distributed, say, to different plants in different cities. In such cases, a block of nonoverlapping numbers may need to be distributed to a separate ID assigner. There are two considerations in this case. First, as we saw earlier, some mechanism must be in place to ensure that there is no overlap in the IDs assigned, or, failing that, there must be some mechanism to cope with a temporary overlap. Second, application systems must not exploit any information that can be inferred from the number range in which an ID occurs. If that information is significant, then it must be recorded as an attribute. This is not a trivial concern. It raises the issue of what we call circumvention paths, which are discussed at the end of this chapter.

14.2.7 Codes

> *Codes are not usually accorded the status of a full identifier due to the often mistaken notion that one is encoding only an attribute rather than an entity.*

Many codes found in systems today are unstable. Codes are not usually accorded the status of a full identifier due to the often mistaken notion that one is encoding only an attribute rather than an entity. For example, the color of a product might be encoded as R (red), B (blue), G (green); or the product line might be encoded as HDL (heavy duty liquid), LDL (light duty liquid), DRY (dry powder), etc. Virtually any attribute is a candidate for encoding for ease of data entry, space savings, and, of course, uniqueness. But virtually any attribute also has the potential to become an entity in its own right about which information is to be kept.

Color, to interested parties as diverse as chemical engineers and advertisers, has numerous relevant attributes: how the color is produced, its reflectivity, its covering ability, its connotations, etc. In a system initially designed to track shipping orders, warehouses were encoded as M (main warehouse), 2 (2nd Street warehouse), and B (Bank Street warehouse).

Not long afterward, it became necessary to maintain information about the warehouses themselves; moreover, six regional warehouses were added, and the Bank Street warehouse became the "main" distribution warehouse.

Codes do not cope well with a change in status from attribute to thing:

- They are often abbreviations subject to duplicates if the number of code values grows.
- They have usually been exempted from referential integrity.
- The corresponding code tables, if they exist at all, are often implemented in some special way, such as by using the DBMS enumeration facility, which is not accessible to the business staff.

There should be no distinction between what is to be encoded and what is to receive proper identifiers. Whatever is to be labeled should receive a system-assigned ID and should be implemented as a normal relation subject to system user maintenance as well as referential and existence integrity checks. Existing codes should be accommodated in the same way as existing IDs by making them external IDs.

The generic-entity cloud (GEC), introduced in Chapter 10, eliminates the possibility of problems caused by codes. Within the GEC, codes are treated as entities. They are subject to referential integrity, and translation tables that are maintained by appropriate customer personnel are automatically provided. In practice, it is reasonable to exempt some codes from this discipline due to their expected very-long-term stability; for example, we all know what a W2 is! An admission: the UniverSIS system, even with its many flexible characteristics, does not employ system-assigned global IDs for codes.

14.2.8 Internet Names

A significant issue in Internet operations concerns the persistence of names. The Web is full of broken strands. In some cases, the object referenced by a link no longer exists; in other cases, the object still exists, but the name that serves as its link has been changed. This is a serious matter that will soon have repercussions that go far beyond the current inconvenience experienced by people who come upon a broken link. As Internet-served data becomes integrated into the operation of application systems, this problem will have the same effects as a system that failed to maintain existence and referential integrity in the databases used by those same applications. Both would be equivalent failures.

The Web currently provides no automatic detection or appropriate response to an attempt to (a) delete an object to which a link points or

(b) establish a link to a nonexistent object. More importantly, even with such an Internet integrity facility, name changes would have the potential to disrupt the processing logic of those back-office applications that use Web-served data. Typical URN (universal resource name), URI (universal resource identifier), and URL (universal resource locator) naming schemes commit virtually all the destabilization errors we outlined in Chapter 7. In particular, they employ embedded information of every stripe and extensive hierarchical qualification. URLs, like any identifier, are designable, and when there is a persistence requirement to be met, then

> designing mostly means leaving information out.... What to leave out — Everything! After the creation date, putting any information in the name is asking for trouble [Berners-Lee, 1998].

The issue for Berners-Lee is how to have name stability while retaining the ability to progressively resolve the name through a distributed server network to a specific servable object.

The difficulty with most proposals to date is their failure to seriously consider the possibility of designing a system that completely separates addressability from identification. For example, conceptually, one could maintain a master identifier-assignment facility that assigns a strictly unique identifier when presented with a new resource address, returns an address when presented with an ID, and updates its ID/address cross-reference when presented with a change of resource address for an existing ID. What is not easily managed, of course, is the scale of such an operation. Nevertheless, the consequences of failing to apply the principle of strict uniqueness are clear. What is not clear is how to apply the basic rule. Where do the informed estimates come from? Just exactly how many digits would the identifier require? And what about the pages within specific Web sites — would they start over with zero or go back to the master assignment facility?

14.3 Circumvention Paths — Back to the Beginning

Flexible systems need stable IDs, and stable IDs need flexible systems.

Customers of automated-world systems are quite ingenious at devising ways to circumvent limitations in the systems with which they work. Customers frequently resort to using identifiers to convey information that is not otherwise maintainable in the system as it currently functions. The authors summarize this as "beware the asterisk"! This does not mean that system users have some diabolical urge to destabilize their systems; it simply shows their understandable and creative reaction to the need to extend the functionality of a system despite the IT maintenance backlog. This phenomenon can be very deeply ingrained. This also illustrates how important it is to do a thorough examination of existing identifiers when analyzing an existing system. Old IDs and how they are interpreted by system users are a source of data items that otherwise might be missed.

For example, Marty, our client, insisted that nonprofit hospital entities have even-numbered identifiers, for-profit hospitals have odd-numbered identifiers, U.S. hospitals have identifiers less than 1000, and Canadian hospitals have identifiers over 1000. He insisted on this coding scheme, even though this information was stored as attributes within the system. After all, we had designed the system to be flexible! He did not recognize that the numeric identification scheme had nothing to do with the real world. His view was shaped by the limitations in the automated-world systems that he had encountered in the past. Marty was so used to circumvention that he circumvented even when it was no longer necessary.

Also, the person or group who is responsible for adding new instances of a thing to a system often acquires the privilege of defining the naming convention for that thing. The definer then exploits this by embedding information that is useful to the definer within the identifier. Worse, the definer then assumes a parochial attitude about the universal appeal of this information to all other users, now and into the future. Indeed, the privileged definer typically designs an elaborately meaningful ID to demonstrate that the privilege has been taken seriously.

System-assigned IDs remove this particular circumvention path. This is a serious matter. The use of meaningless system-assigned IDs is not a technique that can be employed in a vacuum. It must be part of a program to provide flexible systems that are easily maintained and that commits to delivering something like maintenance-on-demand in those cases where a user option for extending system functionality has been eliminated. Flexible systems need stable IDs, and stable IDs need flexible systems.

14.4 Summary

- Stable identifiers used by automated-world systems must be assigned automatically on a next-sequential-number basis.
- Identifiers should also be assigned globally without regard to entity type to preclude duplicate IDs where different entity types become subtypes of a common supertype.

- All internal references in an application database are made via stable identifiers. Any unstable identifiers that are retained for end-user convenience are for external use only as secondary access keys.
- Codes should be given the status of identifiers.

As we saw in Chapter 7, there are numerous forms of unstable identifiers. Stable identifiers are powerfully simple: the next sequential number with sufficient digits to handle all entities likely to be encountered during the lifetime of the system, with a digit to spare. While there may be several complications, depending upon the nature of the automated-world system, designers must not lose track of the simple fact that identifiers must be stable if the system is to be flexible.

Chapter 15

Testing and Maintenance of Flexible Software

It is generally understood that testing is essential, even on a small software modification, to ensure the fidelity of the modification. Testing is required not only for a modification in the system code or information structure, but it is also required for changes in input data if the purpose of the data is to "instruct" the system, i.e., to alter the system's reaction to transactions. Such input data fall into the category of regulatory data.

When testing changes to regulatory data that will result in implementation of new or modified business rules, it is not enough to test entry of the data. The fact that the system accepted the data may mean only that they were entered in correct form using valid values. That in itself does not guarantee that they will produce correct results. Programmers are all too familiar with the distinction between correct program syntax and correct program results.

Testing involves executing system processes and comparing the results with results determined to be correct. Testing occurs in two distinct phases: (a) during development, prior to system operation, and (b) during ongoing operations and modifications. See Exhibit 15.1 for a discussion of real-life testing challenges.

15.1 Errors Encountered in Testing

Errors encountered in testing fall into four categories:

First Concern: Programs Must Not Crash

One of the authors was responsible for the development of an online data-entry negative-option book-club software. Dick, his boss, was a tiger to work for, so our author was very careful with his work. Unfortunately, he had a rather loose programmer, Irvin, working for him doing the GUI screens. At the end of each development point our author would sit down at Irvin's screens and run through various scenarios. All too frequently the programs would crash. At that point, Irvin would say, "What did you do? We will tell the business staff who utilize the system not to do that when they operate it." That was unacceptable, and our author sent Irvin back to correct his program — before Dick saw the problem. Needless to say, regardless of whether the system is flexible or not, one of the first concerns is that the software not crash, but report the problem gracefully to the business staff so that they can correct it and get on with their work.

Getting Rid of Bad Data

One of the authors developed a mailing label system. The system used a match code developed from the data within the name and address when a new address was added. The match code included a check digit produced from the data within the match code. At some point an error was detected in the check digit calculation. After the error was corrected, it was impossible to change or delete label data entered before the error was corrected. So another, nonflexible, change had to be made to the software to bypass the check digit test. This shows how difficult it is to get bad data out of a system once it gets in.

Importance of Correct Results

The service bureau run by one of the authors contracted to take over the payroll of a local company. To do this, they had to write a software product to accept the payroll inputs, do the calculations, and produce the weekly, quarterly, and annual outputs. The contract called for a parallel run that produced outputs that agreed with their existing system. This proved to be an almost intractable problem. Week after week the results from the two systems just did not agree. Finally, our author actually ran hand calculations and found that the service bureau's new software was producing correct results and, that the local company's software was producing erroneous results. It took several rounds to convince the clients that the service bureau's results were correct. This was a very costly lesson in both analyst time and computer resources. Compare the new software's results with results known to be correct—not to results from old software.

Exhibit 15.1. Real-Life Testing Challenges

1. Operator error
2. Invalid data error
3. Processing logic error
4. Hardware and system software error

When researching errors, good programmers typically proceed in the order shown above. They almost never discover that system software (operating system, DBMS, programming language, etc.) is at the root of the problem.

15.1.1 Operator Error

Operator error typically involves recording valid but incorrect data. Because no business rules are violated, the system cannot trap the error. Examples would be typing an individual's address incorrectly, transposing digits in an amount, etc. There is no system protection against valid but erroneous data entry. Operator errors are typically the easiest to detect and correct.

15.1.2 Invalid Data Error

Invalid data typically results from a hole in the business rule logic, an error of omission. Discovery of invalid data will be traced to data validation logic. Rigorous design and testing at initial implementation keeps this type of error infrequent, but any time new data structures and programs are introduced, there is a chance that such errors will occur. This is where a flexible system has an advantage over an inflexible system. The data structures and supporting business rule logic will be stable, i.e., they will not need to change as business staff make system modifications through changes in regulatory data.

15.1.3 Processing Logic Error

Processing logic errors involve either (a) the system doing something it should not do or (b) the system not doing something it should do. Such errors also indicate inadequate testing of scenarios. It is critical that unlikely scenarios be tested as well as likely scenarios.

Unfortunately, when logic errors have resulted in generation of invalid data, IT staff intervention is needed to find and correct the records. It does not matter whether the system that generated the invalid data is flexible or inflexible, or whether the logic was coded or maintained as data by business staff. There is nothing magic about flexible systems in this regard. Correction of records is a highly technical and time-consuming process that can and should be avoided through thorough and rigorous testing.

15.1.4 Hardware and System Software Error

While the three types of errors above are the most common and may account for 99.44 percent of the errors in a software system, hardware and system software errors cannot be totally excluded. The authors, in their careers, have experienced system software errors. One such error caused the operating system to crash whenever the software split a disk sector. Another operating system sort could not handle zero records. The temporary solution was to (a) modify the documentation to indicate that a zero record sort was not possible and (b) make sure to write one dummy record that could be deleted downstream. Even the hardware cannot be assumed to be totally guiltless. Consider, for example, the case of the card reader that intermittently skipped a column and read the contents of an 80-column punched card into 81 columns. The 81st column just happened to be a malicious instruction that caused the next print job to abort. This was a case where cause and effect were far, far removed. These examples of hardware and software errors are relatively old; modern errors lead to situations such as the floating-point error in the early Pentium chip, buffer overruns, and the cases where the authors' word processors blow up and offer to send a message to the vendor, and then do not.

15.1.5 Flexible System Can Reduce Processing Logic Error to Operator Error

In UniverSIS, a processing logic error actually falls in the category of operator error.

Business staff controlling business rules through regulatory data can easily make the same types of errors that programmers make in coding business rules in programs. The good news is that, in a flexible system, what used to be logic errors can become operator (business staff) errors, which are typically easy to detect and correct. For example, within UniverSIS, there is a feature called the Evaluator, discussed in Chapters 13 and 18. The Evaluator allows business staff to define logical conditions in much the same way that programmers write such conditions:

Balance	GT	10.00
GPA	LT	2.00
Major	EQ	History
State	NE	California

It is very easy to set a condition as GT (greater than) by mistake when in fact it should be been LT (less than), or to set a condition as NE (not equal) when it should have been EQ (equal). The system can validate that, for example, "State" is a valid value and that "NE" is a valid value and that "California" is a valid value for "State." It cannot determine that you actually meant to say "State EQ California."

In an inflexible system, such logic would have been in program code. The error would have fallen into the category of "processing logic error." In UniverSIS, it actually falls into the category of "operator error." Detection of the cause of the error may involve approximately equivalent effort, although in the inflexible system a programmer would have to do the research. In the Evaluator example, business staff does the research by examining the data they entered. Correction of the error in the inflexible system would involve a change to program code and all associated testing. Business staff manage correction and testing of Evaluator conditions.

15.2 Two Phases of Testing

Business staff have always been responsible for testing. They have always provided initial business requirements for technical staff and verified the results. With a flexible system, there is an added dimension. Not only do business staff participate in testing the system during initial development, but they also make the modifications during ongoing operation and are responsible for testing to ensure the accuracy of those modifications

15.2.1 System Testing during Development

There will be no possibility of calling the developer from the middle of the ocean. The business staff will have to do their own maintenance.

For initial development of a flexible system, the testing process will be similar to that of traditional development. During this phase, the program information structures and code are tested, which is in effect a test of the accuracy of the communication of business requirements from business staff to the IT staff. Programmers do their best to make their code bug-free and efficient in satisfying the requirements stated by the business experts. But errors occur and misunderstandings arise. Even when there are no errors or misunderstandings, testing may reveal holes in the logic. Errors of omission are common — what we called in Chapter 1 "missed requirements."

It is important to remember here the need to test with an eye on flexibility. Highsmith [2000, p. 168] warns that "without expending considerable effort, developers find it difficult to test for maintainability of an application." It is essential that designers make sure not to reduce flexibility with ill-conceived design features that will lead to expensive and disruptive maintenance.

It may not occur to anyone who has not experienced it that someone might enter data that is completely wrong. The business staff and programmer may have tested the situation in which all data was entered correctly and found that things work perfectly. That is a best-case scenario, and both business staff and programmer must never think in terms of the best-case scenario. They must consider that anything that physically can happen will happen and account for it in the regulatory logic of the system (see Chapter 8, Regulation). There may be a tendency on the part of the business staff to trust that the programmer has done things right, particularly if things have gone well in the past. In the back of their minds may be the thought that the programmer will fix things that are found to be wrong. Business staff must not have this attitude. They should be thinking in terms of a sea voyage. The system has to be seaworthy when it leaves the dock. There will be no possibility of calling the programmer from the middle of the ocean. The business staff will have to do their own maintenance.

In the initial development phase of a flexible system, testing must focus on verifying that the system meets its initial requirements, including the ability to regulate its behavior. Business staff must be satisfied that the regulatory mechanisms work correctly. The system must validate values of individual elements correctly, validate combinations of elements correctly, and execute business rule logic correctly. This would include enforcing rules for entity relationships, triggers for automated system actions, and the like. Once the business staff has verified that the system performs correctly, the work of the programmers should be finished except for assisting business staff with technical tasks related to testing.

In a flexible system, regulatory data enforces the business rules, and maintenance of that regulatory data is the responsibility of business staff. The programmer writes code that does not specify valid values directly but rather enforces validity rules against data entered by business staff. Both business staff and programmers must establish during system development that the business staff will be maintaining the system once it is in production. Business staff, by modifying stored regulatory data values, will modify the system behavior. The point of this testing is to verify that the programmers have done it right in the first place.

When developing a flexible system, programmers generally use an iterative prototyping approach. (See our caution regarding the use of prototyping in Chapter 12, Requirements Determination.) The assumption is that business staff are satisfied only when they have a chance to test-drive a product. The number of iterations can vary, depending on the process and the business staff. Complex processes are often supported by simpler, lower-level processes. Holes in lower-level simple processes are sometimes not revealed until the business staff have had the opportunity to evaluate the upper-level complex process. Discovery of these holes is often prompted during testing by an innocuous-sounding question that begins with "Will the system do such and such?" The response, of course, is that "most likely it will not do anything that you have not told us about." The usual reason for the hole is that the business staff either possesses some knowledge that was not revealed to the programmers or they made assumptions not shared by the programmers. A good tool set and modular design can make such a prototyping approach relatively painless. Yes, "new" concepts such as "agile" have a place in flexible development, but they are not a substitute for it.

15.2.2 Testing during Ongoing Operations

Maintenance will still be required, but who performs the maintenance and how it is performed will change.

The business and its real-world environment are subject to frequent and dramatic change. The information system must be modified to accommodate such change. How that change is accommodated marks the difference between an inflexible system and a flexible system.

In inflexible systems, the rule is that IT professionals (including database administrators) make system modifications by adding or modifying program code and modifying the data structures. In effect, the developers of an inflexible system say to the business staff: "We will gain an understanding of your current business requirements and build a system that meets those requirements. When requirements change, we will modify the system to satisfy the new requirements."

When a term such as "maintenance backlog" is used, it generally refers to the inability of the IT unit to keep up with requests for system modifications. The term "maintenance" is essentially synonymous with system modifications made by IT staff. Eliminating the need for IT staff to perform such maintenance offers great potential for reducing or preventing a backlog.

In flexible systems, the rule is that customers make system modifications by making adjustments to data stored in the system. In effect, the developers of a flexible system say to the business staff: "We will gain an understanding of your current business requirements. We accept that those requirements will change over time. Therefore, we will also gain an understanding of where and how requirements are likely to change. We will build a system that meets today's requirements and provides you with the tools to modify it without our intervention as requirements change."

Business staff modification of the system is a form of system maintenance. Once a flexible system is in place, business staff make most subsequent system modifications. That is, they do most of the system maintenance. The programmers are not involved. Business staff must take care to identify and communicate with all business units that might be affected by the modifications. The fact that changes can be made easily does not mean that they should not be done carefully. As in the example of adding a college in a student information system, the fact that it could be done in UniverSIS (see Section 5.2.5) without programmer intervention does not mean that it was an insignificant change. A great deal of preparation and communication among business units was involved.

We acknowledge a continuum of system flexibility. A system in which every modification must be made by the IT staff is probably rare, as is a system in which every modification is made by business staff. However, we believe that developers can do much to improve the design of information systems, placing more control over modifications in the hands of business staff and thus reducing the need for IT intervention.

Responsibility for ongoing operational testing becomes very clear in a flexible system. Because changes to business rules ideally do not involve changes in program code, the customers must test potential future business requirements and determine what types of system modification, if any, are needed to accommodate such change. They cannot count on their trusted programmer to watch out for them, though the programmer can still provide guidance and consultation regarding techniques for thorough testing.

As with modifications to programs and data structures made by IT staff, the impact of business-controlled changes to regulatory data can be far-reaching, and may be felt in unexpected places at unexpected times — often long after the change is made. Thorough testing is essential whenever new business-controlled regulatory mechanisms are developed or regulatory data of existing mechanisms is modified.

Unless a business staff member has a background in IT, or in another discipline that tests results under varying conditions, we would recommend formal training in principles and practices of testing. Ideally, no individual on the business staff should be entirely responsible for implementing significant regulatory changes. Just as IT staff need to review and test programmer code, business staff need to review and test modifications to regulatory data. Equally important is a correct attitude about testing. Finding holes in a colleague's modifications to business rules does not constitute a personal attack. Good programmers often have colleagues review and test complex code to help ensure that nothing has been overlooked. One of the authors had a colleague who was particularly adept at ferreting out programming oversights. On one occasion, when challenged to "break" what the author thought was rock-solid code, the colleague generated an unanticipated condition on the first keystroke! Despite such occasional embarrassments, the author regularly had this colleague review his work. A working relationship such as this among IT staff helps ensure proper maintenance of the system. Business staff should work with each other in the same way.

As IT staff have learned over time, system modifications can have unintended consequences. Although business staff will be largely responsible for making the necessary changes, IT staff can play a consulting role in assisting with test plans. IT staff will often have access to system support tools such as a data dictionary, database schema, cross-reference facility, etc. not typically available to business staff. These help with analysis of the potential impact of changes. If changes affect batch processes, the IT staff may need to be involved in testing those processes because, in many shops, execution of batch jobs is tightly controlled by the IT department.

15.2.3 Guidelines for Testing

Wherever it resides, business logic must be tested before it is activated in a production environment. Business staff who maintain business rules

```
         Bond   *Evaluation Element                      *OP   *Value
  1       APS   APPL-PROGRAM_____              EQ    15BA_____
  2 AND   APS   APPL-ACAD-AREA_____              EQ    HIST_____
  3 AND         GENDER_____            EQ    F_____
  4    or       _____            EQ    M_____
```

Exhibit 15.2.   Sample Business Condition

must be trained to construct such logic and to test it thoroughly. Just as the correctness of a programmer's code should be verified through thorough testing by business staff, business staff should test the correctness of business rules data that they enter. The operative phrase is "try to break it."

We will look at an Evaluator condition to illustrate some testing considerations and provide some suggestions. The condition shown in Exhibit 15.2 specifies three subconditions. Two elements (APPL-PROGRAM and APPL-ACAD-AREA) are "bound," meaning that they must appear together in a single record. The third element (GENDER) specifies two possible values. A practical testing tool, and one that business staff can typically learn to use quickly, is a decision table. The decision table should lay out all possible combinations with the corresponding expected results. It then functions as a test plan. Note that in the decision table in Exhibit 15.3, we have specified two pairs of application values. This is necessary because the pair members are "bound." The second set of values represents the nth. The point is that all occurrences must be examined, not just the first.

To test this condition, the business staff need to identify all conditions that will yield a true result as well as all patterns that will yield a false result. In Exhibit 15.3, subconditions with a true result are highlighted in gray. Because discrete values have been specified in the condition, the number of true conditions is small, represented in rows 1 to 4. Rows 5 to 7 give a true result for one subcondition but yield an overall result of false. Row 8 gives false results for both subconditions and for the overall condition.

The zip code condition defined in Exhibit 15.4 seems very straightforward: anyone who has a zip code lower than 02100 will be selected. The person constructing this condition undoubtedly knows that zip codes represent geographic areas and that this condition will select only individuals in the Northeast part of the country. Or will it?

This example illustrates a common oversight when specifying ranges of values, one with which programmers are all too familiar. What if HOME-ZIP

	GENDER	APPL-PROGRAM 1	APPL -ACAD - AREA 1	APPL - PROGRAM N	APPL -AC AD - AREA N	RESULT
1	M	15BA	HIST	Not-15BA	Not-HIST	True
2	F	15BA	HIST	Not-15BA	Not-HIST	True
3	M	15BA	Not-HIST	15BA	HIST	True
4	F	15BA	Not-HIST	15BA	HIST	True
5	M	15BA	Not-HIST	Not-15BA	HIST	False
6	F	15BA	Not-HIST	Not-15BA	HIST	False
7	U	15BA	HIST	Not-15BA	Not-HIST	False
8	U	15BA	Not-HIST	Not-15BA	HIST	False

Exhibit 15.3. Decision Table

	Bond	*Evaluation Element	*OP	*Value
1		HOME-ZIP_____	LE	02100_____

Exhibit 15.4. Condition with Value Range

contains no data? What if a blank or null is viewed by the system as less than or equal to 02100, as shown in the decision table in Exhibit 15.5. This means that anyone for whom no zip code is recorded would satisfy the condition. Depending on how the data structures were designed, this might include all individuals with a foreign address. It might be that the intention is to select all individuals whose home address is not in the United States and those who live in the Northeast. But the person doing the testing has to test that possibility and know whether that is the desired result. If those having blank HOME-ZIP are not to be selected, the condition has to be modified as shown in Exhibit 15.6.

	HOME - ZIP	Result
1	02100	True
2	01905	True
3	02101	False
4	Blank	True

Exhibit 15.5. Decision Table for Value Range

	Bond	*Evaluation Element	*OP	*Value
1		HOME-ZIP_____	LE	02100_____
2	and	HOME-ZIP_____	NE	blank_____

Exhibit 15.6. Range Excluding Blank Value

	Bond	*Evaluation Element	*OP	*Value
1		HOME-STATE_____	NE	OH_____
2	and	HOME-STATE_____	NE	KY_____
3	and	HOME-STATE_____	NE	IN_____

Exhibit 15.7. Negative Logic

Similarly, the use of negative logic in a condition can lead to unexpected results. In the condition illustrated in Exhibit 15.7, anyone having a HOME-STATE value not on the list will be selected. As in the HOME-ZIP example, use of the decision table in Exhibit 15.8 to lay out all possible situations may reveal an oversight. It is critical that business staff responsible for recording and testing such business rules have a mechanism to test the rules before they take effect. This may involve use of a separate

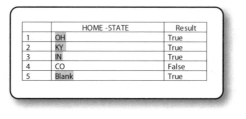

		HOME -STATE	Result
1	OH		True
2	KY		True
3	IN		True
4	CO		False
5	Blank		True

Exhibit 15.8.   Decision Table for Negative Logic

processing environment or, as in the case of the Evaluator, a mechanism for testing the conditions themselves in isolation.

Testing is not unlike talking to an eight-year old who has discovered the magic of complex language. As you begin to scold the child for an infraction, the child will smugly point out to you what "you said," knowing full well that you meant something quite different. That's the difference between a system and an eight-year old. The system understands only what you said. It does not know what you meant. This should provide some perspective. A system is not as intelligent as the average eight-year old. Do not assume that it is.

15.2.4 Testing Platform

For programmers who are accustomed to testing a system, it is a given that modifications are made and tested in a nonproduction environment. This fact may not be obvious to business staff, and so it must be emphasized as part of their training. An approach used in many shops provides a minisystem to test the localized effects of the proposed modifications. Such a minisystem will have a complete set of programs and data structures but a minimal amount of data. A larger test system, a duplicate of the production system, is provided for broader testing, regression testing, etc.

The first step of testing, once the nature of the modification has been determined, is to implement the modifications in the minisystem and validate that they do, in fact, accomplish their purpose. The next step is then to move the modifications to the larger duplicate system and perform thorough testing with more-extensive test data and possibly live data that has been copied to the test system. The purpose here is to ensure that the modifications do only what they are supposed to do, and that they do not cause side effects.

There is an important distinction between production data and test data that experienced testers appreciate. Production data is a crapshoot, being whatever comes up in the course of operating the software. Test data is specifically designed to (attempt to) test all possible conditions. Good test data is not necessarily voluminous, but it should be comprehensive and will normally include data that is not (yet) found in the production data. Test data usually accumulates over time as new conditions are uncovered that require testing. Thus it represents a considerable investment and should be safeguarded as carefully as production data. Modifications should be tested against test data first, then, ideally, against a copy of the production data because we do not know what is in the production data and some as-yet-untested condition may have arisen that will cause a failure.

15.3 Summary

- Testing involves executing system processes and then comparing the results with results determined to be correct. Errors encountered in testing fall into four categories: operator error, invalid data error, processing logic error, and hardware and system software error.
- In a flexible system, what used to be logic errors may become operator (business staff) errors, which are typically easy to detect and correct.
- Testing occurs in two distinct phases: during development and prior to system implementation, and during ongoing operations and modifications.
- Business staff have always been responsible for testing. With a flexible system, there is an added dimension. Not only do business staff test the system during initial development, but they also make the modifications during ongoing operation and do the testing of the modifications.
- Initial system testing must include testing of the regulatory mechanisms within the system.
- In flexible systems, the rule is that customers make system modifications by making adjustments to data stored in the system.
- Eliminating the need for IT staff to perform maintenance offers great potential for reducing or preventing a maintenance backlog.
- With the implementation of an integrated and flexible system, business staff must change their thinking significantly because they have control over changes in system behavior, which may impact other business units besides their own.
- The impact of business-controlled changes to regulatory data can be far-reaching.

- Changes in business rule values entered by business staff must be tested both to ensure that they have the intended effect and to ensure that they have no unintended effects.
- A testing platform to facilitate testing and to protect the production system is a must in all forms of testing, including flexible system testing.

Maintenance does not disappear with the implementation of a flexible system, but responsibility shifts to business staff. This shift in responsibility must be planned with care because it requires a type of thinking that, until now, has been limited to the IT professional. Careful training and mentoring are required for the assumption of this role, with special attention given to the process of system testing.

The good news is that business staff will see the value of flexibility, particularly those staff members who have control over modification. Modifications — system maintenance — can occur according to the business timetable rather than being dependent on availability of scarce IT resources. The bad news, or so it sometimes seems, is that active responsibility for maintaining business rules may appear to involve additional work for the business staff. However, it should not be forgotten that business staff have been essential participants in modifications to inflexible systems as well. They provide the business requirements and then validate the resulting system modifications made by the IT staff. It may be true that a flexible system adds some amount of data maintenance work to the load of the business staff, but the total workload involved in making a modification to a flexible system is significantly lower than that involved in making a comparable modification to an inflexible system.

Chapter 16

Identifying, Managing, and Acquiring Quality Flexible Software

This is the final chapter of Part III, How to Design Flexible Software Systems. In many ways, it is also the final chapter of this book, because Part IV acts rather like an appendix, providing details about UniverSIS and the generic-entity cloud (GEC). Having looked at building systems with flexibility characteristics, we now want to consider applying those design factors to purchased systems. We also want to relate flexibility characteristics to the important issue of software quality and to project management:

- What is the connection between flexible systems and various quality movements?
- How do I manage system development or system acquisition to implement a flexible software system?
- How can I ensure that software acquired (versus built) by our organization is flexible?

16.1 Flexibility and Quality

Several of the authors who went through the quality revolution think that it is relevant to today's enterprises and that its message is germane to flexible software. As novelist Robert Pirsig [1974] stated, "Quality isn't method. It's the goal toward which method is aimed." And Walter Shewhart [1980] declared, "In general, the quality of a thing is that which is inherent in it so we cannot alter the quality without altering the thing."

The objective of this discussion is to shift the focus of software developers from methods of software development to the goal of achieving inherent flexibility in the software. This is a legitimate quality goal in the spirit and substance of the total quality management (TQM) movement of the last decade, and which should continue today. The discoveries of systems behavior made by TQM researchers apply to, and can be positively influenced by, the study of flexibility in software systems.

Taguchi's loss function [1986] parallels the cost rationale underlying the systems maintenance issue discussed in Chapter 1. His concept provides for a quantification of quality: "The quality of a product is the minimum loss imparted by the product to the society from the time the product is shipped. That is, an economic value can be placed on quality by virtue of the customers' perceptions of quality shortfalls in the product." Keen [1991, 1995, 2004], as described earlier, has quantified automated systems in terms of maintenance/development cost ratios. Taken together, these concepts point to a flexibility metric based on the ratio of information technology (IT) system maintenance cost to business staff cost when adjusting to a change in business requirements. Thus, it could be argued that an increase in the flexibility of a system is an increase in the quality of the system in the sense meant by TQM. That is, Keen's ratios (Exhibit 1.1) reflect genuine quality shortfalls — the system's inability to be adjusted economically in proportion to its customers' costs in reacting to changes in requirements.

Similarly, exploiting the knowledge and capability of business staff by designing for the maintenance of business rules directly by business staff (the systems designers' customers) implements the customer-primacy emphasis of TQM. As stated by Radin [1994], "The best way to take advantage of customer input is to believe that your customers are intelligent rational human beings. If you do, they are likely to prove you correct." The shift to business rules automation was echoed by Barker [1992] when he wrote, "Watch for people messing with rules, because that is the earliest sign of significant change."

Most important, however, is that TQM emphasizes *change* in two forms that parallel the flexible system's emphasis on recognizing change in the real world and designing for change in the automated world:

1. *Analysis of environmental changes*: This drives what Drucker [1985] calls systematic knowledge-based innovation. He said, "Systematic innovation ... consists in the purposeful and organized search for

changes, and in the systematic analysis of the opportunities such changes might offer."

2. *Continuous quality improvement (CQI)*: As summarized by Joiner [1994], "Quality processes are designed for change. Specifically, they are designed for continuous and frequent incremental improvements, avoiding wherever possible disruptive structural changes."

It is when making system modifications to accommodate change that the links between flexibility and quality become apparent. Let us examine this in more detail.

It is ironic that, while it enthusiastically enlists "systems thinking" [Senge, 1990], TQM's benefits have not been reliably extended into the application-software arena itself. This is because TQM has largely viewed real-world business systems as processes. It has rightly considered *traditional* systems thinking to be process thinking and therefore particularly applicable to the TQM agenda of quality improvement through business process reengineering (BPR) [Hammer and Champy, 1993]. But we know that really effective systems thinking includes taking information structure into account as well as information processing and, especially, designing within the constraining effect of structure on process to avoid the disruptive effects of structure modifications. Equally ironically, TQM's CQI aims at continuous incremental changes, but this is precisely what is inhibited by rigid application systems that are not designed for change. Factoring this perspective into systems development thinking — as we have argued throughout this book — would improve the flexibility of application systems, thereby allowing more scope for TQM quality improvement initiatives within organizations that are significantly automated.

Joel Barker [1992] wrote, "You manage within a paradigm. You lead between paradigms." The thought leaders of the TQM revolution guided the move from the old to the new business management practices. TQM has become the paradigm within which we manage today. Mutual benefits will accrue to both TQM and software engineering when flexible automated systems become the paradigm within which we do systems development.

16.2 Managing System Development/Acquisition to Achieve Flexibility

Project managers play a key role in achieving flexibility. A project manager (PM) is typically charged with planning and implementing each IT initiative, whether it be a major new system or an improvement of the existing system. The PM becomes a champion for flexibility, representing the best interests of the organization as a whole. There is a strong match between good PM skills and the skills needed to achieve flexibility. According to the Project Management Institute (PMI), the critical skills needed by project managers are [PMI, 2000; Heldman, 2002]:

- Communicating
- Leading
- Team building and human-resource management
- Negotiating and influencing
- Problem solving
- Organizing and budgeting
- Influencing the organization

All of these skills are critical for achieving flexibility. For example, a PM must exercise leadership to influence the organization to invest in flexibility, i.e., to rewrite instead of patch. The PM must employ team building and influencing skills to enforce the flexibility standards, as well as to involve more users in the project. These "soft skills" are essential to the success of today's complex IT projects and particularly for introducing flexibility.

> Leadership and management are not synonymous terms. Leaders impart vision, gain consensus for strategic goals, establish direction, and inspire and motivate others. Managers focus on results and are concerned with getting the job done according to the requirements.... Project managers must exhibit the characteristics of both during different times on the project. Understanding when to switch from leadership to management and then back again is a finely tuned and necessary talent [Heldman, 2002].

A PM has much to deal with. PMI's Project Management Body of Knowledge (PMBOK) breaks the PM's job into nine project management knowledge areas. Managing for flexibility requires attention across all nine areas, as summarized in Exhibit 16.1.

Several aspects of project management and flexibility are discussed in more detail in the following subsections:

1. Managing trade-offs
2. Using teamwork and communications to achieve flexibility
3. Tools for flexible software development
4. Enforcing flexibility as part of daily builds

PM Area	Purpose	Key PM Activities	Managing for Flexibility
Project integration management	• Coordinate the various elements of the project • Make trade-offs among competing objectives and alternatives to meet and exceed stakeholder needs	• Project plan development • Project plan execution • Integrated change control	• Account for life-cycle cost advantages of flexibility • Maintain reference of flexible features; document the ways in which each has been used • Require designers to consider reuse of existing flexible features before inventing new designs • Promote enhancement of existing flexible features to allow broader applicability
Project scope management	• Define and control what is, and is not, included in the project	• Scope planning and definition • Scope verification • Scope change control	• Evaluate trade-offs and implement appropriate level of flexibility • Identify scenarios where multiple requirements can be accommodated with a single flexible design feature; leverage the development effort • Use design reviews and code reviews to ensure flexibility
Project time management	• Develop and control the project rime schedule • Ensure timely completion of the project	• Activity definition and sequencing • Activity duration estimating • Schedule development • Schedule control	• Allow sufficient time for flexible design • Avoid "giving up flexible features" due to schedule constraints
Project cost management	• Ensure project completion within approved budget • Consider effect of project decision on the cost of using the project's product	• Resource planning • Cost estimating and budgeting • Cost control	• Allow sufficient budget for flexible design • Avoid "giving up flexible features" due to budget constraints
Project quality management	• Ensure project satisfies the needs for which it was undertaken • Determine and implement the quality objectives and responsibilities	• Quality planning • Quality assurance • Quality control	• Implement flexibility as a means for continuous process improvement • Develop metrics that recognize increased flexibility as increased quality

Exhibit 16.1. Managing for Flexibility across PMI's Nine Knowledge Areas

16.2.1 Managing Trade-Offs

Project management is all about managing trade-offs and balancing constraints. Flexible systems are also subject to trade-offs. One cannot get something for nothing. Clearly, the programs that access generic-entity clouds will be more complex than programs that access more traditional databases. For a retail organization, for example, the logic for summarizing

PM Area	Purpose	Key PM Activities	Managing for Flexibility
Project human resources management	• Make most effective use of all project stakeholders, including sponsors, customers, partners, and individual contributors • Lead and manage the project team	• Organizational planning • Staff acquisition • Team development	• Train personnel in flexibility techniques • Promote teamwork amongst groups (e.g., development vs. maintenance)
Project communications management	• Provide critical links among people, ideas, and information that are necessary for success • Ensure timely and appropriate generation, collection, dissemination, storage, and disposition of project information	• Communications planning • Information distribution • Performance reporting • Administrative closure	• Help ensure that participants understand the goals, benefits, costs, and challenges of flexibility, as well as the design rationale and standards • Add flexibility metrics to weekly/monthly status review and performance report • Document new business requirements that emerge during the project and are accommodated within existing flexible design Prove the value of flexibility as you go
Project risk management	• Systematically identifying, analyzing, and responding to project risk • Maximizing the probability and consequences of positive events to project objectives, and minimizing the probability and consequences of adverse events	• Risk management planning • Risk identification • Qualitative and quantitative risk analysis • Risk response planning • Risk monitoring and control	• Realistically assess and mitigate flexibility risks (e.g., lack of training, schedule impacts, etc.) • Identify areas where business requirement change is likely to occur and evaluate impact of NOT implementing a flexible design [Avoid the attitude that five minutes after the system goes into production it is someone else's problem]
Project procurement management	• Acquire goods or services from outside the performing organization, as needed to attain project scope	• Procurement planning • Solicitation planning • Solicitation • Source selection • Contract administration • Contract closeout	• Make flexibility an important criterion when evaluating vendor products or services • Compare candidate products to your requirements (that include flexibility) vs. comparing candidate products to each other • Involve both business and technical staff in evaluating flexibility • If outsourcing occurs, at the very least retain project management responsibility internally

Exhibit 16.1.   (continued)

inventory levels by division is simpler for traditional databases because the store-to-division associations are included in the key of the inventory file. Programs that manipulate the GEC-based retail organization, on the other hand, require processing a complex interaction between the information in at least three (logical) files.

The fact that general business rules, referential integrity, cardinality, etc. in a GEC are often supported by data, and thus subject to change, means that much of the system operation is interpreted rather than compiled as fixed code. This has implications for speed of operation and CPU (central processing unit) demand, as well as data storage. However, while processing power and storage are becoming cheaper by the day, intervention by IT personnel to change business rules is becoming increasingly expensive. Outsourcing of programming to foreign countries such as India has become a reality for software vendors in the United States, primarily as a cost-saving measure. It is important to note that IT intervention required for on-site changes to business rules cannot generally be outsourced. More importantly, business disruption caused by erroneous changes or newly revealed requirements are becoming more of an impediment to business each day.

It is essential to understand that the extra effort to develop flexible programs is a one-time investment. Traditional, nonflexible, programs will need modification, testing, etc. each time new organization types are introduced or the associations among types are rearranged. In addition, each time the association of specific stores to specific divisions is changed, the identifier values of the traditional inventory file must be changed. This usually entails unloading the affected records, changing the identifier values, and reloading the records. In a flexible system, inventory records are immune to such changes. Store-to-division association change is performed on the data in the organization's GEC nodes. The result is then automatically reflected in the inventory reporting. Testing, however, is still required to ensure that the correct "data" modifications have been made.

A PM must understand the "life-cycle" advantages of flexibility and constantly influence the organization and the project team to dedicate the necessary resources and time to implement flexibility. This is an ongoing challenge. The authors have seen organizations give up on flexibility features when schedule or budget constraints took over. The value of flexibility hinges on the life-cycle cost, which is driven by the low-maintenance project outcome, referred to by PMI as the "cost of using the project's product":

> Project cost management is primarily concerned with the cost of the resources needed to complete project activities. However, project cost management should also consider the effect of

project decisions on the cost of using the project's product. For example, limiting the number of design reviews may reduce the cost of the project at the expense of an increase in the customer's operating costs. This broader view of project cost management is often called *life-cycle costing*. Life-cycle costing together with Value Engineering techniques are used to reduce cost and time, improve quality and performance, and optimize the decision-making [PMI, 2000].

Realistically, there are varying degrees of flexibility, depending upon what aspect of the computer systems must be modified. We define two distinct levels of flexibility — strong flexibility and medium flexibility — and suggest that possibly an order-of-magnitude reduction in resynchronization and maintenance costs is associated with each level:

- *Strong flexibility*: Only data value modifications are required.
- *Medium flexibility*: Only data value and local procedural code modifications are required.

Below strong and medium flexibility are systems that require changes to information structures. These are effectively inflexible, or rigid, systems. Project managers must help the organization to manage the trade-offs and evaluate life-cycle costs in an effort to determine the appropriate level of flexibility for a particular project.

16.2.2 Using Teamwork and Communications to Achieve Flexibility

Project managers rely heavily on team building and human-resource management skills. A PM sets the tone for the project team — typically formed with people from different parts of the organization — and uses their skills to make the team fully functional. Given that flexibility is a new way of systems development, particular attention to teamwork and communications is required.

It is critical to the success of the project that all members of the team understand the design rationale and have adequate knowledge of and training in software flexibility. Design reviews and code reviews must be enforced as vehicles for ensuring that flexibility has been built into the system. Exhibit 16.2 presents several accounts from UniverSIS where a lack of understanding of the design rationale or lack of standards enforcement led to a compromise in flexibility. Exhibit 16.3 presents an account

---

Part 1

In developing UniverSIS, we discovered that the rules for grading are very complex. Some grades count toward GPA, and some do not. Some grades have credit hours associated with them, and some do not. Some grades show on the student's transcript different from how they were actually recorded. And so on. We designed the data structure for storing the master file of grades to allow the business staff to manage all the rules.

During development of UniverSIS, the Student Records office apparently told a programmer that, for a new business process, five specific grades needed to be handled in a special way. The programmer dutifully coded the logic in his program to handle those five specific grades in that special way. Predictably, several years later the student records office needed to add another grade to the list of special grades. One of the authors happened to get involved. Seeing the hard-coded grades in the program, I asked the student records office whether these grades had common characteristics already controlled by the master grades file. In fact, they did. By modifying the program to look at business rules stored on the grades records, he made it more flexible, allowing the logic to process correctly any grade that followed the specified rule pattern.

This account points out the following:

1. The programmer was not thinking in terms of storing business rules as data. When the student records office identified a list of specific grades, he should immediately have investigated how to avoid hard-coding values in programs. In this case, he would have discovered that existing stored business rules covered the situation. If they had not, he should have analyzed the grades for a pattern that could lead to new stored business rules.
2. The student records office was also not thinking in terms of stored business rules. When questioned about the specific grades and the existing business rule mechanism, the staff member almost immediately recognized that the previous five grades and the new one all followed a pattern.

In other words, both business and IT staff should have known better.

This situation occurred after UniverSIS was in operation for several years, but it could have occurred even during the development phase. Everyone associated with development and support of a system must be aware of the philosophy of the design. When a programmer finds himself ready to hard-code specific values in a program, he should mentally slap himself on the wrist and admonish himself, "We don't do that here."

Exhibit 16.2.   True Confessions from UniverSIS

regarding flexible software at a retail department store chain, underscoring the importance of code reviews in ensuring flexibility and of having all the development players on the same page with respect to flexibility.

In a large IT organization, support for applications might be divided between new development and ongoing maintenance, and a formal or informal status might be associated with one's assignments. Maintenance work, for example, might have lower status than development work. Often senior staff members do development work while newer staff members do maintenance. Development and maintenance groups might have an adversarial relationship, represented by statements like this: "We develop a good system and then the maintenance group screws it up."

Obviously, such an attitude is counterproductive. All of these individuals are important to supporting the system over its life span. For development to flow smoothly into ongoing maintenance, all participants must be aware of the philosophy of the design — flexibility — and carefully trained to build upon that design. Individuals who support a system need to think about how their work fits within the overall design of the system. They therefore need to understand the overall design. A flexible system can easily deteriorate into an inflexible system unless everyone follows the design. Exhibit 16.4 presents a success story from a Fortune 100

Part 2

For some reason, programmers assigned to do batch work view their assignments as somehow being outside the system. Rather than making use of features that already exist, they may invent their own solutions.

A standard problem, when adding an individual's record to a system, is determining whether he is already on the system. Based on the available data, a Yes, a No, or a Maybe, result occurs. Those results lead to the following actions:

· Yes. Individual definitely exists on the system already. Automated processing can proceed. Add new records or update existing records as appropriate.
· No. Individual definitely does not exist on the system. Automated processing can proceed. Establish individual's system identity and add or update records as appropriate.
· Maybe. Individual potentially matches one or more individuals in the system. Automated processing cannot proceed. Report the individual's data. A staff member will do the necessary research to make the Yes/No determination and enter the data manually.

In UniverSIS, the developers created a single, central routine to evaluate the data of incoming individuals, comparing it with data on existing records. A committee of business staff representing all the key business units was involved in establishing the rules. The intent was to use this routine in every process where an individual can be added to the system.

Automated decisions of Yes and No carry a level of risk. An incorrect decision of Yes can result in storing information about one individual on another individual's records. An incorrect decision of No can result in creation of a duplicate set of records for a single individual. The rules in the central routine represented the views of several business units with regard to balancing those risks.

In one batch admissions process that periodically loads a few thousand records into the system, a large number of Maybe results were being generated. As described above, these require manual intervention which, from the point of view of the admissions office, is a bad thing. Rather than initiate a discussion about how—in fact, whether—the existing routine could be modified to yield fewer Maybe answers, the programmer developed his own routine just for that process. He apparently reduced the number of Maybe results and increased the number of No results, but at this point, the results of his "improvement" have not been determined. From the admissions point of view, creation of a duplicate set of application-related records for an individual is not very significant. Turning every Maybe result into a No saves lots of manual effort and presents only minor processing problems. For the student records office, on the other hand, avoiding creation of a duplicate set of records is very important. If a student who has taken a few classes decides to apply for admission to a degree program, it is important to the student records office that all records for that individual be part of a single set. Consolidation of duplicate sets of records can be a nightmare. Obviously, admissions and student records have different priorities. For admissions, the important thing is to avoid manual review of records. The risk of duplicate records is not significant. For student records, creation of a duplicate set of records is a worst-case scenario, to be avoided if at all possible. Manual data entry of the initial set of records is relatively insignificant.

The point is that the programmer, whose job it is to support the admissions office, did not take into consideration the overall needs of the system. By doing something good for admissions, he potentially did something very bad for student records. In an integrated system, the interests of all constituents must be considered. What may be a good thing for one business unit may be a bad thing for another unit.

Exhibit 16.2. (continued)

company where systems development, implementation, and maintenance were coordinated under common standards.

At a minimum, technical managers of the maintenance group need to participate in the design phase of any project. They need to know what is coming their way so that they can prepare their staff. They can also provide valuable insight into the areas of system maintenance that consume most of the time, leading developers to address those areas carefully. During both the development and maintenance phase, design review (Is the design flexible?) and code review (Is the programmer following the intended design?) are important. No one — absolutely no one — should be exempt from such a review.

Project managers can use the following tips to help their project teams practice flexibility for the benefit of the organization:

At the corporate offices of a retail department store chain, some basic flexibility techniques were used in the design of the financial analysis and reporting system. This system was the repository of financial data from eight of the company's nine highly decentralized operating divisions. Hence, the data structure accommodated different organization, product, and inventory location structures, all changing independently from quarter to quarter. The requirements called for the system to allow end users to maintain these changing factors, and the design exploited recursively related generic entities, as described in Chapter 9. The design was not advanced to the level of using a cardinality regulation facility, but it still represented a major improvement in flexibility, achieving a medium level of flexibility.

One of the programs provided an interactive display to enable users to set up and maintain the organization scheme. The programmer had alertly noticed that the design specifications had not allowed for preventing cycles—circular relationships. The programmer solved the cycle problem by coding the program to disallow many-to-many relationships among organization units. By limiting the user to constructing only hierarchical structures, the cycling problem was eliminated. This was an experienced and astute programmer whose solution to a problem effectively eliminated the system's ability to represent networked organizations and negated one of the most important flexibility characteristics of the design.

This problem was discovered and rectified during a code review.

Exhibit 16.3.   Retail Department Store Chain: Code Review Restores Flexibility

In a Fortune 100 company where one of us worked, the progression of systems development and operations went through several phases. First the systems analysis and design group where the system was designed, then the system (along with some personnel) was handed over to the implementation group. From there, the system (again with some personnel for continuity) was handed over to the operations and maintenance group. All phases followed a common set of design and programming standards. When maintenance problems were encountered (lack of flexibility), the cause was determined and the standards modified to, hopefully, avoid the situation in the future. Feedback of maintenance problems and additional flexibility ideas and standards are always in order.

Exhibit 16.4.   Handoffs, Feedback, and Common Standards

- Encourage your teams to design features for multiple uses.
- Keep track of the flexible features and how they were used.
- Before inventing a design specific to a new requirement, review the existing designs. Can they be reused or enhanced with a little tweaking?
- Keep track of success stories. If a requirement that emerges during development can be accommodated with an existing design, that is a success story. Make a note of it, with an estimate of time and effort saved.
- Identify and make use of flexibility "experts," on both the business and IT side. Make use of these experts. Let them review all designs.
- Do not think of the system as something that is "finished" at the end of the project. The project moves the system from one point to another in its life cycle.
- Consider the cost of *not* designing with flexibility in mind.

16.2.3 Tools for Flexible Software Development

We originally planned to include a chapter covering tools for implementation of flexible software systems. After some discussion, we realized that there *are* no tools specifically designed for implementation of flexible software systems, but we still felt that something should be said.

At various points in the book we have talked about tools that help with analysis and design (entity-relationship diagram [ERD], data flow diagram [DFD], etc.). Software products that support these activities fall in the "nice to have" category, but they are not essential. Often a big piece of paper taped to the wall does a great job.

A code generator is a valuable tool for speeding up programming. It is not specific to flexible systems, but because it can be such a time-saver, it may push a management decision in the direction of tearing down and redesigning rather than patching when flaws are discovered. So the code generator may well ease the way for flexible design by reducing recovery time, but it is not essential.

So what is essential? A database management system (DBMS) seems essential for data storage and management these days, but that is not specific to flexible systems. The data dictionary, mentioned several times in this work, is essential as a repository for information about the system: characteristics of data elements; information-structure relationships; identification of modules; cross-referencing of system components, etc. But we think a data dictionary is essential even if one is determined to develop an inflexible system.

There appear to be no tools that are appropriate for the development of flexible system that are not also appropriate for the development of inflexible systems. Even rules engines, like the UniverSIS Evaluator and comparable commercial products, provide benefits in both arenas. The use of an effective rules engine contributes a significant measure of flexibility to an otherwise inflexible system and provides an even greater benefit in a comprehensively flexible system. The same tools that make life easier for development of traditional systems make life easier for development of flexible systems as well.

Flexible system design has to come from the heads of the designers. Acquiring and using software tools will not lead to flexible design. Good tools, like good methods, will help, but they are never a substitute for good thinking.

16.2.4 Enforcing Flexibility as Part of Daily Builds

An important aspect of much of today's software development is the "daily build" in which code produced (modified) during the day is incorporated into the software product. In fact, if you look at the help menu for "about software" on a piece of software you own, you may see something like "software product 9.0.2720," which means that this is the 2720th build of version 9.0 of the software product. Software builds can require a long run, and they are often run overnight.

The project manager or her designee should sit down after each build and test a rotating set of flexibility features. Can we (still) change cardinality between persons and assignments? Can we (still) build a new transaction type by only changing data? Can we (still) move unit X (and all its suborganizations) of an organization, which used to report to unit Q, to now report to unit Z by only changing data? If such features do not work today and they worked yesterday, it is likely an implementation problem. If they never worked, it may be a design problem or lack of understanding of the design on the part of the IT staff. In any case, such problems must be detected and corrected early in the project and continually checked.

16.3 Procuring Flexible Software

Acquisition of packaged software is at an all-time high and continues to grow. According to *Gartner*, the worldwide IT services marketplace — or the market for software, integration, and maintenance services procured externally — was $540 billion in 2002, and it is projected to reach $700 billion in 2007 [Pring, 2003]. The United States is the largest market worldwide, representing half of this world market. Of course, the customization dilemma remains a major issue.

> Many users have come to realize that the cost of software product customizations often outweighs the benefits. This misalignment between cost and benefit is particularly felt in areas of noncore competency for an organization. *Gartner Dataquest*'s view is that application development — of software product and custom code — will change fundamentally over the midterm as declining customization of all aspects of IT environments becomes widely accepted as the norm in the IT industry.... more users we see will accept "good enough," standard, noncustomized solutions for these areas of noncore competency and will seek to customize only applications and business processes that can genuinely deliver competitive advantage. One large insurance company says that its contracts with outside suppliers now stipulate that no more than 25 percent of any new project can be allocated to new code development.... This is a clear indication of the direction in which the industry is going [Pring, 2003].

Some analysts suggest that in-house development is best focused on core business systems that deliver competitive advantage, while packaged products can be particularly cost-effective for noncore business systems.

> Given the direction things are going, you might think that the internally developed application is an endangered species.... These trends, however, are misleading. Custom code is alive and well and serving a vital role at many companies. Proprietary software, crafted by engineers who are close to a company's inner workings and systems, continues to be the secret sauce that gives many businesses an edge. "The stuff that gives you competitive advantage — that's the stuff you need to own and develop in-house," says Jeff Brandmaier, senior VP and CIO at H&R Block [Foley, 2003].

In addition, outsourcing is increasingly used as a strategy to reduce costs. Outsourced resources can be an extension of the in-house team for development of proprietary software, or they can be involved with implementing and maintaining packaged solutions.

> Detroit Edison, a subsidiary of DTE Energy Co., is taking a different path to software-development efficiency. A few months ago, the utility signed up for a service from TopCoder Inc. that lets it submit work requests to the outsourcing company, which uses thousands of freelance developers located in more than 100 countries [Foley, 2003].

Flexibility is an important consideration when evaluating vendor products or outsourcing services. Exhibit 16.5 summarizes the flexibility characteristics discussed in this book in parallel with questions that could be applied to products or services under evaluation. The characteristics are stated in unqualified and unweighted terms for clarity and to provide a baseline. Obviously, the degree to which a particular characteristic can or should be implemented in a particular system is a matter of judgment. For example, one characteristic is that the flexible system shares a common information structure with other related systems. This is an ideal. An actual stand-alone system without a shared database can still exhibit considerable flexibility.

Exhibit 16.5 is aimed primarily at applications systems evaluation. It is not intended for assessment of commercial tools that might be considered business rules engines or business rules systems (BRS). The examples of evaluation questions are aligned approximately with the general categories of flexibility characteristics. It can be difficult to gain access to the internals of a proprietary system, and thus evaluation of some characteristics may

Flexibility Characteristics	Evaluation Questions
1. Does not exist in isolation A flexible system does not exist in isolation. It is integral to a systems ensemble (or supersystem) by virtue of sharing a common information structure.	• Does the system directly access the same sets of physical data files for customer, product, personnel, etc. as do other related systems? • Most purchased systems naturally get a low to zero score because they are inherently stand-alone and can exchange data with other systems only via interfaces. It is essential that the evaluation determine the actual degree of any claimed shared information structure and not rely on vendor statements.

2. Long-term structure/process differentiation that reflects that found in the real world
  a. The information structure reflects only that which can reasonably be expected to remain constant over 20 years.
  b. Characteristics of the real world not constant over 20 years are treated as variables, such that the variations take the form of data item value changes.
	• In general, can anything that has changed in the past about how the business does business be changed now in the system without reprogramming? That is, can such changes be made by business staff manipulating data, rather than by programmers and database administrators manipulating programs and file definitions?
	• For example, has the product line changed; has the back-order policy changed; have payroll deduction types changed; has the chart of accounts changed, have the tax regulations changed; has the organization structure changed?

3. Stable information structure
  a. Least-constrained representation of the things, their properties, and their natural interrelationships about which information is to be kept
    ➤ Generic entities to reflect the flexible generalizations employed in the real world, such as Person as a generalization of employee, manager, dependent, etc.
    ➤ Recursive relationships for generic entities that reflect relationships among different types of the same kind of thing in the real world, such as employee/dependent, etc.
    ➤ Association entities (many-to-many interentity relationships) that reflect what is literally physically possible in the real world and not current business-constrained relationships
  b. The cardinality of current business-constrained relationships is maintained outside the information structure (see item 4, Regulation)
  c. Strictly unique identifiers
    ➤ Used for Internal identification of entity instances and references to entity instances
    ➤ Automatically assigned on a next-sequential number basis
    ➤ Globally assigned regardless of entity type
    ➤ Nonstrictly-unique identifiers used only for external references
    ➤ Internal and external identifiers automatically maintained in 1:1 correspondence
    ➤ Internal identifiers never reused.
  d. Codes treated as entities
  e. Codes preferred to flags
  f. An implementation of the generic-entity cloud building-block construct would include all the factors listed above
	• Can employee, manager, beneficiary, etc. be represented as subtypes of a generic "person" entity such that business staff can define new subtypes without IT intervention? Can the same be done for other basic business entities appropriate to the application -- organizational subtypes, accounting subtypes, product subtypes. etc.?
	• Is the underlying physical association that has been set up in the database between any two or more business entities many-to-many? If a person has one job in the company today, can she have two or more simultaneously tomorrow without reprogramming?
	• The bill-of-material approach is traditionally used to describe product structures. Is the same bill-of-material approach available to business staff to describe the organization structure, the chart of accounts structure, etc.? Can they represent a complex network scheme as well as a traditional hierarchical scheme?
	• Can these structures be interrelated and used by the system in, for example, inventory and financial reporting, so that a change in, say, organization, is automatically reflected in inventory, cost, and revenue for each relevant organization component?
	• Are the identifiers used in the database for recording associations among business entities such as Product ID, Person ID, etc. automatically assigned by the system? Are they completely without any information? Are they assigned so that a Person ID value cannot be the same as a Product ID value or as a Customer ID value, etc.?

Exhibit 16.5. Is Your System Flexible?

also prove difficult. Nevertheless, as much as possible, conduct your own examination and do not rely on vendor statements.

Both business and technical staff need to be involved in such an evaluation. Business staff will know the nature of changes in business policy and practice over time. Technical staff will know how to ask the appropriate questions of the vendor about how such changes would be accommodated within the vendor product. Working together they will be able to make an informed decision.

Flexibility Characteristics	Evaluation Questions

4. Regulation: the system has, or has access to, an extended data integrity facility that provides rules maintenance for cardinality and business policy
  a. Cardinality regulation facility providing the ability to vary the effective cardinality of relationships in the information structure
  b. If/then/else logic representation such that variations in logic are controlled by varying data values. Such rules engines can take different or multiple forms. The first four types listed below support business-staff-enabled rule maintenance:
    ➢ Evaluator-type, in which general Boolean logic is controlled by the software and is based on the selection condition entered by the business staff
    ➢ Condition-search-type, in which choices enacted by the system are controlled by tables of related conditions sequenced by priority
    ➢ Formal predicate logic interpreters of business action rules
    ➢ Extensive parameterization (e.g., SAP), meaning simply that more variables are represented by data value variations and less by program code
    ➢ Extensive use of exit points from standard processing for specialized routines; this requires IT intervention, but it is limited to small, local, modifications
  c. Rules engine access to data dictionary for obtaining metadata regarding data elements of conditions to be evaluated
	•　Can the basic association rules of the enterprise be changed? If the system enforces the rule of one person/one position today, can it be changed to multiple positions (multiple salaries, multiple supervisors, etc.) per person or to multiple persons per position (job sharing) tomorrow without reprogramming?
	•　Are there ways for rules of behavior to be maintained by business staff and be correctly interpreted by the system? Can business staff define, for example, credit terms, pricing structures, eligibility criteria, etc., without requiring substantial IT intervention?

5. Stable processing: a rules engine such as the Evaluator is inherently stable by virtue of being a general purpose tool. Application-determined processing, whether it invokes a rules engine or not, can itself be stable, subject to none-to-minimal local-only modifications. Stable processing:
  a. Exploits stable information structures:
    ➢ Recognizes generic entities
    ➢ Enforces control-type restrictions on generic entities and disallows relationship loops
    ➢ Assumes basic *m:n* relationships
    ➢ Uses cardinality regulation if available
  b. Can do efficient and stable handling of bill-of-material-like recursive file structures:
    ➢ Explosion/assembly (aka roll down/roll up, allocate down/accumulate up) processing of recursive relationships
    ➢ Explosion/assembly processing of nested recursive relationships
    ➢ Exploits direct access to ultimate parent/ultimate child in bill-of-material structure
	•　Can the business staff use generic entities to define and maintain the essential structures of the application? For example, organization charts, product lines and/or bills-of-material; personnel relationships, charts of accounts, etc.?
	•　Can such structures represent networks as well as hierarchies?
	•　Can the business staff define relationships among types of generic entities which the system will enforce on the relationships among instances of the generic entities? For example, in defining an organization, can the staff define that departments are children of subdivisions, which are children of divisions, which are children of companies, and have the system enforce that rule on any relationship the staff defines among instances of companies, divisions, subdivisions, and departments?
	•　Are the relationships above maintained independently of the information they organize? For example, if the product structure were changed would a report of inventory organized by product automatically reflect the new product structure? Ditto for data organized by combinations of structures such as inventory organized by product and location and organization unit, expenses organized by ledger account and person, etc.?
	•　Quantitative data organized by generic entities, such as inventory data, is normally recorded at the lowest levels of the generic entities. Does the system provide automatic re-allocation of lowest level data if a lowest level is changed? If the lowest level is raised, does the system automatically aggregate up; if the lowest level is lowered, does the system provide business staff assistance in allocating down?

Exhibit 16.5.　(continued)

    For those who have been involved in implementation of the large-scale vendor products, the watchword is "customization." Customization translates into modifications of information structures and programming. In other words, customization often means lack of flexibility. When a software project fails or costs two to five times more than the original amount budgeted, it is often because of customization. Keeping the characteristics of flexible systems in mind when evaluating vendor products can help an organization avoid the pitfalls of customization and enjoy the benefits of regulation going into the future.

Some time ago one of our authors participated in a request for proposal (RFP) process in selecting a vendor for a new financial system. One of the more popular candidates on the market was selected. During a vendor presentation, a representative gave a fairly detailed presentation of the features. He mentioned that user-controlled business rules were supported. Further discussion revealed that the design for business rule processing provided for acceptance of user-controlled parameter values but that the conditional logic of the business rules was actually coded in programs. The mechanism for business rules was actually a set of process-specific routines, each having coded logic, rather than a general-purpose tool. This approach does provide a degree of flexibility and is certainly an improvement over hard-coding both values and business rule logic. It may provide enough flexibility to adapt to an organization's changing business requirements. In other words, it may be good enough. In evaluating vendor products, both business and technical staff need to investigate whether a product is in fact good enough. In this case it required an IT professional to look under the covers of the claim for "user-controlled business rules."

Keeping the following myths in mind will help to ensure your success in procuring systems that meet your flexibility needs:

- Myth of comparative evaluation
- Myth of outsourcing

16.3.1 Myth of Comparative Evaluation

Do not compare apples to apples; compare them to a description of the apple you need.

If a packaged system is to be purchased, take care not to fall prey to the myth of comparative evaluation.

Myth: The best product is chosen by comparing candidate products with each other.

Reality: The best product is chosen by comparing candidate products with requirements.

It seems obvious, but the myth persists, so it is worth a reminder. Exhibit 16.6 provides a real-world example of the myth of comparative evaluation in action. Do not compare apples to apples; compare them to

One of the authors was hired as the new systems and programming manager. His first priority was to tackle the monthly business disruption caused by H.I. Publishing's outdated and quirky accounting system. He attempted to form a team to determine the capabilities required for an up-to-date system for the company. Unfortunately, the accounting personnel were unavailable for this. When they were not absorbed by the month-end panic, they were traveling around the country attending demonstrations of packaged accounting systems. Over the manager's objections, a feature-rich "best of breed" accounting package was purchased and installed. Once in operation it was apparent that certain functions vital to the company were missing or deficient and several other functions were superfluous to the business but required significant resources to maintain and operate. At last count the description of the apple that was required had not been produced, and the accounting staff had even less time to work on it. Don't go "system shopping" without a shopping list.

Exhibit 16.6.   The Apples-to-Apples Folly at H.I. Publishing Company (Name Changed)

a description of the apple you need. Also, having the requirements specification first, one that includes flexibility, is a strong aid to keeping the buyer/seller relationship clear.

16.3.2 The Myth of Outsourcing

There is a strong belief that by washing our hands of information technology issues and turning them over to outside experts, effective information technology systems will painlessly appear. This is the myth of outsourcing.

> Myth: We can hire an outside firm with the appropriate expertise that will manage our information technology cheaper and better, and we will avoid the management headaches.
> Reality: It is your business, and you must manage it, including the IT component.

The transformation processes leading to successful IT systems require diligent effort, proper project management, and just plain hard work by management, system customers, and IT professionals alike. This fact of IT life cannot be stressed enough; there is no way around it. If outsourcing occurs, at the very least project management responsibility must be retained internally. This is true even if the bulk of the development work is done by persons outside the enterprise and regardless of whether custom or off-the-shelf IT systems are used. And, as mentioned above in Section 16.2.1, while programming is frequently outsourced to foreign countries, the IT intervention required for on-site changes to business rules cannot generally be outsourced.

16.4 Summary

- The flexibility agenda is consistent with TQM principles and particularly supports the objective of continuous incremental quality improvement.
- As with quality, there is synergy between good project management and flexibility considerations in system development.
- Flexibility should be taken into account in cost/benefit trade-offs.
- Standards and tools are as appropriate to flexible systems as to conventional systems.
- Apply a flexibility characteristics checklist to product acquisition and development outsourcing.

There is evidence that vendors of packaged applications are paying more attention to flexibility. A number of vendors offer business rule engines that can interface with an organization's system. SAP has increased the flexibility of its products: "SAP AG is working on a variety of developer technologies designed to make its notoriously difficult-to-program enterprise software easier to configure and customize and, as a result, faster and less expensive to modify" [Boucher and Mccright, 2003]. The biggest payoff for flexibility may be in packaged and application service providers (ASP)-based applications. The fact that vendors can satisfy multiple customers with the same product provides a powerful incentive for flexible systems. Flexibility can provide virtual customization for different customers without the burden of actual custom coding.

FLEXIBILITY: DELVING DEEPER

IV

Part I introduced flexibility and why it is needed. Part II presented the key ingredients, or techniques, for achieving flexibility. The application of these techniques to design flexible software systems was addressed in Part III. What more could be left to say? The reader now knows what to do and how to do it. Some readers will choose to stop here.

For readers interested in delving more deeply into flexibility, Part IV provides details and case studies on specific flexibility topics. These six chapters enable readers to expand their knowledge of flexibility practices and present possibilities and to venture where very few have trod before.

- Chapter 17 presents a closer look at specific features of UniverSIS, showing how their design is consistent with the approach promoted throughout the book. Each feature includes an overview of the business function that it serves, a discussion of its operation, and implications for flexibility.

- Chapter 18 explains the Evaluator, a flexible tool for maintaining business rules. Examples of increasing complexity are used to show the power of this tool for implementing flexible software.

- Chapter 19 is a case study that contrasts traditional software design with flexible software design. A hypothetical tuition-remission software feature that was developed using traditional methods requires structural and procedural modifications by the IT staff when business requirements change. In contrast, the same system developed with a flexible design utilizing the generic-entity cloud (GEC) accommodates the same changes to business requirements with no intervention by IT staff.

The last three chapters demonstrate the flexibility and power of the GEC.

- Chapter 20 shows how GECs can be used to support regulatory requirements in addition to providing flexible information structures for business information.
- Chapter 21 presents several applications and extensions of the GEC, including the development of a GEC from application requirements, the atomic GEC, a three-ring GEC, and the sub-GEC.
- Chapter 22 presents three aids to facilitate the design and implementation of GEC-based software:
  1. GECAnalyzer: identifies all possible combinations of GECs and externals, thus giving the information-structure designer a tool to ensure that no valid combination is omitted.
  2. GECBuilder: produces a working software system based on GECs and externals provided either manually or by the interaction of the designer, business staff, and the GECAnalyzer. The GECBuilder can be used to:
     - Enter data into a working system in batch or GUI interactive mode
     - Produce indented, nested, recursive, bill-of-materials reports from the data in the GEC-based system
     - Handle cardinality regulation or present the status of a relationship
  3. GECPhazer: after the system is built, generates all possible combinations of typing interactions to ensure that all combinations with a valid business purpose are included.

Chapter 17

A Closer Look at UniverSIS

UniverSIS was introduced in Chapter 5 as a system developed using principles of flexibility. Two of its flexible features were discussed: (a) locators and (b) generic code/code-to-code. The Evaluator function was introduced in Chapter 13. Additional features are presented in this chapter, indicating how their design is consistent with the approach promoted throughout this book.

Before proceeding with discussion of these features, we observe that certain information about an individual is independent of the individual's relationship to the university. Information that falls in this category is stored in the data structure of a Person entity. Examples of such information include date of birth, gender, ethnicity, country of citizenship, social security number, and religious affiliation. The UniverSIS Person entity is a limited implementation of the fully generic entity type discussed throughout the book.

Much of the data stored in UniverSIS is connected to the Person entity, rather than to status-specific entities such as "prospect," "applicant," "student," or "employee." For example, the locator feature mentioned in Chapter 5 allows address information to be recorded for an individual. The connection is made between the Person entity and the locator entity. Any individual, regardless of relationship with the university, will have locator information. In general, unless an individual's information was clearly connected only to a specific status, the designers linked to the Person entity, as we will note in the examples.

293

17.1 Navigation and Security

Online functions in UniverSIS are defined through creation of database records. Each function has identified business owners. Those owners grant access to the functions directly, without IT intervention. Access to functions is also defined to the system through creation of database records. Each member of the business staff works from a personalized menu.

17.1.1 Discussion

Designers of information systems often use a standard menu to present to the staff member the list of available features. A typical approach is to define major groupings in the top-level menu. Selecting a major grouping will lead to a display of subgroupings, which leads to sub-subgroupings, etc. Security features prevent the staff from selecting menu items for which they are not authorized. A drawback of this approach is that it lacks flexibility. As the system grows, the number of menu items increases. At some point, screen-size limitations require reorganization of the groupings. Perhaps most frustrating to the staff member is that he does not know, by looking at his menu, which features he is authorized to use.

UniverSIS allows each staff member's menu to be personalized. The developers identified discrete business activities, called functions, that correspond to the lowest-level items in the chains of a hierarchical menu. The list of available functions serves as an inventory of the online capabilities of the system. A scrolling menu lists the functions that the staff member is authorized to use. As a new function is added to the system, it is made available to the appropriate staff members.

This approach has several benefits. It eliminates the need to redesign menus as the system grows, since all menus are personalized and dynamic. Staff members know that they are authorized to use whatever they see on the menu. No data structures are added or modified as new functions are added to the system. No existing programs need to be modified as functions are added. Identification of functions and assignment of functions to individuals are controlled through maintenance of records by business staff.

A common bottleneck in any organization is IT security. Authorization typically involves signing forms and passing them to the IT security staff, whose job it is to physically perform the task of providing the business staff with the required access to the system. The IT security staff add no value to the process—they are simply carrying out orders in a mechanical way because the person with the actual authority to grant access to the data is unable to do it directly.

```
FUNCTION - Maintain Security Functions

        Function Code: ADMISS-DECISION_
           *Program Module Id: SIAAPOD2

Description...................: Maintain Admissions Decision_____ Users will see this.
*Group Name................: ADMISSIONS_____
Used For Navigation?: Y (Y/N)    Only for programs
*Owner ID.....................: Bruce Johnson
                       Walter W. Woolfolk
                       Cindy Johnson
Access Record Must Match No Updates Criteria? N (Y/N)
No Updates Allowed If Admin Unit Mismatched? N (Y/N)
No Updates Allowed If Department Mismatched? N (Y/N)
Add allowed?..............: N (Y/N)
Modify allowed?..........: Y (Y/N)
Purge allowed?............: N (Y/N)
```

Exhibit 17.1. Function Record

UniverSIS eliminated the paper forms. When a new function is defined, its owners are also defined (Exhibit 17.1). This is the only point where IT security staff is involved. They create the system record for a new function, specifying the function owners — business staff who have the authority to grant access to others. The owners grant such access directly, using an online function designed for that purpose. They determine what type of access a staff member will have and whether that individual's college or business unit will limit access to records. Owners can actually choose not to grant themselves access to the functions they own. It is also possible to designate a function as "public," meaning that individual access authorization is not needed.

Changing ownership of a function involves modifying a single record per Exhibit 17.1. Granting access to a function requires a function owner to modify a single record, shown in Exhibit 17.2. Establishing this security system opened other windows of opportunity. To answer questions such as "How do I know what functions are out there?" and "Whom do I contact to get access to a function?" a simple "function owners" function is available, showing the list of all functions in the system, as well as the names and phone numbers of the function owners. To accommodate the need to copy all the functions from one person's account to another, a copy utility was developed. Adoption of this approach clearly streamlines

```
ACCESS - Maintain Security Access

*Function Code: ADMISS-DECISION_

*User ID: _ Robert Miller
or available to everyone...............................: N (Y/N)

Function Description:
*Group Name..........: ADMISSIONS_____
                      _____
                      _____

Access Attributes
Require Admin Unit Match for Updates?..: N (Y/N)
Require Department Match for Updates?: N (Y/N)
Add Allowed?......................................................: N (Y/N)
Modify Allowed?...............................................: Y (Y/N)
Purge Allowed...................................................: N (Y/N)
```

Exhibit 17.2. Access Record

the process, distributes the workload, and largely eliminates the IT organization from the picture.

There was no way to know what functions would be added, modified, or deleted, but the need to accommodate those activities was evident. Similarly, it was evident that at any time an individual might need to be granted access to a function, to have the type of access modified, or to have access removed. The developers asked the question, "What can change?" with regard to functions and access. The answer led to the flexible design described above.

17.1.2 Implications for Flexibility

Defining both functions and access to those functions as database records is in effect storing business rules as data. The usual benefits come into play. Business staff gain direct control, and IT involvement is reduced. The IT staff is involved only when new functions, requiring new programming, are established. The role of IT security, working from paper forms signed by function owners, is eliminated. Assignment of function access is performed directly by function owners. As staff turnover, reassignment, or reorganization occurs, modifications to access are managed entirely by function owners.

17.2 Documents

Organizations often require individuals to provide credentials and documentation of various types. Through a "document" feature, the developers of UniverSIS generalized this concept, developing a single mechanism that is used to record a variety of credentials and documentation.

17.2.1 Discussion

In gathering business requirements, the UniverSIS developers identified a category of information that could be served by a general-purpose entity. The common thread was recording that an individual had performed some specific activity about which a record needed to be maintained, e.g., submitted a required form, attended a required event, or provided required documentation. The amount of information to be recorded was very limited. In some cases, it was necessary only to record that the activity had been performed and when. In other cases, there was additional qualifying information.

For example, the music department requires an audition of all applicants. The members of an audition committee submit evaluations, from which a single overall rating is determined. Another example involves international students, who are required to submit a federal form that indicates source of financial support. The form has to be resubmitted periodically.

The UniverSIS developers identified a pattern to accommodate these situations and created a multipurpose mechanism called a "document." In addition to its other attributes, the document can have a series of ratings, all business staff-defined. A document recorded for an individual is called a Person-Document. Additional information can be recorded on the Person-Document: date of receipt, date of verification, individual who did the verification, expiration date or term, and free-form notes. Exhibit 17.3 illustrates the document created by the admissions office for music auditions. For each applicant who auditions, a Person-Document is recorded, with the rating the applicant received, as shown in Exhibit 17.4.

To track the international students' financial forms, the Office of International Students created a document corresponding to the standard paper financial form. For each international student, office staff record a Person-Document to indicate receipt of the paper financial form as well as the expiration date of the period covered by that form. Any notes explaining special circumstances are recorded on the Person-Document.

The document mechanism has proved to be a very flexible tool for adding isolated pieces of information to the system without modification

```
┌──────────────────────────────────────────────────────────────┐
│           DOC-DEFINITION - Maintain Credential Documents       │
│                                                                │
│                      Document: AUD_                            │
│                                                                │
│   Description............: CCM Audition_____ │
│   Allow Doc Manual Entry?: Y (Y/N)                             │
│                                                                │
│      Rating      Document Rating Description                   │
│      --------    ---------------------------------------------  │
│   /\ 1 A_  Excellent_____        │
│   || 2 B_  Very Good_____        │
│   || 3 C_  Good_____        │
│   || 4 D_  Fair_____        │
│   || 5 E_  Poor_____        │
│   || 6 __  _____        │
│   || 7 __  _____        │
│   || 8 __  _____        │
│   \/ 9 __  _____        │
│                         5 used of 20                           │
└──────────────────────────────────────────────────────────────┘
```

Exhibit 17.3.   Document Definition

```
┌──────────────────────────────────────────────────────────────┐
│            PERSON-DOC - Maintain Person Documents              │
│                                                                │
│                      ID: 000 99 9365                           │
│                       Jane M. Student                          │
│               *Document......: AUD_ CCM Audition               │
│                    Sequence Number: 1                          │
│                                                                │
│   Received Date.....................: 07 04 2003               │
│   *Document Rating..............: A_ Excellent                 │
│   Rating Completed Date...: 08 15 2003                         │
│   Verification Date.......: __ __ ____   *ID: ___ __ ____      │
│   *Document Valid Thru Term: _____                          │
│   Document Valid Thru Date: __ __ ____                         │
│   /\ 1 Notes: Outstanding range and power._____        │
│   || 2      _____        │
│   || 3      _____        │
│   || 4      _____        │
│   \/ 5      _____        │
└──────────────────────────────────────────────────────────────┘
```

Exhibit 17.4.   Person Document

of programs or information structures. In addition to its use for recording information, the presence or absence of a specific document can be used as the basis for action in various business processes.

Not all new data requirements can be accommodated by the Document/Person-Document structure. However, a significant percentage of those requirements can be accommodated if both developers and business staff are willing to think flexibly, eliminating the need for new data structures and new programming.

17.2.2 Implications for Flexibility

A single, stable information structure is used to record a variety of document types. Because documents are linked to the Person entity, the feature can be used to record information about any individual, regardless of relationship with the university. Business staff can create new types of documents without IT intervention. Standard features can be used in a variety of ways.

17.3 Required Admission Credentials

Building on the document feature described above, this feature allows the admissions office to specify the credentials that applicants to the university's academic programs must provide.

17.3.1 Discussion

The University of Cincinnati (UC) offers over 300 academic programs in a wide variety of academic disciplines. There is a need to record, for each academic program, which credentials an applicant must provide. There is also a need to determine, for an individual applicant, whether all required credentials have been received. The developers were able to use the document feature as the basis for a credential-requirement mechanism.

Credentials take a variety of forms. Transcripts, test scores, letters of recommendation, auditions, and portfolios are examples. Business staff define and maintain credentials as documents. As in the example shown earlier, a credential definition can specify ratings where appropriate, as in the music department's audition ratings.

Business staff define the standard credential requirements of each academic program, as shown in Exhibit 17.5, where three examples are provided:

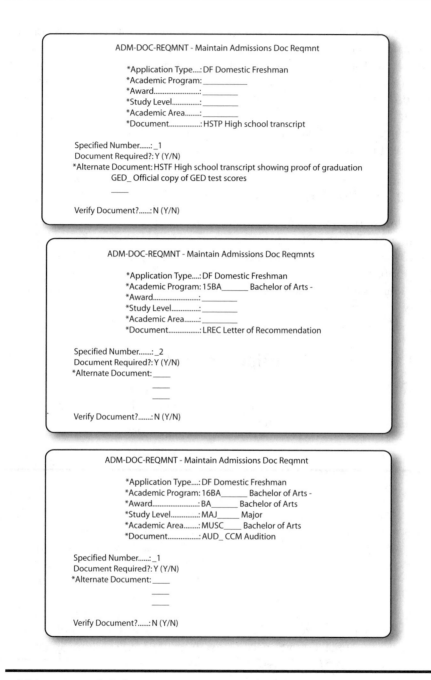

ADM-DOC-REQMNT - Maintain Admissions Doc Reqmnt

*Application Type....: DF Domestic Freshman
*Academic Program: _____
*Award.........................: _____
*Study Level...............: _____
*Academic Area........: _____
*Document.................: HSTP High school transcript

Specified Number.......: _1
Document Required?: Y (Y/N)
*Alternate Document: HSTF High school transcript showing proof of graduation
GED_ Official copy of GED test scores
____

Verify Document?......: N (Y/N)

ADM-DOC-REQMNT - Maintain Admissions Doc Reqmnts

*Application Type....: DF Domestic Freshman
*Academic Program: 15BA_____ Bachelor of Arts -
*Award.........................: _____
*Study Level...............: _____
*Academic Area........: _____
*Document.................: LREC Letter of Recommendation

Specified Number.......: _2
Document Required?: Y (Y/N)
*Alternate Document: ____
____
____

Verify Document?........: N (Y/N)

ADM-DOC-REQMNT - Maintain Admissions Doc Reqmnt

*Application Type....: DF Domestic Freshman
*Academic Program: 16BA_____ Bachelor of Arts -
*Award.........................: BA_____ Bachelor of Arts
*Study Level...............: MAJ_____ Major
*Academic Area........: MUSC____ Bachelor of Arts
*Document.................: AUD_ CCM Audition

Specified Number.......: _1
Document Required?: Y (Y/N)
*Alternate Document: ____
____
____

Verify Document?......: N (Y/N)

Exhibit 17.5. Admission-Document Requirements

- *Levels of specificity*: A credential may be required of all applicants or limited to specific colleges, programs, or majors. For example, "application fee" might be a general requirement but "audition" might be a requirement specific to applicants to music or dance programs.
- *Count*: Multiple credentials of the same type may be required, such as letters of recommendation.
- *Verification*: Upon receipt of a credential, the content and validity might need to be verified separately (letter of recommendation, transcript).
- *Alternatives*: A credential requirement can be met in alternative ways, as when one test result may be substituted for another.

Business staff record receipt of an individual's credentials as documents, i.e., as Person-Document records. Multiple versions of the same document might be recorded for an individual. In addition to the credential information itself, business staff might record expiration date/term and free-form notes.

When an individual applies for admission to an academic program, the system retrieves the set of credential requirements pertinent to that program. These standard requirements are copied to the individual's application profile. The admissions counselor can then customize the applicant's requirements to accommodate special circumstances, such as home schooling, foreign schooling, or the need for English proficiency certification. The list of required credentials functions as a checklist.

As an applicant provides credentials, receipt of each credential is recorded as a Person-Document. The system automatically matches the individual's credential requirements — the checklist — against the documents received. When each item has been checked off, the system changes the status of the application to "ready for decision."

17.3.2 Implications for Flexibility

Business staff can, through adjustment of business rules, accommodate the unique requirements of each academic program. No IT intervention is required to define new credentials or to maintain credential requirements. Unique needs of individual applicants — exceptions to the rules — can be accommodated within the system, without IT intervention.

17.4 Contact Management

To support various recruitment and retention efforts, and to evaluate their effectiveness, the university needs a mechanism for tracking contacts with students and prospective students. The contact-management feature of UniverSIS provides a simple yet flexible tool for this purpose.

17.4.1 Discussion

Customer relationship management (CRM) software appears prominently in vendor marketing materials. The developers of UniverSIS included a simple yet flexible feature for scheduling and maintaining records of personal contacts between business staff and prospects, applicants, and students. The "type" of contact is identified by a "context." Business staff maintain the values for context. Context can be general, such as admissions, student records, and academic advising, or they can be very specific, as the business staff choose. The contact record itself is very simple, as shown in Exhibit 17.6, including elements for the date and time of the contact, the form (personal, telephone, e-mail, etc.), the identifier of the business staff member, follow-up action, and notes about the contact. Future contacts can be scheduled, and a staff member can view a personalized to-do list of scheduled contacts for a given day.

The tool has proved to be flexible and useful in a variety of ways. A telecounseling feature, described in Chapter 5, for example, was built on the contact feature.

17.4.2 Implications for Flexibility

The feature was designed as a general-purpose tool. Through adjustment of data values, business units can use the feature in a variety of ways and for a variety of purposes. It can be used both to prepare for contact

```
                 PERSON-CONTACT - Maintain Prospect Contact

                        *ID: ___ __ ___

                      *Contact Context:____

        *University Contact:___ __ ___
        *Contact Position....:_____
        *Initiator....................:__
        *Contact Form.........:____
        *Action Taken.........:____

        Notes:_____
              _____
              _____
              _____
```

Exhibit 17.6. Person-Contact Document

campaigns and to record the results of such campaigns. Like documents, contacts are linked to the Person entity.

17.5 Correspondence

A university sends a great deal of mail. Typical mailings might be an information packet sent to a prospect, a letter of acceptance to an applicant, and a bill to a student. UniverSIS has a correspondence-management module that allows administrative offices to define such mailings, schedule them for delivery, cancel the delivery if necessary, produce the printed materials, and log the results.

17.5.1 Discussion

The correspondence feature was designed as a general-purpose correspondence tool, available for use by any business unit. Individual processing objects pull specified information from the database management system (DBMS) for insertion into the correspondence, e.g., name, address, salutation, academic program, missing information, etc. New objects can be added without disruption of any existing processes or data structures.

In designing this module as a general-purpose tool, the developers looked carefully at what could be done to make it flexible. Business staff identified the following characteristics of correspondence:

- Mailing items are often sent together as a "packet."
- Some mailing items are personalized; others are not.
- The address to which a mailing is to be sent may vary.
- Each administrative office has its own set of mailings.
- Sometimes a mailing needs to be cancelled because it is no longer necessary.
- Sometimes there is a limit to the number of times a particular mailing is sent to an individual.
- If the output is in paper form, it has to be delivered by operations to the right person or office.
- Rules change over time.

The term "correspondence" identifies the packet (Exhibit 17.7). A particular business area owns each correspondence.

Business staff define different "versions" of a correspondence, specified by date. Correspondence can contain nonpersonalized items such as brochures, informational pamphlets, etc. called "enclosures." Business staff define enclosures in a simple table. Correspondence can contain personalized

CORRESP - Maintain Correspondence

Correspondence ID: MISSINF1
Version Date: 07 05 2000

Description...........: Missing Information letter_____
*Correspondence Locator: /\ 1 TR Temporary Residence
                         || 2 LO Local Address
                         \/ 3 PE Permanent Address

Correspondence Limit..: ___ Unlimited? Y (Y/N)
*Business Area.........: ADMISS Admissions
*Correspondence Type...: APPLICATIONS___ Undergraduate Admissions Applications
*Document Name.........: MISSING INFO LETTER_____
            MAILING LABEL_____
                         _____
                         _____
                         _____
                         _____

*Cancel Requirement....: _____ Version:

*Enclosure:
  /\ 1 GNAPP____ UC Application and Instructions
  || 2 _____
  || 3 _____
  || 4 _____
  || 5 _____
  \/ 6 _____
                    0 used of 20
Do Not Deliver Without Enclosure? N (Y/N)

Output Delivery
*Admin Unit:____   *Department: ____
*Building: EDWARDS_ Edwards Ce *Room: 278___
*Deliver to this Person: 000 99 9694 Mary Staff

Exhibit 17.7. Correspondence

items such as letters, mailing labels, postcards, etc. called "correspondence documents." Business staff define and maintain these items. It is important to note that an enclosure or correspondence document can be associated with multiple correspondences. For example, mailing labels, which are personalized items, are used by many correspondences. Business staff indicate on the correspondence record where output is to be delivered and the number of times the correspondence can be sent to an individual. They also indicate a preferred sequence of addresses. In this example, the admissions office has specified that a "temporary address" is the first choice, followed by a "local address," and finally by a "permanent address." The locator feature, mentioned in Chapter 5, provides the flexibility of an unlimited number of address types. At delivery time, the system uses that sequence to analyze where the missing-information letter will be sent for an individual student based on the sequence and the current date. The address sequence serves as the normal rule, but the rule can be overridden for an individual student. Finally, using the Evaluator mechanism described briefly in Chapter 13 and in more detail in Chapter 18, business staff can define criteria that will cause a correspondence delivery to be canceled at production time if it is no longer necessary. The general-purpose design of the Evaluator pays off once again. A new purpose can be served without any modifications to the Evaluator itself.

This correspondence-management feature has enabled UC to standardize the approach to production of output. In addition, the system maintains a record of what correspondence has been sent, what correspondence documents and enclosures were included, and the address to which it was sent. Such information can be systematically reviewed and analyzed over time. Furthermore, the system permits review of correspondence scheduled for the future, allowing staffing preparation for days when large volumes of output are expected. Although the feature was designed with paper output in mind, it can also be used for electronic correspondence.

17.5.2 Implications for Flexibility

Business staff have full control over both text and insertion of information stored in the DBMS and also control the logic for cancellation of correspondence. While the correspondence feature does not have the full capabilities of a word processor, it does have the significant benefit of integration with the student information system. Once again, because there may be a need to correspond with individuals who have different relationships with the university, the correspondence is linked to the Person entity.

17.6 Correspondence Tracks

The correspondence-track feature builds on the correspondence feature described in Exhibit 17.6. It enables a business unit to identify a sequence of mailings that are to be sent to an individual or identifiable group of individuals. The timing of the mailings, dependencies between mailings, and cancellation of mailings are controlled by rules managed by business staff.

17.6.1 Discussion

UniverSIS provides a correspondence-track feature that can be used to send a series of designated mailings on a personalized schedule to individuals whose personal profile, interests, etc. match specified criteria. The track is tied to a specific academic year. In this example, a series of mailings has been established for admissions applicants to remind them to provide missing documents, shown in Exhibit 17.8. The MISSING INFO requirement defines the criteria for membership in the track, i.e., at least one admission credential document is missing. Once again, the Evaluator provides the

```
                CORRES-TRACK - Maintain Correspondence Track

                                              Corres Track: MIF01_
                    Corres Track Year: 2001

        Description..: Admissions Applicants Acad Year 2000-01_____
        *Requirement (must meet all requirements to qualify for track)
        /\ 1 MISSING INFO___ 05 31 2000 MISSING DOCUMENTS FOR APPLICATION
        || 2 _____
        \/ 3 _____
                                      1 used of 5
        Correspondence Schedule
        /\ 1 *Correspondence......: MISSINF1 Missing Information letter
        ||    Required?      · N (Y/N)
        ||    Send Date...........: __ __ ____
        ||    Pre-Req Corres......: _____
        ||    Elapsed Days Track..: __1
        ||    Elapsed Days Pre-Req: ___

        ||    Elapsed Days Year...: ___
        \/    *Cancel Requirement..: CANCEL MISSING_____ 07 06 2000 Cancel Letter

        Correspondence Schedule
        /\ 2 *Correspondence......: MISSINF2 Missing Information letter
        ||    Required?..........: N (Y/N)
        ||    Send Date...........: __ __ ____
        ||    Pre-Req Corres......: MISSINF1 Missing Information letter
        ||    Elapsed Days Track..: ___
        ||    Elapsed Days Pre-Req: _30
        ||    Elapsed Days Year...: ___
        \/    *Cancel Requirement..: CANCEL MISSING_____ 07 06 2000 Cancel Letter

        Correspondence Schedule
        /\ 3 *Correspondence......: MISSINF3 Missing Information letter
        ||    Required?..........: N (Y/N)
        ||    Send Date...........: __ __ ____
        ||    Pre-Req Corres......: MISSINF2 Missing Information letter
        ||    Elapsed Days Track..: ___
        ||    Elapsed Days Pre-Req: _30
        ||    Elapsed Days Year...: ___
        \/    *Cancel Requirement..: CANCEL MISSING_____ 07 06 2000 Cancel Letter
```

Exhibit 17.8. Correspondence Track

mechanism by which business staff identify the selection criteria. A nightly job evaluates applicants for inclusion in this track. For those who satisfy the MISSING INFO requirement, a series of three mailings is scheduled. The choice of three mailings was a business decision, not a system limitation. The first mailing is scheduled for one day after the individual joins the track. The second is scheduled for 30 days after the first, the third 30 days after the second. Note that each schedule correspondence has a "cancel requirement." If, at the time the correspondence is scheduled to be produced, the individual satisfies the CANCEL MISSING requirement, the correspondence will be cancelled. The CANCEL MISSING requirement specifies that no documents are missing. In other words, if nothing is missing, there is no need to send a "missing information" correspondence. It saves paper and postage and, more importantly, avoids making a bad impression on the applicant. The correspondence-track feature reuses the correspondence feature described in Section 17.5 as well as the Evaluator feature. Several other business units use the correspondence-track feature as well. No unit-specific customizations have been necessary.

17.6.2 Implications for Flexibility

The correspondence-track feature was designed for general use. Any business unit that has a need to send a sequence of mailings can make use of it. The correspondence-track feature itself reused general-purpose system features. Like correspondence, tracks are linked to the Person entity.

17.7 Selected-ID Lists

Business processing often requires that individuals be identified as members of a specific list. The "selected-ID list" feature provides a standard mechanism for recording membership in a list. Business staff can create lists on an ad hoc basis or make use of standard, predefined lists. Members can be added to lists online through a manual process or in a batch process using standard logic.

17.7.1 Discussion

Much of business processing involves identification of individuals to be processed, i.e., creating a list. Business staff might create a list of individuals for purposes of identification, or to support some manual activity such as making phone calls. In many cases, the list is created so that some batch process can act on it. The ideal for batch-processing efficiency is to access only those records that actually need to be accessed.

To accomplish this ideal, the developers established a trigger/list mechanism called the selected-ID list. A selected-ID list is extremely simple. Each list has a name, a category, the ID of the individual, and a few other pieces of optional information. A significant percentage of the UniverSIS batch jobs use these lists to determine the candidates for business processing. An example will illustrate how the triggering mechanism works.

Assessment of tuition and fees is a process that is run nightly, in batch. Certain activities on the part of the student can lead to a change in the amount a student owes, e.g., adding a class, dropping a class, changing academic program, changing health insurance coverage, etc. Except at certain times of the academic term, the information of a typical student does not change from day to day. Because UC has 34,000 students, assessing only those who require processing offered the potential for significant reduction in the use of machine resources. To accomplish this, the developers worked with the business staff to identify the assessment factors, i.e., data-element changes that could lead to changes in the student's tuition and fees. They developed a single module to add an individual to what is called the RE-ASSESSMENT list. They attached the logic to trigger a call to that module for each of the entities that contained an assessment factor. For example, the RE-ASSESSMENT trigger was added to the object used to maintain the enrollment entity. The nightly batch-assessment job processes only those individuals who appear on the RE-ASSESSMENT list, purging them from the list upon completion of assessment. The savings gained by processing only those students who need to be assessed outweighs the overhead of storing the individual's record on the RE-ASSESSMENT list.

The selected-ID-list feature is used for many recurring business processes. A business unit might wish to identify a group of students who meet specified criteria and send them a letter, e.g., the students who are interested in the marching band. Rather than combining the selection process and the business process, the business unit performs the selection first, storing the results in a MARCHING BAND selected-ID list. The size of the list can determine whether the action is taken. If the business group expected a list of 100 and got a list of 1000 instead, it may want to adjust its selection criteria. Having selected the population, the unit can run a correspondence-production job, using the MARCHING BAND list as the source. In the case of RE-ASSESSMENT, the individuals are purged from the list upon completion of the process. However, this is merely an option. Depending on the process, business staff might want to retain the list membership, add members to the list manually, remove members from the list manually, or run another selection with different criteria, adding members to an existing list. The possibilities are endless. The business group can use the lists however it chooses.

```
                SEL-IDS-BY-NAME - Browse Selected IDs by Name

   Action   Selection ID        Name                    Program         Term
   ------   ----------------    ---------------------   ----------     --------
     _      RE-ASSESSMENT       ABBOTT TIFFANY R                          02A
     _      RE-ASSESSMENT       ACKERMAN SCOTT DAVID                      02A
     _      RE-ASSESSMENT       ADAM MATTHEW F                            02A
     _      RE-ASSESSMENT       AIKEN LUKE                                02A
     _      RE-ASSESSMENT       AKI HULUSI SERHAN                         02A
                  ...
   Selection ID: RE-_____   Name: _____
```

Exhibit 17.9.   Selected-ID List

```
              SELECTION-SETS - Browse Selected ID Sets

       Selection Id              Number Of Person In Set
       ------------------        ---------------------------------
       ADM-AUTO-DECISIONS                 7
       PRINT-BILL                         12,156
       RE-ASSESSMENT                      547
```

Exhibit 17.10.   Selected-ID-List Summary

Exhibit 17.9 shows a list of students who need to have charges reassessed as a result of changes in their enrollment, financial aid, etc. The term to be reassessed is specified.

UniverSIS also provides a screen (Exhibit 17.10) that tells the number of entries currently on each list. This feature can be helpful in planning production schedules. For example, processing of very large lists can be staggered across two or more evenings.

The mechanism for maintaining selected-ID lists is stable. Business staff can create new lists and use them in a variety of ways, but modifications to files and programs are not needed to accommodate these lists. However, when a new trigger mechanism must be established, the IT staff does have to write program code. Even in that situation, however, the coding follows an established pattern and can be completed and tested in a few hours.

17.7.2 Implications for Flexibility

Records on the selected-ID list use a standard set of data elements, making the feature essentially generic. Logic for maintaining records is generic, allowing one set of programs to be used to maintain all lists. Business staff can create new lists and modify membership of lists without IT intervention. Because logic for accessing lists for batch processing has been standardized, programmers can reuse that logic when coding new processes involving lists, reducing the amount of development time. Because records are linked to the Person entity, Selected-ID lists are available for use with any individual whose records are stored in the system.

17.8 Tests

Standardized tests can take a variety of forms, using a variety of test components and subcomponents and rules for scoring. UniverSIS provides a flexible mechanism for defining standardized tests and recording student test results.

17.8.1 Discussion

A university uses various types of tests for nonclassroom purposes. Examples include entrance examinations such as the ACT, SAT, and GRE; advanced placement tests; English language proficiency tests; etc. Recognizing that new tests are introduced fairly frequently and that existing tests may undergo revisions, the developers designed a flexible mechanism for defining tests and recording test results. The feature has two principle components: (a) a function for defining tests: TEST-DEFINITION (Exhibit 17.11) and (b) a function for recording an individual's test results: TEST-SCORES (Exhibit 17.12).

TEST-DEFINITION provides an information structure for recording attributes of the test. The structure provides for three levels of scores within a test, i.e., test, test component, and test component subcomponent. Test score ranges are specified. Scores can be nonnumeric. Component or subcomponent scores can be marked as "required."

Note that the fixed limit to the levels of a test represents a departure from the approach that we have generally promoted. However, the reality was that no one had ever encountered a test that had a level below

```
                    TEST-DEFINITION - Maintain Test Definition

            Test Code..: ACT_  Begin Date: 11 01 1989
                           End Date..: __ __ ____
       Description..........: ACT Test After 10/89_____
       Test Low Score....: ____1  High Score: ___36  Score Required? N (Y/N)
       *Document...........: ACT_ ACT Test Score Results
       Non-Numeric Scores Allowed? N (Y/N)
       Show Best Component Score? Y (Y/N)    Sum Components For Total? N (Y/N)
       Component     Description                Low Score  High Score Required?
         1ENG   English_____          ____1     ___36    N (Y/N)
         2MTH   Math_____          ____1     ___36    N
         3RED   Reading_____          ____1     ___36    N
         4SCI   Science Reasoning_____          ____1     ___36    N
         5CMP   Composite_____          ____1     ___36    N
         ____   _____          ____      ____     N
         ____   _____          ____      ____     N


    /\  Component   Description       Low Score        High Score Required?
    ||  1  1ENG  English_____    1____       36____     N (Y/N)
    ||
    ||
    ||  Sub Component  Description      Low Score      High Score Required?
    ||  RHET   Rhetorical Skills_____    1____       18____     N (Y/N)
    ||  USAG   Usage/Mechanics_____    1____       18____     N
    V   ____   _____  ____          ____       N
```

Exhibit 17.11. Test Definition

subcomponent. As we have said, flexibility has its limits. Nevertheless, the mechanism has proved to be very flexible. Data structures and program code have not changed since the feature was introduced. Business staff establish new tests.

On the TEST-SCORES function, entry of a test identifier prompts the system to display the appropriate components and subcomponents for entry of an individual's scores. The presentation of the information is sensitive to the date the student completed the test, selecting the correct version of the test from the TEST-DEFINITION records.

17.8.2 Implications for Flexibility

The format, scoring rules, number of components and subcomponents, etc. comprise, in effect, business rules. These rules are all under business control. Versions of tests, with effective periods, can be maintained.

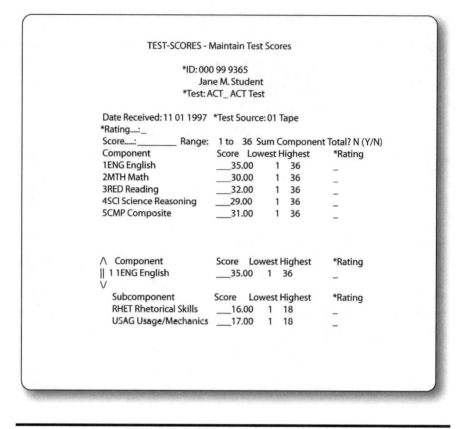

Exhibit 17.12. Student Test Score

Although tests may appear to be specific to an individual's status, they are in fact linked to the Person entity.

17.9 Employee Profile

Although UniverSIS is not a personnel system, a small amount of information about employees is recorded. This information includes a list of functional positions an individual holds. In combination with other general-purpose features, this allows automated assignment of responsibilities.

17.9.1 Discussion

The developers identified a need to maintain within UniverSIS a small amount of information about employees, as shown in Exhibit 17.13. Certain features

```
              EMPLOYEE-PROFILE - Maintain Employee Profile

                                        *ID: 000 99 9998
                              Mary M Staff
                              DREGLMBX
        Active Staff Member?.......: Y (Y/N)
        *Staff Administrative Unit: UREG University Registrar
        *Department.........................: R&S_ Registr & Sched

        If faculty member, enter instructor college and department.
        Active faculty member?...: N (Y/N)
        *Instructor College..............:____
        *Department.........................:____


        *Business Position
         /\ 1 RQ-BILLING Authority for Billing Requirements
         || 2 REGIST____ Registrar Staff
         || 3 ADM03____Admissions Counselor #3
         || 4_____
```

Exhibit 17.13. Employee Profile

used to control access to records and processing capabilities use this information. An employee can have a variety of administrative responsibilities, i.e., wear several "hats." To accommodate this variety of responsibilities, which can change at any time, a business-position element was created. Values for business position are maintained in a generic table, as described in Chapter 5. An individual can be assigned to multiple business positions, and multiple individuals can be assigned to a specified business position. In this example, the individual has been assigned to three business positions.

The feature is used in a variety of ways. For example, as we mentioned above, all correspondence has a designated type (see Exhibit 17.7). A record is maintained in UniverSIS for each correspondence type (Exhibit 17.14). On that record is specified the business position that is permitted to maintain correspondence of that type. The system enforces the rule that only an employee who has the designated business position on his employee-profile record can create or make changes to a correspondence record of that type. Business managers can assign or remove that authorization without IT intervention by modifying data values.

The same approach is used for maintenance of Evaluator conditions and requirements, as shown in Exhibit 17.15. Only an employee who has the specified business position on his employee-profile record can maintain records of a given type.

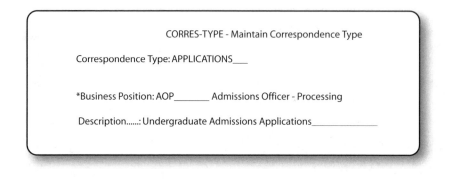

Exhibit 17.14. Correspondence Type

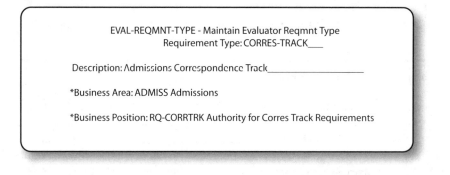

Exhibit 17.15. Evaluator Requirement Type

Another simple mechanism makes use of other general-purpose features to assign admissions counselors to applicants alphabetically (Exhibit 17.16). The generic-table feature, described in Chapter 5, is used here. A generic table containing the 26 letters of the alphabet, called counselor assignment, is created. Using the code-to-code mechanism, also described in Chapter 5, each letter is assigned to a designated business position. The business-position codes are recorded on the counselors' employee-profile records. The program that processes admissions applications contains logic that takes the first letter of the applicant's last name and finds it in the code-to-code table. It then takes the associated business position and finds the first employee-profile record on which that business position is recorded. For example, consider an applicant named William Ross who was assigned to business position ADM03. Mary Staff's employee profile, shown in Exhibit 17.13, includes the ADM03 business position, so William Ross would be assigned to Mary.

```
          Counselor Assignment              Business Position
                  A                              ADM01
                  B                              ADM01
                 ...
                  K                              ADM02
                 ...
                  R                              ADM03
```

Exhibit 17.16. Alphabetic Assignment of Counselors

The same approach has been used in other business units. As staff turnover occurs, it is easy for unit managers to rearrange assignments without any need for IT intervention. This is an example of combining existing features in a creative and flexible way.

17.9.2 Implications for Flexibility

Permission to maintain certain types of data is managed through user-maintained business rules keyed to the business-position feature of the employee profile. Business managers can assign or reassign responsibilities directly, without IT intervention.

17.10 Grades

Grades are familiar to anyone who has attended school. In clarifying business requirements for keeping student grades, the developers discovered that the business rules could be quite complex. It is definitely not as simple as A, B, C.

17.10.1 Discussion

From the screen sample shown in Exhibit 17.17, it is clear that:

- Grades can have a context, defined by "grading system" and "grade type."
- Different grading systems can exist, e.g., undergraduate, graduate, medical school, law school, etc.
- Different types of grades can exist within a grading system, e.g., normal, pass/fail, etc.

```
GRADES - Maintain Grades

        *Grading System: U Undergraduate
        *Grade Type....: N Normal
        Grade.........: A___
        *Begin Term....: 68A_____ Autumn Quarter 1968-69

*End Term................: _____
Description.............: Excellent_____

Grade Shown on Transcript: A___        Include in GPA?..........      : Y (Y/N)
Quality Points.........: __4.0000       Include in Carried Hours?     : Y (Y/N)
                                        Include in Earned Hours?.     : Y (Y/N)
                                        Include in Pass Hours?...     : N (Y/N)
Administrative Use Only?: N (Y/N)       Include in Progress Hours?    : N (Y/N)
*Temporary Convert Grade.: ____         Default Final Grade?.....     : N (Y/N)
Temporary Lapse Periods.: ___           Default Withdrawal Grade?     : N (Y/N)
Temporary Lapse Unit....: _ (T,Y)       Pre-Requisite Invalid?...     : N (Y/N)

This grade cannot be changed to any of these:
        * I___ Incomplete
        N___ No Grade Reported
        Y___ Unofficial Withdrawal
        ____
```

Exhibit 17.17. Grade Maintenance

- There can be versions of a grade, defined by begin and end terms.
- It is possible to show a grade value on the transcript that is different from the actual grade the student received.
- Some grades count toward the student's grade-point average, and some do not.
- Some grades automatically convert to other grades after a specified period of time has elapsed, e.g., incomplete grades.
- Certain grades cannot be changed to other grades.

By providing this data structure, the developers gave business staff a way to maintain control over all aspects of grades. New grading systems can be introduced, and new grades can be introduced within an existing grading system/type. In winter quarter of 1999, approximately nine months before UniverSIS went live, UC introduced plus/minus grading for under-graduates. Modifying the legacy system to accommodate plus/minus grading required hundreds of hours of programming effort. Adding plus/minus grades within UniverSIS would have required no special programming effort. As shown in Exhibit 17.18, introduction of plus/minus grades was

```
                        - Browse Grades -

      Grading  Grade        Begin
      System   Type  Grade  Term              Description
      -------  ----- -----  --------   -----------------------------------------------

        U        N      *     68A
        U        N      A     68A
        U        N      A-    99W
        U        N      B     68A
        U        N      B+    99W
        U        N      B-    99W
        U        N      C     68A
        U        N      C+    99W
        U        N      C-    99W
        U        N      D     68A
        U        N      D+    99W
        U        N      D-    99W
      Grading System: U  Grade Type: N  Grade: ____
```

Exhibit 17.18.   Browse Grades

a matter of adding GRADES records specifying the "begin term" of 99W. Since UniverSIS was implemented, other modifications to grades and grading rules have been introduced. All have been accommodated without IT intervention.

17.10.2 Implications for Flexibility

Storing the business rules associated with grades as data, maintained by business staff, has eliminated the need for IT intervention when the rules change. In addition, the rules themselves are visible and readable. They are not hidden in program code.

17.11 Summary

We have presented ten specific examples of flexible features implemented in UniverSIS, which is in use at the University of Cincinnati. The presentation of each example provided an overview, a discussion of how the feature operates, examples of its use, and a summary of its implications for flexibility and ease of maintenance. Many more examples could have been chosen, but these are sufficient to make our point about the value of flexibility.

The specific features covered are:

- *Navigation and security*: enables assigned business experts to control access to specific functions that they own
- *Documents*: allow business staff to define credentials and required documentation
- *Required admission credentials*: building on the "documents" feature, allows business staff to define credentials an individual must provide when applying for admission to the university
- *Contact management*: enables business staff to track, support, and evaluate contacts made by their offices
- *Correspondence*: enables business staff to create and manage correspondence that merges text with data stored in the system
- *Correspondence tracks*: building on the "correspondence" feature, provides for development and scheduling of personalized sequences of mailings, completely under business staff control
- *Selected-ID lists*: provides a generic mechanism for managing lists of individuals who meet common sets of criteria or who are to be processed together
- *Tests*: provides a mechanism for managing and recording results of an inventory of tests that have a wide variety of formats and scores
- *Employee profile*: enables flexible manipulation of employee roles, which can change frequently
- *Grades*: supports a wide variety of grading systems with differing processing and application rules, all managed by business staff

These examples illustrate what is possible through flexible design. Some of the features are quite simple, despite their flexibility, and others are more complex. Whenever possible, the developers of UniverSIS built general-purpose, reusable features and made use of generic information structures. These examples are presented in the hope that they will move readers to consider how these ideas can be applied to their particular requirements. All of the features described here, as well as others, have contributed to the objective of flexibility, thus giving business staff greater control over changes to system behavior.

Chapter 18

Evaluator: a Flexible Tool for Maintaining Business Rules

In Chapter 8, the discussion of regulation pointed out the benefits of giving business staff control over maintenance of business rules. Simple rules such as "value A is valid and value B is not" have long been represented in software as lists of valid values maintained by business staff. This chapter discusses in detail a technique that gives business staff control over complex business rules.

Changes in business policy account for a significant percentage of the IT effort expended in maintaining inflexible systems. One day the policy states that condition ABC is invalid. The next day, the policy is changed to consider condition ABC valid in some circumstances and invalid in others. The policy is an artificial limit on the behavior of the software — a general business rule — and is subject to change as the business environment changes. When such rules are recorded in programs in the form of traditional IF/THEN/ELSE logic, changes in those rules require modification of program code.

The developers of UniverSIS designed a general-purpose tool — dubbed the Evaluator — that allows business staff to define and maintain complex rules without modifications to programs. The Evaluator has two major components:

- A mechanism to record rules
- A mechanism to evaluate whether an individual case has satisfied those rules

The Evaluator is based on the premise that many business-processing decisions can be constructed with the following components:

- A defined set of decision elements
- A true/false question based on decision elements
- Action to be taken for a true result
- Action to be taken for a false result

The admissions office at the University of Cincinnati uses the Evaluator to automate the process of granting admission to applicants. We provide an overview of this process before getting into more detail about the Evaluator itself.

18.1 Record Rules

An element is a piece of information about an individual that can be used in a business rule. In the case of admissions decisions, the following elements were defined:

- High-school GPA (grade-point average)
- Percentage rank in high-school class
- Ohio high-school proficiency test rating
- Best ACT math score or SAT math score
- Best composite ACT score or SAT total score
- High-school core courses completed indicator

An element is a form of regulatory entity. Before an element can be used, it has to be identified to the Evaluator. Once an element has been established, IT staff need do nothing further with it. Evaluator allows business staff to use elements to construct rules in the form of conditions composed of logical statements. Many administrators were immediately comfortable with this approach because the statements are similar to those they encode on a daily basis to generate reports from UC's data warehouse. The rules can be as simple or as complex as necessary. A rule also has date-sensitive versions, which allows a history of rules to be maintained. It also allows administrative staff to prepare and test new versions of rules without affecting current processes.

```
Condition #1
        High School GPA              GE    3.0
AND     Class Rank Percentage        LE    10
AND     Ohio Proficiency             EQ    PASS
AND     Best ACT Math                GE    24
AND     Best ACT Composite           GE    26
AND     Core Courses Completed       EQ    YES

Condition #2
        High School GPA              GE    3.0
AND     Class Rank Percentage        LE    10
AND     Ohio Proficiency             EQ    PASS
AND     Best SAT Math                GE    550
AND     Best SAT Total               GE    1150
AND     Core Courses Completed       EQ    YES
```

```
EQ = Equal to
NE = Not equal to
GE = Greater than or Equal to
GT = Greater than
LT = Less than
LE = Less than or Equal to
```

Exhibit 18.1. Example of Business Rules Entered for Evaluator

In the fictitious example shown in Exhibit 18.1, the elements were combined into two complex conditions. Satisfying either of the conditions would satisfy the rules for admission to the academic program. A business staff member, sitting at a screen, would enter these conditions and they would be stored in the system.

18.2 Evaluate

The Evaluator provides a mechanism to compare an individual's data, as defined by the elements, to the criteria specified in the rules. This mechanism consists of two parts:

1. A set of modules that retrieves the individual's data
2. An evaluation module that compares the individual's data with the specified rules

In the automated decision example, the retrieval modules assemble the applicant's data for the specified elements. For example, given that the element is high school GPA, a module retrieves the applicant's high school GPA data. The evaluation module compares the applicant's data against the rule, element by element, until it can be determined whether the applicant has satisfied all criteria. If all criteria have been satisfied, the evaluation module returns a result of TRUE. Otherwise, it returns a result of FALSE. The process that is using the Evaluator determines what to do with the result. In the case of automated decisions, a result of TRUE triggers the system to record an offer of admission on the application. The basis of the Evaluator approach is construction of all conditional statements to yield a true or false result.

```
IF  Condition  is  satisfied
    Then  TRUE
ELSE
    FALSE
```

The TRUE/FALSE result is independent of the process that makes use of the result. This allows Evaluator to serve as a general-purpose tool, one that can be used in a variety of business situations. It is being used in UniverSIS in several core business processes, eliminating the need for the IT organization's regular, cyclical program modifications as rules change. Its use is being extended as more business units become aware of and gain confidence in its capabilities.

A significant cost to the Evaluator approach was the time spent developing and testing the mechanism itself. It is complex. Once completed, however, it is available to any business purpose that requires evaluation of records. Additional Evaluator programming, in the traditional sense of the IT staff writing code, occurs only when new selection elements are required or when a new process making use of the Evaluator is developed, as shown in Exhibit 18.2. The selection element programs can typically be written and tested in two hours or less. For example, the registrar's office might have a process that selects students using the Evaluator and produces mailing labels for those students. If a new selection element is needed, e.g., ACADEMIC-MAJOR, a programmer writes a specialized program that will retrieve that information for the Evaluator. Once ACADEMIC-MAJOR is added to the pool of selection elements, it is now available for use by any business area, not just the registrar's office, and for any purpose, not just production of mailing labels. The programmer does not need to be concerned with how or where the ACADEMIC-MAJOR routine is being used. It is a tool in the toolbox of the business staff. System modifications — made in the past by IT staff doing programming by modifying code — can be made by business staff doing "programming" by adding or modifying Evaluator conditions.

Several years after the initial implementation of UniverSIS, a new process was developed to assign students to groups for early registration. The new data structure includes a place for the Evaluator requirements. Because the new process involved recording new information, new data structures and programming were required, but the only modification to the Evaluator itself was the addition of new selection elements. Business staff define the groups and then define the Evaluator requirements that

```
                        Maintain Regist Priority Group

    Action (A,B,C,D,M,N,P)  _      *Term: 04A_____ Autumn Quarter 2004-05
                                    Group: 2D


    Sequence Number: 80_
    Description....: Undergraduates with 90+ Hours_____
    Begin Date.....: 05 11 2004
    End Date.........: 05 12 2004


    *Requirement (must meet all requirements to qualify for group)
       1 PRIORITY 90+___ 03 17 2004  Priority Matriculated Undergraduate Student
       2 _____
       3 _____
       4 _____
       5 _____
```

Exhibit 18.2.   Adding a New Process to the Evaluator

assign students to those groups using the Evaluator capabilities. They can add or subtract groups, change requirements, change dates, etc. without any modifications to information structures or program code.

The process to assign students runs in batch mode. The programming includes the standard logic to activate the Evaluator and take the appropriate action based on the result. For each student, the processing goes through the groups one by one, invoking the Evaluator each time, until it finds a group for which the student satisfies the Evaluator requirement. It then assigns the student to that group, much like the dynamic condition search in Chapter 13.

When developing a new business process that makes use of the Evaluator, a programmer must establish the connection. Like any reusable module, the Evaluator must be invoked via program logic. Data is passed back and forth between the calling module and the Evaluator. The Evaluator itself need not be touched, however, because it is independent of any process that uses it. The technical steps involved in establishing the connection to the Evaluator follow a simple, standard pattern. Programming effort is involved only when the new process is established. Once the process is in place, with a connection to the Evaluator, further maintenance of that process is not required.

18.3 Evaluator: the Details

This section explains the data structures and some of the processing that underlie the Evaluator. This discussion is presented for readers who are interested in the details. In designing the Evaluator, the challenge was to develop a tool that could store, retrieve, and evaluate business logic and allow users to maintain not only data values, but also the business logic itself. The business logic was broken into conceptual components:

- Elements
- Values
- Relational operators
- Logical operators
- Subconditions
- Conditions
- Rules
- Business requirements
- Results
- Business decisions

Evaluation criteria are recorded in the form shown in Exhibit 18.1. The evaluation process receives the identifier of a person, evaluates the person's data according to the specified criteria, and returns a result of TRUE or FALSE. The result is passed to the module that makes the required business decision. In UniverSIS, the Evaluator is used only to evaluate persons, though it could be adapted for use with any entity.

18.3.1 Building Evaluator Requirements

The lowest level of logic is called a subcondition. A logical statement or statements expressing a relationship between a single element and a value or set of values forms a subcondition. The relational operator defines the relationship; six values are possible. As shown in Exhibit 18.1, they are EQ, NE, GT, GE, LT, and LE. An example would be:

```
ACAD-PROGRAM     EQ     15BA
```

The statement must be true for the subcondition to be satisfied. Logical operators (and/or) can be components of a subcondition. The subcondition is composed of a statement or statements referring to a single element and giving a single result. For example:

```
        ACAD-AREA     EQ     HIST
or      ACAD-AREA     EQ     ECON
```

Subconditions can specify ranges of values as well as individual values. In the following improbable example, to satisfy the subcondition would require a score between 500 and 800, excluding 591 through 659.

	SAT-BEST-MATH	GE	500
and	SAT-BEST-MATH	LE	590
or	SAT-BEST-MATH	GE	660
and	SAT-BEST-MATH	LE	800

A condition can have multiple subconditions. The following condition has three subconditions, one for each element. Each subcondition must be satisfied for the parent condition to be satisfied.

	ACAD-PROGRAM	EQ	15BA
AND	ACAD-AREA	EQ	HIST
or	ACAD-AREA	EQ	ECON
AND	SAT-BEST-MATH	GE	550

At the next level is a rule. A rule can specify one or more conditions. At least one condition must be satisfied for the parent rule to be satisfied and return a value of TRUE. In Exhibit 18.1 we showed a rule having two conditions. If, for an individual, either of the conditions were satisfied, the individual would have satisfied the rule.

At the next level is the business requirement, which can specify one or more rules. All rules must be satisfied for the business requirement to return a result of TRUE.

The relationships among the components are shown in Exhibit 18.3. The simplest business requirement would have one rule that has one condition that has one subcondition. The most complex business requirement could have any number of rules, each having any number of conditions. There is effectively no limit on the complexity of the business requirements that can be constructed with the Evaluator.

A data retrieval module is coded for each element. Each retrieval module is coded to perform a small, specific task, which is to retrieve an explicit value or set of values from a defined storage location. In the example above, ACAD-PROGRAM, ACAD-AREA, SAT-BEST-MATH, SAT-BEST-VERBAL, etc. were identified as evaluation elements. The developers could have coded modules for every element in the system, but as a practical matter not all elements are used to make business decisions. The value for an evaluation element can be obtained in two ways:

1. Retrieved directly from stored data
2. Derived from stored data

IF

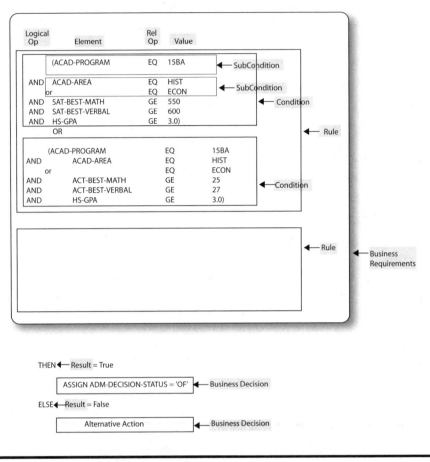

Exhibit 18.3. Evaluator Components

For example, modules that retrieve the values for elements such as "Home Zip Code" or "Home State" would retrieve them directly from stored data. Modules that retrieve values for elements such as "Highest Test Score," "Grade Point Average," and "Enrollment Hours" would analyze multiple records to derive and return a single value.

SAT-BEST-MATH provides an example of retrieving a derived value. An individual can take the SAT multiple times. The test has two components, math and verbal. In certain business processes, an individual's best SAT math score may determine eligibility for an action, in this case admission to the university. The retrieval module for SAT-BEST-MATH is

```
              EVALELEM - Maintain Evaluator Element

  Element: GENDER_____

  Description...: Person's Gender Code_____
  *Bond Group....: ___
  *Standard Field: GENDER-CODE_____
  *Value Help Pgm: SITABS03
  Element ID....: 003
  Object Subprogram: SIEVE003
```

Exhibit 18.4.   Evaluator Element Data

coded to look at every occurrence of an individual's SAT test results, keeping track of the highest math score. The highest score is then compared with the value specified in the logical condition.

Although it does not appear in the diagram above, "University Grade Point Average" (U-GPA) provides another example of retrieving a derived value. A student's grade point average is not stored. Instead, whenever U-GPA is needed for evaluation, the retrieval module derives the value by reading the student's enrollment records and averaging the grades. The derived U-GPA value is then compared with the value specified in the logical condition.

The information shown in Exhibit 18.4 is recorded for each evaluation element.

- *Bond Group*: If two or more fields are to be bound together, they must have the same bond-group ID. Bond-group IDs are maintained in a system table. "Bound" elements would be members of a stored group of related elements for which multiple records may exist. For example, an individual could have multiple applications. The elements mentioned in Exhibit 18.5, APPL-ACAD-AREA and APP-TERM, would be "bound."
- *Standard Field*: The standard field that defines the format and length for the element. Standard fields are a feature of the data dictionary used by UniverSIS.
- *Value Help Pgm*: The program that provides help for values as the business staff member is entering a condition.

```
        EVALELEM - Maintain Evaluator Element

Element: APPL-ACAD-AREA_____

Description...: Academic Area of Application_____
*Bond Group....: APP
*Standard Field: ACAD-AREA_____
*Value Help Pgm: SIACAS03
 Element ID....: 024
 Object Subprogram: SIEVE006
```

```
        EVALELEM - Maintain Evaluator Element

Element: APP-TERM_____

Description...: Term of Application_____
*Bond Group....: APP
*Standard Field: TERM-ID_____
*Value Help Pgm: SITERS01
 Element ID....: 016
 Object Subprogram: SIEVE006
```

Exhibit 18.5.   Bond Group Example

- *Element ID*: The numeric identifier for the element. This numeric identifier is used when storing Evaluator conditions rather than the text name.
- *Object Subprogram*: The data retrieval subprogram developed for this element.

18.4 Working through Examples

Exhibit 18.6 shows a partial list of Evaluator elements used in subsequent examples. Note that each element has both a name and a numeric ID. The element ID is a five-digit number that follows the basic rule for generating stable IDs (the leading zeros are suppressed).

A condition is a set of logic statements in Boolean form. Users identify the element by name, use a relational operator to indicate the type of comparison to be made, and specify a value. The following condition

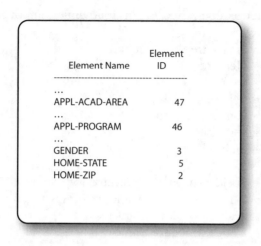

```
                         Element
        Element Name       ID
----------------------------- -----------
        ...
        APPL-ACAD-AREA          47
        ...
        APPL-PROGRAM            46
        ...
        GENDER                   3
        HOME-STATE               5
        HOME-ZIP                 2
```

Exhibit 18.6. Evaluator Elements

```
     Condition ID: TEST CASE

     Bond  *Evaluation Element      *OP  *Value
  1        GENDER_____     __  EQ M_____
  2        _____     __  _____
  3        _____     __  _____
  4        _____     __  _____
  5        _____     __  _____
  6        _____     __  _____
  7        _____     __  _____
  8        _____     __  _____
  9        _____     __  _____
                                              1 used of 25
```

Exhibit 18.7. Defining a Simple Condition

(Exhibit 18.7) presents the simplest possible example. The condition has one subcondition having a single statement: GENDER EQ M. The Evaluator converts the condition entered by the user and stores the condition in a tabular format that represents a binary tree. The values specified in the condition are stored in a separate table, referenced by number. As mentioned previously, the elements are stored in a master list in the system, referenced by name and number.

The binary tree is composed of the following components:

Node   = binary tree unit identifier
    E = Element
    V = Value
    R = Relational operator
    L = Logical operator
LC   = Left child
RC   = Right child
PR   = Parent
NEG   = Positive/negative indicator for evaluation result (+/−)
PCV   = Parse completion value; indicates when to stop evaluating (T or blank)
Log Op = Logical operator value
    A = And
    O = Or
Bond   = Indicates element of a related group of elements
    B = Bound
    U = Unbound
Rel Op = Relational operator value (EQ, NE, GT, GE, LT, LE)
El   = Element ID
Val   = Value ID

The stored condition references the element and values numbers. The example shown in Exhibit 18.7 is entered in this format:

```
GENDER    EQ    M
```

The Evaluator translates that condition into this:

```
Element #3    EQ    Value #1
```

It is actually stored in this format. GENDER has an element ID of 3 and M is the first (in this case, the only) value on the list. Note that the E node refers to Element #3 and that the V node refers to Value #1 (Exhibit 18.8). In pictorial form Exhibit 18.8 would look like Exhibit 18.9.

In evaluating this condition, the evaluating mechanism would start with Node #1. Because it is an R node, it "knows" to look to the left child for the E node, which tells it to retrieve the individual's data for Element #3. Then it looks to the right child for the V node containing the value to which the individual's value is to be compared, in this case Value #1, which is M. The result will be true or false.

The Evaluator is designed to retrieve and compare multiple values from the individual's record. That is, it assumes a one-to-many cardinality relationship between the individual and the value on the individual's

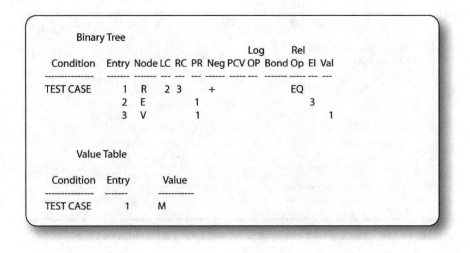

Binary Tree

Condition	Entry	Node	LC	RC	PR	Neg	PCV	Log OP	Rel Bond	Op	El	Val
TEST CASE	1	R	2	3		+				EQ		
	2	E		1							3	
	3	V		1								1

Value Table

Condition	Entry	Value
TEST CASE	1	M

Exhibit 18.8.   Evaluator Binary Tree: Internal Representation

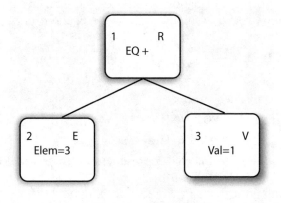

Exhibit 18.9.   Evaluator Binary Tree: Graphical Representation

record for the specified element. If in fact only one occurrence exists, that is just the special one-to-one case. For positive relational operators, (*not* NE) the Evaluator will compare all available values until a "true" is returned or the list is exhausted. In the case of the NE relational operator, it will do the same thing, but when it reaches a result, it will reverse it. The NE operator is therefore actually more like "never equal."

Exhibit 18.10 shows a slightly more complex case. Two values have been specified for the same element, so two statements are needed within

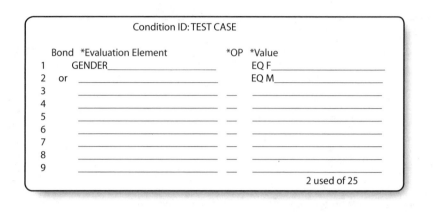

Exhibit 18.10. Example of Multiple Statements within a Subcondition

the subcondition. The logical operator connecting them is "or." By convention, the Evaluator displays lowercase "or" and "and" between statements within a subcondition. Uppercase "AND" is displayed between subconditions.

Again, the stored information references the element and value numbers. The stored order is actually the reverse of the order entered by the user.

```
        GENDER   EQ   M

or               EQ   F
```

The Evaluator translates to this:

```
        Element  #3  EQ   Value  #2

Or                   EQ   Value  #1
```

Exhibit 18.11 shows the internal representation. In pictorial form, Exhibit 18.11 would look like Exhibit 18.12.

The evaluating mechanism would start with Node #1. Because it is an L node, it "knows" to look to the left child for an R node or another L node. In this case, it is an R node. Because it is an R node, as above, it "knows" to look to the left child for the E node, which tells it to retrieve the individual's data for Element #3. Then it looks to the right child for the V node containing the value to which the individual's value is to be compared, in this case Value #2. The result will be true or false. That result is then passed back to the parent L node. Because the logical operator is "O" (or), if a true has been returned from Node #2, the logical operator has what it needs for a decision. It is not necessary to look at Node #5. If the result passed from Node #2 had been false (not equal to Value #2), the Evaluator would have examined Node #5.

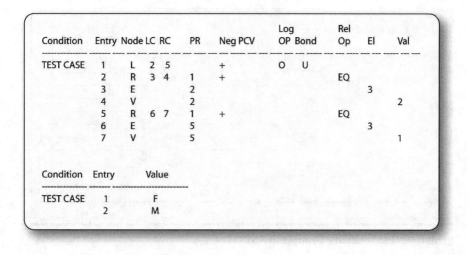

Condition	Entry	Node	LC	RC	PR	Neg	PCV	Log OP	Bond	Rel Op	El	Val
TEST CASE	1	L	2	5		+		O	U			
	2	R	3	4	1	+				EQ		
	3	E			2						3	
	4	V			2							2
	5	R	6	7	1	+				EQ		
	6	E			5						3	
	7	V			5							1

Condition	Entry	Value
TEST CASE	1	F
	2	M

Exhibit 18.11. More-Complex Example of Evaluator Binary Tree: Internal Representation

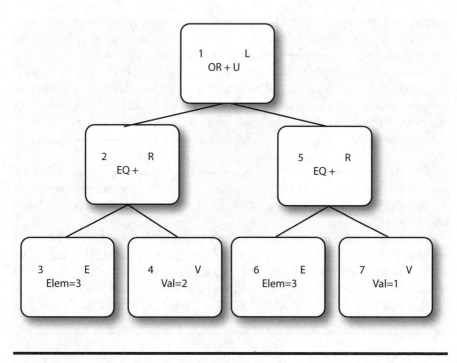

Exhibit 18.12. Example Test Case: Graphical Representation

```
    Condition ID: TEST CASE

        Bond  *Evaluation Element              *OP  *Value
    1    APS   APPL-PROGRAM_____     EQ   15BA_____
    2 AND       GENDER_____    EQ   F_____
    3   or       _____    EQ   M_____
    4             _____    _    _____
    5             _____    _    _____
    6             _____    _    _____
    7             _____    _    _____
    8             _____    _    _____
    9             _____    _    _____
                                                        3 used of 25
```

Exhibit 18.13.   Adding Complexity to Test Case

We can keep increasing the complexity of the condition, as shown in Exhibit 18.13. Note that because two Evaluator elements (APPL-PROGRAM and GENDER) are specified, the condition has two subconditions, connected by uppercase AND. The resulting binary tree becomes increasingly complex as well. We invite the reader to draw the pictorial representation. The internal representation is shown in Exhibit 18.14.

In the next example (Exhibit 18.15 and Exhibit 18.16), we see "bound" elements. An individual might have applied to more than one academic program, each program having an academic area (major). The condition specifies a program of 15BA and an academic area of HIST. The "bound" designation means that the two specified values must be found on the same record. That is, an application having a program of 15BA with a non-HIST academic area would not satisfy the condition, nor would an application having a non-15BA program with a HIST academic area.

In Exhibit 18.17 and Exhibit 18.18, the Element HOME-STATE has been added with a sequence of values.

Building on the previous example, add Element HOME-ZIP (Exhibit 18.19 and Exhibit 18.20), specifying a range of zip codes, with certain exclusions in the middle of the range. This example contains some real-world redundancy, as the zip code will tell you the name of the state. The point of the example is to show the type of selection complexity that the Evaluator can accommodate.

Condition	Entry	Node	LC	RC	PR	Neg	PCV	Log OP	Bond	Rel Op	El	Val
TEST CASE	1	L	2	9		+		A	U			
	2	L	3	6	1	+		O	U			
	3	R	4	5	2	+				EQ		
	4	E			3						3	
	5	V			3							3
	6	R	7	8	2	+				EQ		
	7	E			6						3	
	8	V			6							2
	9	R	10	11	1	+				EQ		
	10	E			9						46	
	11	V			9							1

Condition	Entry	Value
TEST CASE	1	15BA
	2	F
	3	M

Exhibit 18.14. Adding More Complexity to Test Case

Condition ID: TEST CASE

	Bond	*Evaluation Element	*OP	*Value
1	APS	APPL-PROGRAM_____	EQ	15BA_____
2 AND	APS	APPL-ACAD-AREA_____	EQ	HIST_____
3 AND		GENDER_____	EQ	F_____
4 or		_____	EQ	M_____
5		_____	__	_____
6		_____	__	_____
7		_____	__	_____
8		_____	__	_____
9		_____	__	_____

4 used of 25

Exhibit 18.15. Test Case with Bound Elements

Condition	Entry	Node	Log LC	Rel RC	PR	Neg	PCV	OP	Bond	Op	El	Val
TEST CASE	1	L	2	9		+		A		U		
	2	L	3	6	1	+		O		U		
	3	R	4	5	2	+				EQ		
	4	E			3						3	
	5	V			3							4
	6	R	7	8	2	+				EQ		
	7	E			6						3	
	8	V			6							3
	9	L	10	13	1	+	T	A	B			
	10	R	11	12	9	+				EQ		
	11	E			10						47	
	12	V			10							2
	13	R	14	15	9	+				EQ		
	14	E	13								46	
	15	V	13									1

Condition	Entry	Value
TEST CASE	1	15BA
	2	HIST
	3	F
	4	M

Exhibit 18.16. Adding Complexity with Bound Elements

Condition ID: TEST CASE

		Bond	*Evaluation Element	*OP	*Value
1		HOM	HOME-STATE_____	EQ	IN_____
2		or HOM	_____	EQ	KY_____
3		or HOM	_____	EQ	OH_____
4	AND	APS	APPL-PROGRAM_____	EQ	15BA_____
5	AND	APS	APPL-ACAD-AREA_____	EQ	HIST_____
6	AND		GENDER_____	EQ	F_____
7		or	_____	EQ	M_____
8			_____	—	_____
9			_____	—	_____

7 used of 25

Exhibit 18.17. Add Home State in the Cincinnati Area

Condition	Entry	Node	LC	RC	PR	Neg	PCV	Log OP	Bond	Rel Op	El	Val
TEST CASE	1	L	2	9		+		A	U			
	2	L	3	6	1	+		O	U			
	3	R	4	5	2	+				EQ		
	4	E			3						3	
	5	V			3							7
	6	R	7	8	2	+				EQ		
	7	E			6						3	
	8	V			6							6
	9	L	10	17	1	+		A	U			
	10	L	11	14	9	+	T	A	B			
	11	R	12	13	10	+				EQ		
	12	E			11						47	
	13	V			11							5
	14	R	15	16	10	+				EQ		
	15	E			14						46	
	16	V			14							4
	17	L	18	21	9	+	T	O	B			
	18	R	19	20	17	+				EQ		
	19	E			18						5	
	20	V			18							3
	21	L	22	25	17	+		O	B			
	22	R	23	24	21	+				EQ		
	23	E			22						5	
	24	V			22							2
	25	R	26	27	21	+				EQ		
	26	E			25						5	
	27	V			25							1

Condition	Entry	Value
TEST CASE	1	IN
	2	KY
	3	OH
	4	15BA
	5	HIST
	6	F
	7	M

Exhibit 18.18. Internal Representation at This Stage of Complexity

Condition ID: TEST CASE

	Bond	*Evaluation Element	*OP	*Value
1		HOM HOME-ZIP_____	GE	40000_____
2	and	HOM _____	NE	45221_____
3	and	HOM _____	NE	45222_____
4	and	HOM _____	LE	50000_____
5	AND	HOM HOME-STATE_____	EQ	IN_____
6	or	HOM _____	EQ	KY_____
7	or	HOM _____	EQ	OH_____
8	AND	APS APPL-PROGRAM_____	EQ	15BA_____
9	AND	APS APPL-ACAD-AREA_____	EQ	HIST_____
10	AND	GENDER_____	EQ	F_____
11	or	_____	EQ	M_____

11 used of 25

Exhibit 18.19. Specific Zip Codes within Neighboring States

Condition	Entry	Node	LC	RC	PR	Neg	PCV	Log OP	Bond	Rel Op	EI	Val
TEST CASE	1	L	2	9		+		A	U			
	2	L	3	6	1	+		O	U			
	3	R	4	5	2	+				EQ		
	4	E			3						3	
	5	V			3							11
	6	R	7	8	2	+				EQ		
	7	E			6						3	
	8	V			6							10
	9	L	10	17	1	+		A	U			
	10	L	11	14	9	+	T	A	B			
	11	R	12	13	10	+				EQ		
	12	E			11						47	
	14	R	15	16	10	+				EQ		
	15	E			14						46	
	16	V			14							8
	17	L	18	29	9	+	T	A	B			
	18	L	19	22	17	+		O	B			
	19	R	20	21	18	+				EQ		
	20	E			19						5	
	21	V			19							7
	22	L	23	26	18	+		O	B			
	23	R	24	25	22	+				EQ		
	24	E			23						5	
	25	V			23							6
	26	R	27	28	22	+				EQ		
	27	E			26						5	
	28	V			26							5
	29	L	30	33	17	+		A	B			
	30	R	31	32	29	+				LE		
	31	E			30						2	
	32	V			30							4
	33	L	34	37	29	+		A	B			
	34	R	35	36	33	-				EQ		
	35	E			34						2	
	36	V			34							3
	37	L	38	41	33	+		A	B			
	38	R	39	40	37	-				EQ		
	39	E			38						2	
	40	V			38							2
	41	R	42	43	37	+				GE		
	42	E			41						2	
	43	V			41							1

Condition	Entry	Value
TEST CASE	1	40000
	2	45221
	3	45222
	4	50000
	5	IN
	6	KY
	7	OH
	8	15BA
	9	HIST
	10	F
	11	M

Exhibit 18.20. New Binary Tree Elements

18.5 Summary

- In the Evaluator, criteria for business decisions are defined as a set of conditional statements.
- When evaluated, conditional statements yield a true or false result.
- The Evaluator mechanism is independent of any business process for which it is used.
- The Evaluator approach has flexibly handled all logical business decision criteria encountered that could be defined in terms of data stored in the system as evaluator rules, conditions, and subconditions.
- The Evaluator is a general-purpose tool, a flexible tool.
- The Evaluator mechanism itself has been completely stable since its implementation. No modifications of data structures or program code have occurred.
- The UniverSIS Evaluator has been incorporated into the business logic of admission decisions, charging, correspondence tracks, and other business decision processes.
- New Evaluator elements have been added over the years, which has required coding of individual data-retrieval modules. These modules follow a standard template and typically require only a few hours to code and test.
- As new business processes have been added to the system, new uses for the Evaluator have been identified.

The Evaluator illustrates the potential for transferring control over business rules to business staff and simultaneously reducing IT maintenance effort. The tool makes use of stable data structures and generic processing patterns. Evaluator can and does serve a variety of business purposes and can be deployed easily as new purposes are identified. In Chapter 19, we provide a case study showing how two software tools — the generic-entity cloud (GEC) and the Evaluator — can be used together to provide a flexible system.

Chapter 19

Tuition-Remission Case Study: Traditional versus Flexible

In this chapter, we review previous material by examining a business process and demonstrating how a software system can be designed to support it. First, we describe how a more traditional method of system design would approach the task. Then we approach the same task using some of our flexibility tools — the generic-entity cloud (GEC) and the Evaluator. For readers who have grasped fully the concepts of those tools, this chapter may be unnecessary. For those who are less confident, we believe that the comparison of the two approaches will reinforce understanding of the difference between inflexible and flexible design.

At some universities, tuition is remitted or waived for individuals who are university employees or who have specified relationships with university employees. We will consider only the case of children of employees. A typical business rule for tuition remission can be stated simply:

> The child of an employee is eligible for tuition remission.

The process under discussion is "award tuition remission." That process determines whether a given student is eligible for tuition remission. If the student is eligible, the process will store a record of eligibility in the system.

Our test case will involve John and Mary. Their statuses and relationships are as follows:

- John is an employee.
- John is also a student.
- Mary is a student.
- Mary is John's child.
- John is Mary's parent.

We are assuming that the gender of the child and parent do not matter. The "award tuition remission" process needs to be able to determine whether Mary is eligible for tuition remission and, if she is, to store a record of that eligibility.

19.1 Traditional Approach

It is very common for analysis of business processes to drive system design. We will perform such a process-oriented analysis as our example of the traditional approach.

The output of the process is a record of a student's eligibility for tuition remission. Discussion with the business staff reveals that tuition remission is awarded on a term-by-term basis. Because we want our process to determine whether a student is eligible for tuition remission in a given term, the basic inputs are Student ID and Term. We know that not all students are eligible for tuition remission. The business rule stated earlier defines who is eligible.

To enforce the rule, the process needs access to pertinent information. The business rule contains the words "child," "employee," and "tuition remission," which indicates the need to store data about these entities. Applying some common sense, we conclude that the "child" must be a student. We also conclude that we need to keep information about the academic terms. We therefore need data found in four (logical) data stores: Employee, Student, Term, and Student Term Tuit-Rem.

For purposes of this discussion, we specify very simple data stores, having the elements shown in Exhibit 19.1. Note that we have anticipated the possibility of an employee having multiple children. For ease of reading, we have omitted system-assigned identifiers.

A data flow diagram (DFD) is often used for recording the results of an analysis, as illustrated in Exhibit 19.2. In Exhibit 19.2, we see that the basic Input (Student ID and Term) parameters are passed to the "award tuition remission" process. The process receives information about

```
Employee
            Employee-Name
            Employee-ID
            Child-Name-1
            Child-ID-1
            Child-Name-2
            Child-ID-2
            Child-Name-3
            Child-ID-3

Student
            Student-Name
            Student-ID
            Birth-Date
            Father-Name
            Father-ID
            Mother-Name
            Mother-ID

Term
            Term-Name

Student Term Tuit-Rem
            Student-ID
            Term-Name

We establish records in these files for our example.

Employee
            Employee-Name:      John
            Employee-ID:        123-45-6789
            Child-Name-1:       Mary
            Child-ID-1:         234-56-7890
            Child-Name:
            Child-ID 2
            Child-Name-2
            Child-ID-3

Student
            Student-Name:       Mary
            Student-ID:         234-56-7890
            Birth-Date:         1980-01-01
            Father-Name:        John
            Father-ID:          123-45-6789
            Mother-Name:        Jane
            Mother-ID:          345-67-8901

Term
            Term-Name:          Fall2003

Student Term Tuit-Rem
            Student-ID
            Term-Name
```

Exhibit 19.1. Data Stores for Academic Terms

Employee, Student, and Term. The logic of the process determines whether Mary is eligible for tuition remission. If she is, the process records her eligibility on a Student Term Tuit-Rem record.

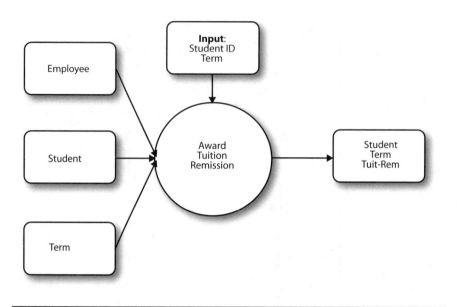

Exhibit 19.2. Data Flow Diagram for Award Tuition Remission: Traditional Approach

The logic of the process must be programmed. From this diagram, a programmer can see that several basic things are going on. Summarized briefly, they are:

- Receive input
- Read Term file
- Read Student file
- Read Employee file
- Write Student Term Tuit-Rem record

Programming of activities such as these will follow a standard pattern. Writing of the Student Term Tuit-Rem record will be conditional upon the student being eligible.

The programming specific to the "award tuition remission" process will reflect the logic of the original specification: *The child of an employee is eligible for tuition remission.* Adding Term to the specification, we would end up with a condition like the following. It is this logic that the programmer must encode in the "award tuition remission" process.

```
If the specified term is valid
And Mary is a Student
And Mary is the Child of a Person who is an Employee
Then Mary is eligible for Tuition Remission
```

```
BEGIN PROGRAM.

Define True-False Switches (SW):

#TERM-VALID-SW
#STUDENT-SW
#CHILD-SW

Define Input Fields:

#INPUT-STUDENT-ID
#INPUT-TERM-NAME

Receive Input Parameters

INPUT #INPUT-STUDENT-ID #INPUT-TERM-NAME

READ Term File
IF Term.Term-Name = #INPUT-TERM-NAME
            Set #TERM-VALID-SW = TRUE
END-IF
END-READ

READ Student File
IF Student.Student-ID = #INPUT-STUDENT-ID
            Set #STUDENT-SW = TRUE
END-IF
END-READ

READ Employee File
IF Employee.Child-ID-1 = #INPUT-STUDENT-SSN
            OR Employee.Child-ID-2 = #INPUT-STUDENT-ID
            OR Employee.Child-ID-3 = #INPUT-STUDENT-ID
            Set #CHILD-SW = TRUE
END-IF
END-READ

IF #TERM-VALID-SW = TRUE
            AND #STUDENT-SW = TRUE
            AND #CHILD-SW = TRUE
            Write Student Term Tuit-Rem Record
END-IF

END PROGRAM
```

Exhibit 19.3. Pseudocode Example of Award Tuition Remission: Traditional Approach

Exhibit 19.3 presents a pseudocode example of how the programmer might accomplish this. If we follow the logic of the program for Mary and Term Fall2003, we find that:

```
Fall2003 is a valid Term
Mary is a Student
Mary is the Child of John who is an Employee
```

Therefore: Mary is eligible for tuition remission in Fall2003 and we write a Student Term Tuit-Rem record for her.

There is nothing wrong with this solution when only the original specification is considered. However, "What happens when something changes?" Here are three possibilities and what is likely to be done about them given the original design:

- An employee has more than three children.
- Spouses become eligible for tuition remission.
- An age limit of 23 is placed on tuition remission eligibility for children.

19.1.1 Traditional Approach: an Employee Has More than Three Children

The original design of the Employee file specified a maximum of three children. The likely modification will be to estimate a larger maximum, say ten, and modify the Employee file to accommodate ten occurrences of Child-Name and Child-ID. The logic of the program will need to change as shown in Exhibit 19.4.

19.1.2 Traditional Approach: Spouses Become Eligible for Tuition Remission

The original design of the Employee file did not provide for a spouse. The likely solution will be to add Spouse-ID and Spouse-Name to the Employee file. The program will need to be modified to add a #SPOUSE-SW. The logic of the READ of the Employee file will need to change as shown in Exhibit 19.5.

```
READ Employee File
IF Employee.Child-ID-1 = #INPUT-STUDENT-ID
            OR Employee.Child-ID-2 = #INPUT-STUDENT-ID
            OR Employee.Child-ID-3 = #INPUT-STUDENT-ID
... (and so on)
            OR Employee.Child-ID-10 = #INPUT-STUDENT-ID
            Set #CHILD-SW = TRUE
END-IF
END-READ
```

Exhibit 19.4. Employee File Modification for More than Three Children

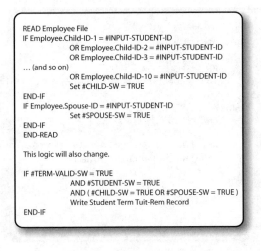

```
READ Employee File
IF Employee.Child-ID-1 = #INPUT-STUDENT-ID
            OR Employee.Child-ID-2 = #INPUT-STUDENT-ID
            OR Employee.Child-ID-3 = #INPUT-STUDENT-ID
... (and so on)
            OR Employee.Child-ID-10 = #INPUT-STUDENT-ID
            Set #CHILD-SW = TRUE
END-IF
IF Employee.Spouse-ID = #INPUT-STUDENT-ID
            Set #SPOUSE-SW = TRUE
END-IF
END-READ

This logic will also change.

IF #TERM-VALID-SW = TRUE
            AND #STUDENT-SW = TRUE
            AND ( #CHILD-SW = TRUE OR #SPOUSE-SW = TRUE )
            Write Student Term Tuit-Rem Record
END-IF
```

Exhibit 19.5.   Employee File Modification to Add Spouse

19.1.3 Traditional Approach: an Age Limit of 23 Is Placed on Tuition-Remission Eligibility

Birth date is already available on the Student record. Within the program, we would add a field for #STUDENT-AGE, and logic would be added to calculate #STUDENT-AGE by comparing the student's birth date with the current date. The logic for writing the Student Term Tuit-Rem record would need to be modified to something like that shown in Exhibit 19.6.

19.1.4 Discussion

> *Three fairly simple changes ... necessitated modifications to program code and, in two of the three cases, modifications to data structures. This is what is meant by a high-maintenance system.*

These examples illustrate the typical problems found in an inflexible design. It is not that the original work has been performed incorrectly. The process-oriented approach effectively identified and accommodated the original requirements. The logic of awarding tuition remission was isolated in a single module. Modularity is a sound design principle for both traditional and flexible software. Input to the process is provided

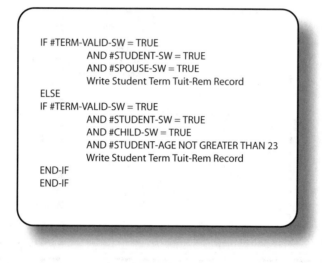

```
IF #TERM-VALID-SW = TRUE
        AND #STUDENT-SW = TRUE
        AND #SPOUSE-SW = TRUE
        Write Student Term Tuit-Rem Record
ELSE
IF #TERM-VALID-SW = TRUE
        AND #STUDENT-SW = TRUE
        AND #CHILD-SW = TRUE
        AND #STUDENT-AGE NOT GREATER THAN 23
        Write Student Term Tuit-Rem Record
END-IF
END-IF
```

Exhibit 19.6.   Employee File Modification to Add Age

via parameters, also a good technique. The designer/programmer might justifiably believe that this was a job well done.

Yet three fairly simple changes in business requirements necessitated modifications to program code and, in two of the three cases, modifications to data structures. This is what is meant by a high-maintenance system. Each of these modifications may be fairly easy to make, but the IT staff needs to make and test the modifications. This is a small component of a large system. If the rest of the system follows a similar design, the number of modifications requiring IT staff intervention could be very large. In addition, the changes to the data structures have potentially nonlocal effects, possibly requiring modifications to programs that access these files for reasons entirely unrelated to the determination of tuition-remission eligibility.

19.2 Flexible Approach

Let us look at how the same business requirements might be implemented in a system designed with flexibility in mind. We would start with a careful GEC analysis of data structures. The GEC diagram in Exhibit 19.7 represents the way in which the data pertaining to employees and students would be organized. We identify employee and student as types of a more general entity called Person." We identify parent and child as relationships between

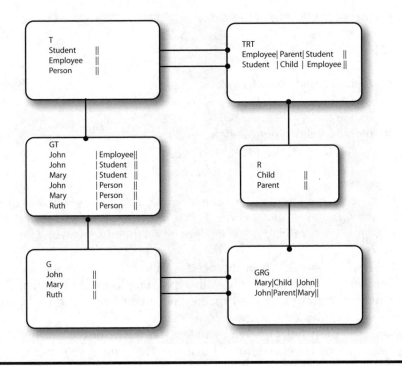

Exhibit 19.7. Person GEC

persons. Within the GEC structure for Person, we can, therefore, record information about persons and their relationships with each other. John, Mary, and Ruth have been defined as Persons in this example.

19.2.1 *Review of the GEC-Building Process*

- Define the generic node (G)
- Define the type node (T)
- Define the role node (R)
- Define the type-role-type node (TRT)
- Define the generic-type node (GT)
- Define the generic-role-generic node (GRG)

We are not showing all the detail of the steps identified above. Included in the activities of definition will be identification of the data elements of each node. For this illustration we show only representations of the IDs of the node records.

- Identify valid type (T) values
    Student
    Employee
    Person
- Identify valid role (R) values
    Child
    Parent
- Identify valid type-role-type (TRT) values
    Student | Child | Employee | |
    Employee | Parent | Student | |

Up to this point, we have identified only data integrity rules that apply within the GEC. The values in the T, R, and TRT nodes form the pools of valid values. Their validity does not depend on their use with any instances of Generic (G).

The valid T values reflect the needs of the business. In this example, the business is concerned only with types Employee and Student. The Type node will always have a Type instance that corresponds to the name of the GEC, in this case Person.

Similarly, the valid TRT values reflect the needs of the business. The business experts have determined that the TRT values shown above are needed.

The following values are not needed currently but could be added as business needs change:

    Student | Parent | Employee | |
    Employee | Child | Student | |

Although not shown here, the rules represented by these node entries could be date-sensitive, because rules may change over time.

19.2.1.1 Add Generic and Generic Type (G and GT) Values

At this point we are ready to add instances of the G node. The GEC requires recording of at least one GT instance for each instance of the G node, but GRG instances are not required. GT values must be validated against instances in the G and T nodes.

In the example above, Mary was added as an instance of G. Because three valid values of T exist, it was possible to create one or two GT records for Mary. We defined two.

    Mary | Student | |
    Mary | Person | |

John was added as an instance of G. He is both a student and an employee. Therefore, three GT values were recorded for him.

John | Student ||
John | Employee ||
John | Person ||

Ruth was added as an instance of G. She is neither a student nor an employee. She has one GT record.

Ruth | Person ||

19.2.1.2 Add Generic Role Generic (GRG) Values

The GEC can be used to express relationships between instances of G. The original specification stated that Mary is John's child and that John is Mary's parent. The GRG node is used to record these relationships, subject to the data integrity rules of the GEC, specifically the type validation rule presented in Chapter 9.

The valid TRT values have been identified. The TRT and GRG records are always read from left to right.

Student | Child | Employee || (Student is a Child of an Employee)
Employee | Parent | Student || (Employee is a Parent of Student)

We would like to record the following GRG values:

Mary | Child | John || (Mary is the Child of John)
John | Parent | Mary || (John is the Parent of Mary)

The following corresponds to validation programming that would be standard for any GEC.

Let us look at Mary | Child | John ||. First check that Child is a valid value of R. It is.

Now match the TRT to the proposed GRG. The left T of the TRT is matched against the left G of the GRG.

Mary | Child | John || (GRG)
Student | Child | Employee || (TRT)

In this example, GEC processing checks whether Mary is a student by looking for a GT record containing the value Mary | Student ||. It finds one. So far, so good — now it checks for a GT record containing the value John | Employee ||. It finds one. The GRG value Mary | Child | John || is therefore valid.

GEC processing will follow the same steps for GRG value John | Parent | Mary || and find that it is also valid. In contrast, an attempt to add GRG value John | Child | Mary || would result in an error condition. The GEC would find a GT record with a value of John | Student || but would not find a GT record with a value of Mary | Employee ||.

Exhibit 19.8 shows the general case of the external Person-Tuit-Rem-Term as a connection between Person and Term. Exhibit 19.9 shows the specific case of Mary the Student and John the Employee.

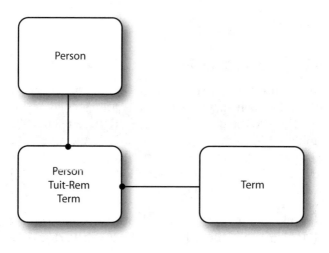

Exhibit 19.8. General Case

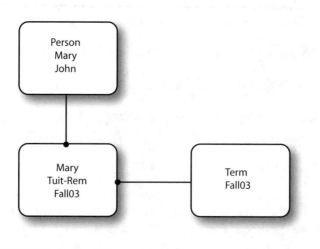

Exhibit 19.9. Specific Instance

The GEC maintains the integrity of the data contained within its nodes. Although we did not show how the traditional approach would maintain the integrity of the data in the data stores, it is likely that the traditional approach would be correct but inflexible.

19.2.2 Using the GEC to Apply Business Rules

Stated simply once again, the business rule for tuition remission is this:

> The child of an employee is eligible for tuition remission.

More precisely stated, the rule is:

> A Person who is both (a Student) and (a Child of a Person who is an Employee) is eligible for tuition remission.

We can use a DFD to represent the process of awarding tuition remission (Exhibit 19.10). In contrast to Exhibit 19.2, Employee and Student have been replaced by a single entity — Person — and the Student Term Tuit-Rem entity has been renamed to Person Term Tuit-Rem. The logic described for the traditional approach will be needed in the flexible approach as well.

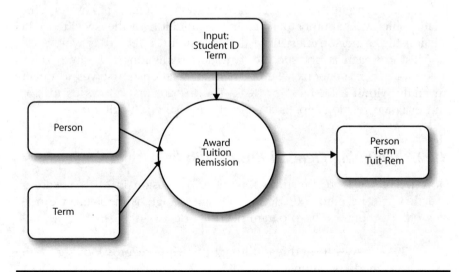

Exhibit 19.10. Data Flow Diagram for Award Tuition Remission: Flexible Approach

We need to determine whether Mary is eligible for tuition remission. The rule is:

```
If the specified term is valid
And Mary is a Student
And Mary is the Child of a Person who is an Employee
Then Mary is eligible for Tuition Remission
```

Although not shown, there is a Term GEC. Validation of the term would simply check for the presence of a GT node in the Term GEC that matches the Input Term.

Validating Mary's eligibility is slightly more involved. We can make this determination by searching for two records in the Person GEC. First we look for a GRG record in which the left G value is "Mary" and the R value is "Child." We find one.

Mary | Child | John | | (GRG)

Next we look for a GT record indicating that Mary is a Student. We find one.

Mary | Student | | (GT)

Having found both records, we know that Mary is eligible for tuition remission. Although finding the GRG record is sufficient in this example, it is insufficient in the general case. A nonstudent can have a Child relationship with another person. In the addition to the specified GRG relationship, a person must have the specified GT record as well.

This approach is not specific to tuition remission. The same pattern holds for other situations where a defined relationship serves to qualify an entity within a business process. The feature that allows us to store and evaluate relationships is a general-purpose and flexible tool.

19.2.3 Defining General Business Rules

How might we store the rules for tuition remission in our software so that they can be enforced? Because business logic is involved, we need to write a program. The program needs to do two things:

1. Take Mary's ID and read through the GRG records looking for the specified condition.
2. Take Mary's ID and read through the GT records looking for the specified condition.

```
Assign RESULT = 'FALSE'
Assign GENERIC-ID = Mary-ID
Assign R-ID = 'Child'
Perform VALIDATE-PERSON-GRG

ROUTINE VALIDATE-PERSON-GRG
            GRG-READ-LOOP.
READ GRG Record
            IF Left G = GENERIC-ID
            AND R = R-ID
                        THEN
                        RESULT = 'TRUE'
                        Escape from GRG-READ-LOOP.
            END-IF
END-READ
END-VALIDATE-PERSON-GRG
```

A RESULT value of 'TRUE' would indicate that Mary has passed this test for Tuition Remission eligibility. A value of 'FALSE' would indicate that she has not.

Assuming that Mary has passed the GRG test, the system would need to test for the required GT value using logic nearly identical to that of the GRG test.

```
Assign RESULT = 'FALSE'
Assign GENERIC-ID = Mary-ID
Assign T-ID = 'Student'
Perform VALIDATE-PERSON-GT

ROUTINE VALIDATE-PERSON-GT.
            GT-READ-LOOP.
READ GT Record
            IF G = GENERIC-ID
            AND T = T-ID
                        THEN
                        RESULT = 'TRUE'
                        Escape from GT-READ-LOOP.
            END-IF
END-READ
END-VALIDATE-PERSON-GT
```

Again, a RESULT value of 'TRUE' would indicate that Mary has passed this test for Tuition Remission eligibility. A value of 'FALSE' would indicate that she has not.

A 'TRUE' result from both of these tests indicates that Mary is in fact eligible for Tuition Remission.

Exhibit 19.11. Pseudocode Example of Award Tuition Remission: Flexible Approach

The first process could be expressed as in Exhibit 19.11. We specify that values are to be passed as parameters rather than hard-coded into the program.

As in the traditional approach, we coded logic in a program. The difference is that in the traditional approach, the logic was specific to the process. In the flexible approach, these routines would be coded once and could be used to evaluate GRG and GT records for any specified relationship and any process.

To take advantage of this flexible approach, we need mechanisms by which the business staff can maintain the business rules. The following approach provides flexibility. We define a regulatory entity for GRG rules (Exhibit 19.12). Note that the VALIDATE-PERSON-GRG routine and the VALIDATE-PERSON-GT are specific to the PERSON GEC. For OTHER GECs, there would be VALIDATE-OTHER-GRG and VALIDATE-OTHER-GT. Each record is associated with a specified entity and a process that acts on that entity. On each record the business staff would specify the routine and the appropriate relationship. The process "award tuition remission" would be coded to look for any associated GRG rules, execute the specified routine, and take appropriate action based on the result. Note that it would be possible to have multiple GRG rules for "award tuition remission," though as currently specified, only a relationship of Child qualifies an individual for tuition remission.

Similarly, we would need a GT rule (Exhibit 19.13).

The process "award tuition remission" would be programmed to look for all GRG and GT rules on which the process name is stored, pass the appropriate parameters to the specified routines, and take appropriate

```
                    GRG Rule

        Rule ID      : GRG 001
        Entity       : Person Tuit-Rem Term
        Process      : Award Tuition Remission

        Routine                  Relationship
        VALIDATE-PERSON-GRG      Child
```

Exhibit 19.12. GRG Rule

```
                    GT Rule

        Rule ID      : GT 001
        Entity       : Person Tuit-Rem Term
        Process      : Award Tuition Remission

        Routine                  Type
        VALIDATE-PERSON-GT       Student
```

Exhibit 19.13. GT Rule

action based on the results. In other words, the process would award tuition remission if the student were found to be eligible.

This flexible approach yields results that satisfy the original business requirements. But so did the traditional approach. The flexible approach appears to be more complex and might take longer to develop. The reader might justifiably ask, "Why bother?" Once again, we ask, "What happens when something changes?" We will address the same three changes that occurred in the traditional approach:

1. An employee has more than three children.
2. Spouses become eligible for tuition remission.
3. An age limit of 23 is placed on tuition-remission eligibility for children.

19.2.4 Flexible Approach: an Employee Has More than Three Children

For the flexible approach, accommodating an employee who has more than three children proves to be trivial. Student and Employee are types of Person. Every individual on the system has a Person record. Subject to the data integrity rules of the GEC, simply adding a new GRG record can represent a relationship between any two Persons. No IT intervention is required to increase the number of children that can be recorded for an employee because whatever limits exist are adjustable through cardinality regulation. The flexible approach has indeed proved flexible in this case.

This particular bit of flexibility is a natural by-product of normalization when analyzing data requirements. The authors do not claim to have invented data normalization. Normalization is a good data analysis tool, but it is not at all unusual for system designers to design data structures that are not fully normalized. When they do, however, they must recognize the potential for inflexibility. In designing the system, they must take into consideration not only today's requirements, but tomorrow's potential changes.

19.2.5 Flexible Approach: Spouses Become Eligible for Tuition Remission

Let us say that this is the new situation, as illustrated in Exhibit 19.14.

- John is an employee.
- John is also a student.
- Mary is a student.

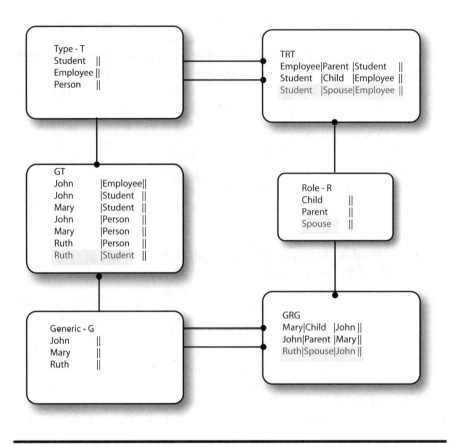

Exhibit 19.14. Person GEC with Spouse Role

- Mary is John's child.
- John is Mary's parent.
- Ruth is a student.
- Ruth is John's spouse.

We need to take the following actions to synchronize the GEC in Exhibit 19.14 with the new business situation.

- Identify additional valid T values
  No additional values needed
- Identify additional valid R values
  Add Spouse (in gray)
  Identify additional valid TRT values
  Add Student | Spouse | Employee || (in gray)

We did not add the value Employee | Spouse | Student | | to the list of valid TRT values because our business experts said that this relationship is of no interest to them. If it is needed for another business purpose at a later date, it can be added at that time.

- Identify additional GT values
  Add GT value for Ruth-Student (in gray)
- Identify GRG values
  Add the value Ruth | Spouse | John | | (in gray)

Matching this GRG value against the new TRT value, we see that the GRG value is valid.

Student | Spouse | Employee | | (TRT)
Ruth | Spouse | John | | (GRG)

The standard GEC logic checks whether Ruth is a student by looking for a GT record containing the value Ruth | Student | |. It finds one. So far, so good. Now it checks for a GT record containing the value John | Employee | |. It finds one. The GRG value Ruth | Spouse | John | | is therefore valid.

If we had attempted to add GRG value John | Spouse | Ruth | |, the GEC would have found it to be in violation of the type validation rule, as we have no supporting TRT value of Employee | Spouse | Student | |.

With the GEC we were able to record a new generic-entity type and define a new relationship between types. We were able to take an existing entity instance (Ruth) and express her relationship with another entity instance (John). Unlike the traditional approach, all this was accomplished with the addition of data values and without modification to information structures or program code.

What about adjustment of the business rules?

We designed VALIDATE-PERSON-GRG as a generic GRG evaluation routine. Until now, the only relationship that qualified for tuition remission was Child. Because the rules have changed, we need a new rule. The rule now looks like this:

The child or spouse of an employee is eligible for tuition remission.

More precisely stated, the rule is:

A Person who is (a Student) and either ((a Child of a Person who is an Employee) or (a Spouse of a Person who is an Employee)) is eligible for tuition remission.

```
                        GRG Rule

        Rule ID      :GRG 002
        Entity       :Student Tuit-Rem Term
        Process      :Maintain Student Tuit-Rem Term

        Routine                        Relationship
        VALIDATE-PERSON-GRG            Spouse
```

Exhibit 19.15. Second GRG Rule

Business staff can accommodate the change by recording a second GRG rule (Exhibit 19.15). No additional GT rule is needed.

The process "award tuition remission" is written to look for associated GRG rules, execute the specified routines, and take appropriate action based on the result. With these modifications, the process would find two GRG rules to be evaluated. It would find that Ruth does not qualify for tuition remission based on the first rule, but she does qualify based on the second.

The GEC was again able to accommodate a change in tuition-remission rules with addition of data values and without changes to data structures or program code, in contrast to the traditional approach.

19.2.6 Flexible Approach: an Age Limit of 23 Is Placed on Tuition-Remission Eligibility

Our GRG and GT rule mechanisms cannot accommodate this business requirement. The GRG rule, though flexible in its way, is very specific to relationships in the GEC. The GT rule is very specific to control type in the GEC. We need a different mechanism for evaluating the age of the child.

Would it be possible to design an evaluation mechanism that works for this new requirement as well as many others? The answer is yes. In Chapter 18 we describe such a mechanism, called Evaluator — a general-purpose evaluation tool based on the premise that any business processing decision can be constructed with the following components:

- A predefined set of decision elements
- A true/false question based on decision elements
- Action to be taken for a true result
- Action to be taken for a false result

```
Rule ID      : RULE 001
Entity       : Student Tuit-Rem Term
Process      : Award Tuition Remission
GEC          : PERSON

             AGE                    LE  23
```

Exhibit 19.16.   Business Rule

Business staff record rules in the system using the decision elements they have identified. Rules have effective begin and end dates, which means that a history of rule changes can be maintained. Business processes that require business decision logic are programmed to make use of the business staff-maintained rules. The business decision logic is not coded directly.

For the "award tuition remission" example, we define a decision element:

> AGE. Its data retrieval module will use the stored Birth Date
> to determine the individual's age.

Using the Evaluator approach, business staff can record this business rule. To the "award tuition remission" process, we add logic that will look up related business rules, invoke the Evaluator, and take action based on the result. In this case, after getting successful GRG and GT rule results for Mary, the process would check business rule RULE001 (Exhibit 19.16). A result of "true" means that Mary is eligible.

Because the Evaluator mechanism already existed and Birth Date was already present on the Student record, the only system modification was coding of the data retrieval module that provides the student's age for evaluation. This is significantly less effort than was required with the traditional approach.

19.2.7 Additional Thoughts

Let us not stop here. The Evaluator mechanism actually provides enough flexibility that it can be used to enforce the GRG and GT rules as well as the AGE rule, making the VALIDATE-PERSON-GRG and VALIDATE-PERSON-GT routines unnecessary. In addition to AGE, we define two other decision elements:

- PERSON-RELATIONSHIP: The data retrieval module for PERSON-RELATIONSHIP will be coded to retrieve all GRG values for the specified individual.
- PERSON-TYPE: The data retrieval module for PERSON-TYPE will be coded to retrieve all GT values for the specified individual.

Using the Evaluator approach, business staff can record these two rules in Exhibit 19.17 and Exhibit 19.18.

The process "award tuition remission" would be coded to look for any associated business rule records, invoke the Evaluator, and take appropriate action based on the result. A result of true for either rule would qualify the student for tuition remission. Note that the GRG and GT rules specified earlier are incorporated in the Evaluator logic, along with the new age-related rule.

Business Rule

Rule ID	:RULE 001		
Entity	:Student Tuit-Rem Term		
Process	:Award Tuition Remission		
GEC	:PERSON		
	AGE	LE	23
AND	PERSON-RELATIONSHIP	EQ	Child
AND	PERSON-TYPE	EQ	Student

Exhibit 19.17. Evaluator Business Rule 001

Business Rule

Rule ID	:RULE 002		
Entity	:Student Tuit-Rem Term		
Process	:Award Tuition Remission		
GEC	:PERSON		
	PERSON-RELATIONSHIP	EQ	Spouse
AND	PERSON-TYPE	EQ	Student

Exhibit 19.18. Evaluator Business Rule 002

Mary, the child of John, would qualify only up to the age of 23 according to RULE001 (Exhibit 19.17). Ruth, the spouse of John, would qualify according to RULE002 (Exhibit 19.18).

The Evaluator approach adds an additional layer of flexibility. The same business-rule mechanism can be used with any number of business processes. Such a mechanism can be structured to support all the AND/OR Boolean logic typically found in IF/THEN/ELSE logic of program code. As long as existing decision elements are used in constructing new business rules, no modification to information structures or program code is required. If a new decision element is required, a developer will code the appropriate data retrieval routine and add the new decision element to the pool of available elements. This effort is typically measured in hours and existing business rules are not affected. Business staff can create new business rules or new versions of existing business rules without IT intervention.

19.3 Comparison of Traditional and Flexible Approaches

Once change was introduced,... the traditional approach required significantly more IT intervention than the flexible approach.

Both the traditional and flexible approach resulted in systems that met the original business requirements. Once change was introduced, however, the traditional approach required significantly more IT intervention than the flexible approach. The flexible approach does in fact prove to be the low-maintenance option.

19.4 Summary

- In this case study, we compared a traditional process-oriented approach to a flexible, information-structure-oriented approach.
- Both approaches yielded good results in the initial implementation.
- As changes in business requirements occurred, the traditional approach required modifications to both program code and information structures, even when the changes in requirements appeared to be fairly minor.
- With the flexible approach, the same changes were accommodated without modification to either information structures or program code.
- Thoughtful design offers the possibility of generic data structures and generic program code for recording and evaluating business rules. Such generic tools can be reused in a variety of business situations. The GEC and the Evaluator are examples of such generic tools.

An additional consideration in some organizations is the method by which work done by the IT unit is funded. It is not unusual to require business units to pay for IT service. This approach inevitably leads to a gap between the "have" units and the "have-nots" with regard to ability to pay. Obviously, a flexibly designed system that requires no IT intervention as business requirements change benefits both the "haves" and the "have-nots" impartially.

Chapter 20

Regulatory GECs

In Chapter 10, we introduced the generic-entity cloud (GEC) and discussed its internal regulatory capabilities. In Sections 10.3 and 10.6, we indicated that the GEC approach also provided for regulation of the relationships between GECs via data structures called "externals." This chapter looks at specific examples to see how the combination of GECs and externals provides business staff with control over the characteristics of entities and the relationships between them. In the initial example we look at financial transactions involving tuition charges and payments at a university.

Exhibit 20.1 presents an example Person GEC. Every GEC has a default multivalued element (MVE) having the same name as the GEC itself and a default instance of the MVE having the same name as the GEC itself. The Person GEC therefore has an MVE called Person (T-Person) that has an instance called Person. For this discussion, we also define one non-default T-Person instance: Student. We have identified Jane as a Person who has Person-Type (GT-Person|Person) values of Student and Person. By default, the T node designates a multivalued attribute (MVA) rather than a control type (CT), so the type (T), type-role-type (TRT), and generic-role-generic (GRG) nodes are inactive and are shown in gray.

Next, Transaction is presented as a GEC in Exhibit 20.2. It has two values, Charge and Payment. It has only the default type of transaction (T-Transaction), which has two values, Tuition and Cash. Charge-Tuition and Payment-Cash are identified as valid generic-type (GT) values. Again, because the T node is an MVA, not a CT, no role (R), type-role-type (TRT), or generic-role-generic (GRG) values are present.

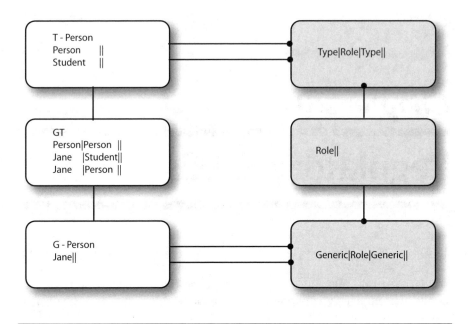

Exhibit 20.1. Example Person GEC

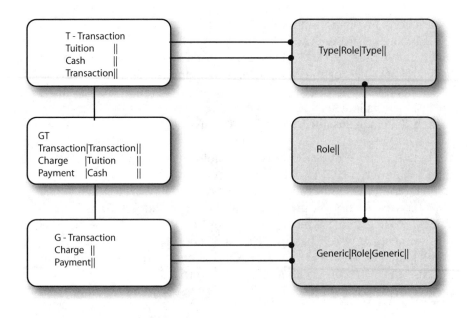

Exhibit 20.2. Example Transaction GEC

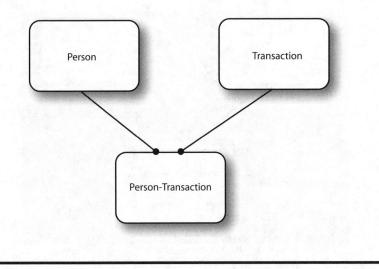

Exhibit 20.3. Person Transaction External

Note that in the GEC in Exhibit 20.2, we have not shown GT records for Charge | Transaction | | or Payment | Transaction | |.

To show the relationship between Jane and her transactions, the GEC rules require an external called Person-Transaction, shown in Exhibit 20.3. While the GEC external in Exhibit 20.3 is shown connecting to the G node, such connections are actually implemented slightly differently. In truth, Jane's charge and payment result from her being a person with a type of Student, so the connection actually occurs between GT nodes (Exhibit 20.4).

Exhibit 20.1 through Exhibit 20.4 demonstrate some of the flexibility of the GEC/external approach. With these data structures alone, business rules can be established and enforced. Moreover, business staff can change business rules via modification of data values. New Person types can be introduced. New transactions can be introduced. New relationships between them can be established.

20.1 Attached versus Detached Regulation of GT Values

An essential aspect of GEC regulatory activity is validation of values. There are two forms of value validation:

1. *Attached regulation*: attached to a specific GEC
2. *Detached regulation*: detached through the use of externals attached to an additional GEC

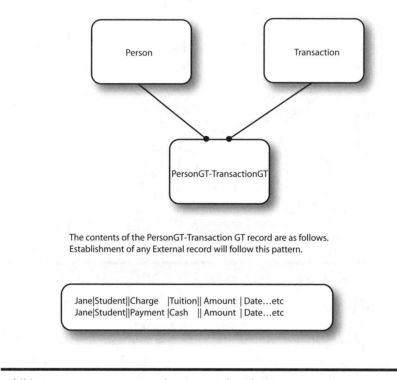

The contents of the PersonGT-Transaction GT record are as follows. Establishment of any External record will follow this pattern.

```
Jane|Student||Charge  |Tuition|| Amount | Date...etc
Jane|Student||Payment |Cash   || Amount | Date...etc
```

Exhibit 20.4. Person Transaction External with GT Connections

We have shown that a value recorded in the GT node represents a connection between a value in the G node and a value in the T node. If no additional validation of that GT value is performed, the system has applied what we call attached regulation. That is, the list of valid values is attached to the GEC by means of the T node. Jane|Student|| is a valid GT value because Jane is a valid G value and Student is a valid T value. We could not have recorded Jane|Employee|| or Joseph|Student|| because no T value of Employee exists and no G value of Joseph exists.

In addition to the attached regulation of the GT value, it may be necessary to validate its value against an external list of valid values. Such validation is called detached regulation. That is, the list of valid values is detached from the specific GEC recorded in a central GEC, where it can be shared by multiple specific GECs. The idea is that the GT value must be consistent with the system as a whole, not only consistent with the structure of its GEC. The following section discusses how detached regulation is supported within a GEC-based system.

20.2 GEC Validation Tables

We generally think of GECs as containing application information about persons, places, or things. It is also possible to construct entire GECs whose only purpose is regulatory.

A great deal of regulatory data may reside in a system in the form of tables of "valid values," sometimes called "domains." Domains are often implemented within the database in such a way that modification requires the intervention of IT professionals. The approach shown here uses GECs to store and control tables of valid values. The data elements of State and Country are used to illustrate how this occurs.

State and Country often serve different purposes in a system, yet those purposes should share a common set of values. It does not make sense to have separate — and identical — sets of valid values for each purpose. All purposes should be served by the same set of values.

We can use the GEC mechanism. Start by identifying a State GEC. It has the usual default MVE (T-State) and the default instance of T-State (State). Establish the State T node as an MVA, not a CT. Therefore, only the T, G, and GT nodes are shown. Exhibit 20.5 shows five possible instances

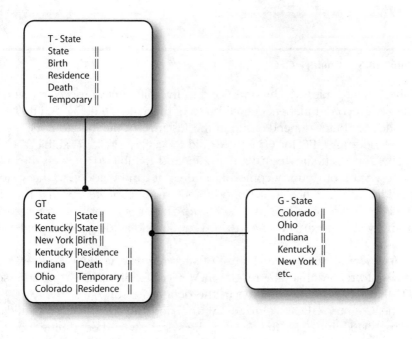

Exhibit 20.5. State GEC

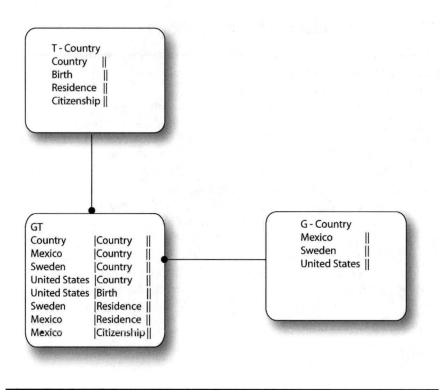

Exhibit 20.6. Country GEC

of the T-State node, which correspond to five different purposes for storing State on a record. Independent attributes of the State are defined in the State G node. Attributes dependent upon the instance of the T-State node are in the GT node. A GEC for Country would look very similar (Exhibit 20.6).

The approach shown in Exhibit 20.5 and Exhibit 20.6 is very flexible. If a new State or Country comes into being, it can be added to the system by adding an instance to a G node and to appropriate instances to the GT node. If we need to add a new purpose for State or Country, we can do so by adding an instance to a T node and adding appropriate GT instances.

How would a system make use of such regulatory GECs? Suppose that we wish to record that Jane resides in Mexico. Exhibit 20.7 shows a Person GEC that has no types other than the default Person.

The Country GEC is utilized by applying the logic used to validate externals (Exhibit 20.8). In this case, the system would determine whether it is valid to store an external that links Jane's Person-GT record to the Country GEC's GT record. Because both Jane|Person|| and Mexico|Residence|| exist, such an external is valid, and a record can be stored. It is likely that such a record would have elements to store the effective

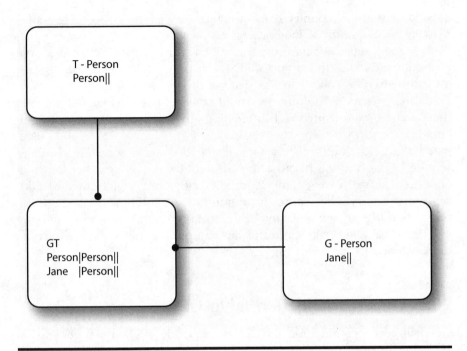

Exhibit 20.7.   Person GEC

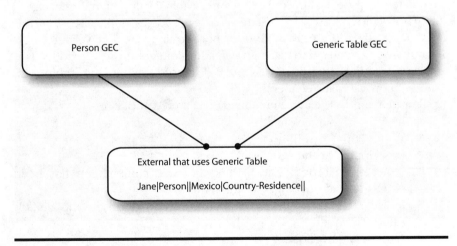

Exhibit 20.8.   External Validating Jane's Country of Residence

dates of residence. Had Jane been a resident of Sweden for some period of time before becoming a resident of Mexico, she could have two external records. Note that we could not record that Jane's country of birth is

Mexico or that her country of citizenship is Sweden, as no such entries exist in the GT node of Exhibit 20.6.

Designers must ask the question, "What can change?" What if a new element is added to the system and we wish to validate its values against an external GEC? Following the pattern above, we would create a new GEC (and external). The process would be very straightforward, following the standard pattern involved in creating any GEC. The entire operation could be performed using the GECBuilder (see Chapter 22) to add GECs, externals, fields, and relationships as needed. This would technically require IT intervention because the GECBuilder is, among other things, a code generator. However, the IT modifications are straightforward add-ons that are unlikely to cause disruption to the existing software, and the business staff can immediately begin to control the new operation by entering data values. But even this amount of IT effort is unnecessary, as demonstrated in the following section.

20.3 Generic Validation Table GECs

GEC support for validation tables can be made even more generic by changing the approach slightly. Instead of defining separate GECs for State and Country, define a single GEC called Table, as shown in Exhibit 20.9.

T values in this GEC are formed by combining G value and "purpose," e.g., State+Purpose and Country+Purpose. Each T value identifies a logical "table" of valid values. The instances of each logical table are stored as GT records. To add a new table does not require a new GEC, just a new T value and G values and their appropriate linkage in the GT node. This approach requires that all G, T, and GT records within the Table GEC use common GT data elements.

Consider the following elements to be likely candidates:

- Value+Purpose: GT node
- Description of the Purpose: T node
- Indicator to report that a Value+Purpose combination has been retired and is no longer valid: GT node
- Indicator to show that, for a given purpose, this is the default value: GT node
- Audit-User: All nodes
- Audit-Timestamp: All nodes

When a new element is introduced into the system, it is defined in the data dictionary. Once defined, it can be established as a T value in the generic table GEC. A new logical table can then be created within

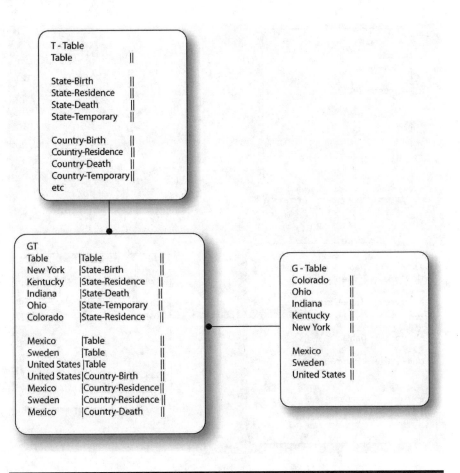

Exhibit 20.9. Generic Table GEC: Combining State GEC and Country GEC

the generic table GEC without modification of data structures or program code. This is flexible!

For example, if we introduce the element Gender to the system and it has just one purpose, we would follow the steps listed below:

- Add Gender to the data dictionary.
- Add a T instance in the generic table GEC's T node for Gender.
- Add values to the G node for every valid value of Gender.
- Add values to the GT node linking the Gender values with the T instance of Gender.

The new entries are shown in Exhibit 20.10 in gray. We can now record that Jane is a female, because the system will find the external Jane|Person||Female|Gender|| to be valid.

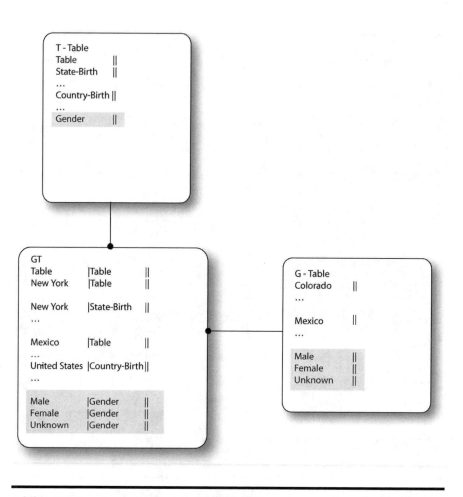

Exhibit 20.10. Gender Added to "Table" GEC

Note that although T nodes in the generic table GEC default to MVAs, they can be changed to CTs, adding another degree of flexibility as, for example, in the value-to-value translation presented in Section 20.5. The only purpose of the generic table GEC is that of regulation. The values stored in the GT nodes serve as reference data. "Reference data is any kind of data that is used solely to categorize other data found in a database, or solely for relating data in a database to information beyond the boundaries of the enterprise" [Chisholm, 2004]. This can all be handled without IT intervention.

There is a potential problem with the generic validation table approach. The various "tables" within the generic table are being treated as instances of a generic entity rather than as entities themselves. Therefore, a structure change will be needed if an instance were to acquire additional attributes and need to function as an entity in itself. It is interesting that a technique that increases flexibility in one way can also inhibit flexibility in another way. It is the old trade-off business again. In this case, for any validation table that can be expected to always share the same set of attributes with other such tables, then the trade-off is in favor of the approach using the generic validation table.

20.4 When to Use Attached or Detached Regulation

The choice of whether to use attached or detached regulation is made by the designer. If a T node will share a list of valid values, the use of detached regulation is recommended. This will ensure that only one set of values needs to be maintained. For example, if T values for Country-Residence and Country-Birth share the same list of valid countries, entry of Country-Residence and Country-Birth values for a Person should be validated against a single central list. It would not make business sense to maintain parallel lists, as that requires a process, manual or automated, for keeping the lists synchronized. And remember, when data exists in two places, it will not necessarily be the same in both places. Although this has nothing to do with flexibility per se, the ability to maintain a nonduplicate list in a flexible manner means that it is much more likely to be done, and it enables business experts to improve the operation of their systems.

Even in the unlikely case that the lists of valid Country-Residence and Country-Birth are not the same, all the involved countries can be listed in the G node. Subsets of the G node values can be established for Residence and Birth using the GT node.

The GEC is flexible in this regard. Attached regulation can be declared initially and later changed to detached regulation through a change in or addition to data values in the T node, thus establishing a logical table in the generic table GEC and connecting to system data via one or more externals.

20.5 Value-to-Value Translation

Value-to-value translation is one of the most elegant uses of the generic table GEC. We think of it as a kind of regulatory Rosetta stone. There are times when a system process requires translation of one value to another value or values. This discussion looks at how to implement an automated mechanism to serve this purpose by making use of the previously described generic table GEC.

In this example, from a student information system, we have two logical tables, or instances, of the generic table GEC's T node:

Interest   = Academic Interest
Enclosure = Informational Material

The business requirement is to make a connection between the two. If a student expresses interest in a particular academic subject, certain informational material about that subject needs to be sent to the student.

Earlier, we stated that the default T values in the generic table GEC were MVAs. This means that no R, TRT, or GRG nodes will be active. However, in this case, our T values are CTs (control types), which provides additional flexibility.

To begin, we establish a Role (R) instance called Mail. Then we establish a TRT instance for Interest | Mail | Enclosure. The TRT relationship can be expressed as "a specific Interest leads us to Mail one or more Enclosures."

The GEC is shown in Exhibit 20.11. Note that the previously discussed entries for State, Country, and Gender are not shown here, but they could exist. Only the entries related to the current discussion are shown.

In the GT nodes, the G values are associated with the appropriate type. Biology, for example, designates an Interest rather than an Enclosure.

The TRT node represents the value translation that we want to occur.

The GRG node represents instances of the TRT relationship. An Interest value of Biology should result in enclosures B1 and H1 being mailed. An Interest value of History should result in H1 being mailed. Note that an Interest value of History should *not* result in B1 being mailed. If the business requirements changed and B1 should be mailed to those having an interest in history, adding the appropriate GRG instance would establish that relationship between HIST and B1.

This mechanism has many uses. Within UniverSIS, our example student information system, mailing of informational materials is managed in this way. The same mechanism can be used in other situations where it is necessary to translate one value to another. Such a situation occurs when data comes into a system from an external system and values do not map precisely between the two systems.

For example, a university student information system might receive a file from a national testing service that includes information about the student's academic interests. The university's list of potential academic interests may differ from the list provided by the testing service. Recording the list of testing service values as a logical table within the generic table GEC would allow use of the value-to-value translation mechanism. Business staff could map one or more interests from the testing service list to one or more interests in the university's list. Biology, Microbiology, and

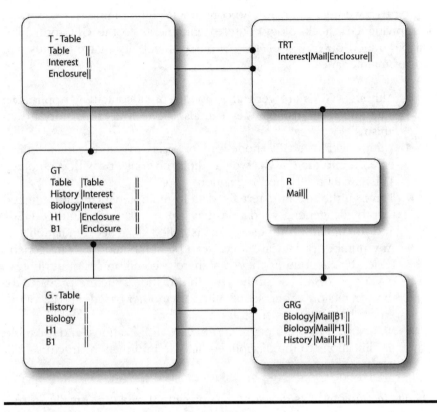

Exhibit 20.11. Code-to-Code Generic Table

Biochemistry, for example, might all be mapped to Biology. Biochemistry might be mapped to both Biology and Chemistry. How the value translations are mapped is entirely under the control of the business staff. As in the previous Interest/Enclosure example, the mapping of the testing service values to the university system values occurs in the GRG node.

In general, because a 1:1 correspondence is a special case of an *m:n* correspondence, this facility, combined with a cardinality restriction, could be used for any cross-reference requirement that entails establishing a 1:1 correspondence between the elements of two lists. In particular, it could apply to the maintenance of the necessary 1:1 correspondence between internal and external identifiers discussed in Chapter 14.

20.6 Summary

The GEC principles described in this book provide a solid foundation for flexible software design. At the same time, GEC design remains a work in progress. We urge the reader to continue to think of and test new ways of applying GEC technology. Future refinements to the GEC principles will be judged on how well they promote flexibility that translates into ease of maintenance.

- Although GECs are generally thought of as containing application data and relationships, they can also be used as regulatory mechanisms.
- Values within a GEC node can be used to validate data values entered into the GEC as well as their relationships with each other. This is called attached regulation.
- Through the use of externals, data in multiple GECs can be linked to provide generic validation that can be used by multiple GECs and for multiple purposes. This is called detached regulation.
- Any number of logical "tables" can be combined into one generic table GEC as long as they can share a common set of attributes.
- A very powerful use of the GEC information structure provides for the conversion of one set of values to another based on data values entered by business staff.
- We expect to find many more GEC applications and possible modifications to the disciplined flexible information structures that it provides.

GEC technology was developed to provide flexible information structures for the persons, places, and things that make up a software system. It allows easily modified cardinality enforcement, relationships, and data validation. GEC technology also provides an extremely flexible means of declaring and enforcing general business rules.

Chapter 21

GEC Applications and Extensions

This chapter covers several GEC-oriented topics. Some have to do with the application of the GEC approach. Others are extensions of the basic GEC presented elsewhere in the book. Still others are ideas of how to extend the GEC to make it an even more valuable tool for achieving system flexibility.

21.1 Developing a GEC

In Chapter 10, we introduced the GEC, showing an example of how information pertaining to positions could be managed. We begin this chapter by exploring another GEC that has only one ring, showing how the Course entity from UniverSIS can be implemented as a GEC. See Exhibit 21.1.

A course is the basic unit of academic instruction at a university. Each course has a system-assigned identifier. A course has numerous attributes such as title (name), subject matter, home college, credit hours, etc. All of this can be accommodated by identifying a Course entity in its simplest form, without use of the GEC. However, using the GEC as a design aid, we are prompted to ask additional questions:

1. What are the course names?
2. Are there (or could there be) different types of courses? If so, we need to define them in the T node.

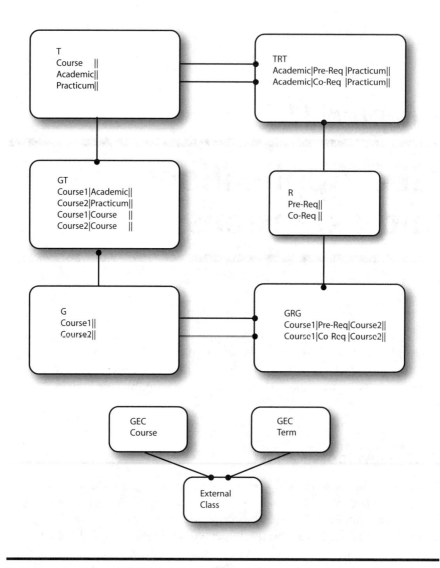

Exhibit 21.1. Course GEC and Class External Shown as Connection from Course and Term GECs

3. Are there (or could there be) relationships among different courses? If so, we need to define them in the R node.
4. What are the valid relationships between types? These must be defined in the TRT node.
5. What is the type of each instance of Course? These must be defined in the GT node.
6. What are the valid relationships between instances of Course entity? These must be defined in the GRG node.

In answer to question 1, we have Course1 and Course2.

The answer to question 2 is "yes." Although there may traditionally have been only one type of course, the possibility of multiple types has always existed. For example, the nature of instruction at a university is changing, with emphasis on preparation for employment. In addition to traditional academic courses, universities may offer practicum courses that focus on application of material learned in academic courses. Such courses would not be included in the student's academic transcript or grade-point average. In other words, the rules governing practicum courses are different from the rules governing academic courses. Every entity will have at minimum an identity value in the T node. For the Course entity, this means a T value of Course. In Exhibit 21.1, we identified the two additional type values in the T node: Academic and Practicum.

The answer to question 3 is also "yes." A student may be required to complete Course1 before taking Course2. The relationship between the courses is that Course1 is a prerequisite of Course2. A student might be required to take Course1 at the same time as Course2, in which case the relationship is that of corequisite. In Exhibit 21.1, we identify two values in the R node: Pre-Req and Co-Req.

In addressing question 4, we determine from our business experts that an academic course may be a prerequisite for a practicum course or a corequisite with a practicum course. A practicum course is never a prerequisite for an academic course. We therefore identify two relationships in the TRT node:

Academic | Pre-Req | Practicum ||
Academic | Co-Req | Practicum ||

In answer to question 5, we identify two relationships between Course and Type in the GT node:

Course1 | Academic ||
Course2 | Practicum ||

All courses are of type Course, the identity type. In answer to question 6, we determine the relationship between instances of the Course entity. We identify relationships in the GRG node:

Course1 | Pre-Req | Course2 ||
Course1 | Co-Req | Course2 ||

In business terms, this means that the student can register for Course2 if she either has completed Course1 or is simultaneously taking Course1. There can be no GRG relationship between Course1 and Course2 based on the T value of Course because the TRT node specifies no relationship based on a T value of Course.

As a result of answering the six questions above, we observe that:

■ A course always has at least one type, that of the entity identity. In this example, the entity Course has the identity type of Course. In addition to the identity type, a single course could in principle have multiple types, one type, or no types — implemented via cardinality regulation.

■ It appears that a course could have a GRG relationship with itself, but in the case of Pre-Req and Co-Req, that does not make business sense. Allowing parent and child nodes in the GRG to be identical opens the possibility of an endless loop in a bill-of-materials (BOM) relationship. The GECBuilder operation presented in Chapter 22 checks for and disallows this condition.

Going one step farther, we can visualize the existence of another GEC to define Term. A Class would be an external that relates the Course GEC and the Term GEC, as shown at the bottom of Exhibit 21.1.

In addition to Course, Term, and Class, a university may have additional entities such as Meeting, Instruction Unit, etc. By Instruction Unit we mean the format in which instruction occurs. Examples would be lecture, lab, seminar, recitation, etc. A Meeting entity would include the time and place where the instructor and students gather for the Instruction Unit. For example, if a class had a lecture every Monday, Wednesday, Friday at 10:00 A.M. in Room 123 from September 25 through December 15, we would identify three Meetings. We encourage the readers to design information structures for these entities utilizing GECs and externals.

21.2 GEC with Business Rules

The GEC information structure takes us only part way toward full satisfaction of business requirements. It provides support for data structures and relationships within those structures. With the Role node of the GEC, we can specify a relationship between types, but that may not provide the system with all the business rules related to specific business processes. For example, the role Pre-Requisite means that the student cannot register for the course of the type on the right side of the TRT until he has completed the course of the type on the left side of the TRT.

To support our earlier example, Course1|Pre-Req|Course2||, the registration process requires logic that tells the system to look for a previous enrollment in Course1 before allowing a student to register for Course2.

Corequisites are even a little trickier; all that can be said is that the relationship is validated via the TRT/GRG connection. Thus business rules to control processing must be declared as shown below.

From our earlier example, we know that an academic course can be a Pre-Req of a practicum course. Exhibit 21.2 shows the relevant TRT.

Exhibit 21.3 shows the GRG for a specific pairing of courses, validated against the TRT. To accommodate the prerequisite logic for the registration process, we would develop a data structure to record business processes (Exhibit 21.4). Each business process would have associated with it the name of a module to be executed by the system. For this discussion, we

TRT

Academic | Pre-Req | Practicum ||

Exhibit 21.2.   Example TRT

GRG

Course1 | Pre-Req | Course2 ||

Exhibit 21.3.   Example GRG

```
Process ID  : PROC001
Name        : Registration
GEC         : Course
Role        : Pre-Req
Module ID   : Evaluator
```

Exhibit 21.4.   Business Process Record

```
GRG

Course1 | Pre-Req | Course2 ||

Process              : Registration
Requirement ID       : Rule001
```

Exhibit 21.5. Revised GRG

```
Rule001

STUDENT-COMPLETED-COURSE     EQ 'Course1'
STUDENT-REG-TERM             LT CURRENT-TERM
```

Exhibit 21.6. Evaluator Rule001 for Pre-Requisite

will assume that the module is the Evaluator, described in Chapter 18. A master list of system processes will be maintained as data within the system. "Registration" would be one value on that master list. Others might include Award Scholarship, Grant Admission, etc. Technical staff would maintain that list as new processes were added to the system.

The elements (Name, GEC, and Role) together serve as a search argument. Finding a match on the search argument, the business process would execute the Module ID, in this case Evaluator, and use the result.

Exhibit 21.5 shows the revised GRG for the specific pairing of Course1 and Course2. To this record, we attach a Process ID and an Evaluator Requirement ID.

Exhibit 21.6 shows the Evaluator requirement identified as Rule001, which states that to get a TRUE result, the student must have completed Course1 some time before the current term.

The registration process would behave as follows. We will assume that Jane is attempting to register for Course2.

■ The registration process needs to "know" its own identify. It would combine Process=Registration, GEC=Course, and Role=Pre-Req to construct a search argument.
■ The search argument would find a match on PROC001, which states that Evaluator must be executed.

- The system would find the GRG record containing Course2 and retrieve the information that Rule001 must be observed.
- The registration would pass to the Evaluator Jane's ID and the Requirement ID=Rule001.
- The Evaluator would return a TRUE or FALSE value.
- Depending on the Evaluator result, Jane either would or would not be permitted to register for Course2.

We have used a simple example having only one matching Process record and one Evaluator Requirement, but there would be no inherent limit to the number of related Process records or Requirements. As new processes are introduced, they are added to the master list. From that point forward, business staff can use the Evaluator to establish business rules and connect them to business processes.

21.3 Multi-Ring (3) GEC

In Chapter 10 we mentioned that a GEC could have multiple rings. The following example shows a GEC-based Person entity having three rings corresponding to three T nodes.

- Ring 0: T-Employee
- Ring 1: T-Student
- Ring 2: T-Relationship

The reader will note that we took the business requirements of Chapter 19's tuition remission example and implemented them in a different way within the GEC structure. Rather than declaring Student and Employee as values of a single T node as in Chapter 19, we declare separate T nodes (and rings) for Student and Employee. Rather than declaring Child, Parent, and Spouse as values of the Person R node, we declare a T node for Relationship. We show this alternative approach to illustrate that the designer can exercise judgment about how to use the GEC structures within the context of the organization's business requirements.

All the rings share the generic entity file (G). Each ring has a separate file for each of the following: Type (T), Generic Type (GT), Type Role Type (TRT), Role (R), and Generic Role Generic (GRG). In Exhibit 21.7 these are labeled R0, R1, and R2, indicating the ring in which they reside.

To demonstrate how these rings work, we populate the nodes with data. The data is presented in list format, as it is much easier to follow than placing data in the nodes of Exhibit 21.7. Also, for ease of presentation, we will treat the data values in these files as if they were the identifiers controlling internode connections.

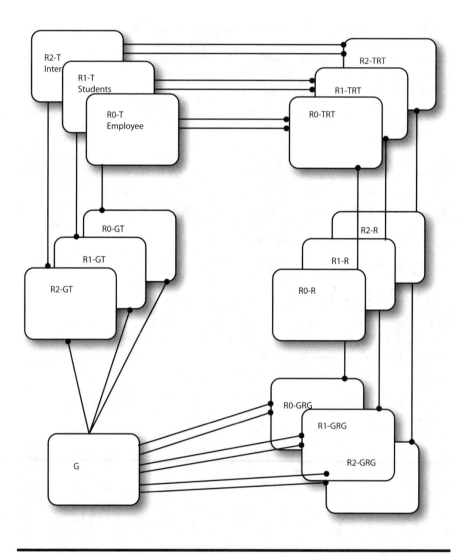

Exhibit 21.7. Multi-Ring (3) GEC (R0 Employee; R1 Student; R2 Interpersonal Relationship)

In the R0-Type file: control types of Employees (i.e., persons who get paid by the university).

- TA (teaching assistant)
- Assistant (professor)
- Professor
- Associate (professor)

- Dean
- Provost
- President
- Vice (President)
- Chair (of department)
- Janitor
- Supervisor

In the R1-Type file: control types of Students (i.e., persons who pay the university, either directly or indirectly through scholarships or assistantships).

- Graduate
- Undergraduate

In the R2-Type file: control types of interpersonal Relationships.

- Child
- Parent
- Spouse

In the TRT nodes, the allowable relationships are set up as follows; we will populate the Relationship files at the same time.

- R0-Role reports to T0-TRT. This is essentially the organizational chart (Exhibit 21.8).
- R1-Relationship (For students who have no specific relationships, the file is empty. R1-TRT is also empty.)

Parent	Role	Child
Provost	Reports to	President
Dean	Reports to	Provost
Chair	Reports to	Dean
Professor	Reports to	Chair
Associate	Reports to	Chair
Assistant	Reports to	Chair
TA	Reports to	Professor
Vice	Reports to	President
Supervisor	Reports to	Vice
Janitor	Reports to	Supervisor

Exhibit 21.8. TRT for Employee Relationships

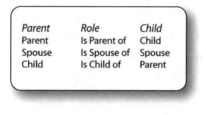

Parent	Role	Child
Parent	Is Parent of	Child
Spouse	Is Spouse of	Spouse
Child	Is Child of	Parent

Exhibit 21.9. TRT for Interpersonal Relationships

- R2-Relationship
  - Is Parent of
  - Is Spouse of
  - Is Child of
- R2-TRT, allowable interpersonal relationships are shown in Exhibit 21.9.

At this point, we have declared the business rules, i.e., regulatory data associated with our application that can be set up using the GEC. Now we will declare some entities (persons) and their various types and see how the business rules established above control our application.

The persons who are associated with our organization are listed below.

- Bruce is a janitor.
- Bo is a teaching assistant and graduate student.
- Cindy is president.
- Walt is provost.
- John is a department chair and professor.
- Carmen is a supervisor and a graduate student.
- Linda is an undergraduate student.
- Dell is an assistant professor.
- Gates is a janitor.
- Peter is Martin's father.
- Cindy is Russell's sister.
- Martin is a graduate student.
- Michele is Russell's spouse.
- Spencer is a graduate student.
- Ursula is an undergraduate student.
- Russell is Ursula's father
- Russell is an associate professor.
- Joe is vice president of facilities.

Other types and relationships are possible, but they are not of interest to our application at this time.

Using the information above, we populate the Person generic node:

- Bruce
- Bo
- Cindy
- Walt
- John
- Carmen
- Linda
- Dell
- Gates
- Peter
- Martin
- Michele
- Spencer
- Ursula
- Russell
- Joe

Next we populate the GT (generic-type) nodes, as shown in Exhibit 21.10. And finally, we populate the GRG nodes to indicate specific reporting lines and interpersonal relationships, as shown in Exhibit 21.11.

The R1-GRG is empty. Note that at this time we have no TRT or GRG relationship for siblings, as they are of no interest. Thus Cindy as the sister of Russell is not recorded.

How would we use this information structure? Let us revisit the tuition remission example from Chapter 19, using the following business policy to guide us. Note that its terms are more specific than in Chapter 19.

> An undergraduate student who is the child or spouse of an employee is eligible for tuition remission, but only if the employee is an associate professor.

Using the single-ring GEC in Chapter 19, we were able to enforce the policy using data stored in the GEC structures. Here we will illustrate the same capability when the data is stored in three GEC rings rather than one.

- To see if Bruce is eligible for tuition remission, we first check the R0-GT node to determine whether he is an undergraduate. Since we find no entry for him, he is *not eligible.*
- To see if Linda is eligible, we check the R0-GT node and find that she is an undergraduate. However, in R2-GT we find that she is not the child or spouse of an employee. She is *not eligible.*

R0-GT	*GT Node for Employees*
Bruce	Janitor
Bo	TA
Cindy	President
Walt	Provost
John	Department Chair
John	Professor
Carmen	Supervisor
Dell	Assistant Professor
Gates	Janitor
Russell	Associate Professor
Joe	Vice President

R1-GT	*GT Node for Students*
Bo	Graduate
Carmen	Graduate
Linda	Undergraduate
Martin	Graduate
Spencer	Graduate
Ursula	Undergraduate

R2-GT	*GT Node for Relationships*
Russell	Parent
Ursula	Child
Russell	Spouse
Michele	Spouse
Cindy	Parent
Martin	Child
Peter	Parent

Exhibit 21.10. GT Nodes for Employees, Students, and Interpersonal Relationships

- To see if Bo is eligible, we check R0-GT and find that he is not an undergraduate student. He is *not eligible.*
- To see if Martin is eligible, we check the R0-GT node and find that he is an undergraduate. We find in R2-GRG that Martin is the child of Peter. Looking at R0-GT, however, we find no entry for Peter. Martin is *not eligible* for tuition remission.
- To see if Ursula is eligible, we check the R0-GT node and find that she is an undergraduate. Checking R2-GRG, we find that Ursula is the child of Russell. Checking R0-GT, we see that Russell is an associate professor. Ursula is *eligible* for tuition remission.

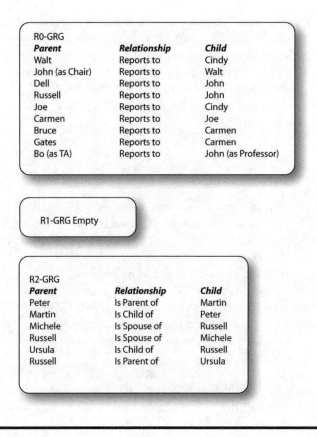

Exhibit 21.11. GRG Nodes for Employees, Students, and Interpersonal Relationships

- To see if Michele is eligible, we check R0-GT and find that she is not an undergraduate. Michele is *not eligible* for tuition remission. Note that we find in R2-GRG that she is the spouse of Russell, who is an associate professor. If Michele becomes an undergraduate student, she will be eligible for tuition remission.

This GEC-based information structure supports a flexible approach to our process of tuition remission. The status, relationship, etc. of persons connected to the process can be easily manipulated by business staff. Of course, general business rules utilizing these structures must be established in the system, as shown in Chapter 19 and in the course example earlier in this chapter. That step has been omitted here so as to concentrate on the multi-ring aspect of the GEC, but the concept will be the same. The business-rule mechanism will enforce the rules by gathering and evaluating stored data.

GEC nodes record referential integrity rules for allowable relationships inside a given GEC ring. Rules can be enforced across rings only through external rules declaration. For example, if there were a business rule that graduate students cannot work as janitors, the GEC structures could not be used directly to enforce that rule because two rings are involved. However, an external rule declaration, such as a modification to Exhibit 21.4 and Exhibit 21.6, would provide for this.

21.4 The Atomic GEC

Never content with our work, we ask whether additional flexibility can be incorporated into the GEC design. This section describes what may be the ultimate form of the GEC: the atomic GEC. As a practical matter, this approach may not be ideal, but it provides food for thought. Assume infinite speed and storage and keep an open mind.

What if the system designer decides that all attributes describing the entity are to be implemented as multivalued entities (MVEs)? There would be a (potential) ring for each attribute. Any attribute could have zero, one, or more optional values (in addition to the identity value) dynamically. This is the atomic GEC!

This approach may not seem to make sense for "obviously" single-valued elements like birth date, amount owed, name, etc. However, even elements such as these deserve a closer look. One of our authors developed a personnel records system that had no input of its own; it rummaged through existing systems such as payroll, plans, medical, etc. and extracted specific field values such as birth date. It occasionally uncovered more than one value. When this happened, both were reported and stored until the right one was determined and the wrong one deleted via manual data entry. The same thing happens in the case of name. Names can and do change. One of our authors has dropped his middle initial/name and Jr. since his father died. But in some legal situations, he must keep one or the other or both, yielding up to four possible names for the same person.

This again shows the value of cardinality regulation, which can be used to shut down portions of the ring that are not needed initially. Even if all attributes are designated as MVEs, most will be implemented with one occurrence, and most will not need R, TRT, or GRG nodes for either their entity values or their control-type values. However, by including at initial implementation time the capability to extend and refine the meaning and use of an attribute without IT intervention, designers provides great — one might say "atomic" — power to the system.

G-Person	T-Person	Sub-T-Person	Sub-Sub-T-Person
	Person		
	Employee	Faculty	Tenured
	Employee	Faculty	Adjunct
	Employee	Staff	
	Student	Degree-Seeking	
	Student	Non-Degree-Seeking	

Exhibit 21.12. Person Sub-Subclassifications

21.5 SubGECs

The evolution of GEC design is ongoing. This section presents ideas on what we call the "SubGEC." The MVE typing ring of the GEC allows a great deal of flexibility in typing and categorizing people, and, as shown above, the use of the multi-ring features allows multiple typing within a given GEC. However the multi-ring feature does not recognize the hierarchy of types that actually exists.

There may be another way to handle the situation, as shown in Exhibit 21.12. Under the T-Person node, we have the values shown. Presumably, we would record the same information about every person, every employee, and every student. What if we record additional information for degree-seeking students that is different from the additional information for non-degree-seeking students? What about employee/faculty versus employee/staff? To make it more complex, what if we record different additional data for tenured and adjunct faculty?

One approach is to make each Type value in the T node of the GEC a combination of Type and Purpose. For example, in a T node for Country, the values could be Country-Residence, Country-Birth, etc. This approach seems to work well for Country because the possibility of subpurposes seemed fairly remote. We should, however, recognize the lack of flexibility to handle subpurposes should the need for them arise.

Another approach would be to connect the GT node in a Parent GEC to the G node in a Child GEC, as seen in Exhibit 21.13, which shows only the Employee SubGEC. The same approach would be used for a Student SubGEC. The R, TRT, and GRG nodes would be available within the SubGECs as well, though we have not shown them in the exhibit.

With the SubGEC approach, we have an information structure in which data about and relationships between persons as persons can be handled

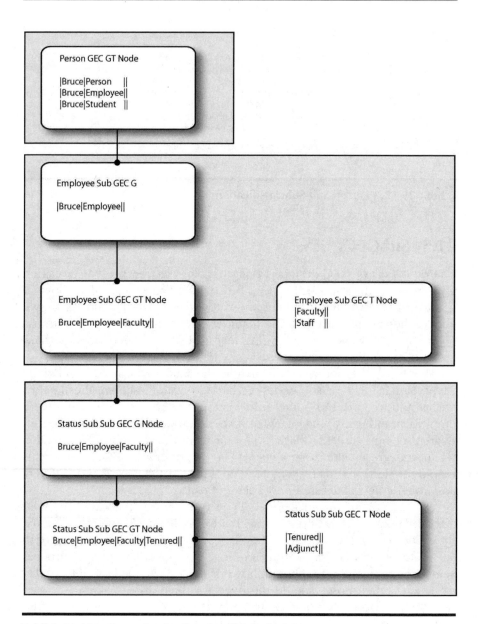

Exhibit 21.13. Example of a Two-Level Sub-GEC Structure

in the top-level Person GEC. Data about and relationships between Person-Employees can be handled by the next-level sub-GEC Employee. Data and relationships unique to Faculty are stored in the Status Sub-Sub-GEC. The number of sublevels is unlimited.

Referential integrity and cardinality regulation can be managed through the normal mechanism of the GEC. Existing processes manage additional layers of complexity.

21.6 Summary

This chapter has demonstrated the following:

- The development of a GEC showing how each node is used
- The inclusion of general business rules to utilize the information-structure enforcement inherent in the GEC
- The possibility of an atomic GEC in which every attribute of a generic entity is implemented as a multivalued element (MVE)
- The multiple ring feature of the GEC, which can be used to support and enforce relationships required for the enforcement of complex business rules
- The evolution of GEC technology, which is undergoing continuing development and refinement in the constant quest for more-flexible software systems

The GEC approach provides a way to design information structures that are stable and flexible, resulting in reduction or elimination of maintenance by the IT staff. This chapter provided various examples of GEC applications and extensions. Chapter 22 presents several tools to facilitate the use and extension of the GEC approach.

Chapter 22

GEC Aids

The rigor and discipline of the generic-entity cloud (GEC) information structure enables us to create aids for the development and operation of GEC-based flexible software. The GECAnalyzer and GECBuilder are implementation aids; the GECPhazer is an operational aid.

This chapter is meant for the reader who is interested in the details, who wants to know more about GEC operation, and who has thoughts of developing or utilizing similar aids. These aids are described in the sequence in which they are used to develop and implement the information structures:

- *GECAnalyzer*: Once the GECs have been chosen, the GECAnalyzer generates all possible combinations of GECs that may yield external entities in the information structure. This helps ensure that the analyst/designer will not overlook valid combinations, even if they are not currently needed.
- *GECBuilder*: The GECBuilder actually builds the files and fields, and provides for raw data entry. The GECBuilder can receive data three ways: (a) from specifications automatically provided by the GECAnalyzer, (b) interactively via GUI screens, and (c) from specification files created with an editor.
- *GECPhazer*: After the work of the GECBuilder has been completed, lists of control types and role values are entered into the operational software. We are, in effect, in "maintenance" mode at this point. The GECPhazer generates all possible combinations of the GT (generic-type) node and the TRT (type-role-type) nodes. The business

staff identifies the ones that are currently valid. As with the GECAnalyzer, this approach should ensure that no valid combinations are overlooked.

The GECAnalyzer/GECBuilder/GECPhazer tool set facilitates development and maintenance of a generic, flexible information structure, which is the foundation of a flexible system. These aids make flexible systems easier to develop and also serve to validate the GEC approach. The GECAnalyzer and the GECPhazer are simple combination tools, and thus they can be implemented quite easily in any programming language. The GECAnalyzer, for example, was developed in NATURAL, Software AG's 4GL programming language. The output can be in the form of reports or import files that the GECBuilder can use directly. A GECBuilder prototype has been developed in Java to show the feasibility of having aids that support this kind of functionality. Vendor products that provide these capabilities can support GEC design.

22.1 The GECAnalyzer

A simple corporate organizational structure is used to illustrate the GECAnalyzer. Analysis of this sample corporate "system" leads to identification of three generic entities: Organization, Position, and Person. The GECAnalyzer identifies all possible pairings of those generic entities. Discussion with the business staff reveals which pairings are needed as externals. The process is iterative. Initially, the externals associated with generic entities are identified and marked "yes" or "no." In the next round, all possible pairings are identified, including those paired with newly created externals, and marked for inclusion or exclusion. Iterations continue until a round results in identification of no new externals. In Exhibit 22.1, we show the process of generating possibilities and accepting or rejecting them. The names of the resulting entities shown as entries in the table are simply the accumulation of the names of the parent entities.

In Exhibit 22.2, we show the net result of the GECAnalyzer's work. At this point, the analyst and business staff should agree on more meaningful names for the resulting entries. Note that one parent of the Assign external is a GEC, and the other is itself an external.

Exhibit 22.3 illustrates the GEC-based flexible software system resulting from the analysis shown in Exhibit 22.2.

The output from the GECAnalyzer is fed to the GECBuilder. It would look like Exhibit 22.4 (only the GECs and externals are shown). The left-hand column is the actual "code," the right-hand column is the explanation. In Exhibit 22.4, the Org and Pos GECs have as their MVEs (multivalued

Needed	Name	Category	Parent 1	Parent 2		
	These are the three Generics					
Yes	Org	G				
Yes	Pos	G				
Yes	Per	G				
	First wave of potential Externals					
	All possible G/G combinations					
Yes	Org-Pos	E	Org	Pos		
No	Org-Per	E	Org	Per		
No	Pos-Per	E	Pos	Per		
	Second wave of potential Externals					
	All possible combination of G nodes with yes E nodes					
No	Org-Org-Pos	E	Org	Org-Pos		
No	Pos-Org-Pos	E	Pos	Org-Pos		
Yes	Per-Org-Pos	E	Per	Org-Pos		
	Third wave of potential Externals					
	All combinations of G nodes and with "Yes" E nodes and E nodes with "Yes" E nodes					
No	Org-Per-Org-Pos	E	Org	Per-Org-Pos		
No	Pos-Per-Org-Pos	E	Pos	Per-Org-Pos		
No	Per-Per-Org-Pos	E	Per	Per-Org-Pos		
No	Org-Pos-Per-Org-Pos	E	Org-Pos	Per-Org-Pos		
	All "No" results. We are finished.					

Exhibit 22.1. Analysis of Combinations Generated

Needed	Name	Category	Parent 1	Parent 2
Yes	Org	G		
Yes	Pos	G		
Yes	Per	G		
Yes	Org-Pos	E	Org	Pos
Yes	Assign	E	Per	Org-Pos

Exhibit 22.2. Final GECAnalyzer Results

elements) control types (CTs) so that TRT and generic-role-generic (GRG) relationships will be developed. The Per GEC has MVA (multivalued attribute) as its MVE, which means that the TRT and GRG relationships will not exist. The decision about CT or MVA is based on the needs of the business. The Per hierarchical or network relationships will be established

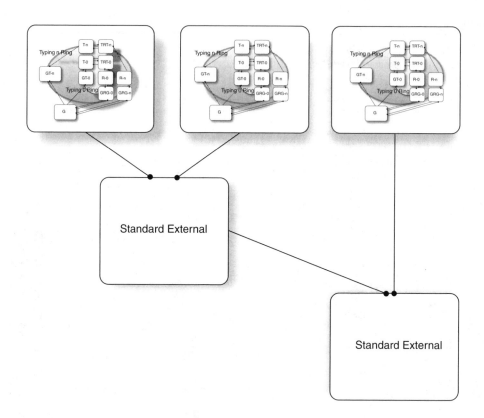

Exhibit 22.3. **GEC-Based Software System — Results from the GECAnalyzer**

"Code"	Explanation
New Corporate System	Starting a new flexible software system Initialize all files
GOrg,,CT	Establish a GEC (with six nodes) named Org with Org as a default MVE Control Type
GPos,,CT	Establish a GEC (with six nodes) named Pos with Pos a default MVE Control Type
GPer,,MVA	Establish a GEC (with six nodes) named Per with Per as a default MVE MVA
EOrgPer,Org,Per	Establish an External named OrgPer with parents Org and Per
EAssign,Per,OrgPer	Establish an External named Assign with parents Org and OrgPer

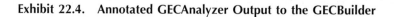

Exhibit 22.4. **Annotated GECAnalyzer Output to the GECBuilder**

through connections with the Org and Pos GECs, as shown below. Note that in Exhibit 22.4, the GECs Org and Per were established before the external OrgPer could be established and that the external OrgPer was established before the external Assign could be established.

The GECAnalyzer/GECBuilder relationship is not necessarily a one-time, start-up operation. It makes sense to use the GECAnalyzer to generate new potential combinations of GECs and externals whenever new GECs are added to the system.

How the GEC-based system comes into existence may not be important, i.e., generated by a GECBuilder or established manually by a DBA (database administrator). The same structures can be implemented in different ways in different environments. There are many successful ways of designing software. However, some detail about how application data fits into the foundation structures is very important, which can be seen from an examination of the GECBuilder operations.

22.2 The GECBuilder

The next two sections describe the GECBuilder operation. First we provide a general description, and then we use a portion of the system above to show samples of the GECBuilder in operation.

22.2.1 The GECBuilder: General Operation

Once the combinations of GECs and externals have been analyzed and generated in the GECAnalyzer (or manually), the GECBuilder is then used to develop a GEC-based system from an input file. Exhibit 22.5 shows that the GECBuilder is itself made up of GECs and externals. The information structure of the GECBuilder has five GECs represented by boldly outlined boxes (Barber, Role, GE (generic entity), Field, and File) and four externals represented by the lightly lined boxes (GE/Field, File/Field, File/Instance, and Field/Instance). The File-GRG file, which is internal to the File GEC, serves as the Relationship file, which supports cardinality regulation.

The GECBuilder is implemented as an atomic database with elementary pieces stored as atomic items. For example, each field value is stored in a separate GECBuilder record so that assembly of an application file record requires access to the GECBuilder field/instance record for each field in an application record instance. This may not be very efficient operationally, but it simplified the implementation of the prototype. The feasibility and practicality of operating an atomic system in a production environment has provided much food for thought and conversation for system designers over the years. We will not review those discussions here. We chose this approach simply because we found it to be an effective way to illustrate our points.

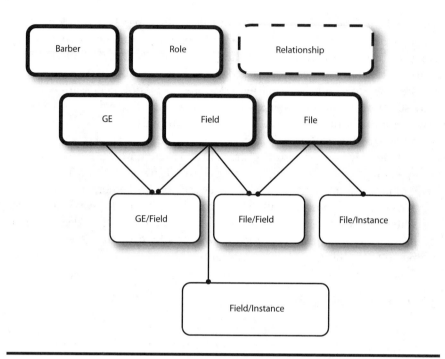

Exhibit 22.5.   The GECBuilder Information Structure

The purpose of each GEC and external is described below. A conventional data dictionary would manage many of these functions.

- The Barber (a real barber says "next!") node is used by the routine that presents the next sequential number for identifier assignment.
- The Role node contains values of roles between entities in relationships with other entities or themselves.
- The Relationship node is implemented via the File-GRG file, which is internal to the File GEC. The File-GRG node contains, among other things, the information that supports cardinality regulation.
- The GE node stores the application system's generic entities.
- The Field node records application system fields. All fields are declared here, regardless of the records in which they are used. This node serves as a portion of a data dictionary, thus ensuring consistent field-naming conventions.
- The File node is used to declare files, including files within GEC rings, as well as externals. Like the Field node, it serves a data dictionary function.

- The GE/Field node indicates which fields are MVEs. Some MVEs are MVAs (multivalued attributes), which do not require a full ring of five nodes. Others are CTs (control types) that do require a full ring of five nodes.
- The File/Field external node defines records by indicating which fields (from the Field node) are in which files (from the File node). This is another data dictionary feature.
- The File/Instance external node records record instances, indicating which instances from the global ID assigner (Barber) are in which record. This provides access from file to instance.
- The Field/Instance node indicates which fields belong to a given record instance. Thus, knowing the instance, a process can gather individual fields into logical records.

The purposes of the nodes described above can be summarized briefly:

- The application database data consists of the File/Instance node and the Field/Instance node.
- The bill-of-materials (BOM) capabilities of the field GEC (Field-GRG) is meant to support grouped items. This feature has not been implemented in the current version of the GECBuilder.
- The GE, GE/Field, Field, File, and File/Field nodes contain the application metadata and thus correspond to a data dictionary.
- All the nodes shown in Exhibit 22.5 contain GECBuilder data to which application metadata is posted as the GECBuilder is run to build or modify (regulate) the application and to which data is posted as the application is operated.

An integral part of the GECBuilder is utilitylike routines necessary to process the information structures that are built. These routines include the Bill-of-Materials Exploder, which handles nested recursive relationships. These routines are components of the GECBuilder prototype. Much of the work done by these components would otherwise need to be coded by an application programmer for *every* application. Thus, although the processing of a GEC-based flexible software system sounds (and is) complex, this complexity is hidden from the applications programmer and needs to be written only once. Furthermore, the programming work done automatically by the GECBuilder saves time and effort for the programmer every time an application must be written. Readers who have had experience with code generators can appreciate such savings. But the GEC and GECBuilder provide more than a code-generation tool set.

22.2.2 The GECBuilder: Examples of Operation

Exhibit 22.6 shows part of the system created by the GECBuilder from the file produced in Exhibit 22.4. The first line shows the header of the file generic node, its time produced in the same format as above, its association order, the record length of the records that follow (52 bytes), and a filler. Note that the | delineates fields in the report.

```
Record length- - - - - - - - - - - -┐
Association Order- - - - - - - - -┐ ¦
Date/Time Stamp- - - - -┐        ¦  ¦
Node- -┐                ¦        ¦  ¦
ID     ¦                ¦        ¦  ¦
 ¦     ¦                ¦        ¦  ¦
000002|File       |20040517121346|1|052|**filler**|


End of Record Indicator - - - - - - - - - -┐
Association Order- - - - - - - - - - - -┐ ¦
Max Allowable Records - - - - - - - -┐  ¦  ¦
Records in file   - - - - - - -┐     ¦  ¦  ¦
Name- -┐                       ¦     ¦  ¦  ¦
ID     ¦                       ¦     ¦  ¦  ¦
000135|Org.          |000000|999999|0|!|
000136|Org.GRG       |000000|999999|3|!|
000137|Org.T         |000000|999999|0|!|
000138|Org.TRT       |000000|999999|3|!|
000139|Org.R         |000000|999999|0|!|
000140|Org.GT        |000000|999999|2|!|
000143|Pos.          |000000|999999|0|!|
000144|Pos.GRG       |000000|999999|3|!|
000145|Pos.T         |000000|999999|0|!|
000146|Pos.TRT       |000000|999999|3|!|
000147|Pos.R         |000000|999999|0|!|
000148|Pos.GT        |000000|999999|2|!|
000151|Per.          |000000|999999|0|!|
000152|Per.GRG       |000000|000000|3|!|
000153|Per.T         |000000|999999|0|!|
000154|Per.TRT       |000000|000000|3|!|
000155|Per.R         |000000|000000|0|!|
000156|Per.GT        |000000|999999|2|!|
000157|OrgPer.       |000000|999999|2|!|
000160|Assign.       |000000|999999|2|!|
```

```
Record length- - - - - - - - - - - - - -┐
Association Order- - - - - - - - - - -┐ ¦
Date/Time Stamp- - - - - - - -┐       ¦  ¦
Node- - - - -┐                ¦       ¦  ¦
ID           ¦                ¦       ¦  ¦
 ¦           ¦                ¦       ¦  ¦
000003|FileGRG     |20040517132014|3|051|**filler**|


End of Record Indicator - - - - - - - - - - -┐
Actual Children- - - - - - - - - - - - -┐  ¦
Min Children - - - - - - - - - - - -┐   ¦  ¦
Max Children- - - - - - - - -┐       ¦   ¦  ¦
ChildID               ¦       ¦       ¦   ¦  ¦
RelationID- -┐        ¦       ¦       ¦   ¦  ¦
ParentID     ¦        ¦       ¦       ¦   ¦  ¦
000135|000101|000136|999999|000000|000000|!|
000136|000101|000135|999999|000000|000000|!|
000137|000101|000138|999999|000000|000000|!|
000138|000101|000137|999999|000000|000000|!|
000139|000101|000136|999999|000000|000000|!|
000139|000101|000138|999999|000000|000000|!|
000135|000101|000140|999999|000000|000000|!|
000137|000101|000140|999999|000000|000000|!|
000143|000101|000144|999999|000000|000000|!|
000144|000101|000143|999999|000000|000000|!|
000145|000101|000146|999999|000000|000000|!|
000146|000101|000145|999999|000000|000000|!|
000147|000101|000144|999999|000000|000000|!|
000147|000101|000146|999999|000000|000000|!|
000143|000101|000148|999999|000000|000000|!|
000145|000101|000148|999999|000000|000000|!|
000151|000101|000152|000000|000000|000000|!|
000152|000101|000151|999999|000000|000000|!|
000153|000101|000154|000000|000000|000000|!|
000154|000101|000153|999999|000000|000000|!|
000155|000101|000152|000000|000000|000000|!|
000155|000101|000154|000000|000000|000000|!|
000151|000101|000156|999999|000000|000000|!|
000153|000101|000156|999999|000000|000000|!|
000140|000101|000157|999999|000000|000000|!|
000156|000101|000157|999999|000000|000000|!|
000156|000101|000160|999999|000000|000000|!|
000157|000101|000160|999999|000000|000000|!|
```

Exhibit 22.6. Part of the File GEC Output from a GECBuilder Run

The file records for each File (node) are shown next, after the header. The record includes the file ID, name, actual number of records in the file (none, as no application data has been entered), and the maximum number that can be entered (note that it is 999999 for most files but that it is 000000 for the GRG, TRT, and R nodes of the Per GEC because it was declared as an MVA rather than a CT).

The File-GRG node shows the parent-child relationship of the files shown above. The format is as follows: the Parent file ID, the Relationship ID, and the Child file ID. Next are shown the maximum number of children the relationship can have, the actual number, and the minimum number. Note that the maximum number of children in the Per. to the Per.GRG (151 to 152) is zero. This is also the case for the Per.T to Per.TRT relationship (153 to 152), the Per.R to the Per relationship (155 to 152), and the Per.R to Per.TRT relationship (155 to 154) because the Per GEC has a MVA ring, whereas the Org. and Pos. GECs have CT rings. As can be seen from the above, the File-GRG node is used to implement cardinality regulation.

Exhibit 22.7 demonstrates additional features of the GECBuilder using the Org GEC. In Exhibit 22.7 the G again stands for GEC. The F designates a field to be added to the file. The GUI modules of the GECBuilder prototype

Code	Explanation
New Org System	Starting a new flexible software system Initialize all files
GOrg,,CT	Establish a CT MVE GEC named Org
FOrg,Description,Description	Add a field named Description of type Description to the Org. file
FOrg,F4,Description	Add a field named F4 of type Description to the Org. file
FOrg.T,F3,Description	Add a field named F3 of type Description to the Org.T file
FOrg.T,F4,Description	Add a field named F4 of type Description to the Org.T file
FOrg.R,Name,Name	Add a field named Name of type Name to the Org.R file
FOrg.R,F3,Description	Add a field named F3 of type Description to Org.R file
FOrg.R,F4,Description	Add a field named F4 of type Description to the Org.R file
FOrg.GT,Date,Date	Add a field named Data of type Date to the Org.GT file

Exhibit 22.7. Input to the GECBuilder for an Organization System

Org.		ID	Identifier *GEC Declared
Org.		Name	Name *GEC Declared
Org.		Description	Description
Org.		F4	Description
Org.T		ID	Identifier *GEC Declared
Org.T		Org	Name *GEC Declared CT field
Org.T		F3	Description
Org.T		F4	Description
Org.GT		ID	Identifier *GEC Declared
Org.GT		GID	Identifier *GEC Declared
Org.GT		TID	Identifier *GEC Declared
Org.GT		Date	Date
Org.R		ID	Identifier *GEC Declared
Org.R		Name	Name
Org.R		F3	Description
Org.R		F4	Description
Org.GRG		ID	Identifier *GEC Declared
Org.GRG		PID	Identifier *GEC Declared
Org.GRG		RID	Identifier *GEC Declared
Org.GRG		CID	Identifier *GEC Declared
Org.TRT		ID	Identifier *GEC Declared
Org.TRT		PID	Identifier *GEC Declared
Org.TRT		RID	Identifier *GEC Declared
Org.TRT		CID	Identifier *GEC Declared

Note: The *GEC Declared fields were declared when the GEC was created.

Exhibit 22.8. Org GEC Records Produced by the GECBuilder

operate with four fields in each record (as shown later in Exhibit 22.11). In Exhibit 22.7, when the GEC was created, the Org. record had two fields already assigned: ID and name. Two more were added: Description and F4. For the T node, two fields were assigned as the GEC was created: ID and Org CT. Two placeholder fields were added — F3 and F4 — both of type Description. The R node needs three additional fields, as only the ID was assigned at GEC creation time. The GT file needs only one additional field, as its ID as well as the GID (generic ID) and the TID (type ID) were assigned at GEC build time. Exhibit 22.8 shows the layout of the GEC records after the GECBuilder was executed with the data in Exhibit 22.7.

A. A Networked Organization as an Organization Chart

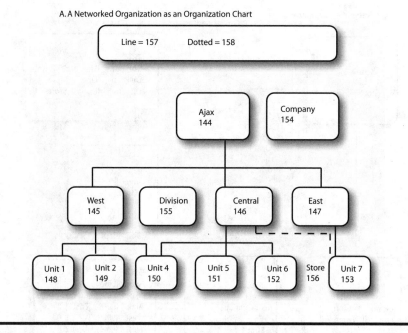

Exhibit 22.9.   Representations of a Networked Organization

The GECBuilder also supports application data, a feature used to create the organization chart shown in Exhibit 22.9. The networked organization in Exhibit 22.9 can be demonstrated by running the BOM Exploder module of the GECBuilder, as demonstrated in Exhibit 22.10. Choose the GEC and whether you wish the MVA or the CT (MVA is the default; MVE, the name of the MVE field, or blank will produce the MVE, TRT, or Generic GRG, respectively, and a Starting ID) and click Enter. The results are in a file starting with EXP and a function of the date and time with a .dat extension. Exhibit 22.10 shows that the BOM Exploder and the GECBuilder support nested recursive bill-of-materials structures, which are essential for flexible software.

There is much more to the GECBuilder. For brevity, two more features are presented: online manipulation and the cardinality regulator.

B. A Networked Organization as a GEC Diagram

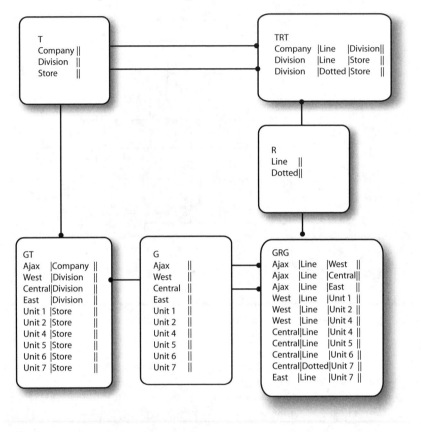

Exhibit 22.9. (continued)

Exhibit 22.10. The BOM Exploder Module of the GECBuilder

```
BOM Explosion for Org Generic Start ID = 000144
/20040515090035

000144 Ajax
   000145 West                              Line
              000148 Unit 1                 Line
              000149 Unit 2                 Line
              000150 Unit 4                 Line
   000146 Central                           Line
              000150 Unit 4                 Line
              000151 Unit 5                 Line
              000152 Unit 6                 Line
              000153 Unit 7                 Dotted
   000147 East                              Line
              000153 Unit 7                 Line

Explosion Complete @ 20040515090043

Or (screen not shown)

BOM Explosion for Org  Start ID = 000154
/20040515090852

000154 Company
   000155 Division              Line
              000156 Store       Line
              000156 Store       Dotted

Explosion Complete @ 20040515090853
```

Exhibit 22.10.   (continued)

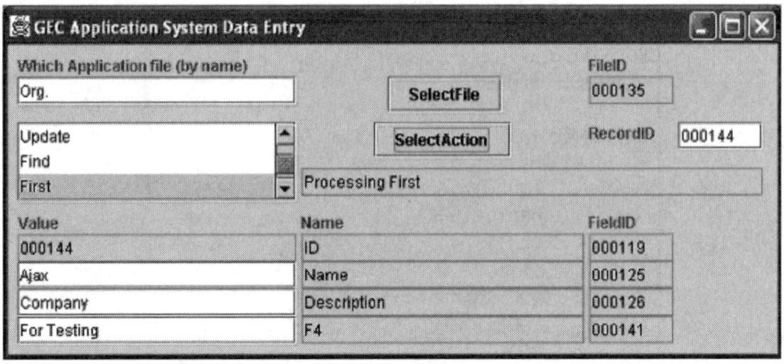

Exhibit 22.11. GEC Application Data Manipulation in GECBuilder

Exhibit 22.11 shows the GEC Application System Data Entry screen. To use this screen, one enters a file name and then clicks SelectFile. For the Org GEC, the file names as given above are: Org., Org.T, Org.GT, Org.R, Org.GRG, and Org.TRT. Note the period after the GEC Org to produce the Org. generic file. Once the file is displayed, various actions can be performed. The one shown is FIRST; it reads the first record in the file (in the order entered). Other actions available are: ADD, DELETE, UPDATE, FIND, and NEXT. When records or files cannot be found, *EOF* is shown in the appropriate window.

To use the cardinality regulator, shown in Exhibit 22.12, one enters the parent and child file names and clicks on SelectFiles. The maximum, minimum, and actual number of children in the relation are shown. The maximum or minimum can be changed here, as long as the maximum is set equal to or less than the actual or the minimum is set to equal to or more than the actual. If files are entered that are not in a parent-child relationship, *EOF* will show in the minimum, maximum, and actual children fields.

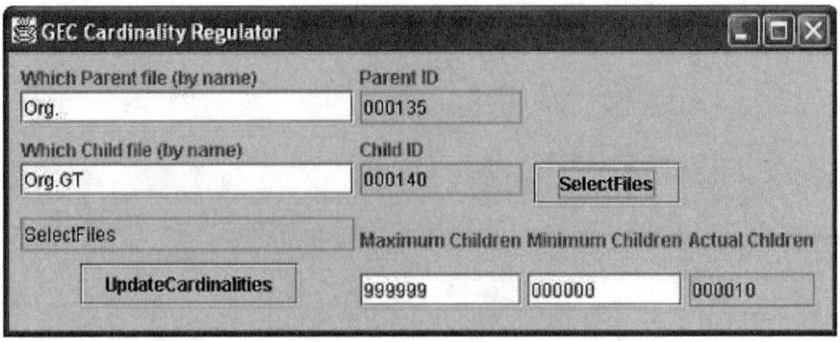

Exhibit 22.12. The Cardinality Regulator in GECBuilder

The various examples of GECBuilder operation illustrate how GEC-based flexible software systems can be developed, implemented, and operated effectively. Using the GECBuilder, GECs, externals, and fields can be added to running systems. MVAs can be converted to GTs (provided that the R, GRG, and TRT nodes are empty) and vice versa.

Features not currently available in the Java prototype GECBuilder, but which could be added, include:

- The ability to add additional rings to an existing GEC (only one ring is currently supported)
- More extensive field manipulation capabilities, including grouped fields (currently all fields, regardless of declared types, are treated as 20-byte character fields)
- Generation of data declaration statements for selected database management systems (DBMSs)

22.3 The GECPhazer

It helps clarify how truly complex the task of building an information system really is.

Just as the GECAnalyzer can help the designer include all valid externals, the GECPhazer can help business staff to include all valid combinations of values in the GT and TRT nodes. Once a GEC-based system has been established and data entered into the T and G nodes as presented in the sections above, then the GECPhazer can be used to make sure that no valid business combinations are missed.

Exhibit 22.13 shows a Person GEC based upon Exhibit 10.14 with positions and persons managing themselves. While we do not think it makes sense for an executive to manage himself or herself, nor for the HR director to manage himself or herself, we have seen such situations in organizations. That is the beauty of the GECPhazer aid. It presents all possible combinations for review. The business staff determines validity. If it is invalid, exclude it; if it is valid, include it.

Having defined the valid values for Position, Type, and Role, we can generate all possible combinations for Position|Type|| and Type|Role|Type||. It is likely that not all are current business realities. A business decision must be made regarding which of the possibilities reflects reality. However, the process of generating all the mathematical possibilities and then having business staff review them in a systematic way helps avoid the "oh, I forgot about that" situation. Plus it helps clarify how truly complex the task of building an information system really is.

Position GEC		
Type		
Pos-Type-ID	**Pos-Type-Name**	
17	Executive	
18	Management	
19	Staff	
23	Supervisor	
Position		
Pos-ID	**Pos-Name**	
20	HR Director	
21	Dept Manager	
22	Clerk	
24	Shift Leader	
49	Secretary	
50	Store Manager	
51	Night Supervisor	
Position/Type		
Mathematical Possibilities	**Pos-ID**	**Pos-Type-ID**
	20	17
	20	18
	20	19
	20	23
	21	17
	21	18
	21	19
	21	23
	22	17
	22	18
	22	19
	22	23
	24	17
	24	18
	24	19
	24	23
	49	17
	49	18
	49	19
	49	23
	50	17
	50	18
	50	19
	50	23
	51	17
	51	18
	51	19
	51	23
Current Reality	Position-ID	Type-ID
	20 (HR Director)	17 (Executive)
	21 (Dept Manager)	18 (Management)
	22 (Worker)	19 (Staff)
	24 (Shift Leader)	23 (Supervisor)

Exhibit 22.13.   GECPhazer Output for Position GEC Values

Role			
Role-ID	**Role-Name**		
47	Manages Directly		
48	Manages Indirectly		
Type/Role/ Type			
Mathematical Possibilities			
	Parent-ID	**Role-ID**	**Child-ID**
	17	47	17
	17	47	18
	17	47	19
	17	47	23
	18	47	17
	18	47	18
	18	47	19
	18	47	23
	19	47	17
	19	47	18
	19	47	19
	19	47	23
	23	47	17
	23	47	18
Disallowed	~~23~~	~~47~~	~~19~~
	23	47	23
	17	48	17
	17	48	18
	17	48	19
	17	48	23
	18	48	17
	18	48	18
	18	48	19
	18	48	23
	19	48	17
	19	48	18
	19	48	19
	19	48	23
	23	48	17
	23	48	18
	23	48	19
	23	48	23
Current Reality			
	17 (Executive)	47 (Manages Directly)	17 (Executive)
	17 (Executive)	47 (Manages Directly)	18 (Management)
	17 (Executive)	47 (Manages Directly)	19 (Staff)
	18 (Management)	47 (Manages Directly)	23 (Supervisor)
	18 (Management)	47 (Manages Directly)	19 (Staff)
	23 (Supervisor)	48 (Manages Indirectly)	19 (Staff)

Exhibit 22.13. (continued)

Any Position|Role|Position|| relationship must respect the rules encoded in the other nodes of the GEC. For example, if current reality (in Type|Role|Type||) does not allow a Supervisor (Parent-ID = 23 to Manage Directly (Role ID = 47) Staff (Child-ID = 19), then no position

Position-Role-Position			
	Parent- ID	**Role-ID**	**Child-ID**
	20 (HR Director)	47 (Manages Directly)	20 (HR Director)
	20 (HR Director)	47 (Manages Directly)	21 (Dept Manager)
	21 (Dept Manager)	47 (Manages Directly)	22 (Worker)
	20 (HR Director)	48 (Manages Indirectly)	22 (Worker)
	24 (Shift Leader)	48 (Manages Indirectly)	22 (Worker)
	21 (Dept Manager)	48 (Manages Indirectly)	24 (Shift Leader)

Exhibit 22.13. (continued)

whose type is Supervisor may manage directly a position whose type is Staff. Thus, in the example above, no Shift Leader (who in this instance is defined as a Supervisor) may Manage Directly a Worker (who in this instance is defined as type Staff). According to the type validation rule, only the role Manages Directly may connect Shift Leader and Worker.

Of course, adding a new value for Position, Position | Type | |, or Role results in a proliferation of new possibilities, just like the real world. The GECPhazer allows the identification of all the possibilities and allows business staff to systematically include or exclude them, helping to avoid the all too common situation where a possibility is overlooked.

22.4 Summary

The rigor and discipline of the GEC information structure enabled the building of three aids for development and operation of GEC-based flexible software. The first two, GECAnalyzer and GECBuilder, are implementation aids; the third, GECPhazer, is an operational aid. Readers can develop similar aids or procure vendor products that provide such capabilities to support GEC design.

- *GECAnalyzer*: This module identifies all possible combinations of GECs and externals, thus aiding the information-structure designer in ensuring that no valid combination is omitted.
- *GECBuilder*: This module produces a working software system based on GECs and externals designed either manually or by the interaction of the designer, business staff, and the GECAnalyzer. The GECBuilder can be used to:
    - Enter data into a working system in batch or GUI interactive mode

- ▪ Produce indented, nested, recursive, bill-of-materials reports from the data in the GEC-based system
- ▪ Handle cardinality regulation or present the status of a relationship
- ▪ *GECPhazer:* This module, used after the system has been built, generates all possible combinations of GT and TRT interactions to ensure that all combinations with a valid business purpose are included.

Aids such as the GECAnalyzer/GECBuilder/GECPhazer tool set facilitate development and maintenance of a generic, flexible information structure, which is the foundation of a flexible system. These aids make flexible systems easier to develop and promote consistency. Development of such aids is a one-time cost that can be recouped many times over during the operation of the system.

You have reached the end of the book. We look forward to hearing your ideas about the implementation of flexible systems in the near future.

Appendix A

Bibliography and References

Agile Manifesto; available online at http://agilemanifesto.org/principles.html, 3/25/05.

Babcock, C., Software lets insurers play by the rules, *Information Week,* Aug. 16, 26, 2004.

Bach, J., The challenge of good-enough software, *Am. Programmer,* 8, 3–11, 1995.

Baker, T.F., Chief programmer team management of production programming, *IBM Syst. J.,* 1, 1972.

Barker, J., *Paradigms: the Business of Discovering the Future,* Harper Collins, New York, 1992.

Berners-Lee, T., Axioms of Web Architecture: 2 — the Myth of Names and Addresses, 1996; available online at http://www.w3.or g/DesignIssues/NameMyth.html.

Berners-Lee, T., Cool URIs Don't Change, 1998; available online at http://www.w3.org/Provider/Style/URI.html.

Boehm, C. and Jacopini, A., Flow diagrams: Turing machines and languages with only two formation rules, *Commn. ACM,* 9, 366–371, 1996.

Boogaard, M., *Defusing the Software Crisis: Information Systems Flexibility through Data Independence,* Book 79, Tinberg Institute Research Series, 1994.

Boucher, R.F. and Mccright, J.S., SAP eyes web services development, *eWeek,* Nov. 17, 2003.

Brandel, M., Educating Your CXO (sidebar), *Computerworld,* July 26, 2004.

Brooks, F., *The Mythical Man Month: Essays on Software Engineering,* Addison-Wesley, Reading, MA, 1975.

Brooks, F., No silver bullet: Essence and accidents in software engineering, *Computer,* Apr. 1987, pp. 10–19.

Business Rules Group, The (BRG), 2004; available online at http://www.business-rulesgroup.org/brmanifesto.htm.

Chabrow, E., Some see I.T. as the problem, *Information Week*, Aug. 30, 2004.

Chapman, G., *The Complete Monty Python's Flying Circus: All the Words*, Vol. 1, Pantheon Books, 1989.

Chisholm, M., Normalizing reference data, *DM Rev.*, 14:4, 38, Apr. 2004.

Conner, D.R., *Managing at the Speed of Change*, Villard Books, 1992.

Cox, B.J., *Object Oriented Programming*, Addison-Wesley, Reading, MA, 1986.

Dadashzedah, M., Database management systems: the foundation for information architecture, in *Information Technology Resources Utilization and Management: Issues and Trends*, Mehdi and Yaverbaum, G., Eds., Idea Group, 1990.

Date, C.J., *What, Not How: the Business Rules Approach to Applications Development*, Addison-Wesley, Reading, MA, 2000.

Date, C.J., *An Introduction to Database Systems*, Vol. II, Addison-Wesley, Reading, MA, 1984.

DeMarco, T., *Why Does Software Cost So Much?* Dorset House Publishing, 1995.

Dent, C., Making an Adaptive KB, Apr. 2004; available online at http://www.burningchrome.com/~cdent/arts/my/2.1.wiki.

Dijkstra, E.W., Go-to statement considered harmful, *Commn. ACM*, 11:3, 147, 1968.

Drucker, P., *Innovation and Entrepreneurship: Practice and Principles*, Harper & Row, New York, 1985.

Elkins, W., Maximizing ROI by implementing a project office, *Electronic Commerce World*, 11, 2001.

Foley, J., In-house innovation, *InformationWeek*, Sep. 15, 2003; available online at http://www.informationweek.com/story/showArticle.jhtml?articleID=14704726.

Gause, D.C. and Weinberg, G.M., *Exploring Requirements: Quality before Design*, Dorset House Publishing, 1989.

Gould, S.J., *Dinosaur in a Haystack: Reflections in Natural History*, Harmony Books, New York, 1995.

Greenbaum, J., Build vs. Buy in the 21st Century, *Intelligent Enterprise*, Apr. 22, 2003; available online at http://www.intelligententerprise.com/030422/607feat2_1.jhtml?requestid=72682.

Hammer, M. and McLeod, D., Database description with SDM: a semantic database model, *ACM Trans. Database Syst.*, 6, 351–386, 1981.

Hammer, M. and Champy, J., *Reengineering the Corporation: a Manifesto for Business Revolution*, Harper Collins, New York, 1993.

Haughey, T., Is dimensional modeling one of the great con jobs in data management history? Parts 1 and 2, *DM Rev.*, Mar., Apr. 2004.

Hay, D.C., The Zachman Framework, 2000; available online at http//www.essentialstrategies.com/publications/methodology/zachman.htm.

Hay, D. and Healy, K.A., Eds., Defining Business Rules: What Are They Anyway? Rev. 1.3, The Business Rules Group (formerly known as the GUIDE Business Rules Project), July 2000; available online at http://www.businessrulesgroup.org. (The group's Business Rules Manifesto is in an appendix to Chapter 8.)

Hayes, F., IT: Nifty at 50? *Computerworld*, 78, Jan. 29, 2001a.

Hayes, F., Flood of Troubles, *Computerworld*, 70, Nov. 5, 2001b.

Hayes, I.S., Easy maintenance should be an objective of new application design, *Appl. Dev. Trends*, 59, Nov. 1995.

Hayes, I.S., The value of business software maintenance, *Appl. Dev. Trends*, Nov. 1996.

Heldman, K., *PMP: Project Management Professional Study Guide*, Sybex Inc., 2002, pp. 57–60.

Highsmith, J.A., III, *Adaptive Software Development: a Collaborative Approach to Managing Complex Systems*, Dorset House Publishing, 2000.

Highsmith, J., Thriving in turbulent times, *Appl. Dev. Strategies*, 10, 1–16, 1998.

Horowitz, A.S., Are You Annoying? *Computerworld*, 34, July 26, 2004.

Johnson, B. and Ruwe, M., *Professional Programming in COBOL*, Prentice Hall, New York, 1991.

Johnson, B., Woolfolk, W.W., and Ligezinski, P., Counterintuitive management of information systems technology, *Bus. Horizons*, Mar.-Apr., 1999.

Johnson, B., Woolfolk, W.W., and Ligezinski, P., Nightmares and Myths of OO, presented at Unix Austria Conference on Open Systems, Vienna, Austria, Oct., Dec., 1994.

Johnson, B. and Woolfolk, W.W., Generic entity clouds: A stable information structure for flexible computer systems, *Systems Dev. Manage.*, Oct. 2001.

Johnson, B., More lessons from civil engineering, *IEEE Software*, Nov. 1995.

Johnson, B., Data processing — out of control, *Operations Manage. Rev.*, 2, 2, 1984.

Johnston, T., Primary Key Reengineering Projects, *DM Rev.*, Feb., Mar. 2000.

Joiner, B.L., Fourth Generation Management: the New Business Consciousness, McGraw-Hill, New York, 1994.

Kaplan, J. and Bernays, A., *The Language of Names*, Simon & Schuster, New York, 1997.

Kavi, K., Brown, J.C., and Tripathi, A., The Pressure Is On, *Computer*, Jan. 1999.

Keen, P.G.W., personal communication, July 21, 2004.

Keen, P.G.W., *Every Manager's Guide to Information Technology: a Glossary of Key Terms and Concepts for Today's Business Leader*, 2nd ed., Harvard Business School Press, Cambridge, MA, 1995.

Keen, P.G.W., *Shaping the Future: Business Design through Information Technology*, Harvard Business School Press, Cambridge, MA, 1991.

Kent, W., *Data and Reality: Basic Assumptions in Data Processing Reconsidered*, North-Holland, Amsterdam, 1978.

Ligezinski, P., Zero-Maintenance Systems, unpublished, 2nd place winner 1988 SIM paper competition, 1988.

Lytton, N., Maintenance dollars at work; Software vendors have it right: Maintenance work can double as development, *Computer World/ROI*, July 16, 2001.

Martin, J., *Strategic Data-Planning Methodologies*, Prentice Hall, New York, 1982.

Mayne, E., From the Front: Duplicate VINs Pose Issue, *Detroit News* as reported in *Denver Post*, July 2, 2004, p. 15A.

McConnell, S., *Rapid Development*, Microsoft Press, 1996.

Mello, A., 4 trends shaping ERP, *Tech Update*, Feb. 7, 2002.

Miller, R.W., Johnson, B., and Woolfolk, W.W., UniverSIS: flexible system, easy to change, *Educause Q.*, 253, 44, 2002.

Moyers, W., *A World of Ideas*, Doubleday, New York, 1990.

Murphy, M., personal communication, July 11, 2004.

Nolan, R.L., Managing the crisis in data processing, *Harvard Bus. Rev.*, Mar.-Apr. 1979.

Pant, S. and Hsu, C., Strategic Information Systems Planning: a Review, 1995 Information Resources Management Association International Conference, May 1995, Atlanta.

Parnas, D.L., Designing software for ease of extension and contraction, *IEEE Trans. Software Eng.*, Mar. 1979.

Pirsig, R., *Zen and the Art of Motorcycle Maintenance*, Bantam Books, 1974.

Pring, B., Worldwide IT Services Marketplace 2Q03 Review: Focus Report, *Gartner*, June 17, 2003, pp. 17–18.

Project Management Institute, A Guide to the Project Management Body of Knowledge, 2000.

Radin, D., *Building a Successful Software Business*, O'Reilly & Associates, 1994.

Roget's II, *The New Thesaurus*, 3rd ed., Houghton Mifflin, Boston, 2003.

Ross, R.G. and Healy, K.A., Eds., Organizing Business Plans: the Standard Model for Business Rule Motivation, Rev. 1.0, Business Rules Group (formerly GUIDE Business Rules Project), Nov. 15, 2000; available online at http://www.businessrulesgroup.org.

Ross R.G., *Principles of the Business Rules Approach*, Addison-Wesley, Reading, MA, 2003.

Rubin, K., Survival of the Fittest, *Intelligent Enterprise*, 48, Jan. 26, 1999.

Schaffer, R.H. and Thompson, H.A., Successful change programs begin with results, *Harvard Bus. Rev.*, 70, 80–89, 1992.

Scheuer, J.A., personal communication, June 5 and July 20, 2004.

Seeley, R., Requirements required, *Appl. Dev. Trends*, Dec., 31–35, 2003.

Senge, P., *The Fifth Discipline: the Art and Practice of the Learning Organization*, Doubleday Currency, 1990.

Shewhart, W., Economic Control of Manufactured Products, ASQC, 1980.

Shirky, C., Situated Software, 2004; available online at http://www.shirky.com/writings/situated_software.html.

Software AG, Rapid Application Development (RAD) Project Fundamentals, MTH-RPJ-002, Sep. 1994.

Software AG, ADABAS Concepts and Facilities, 1999.

Taguchi, G., *Introduction to Quality Engineering*, Asian Productivity Organization, 1986.

von Halle, B., *Business Rules Applied: Building Better Systems Using the Business Rules Approach*, Wiley Computer Publishing, New York, 2002.

Wand, Y. and Weber, R., Mario Bunge's ontology as a formal foundation for information systems concepts, in *Studies on Mario Bunge's Treatise*, Weingartner, P. and Dorn, G.J.W., Eds., Rodopi, 1990.

Ward, J. and Peppard, J., *Strategic Planning for Information Systems*, 3rd ed., Wiley, New York, 2002.

Waters, J.K., Extreme method simplifies development puzzle, *Appl. Dev. Trends*, July 1, 2000.

Weinberg, G.M., *Systems Thinking*, Vol. 1, Quality Software Management, 1992; *First-Order Measurement*, Vol. 2, Quality Software Management, 1993; *Congruent Action*, Vol. 3, Quality Software Management, 1994; *Anticipating Change*, Vol. 4, Quality Software Management, 1997, Dorset House Publishing.

Weinberg, G.M., *An Introduction to General Systems Thinking*, John Wiley & Sons, 1975.

Weinberg, G.M. and Weinberg, D., *On the Design of Stable Systems*, John Wiley & Sons, 1979.

Weinberger, D., *Small Pieces Loosely Joined*, Perseus Books, 2002.

Whitener, T., Primary identifiers: the basics of database stability, *Database Programming Design*, Jan. 1989.

Whitmarsh, J., Letter from the editor, *Chief Inf. Off.*, 9, 10, 1995.

Woolfolk, W.W. and Johnson, B., Information-free identifiers: a key to flexible information systems, parts I and II, *Data Base Manage.*, July, Aug. 2001.

Woolfolk, W.W., Ligezinski, P., and Johnson, B., The Problem of the Dynamic Organization and the Static System: Principles and Techniques for Achieving Flexibility, in *Proc. 29th Annual Hawaii International Conference on System Sciences*, HICSS-29, Vol. 3, 1996, pp. 482–491.

Yourdon, E., Whitehead, K., Thomann, J., Oppel, K., and Nevermann, P., *Mainstream Objects: an Analysis and Design Approach for Business*, Prentice-Hall, New York, 1995.

Zachman, J.A., A framework for information systems architecture, *IBM Syst. J.*, 26, 3, 276, 1987.

Zachman, J.A., The Zachman Framework and Its Implications for Methods and Tools, in *Proc. Second Annual Conference on Software Methods,* Orlando, FL, Mar. 23, 1993.

Use of Our Earlier Material

We have made extensive use of material that we have published earlier. We have taken the original computer text files and molded them to fit with various sections of the book. Here we acknowledge this material and these publishers.

Our first publication treating the subject of flexible software systems was "The Problem of the Dynamic Organization and the Static System: Principles and Techniques for Achieving Flexibility," published in *Proceedings of the 29th Annual Hawaii International Conference on Systems Sciences*, HICSS-29, Vol. III, p. 482, IEEE Computer Society Press. Maui, Hawaii, January 1996 [Woolfolk, Ligezinski, and Johnson, 1996] (© 2004 IEEE).

Some of the material relating to the Generic Entity Cloud (GEC) has been taken from "Generic Entity Clouds: a Stable Information Structure for Flexible Computer Systems," *Systems Development Management*, October 2001 [Johnson and Woolfolk, 2001].

Portions of the material relating to the use and misuse of entity identifiers has been adapted from "Information-Free Identifiers: a Key to Flexible Information Systems," *Data Base Management*, Part I, July 2001, Part II, August 2001 [Woolfolk and Johnson, 2001].

The sections about UniverSIS, the flexible student information system at the University of Cincinnati, are in part derived from "UniverSIS: Flexible System, Easy to Change," *Educause Quarterly*, 25, 344 (Fall), 2002 [Miller, Johnson, and Woolfolk, 2002].

The myths regarding the management and use of information technology have been adapted from "Counterintuitive Management of Information Systems Technology," *Business Horizons*, 42, 2, March-April 1999 [Johnson, Woolfolk, and Ligezinski, 1999].

We graciously thank these publishers for their permission to use this material.

Index

423

E

F

H

I